MAKE-BELIEVE

Also by Laurence Leamer:

The Paper Revolutionaries
Playing for Keeps in Washington
Assignment
Ascent: The Spiritual and Physical Quest of Willi Unsoeld

MAKE-BELIEVE

THE STORY OF NANCY & RONALD REAGAN

LAURENCE LEAMER

7492

Laura Elliott, Research Associate
Vincent Virga, Photo Editor

1817
HARPER & ROW, PUBLISHERS, New York
Cambridge, Philadelphia, San Francisco
Mexico City, São Paulo, Sydney

Grateful acknowledgment is made for permission to reprint: "Rainbow Stew." Lyrics by Merle Haggard. Copyright © 1981 by Shade Tree Music, Inc. Reprinted by permission of Shade Tree Music, Inc. "To Love a Child." Lyrics by Hal David. Copyright © 1982 by Casa David and Jonico Music. Reprinted by permission of Hal David. Portions of this book, in slightly different form, have appeared in *California Magazine, Ladies' Home Journal, The Washingtonian.*

FIRST EDITION

Designer: Abigail Sturges

Library of Congress Cataloging in Publication Data

Leamer, Laurence.
  Make-believe.

  Includes index.
  1. Reagan, Ronald.   2. Reagan, Nancy, 1923–
3. Presidents—United States—Biography.   4. Presidents—United States—Wives—Biography.   I. Title.
E877.L4 1983   973.927′092′2 [B]   82-48123
ISBN 0-06-015102-1

83 84 85 86 87 10 9 8 7 6 5 4 3 2 1

For
Carol Mann

CONTENTS

ILLUSTRATIONS

ACKNOWLEDGMENTS

I wrote *Make-Believe*, but it is not simply my book. Laura Elliott, my research associate, did everything from tedious research and editing to the most sensitive and difficult reporting. Early on she spent a week sitting on the floor in the stacks at the Library of Congress going through hundreds of uncataloged magazines. She interviewed many people who had not been interviewed before. Toward the end there was a hole in the research, and I simply didn't have the time to go out to Los Angeles again. So Laura flew out and came back a week later exhausted but with some of the best material in the book. She is a superb journalist, and I miss her counsel, good cheer, and moral strength. I hope that anyone who finds value in this book will realize how strong a contribution she made.

I am very fortunate in having so many good friends, and in this case doubly fortunate that so many of them are journalists. My dear friend Elizabeth Mehren of the *Los Angeles Times* covered Mrs. Reagan and the White House for the first year of the administration, doing some of the best reporting anyone did. Elizabeth's work and material vastly enriched my own reporting. Ellen Farley and William Knoedelseder, Jr., wrote the definitive magazine piece on Ronald Reagan's Hollywood years. They gave me their notes and research materials. Jane Winebrenner of *New York* magazine was helpful. Kitty Kelley proved as good a colleague as a friend. Several other prominent journalists gave me their notes, tapes, and background material. They chose to remain anonymous, but I want them to know how much their generosity has meant to me and to this book. Bill Steinmetz, a Los Angeles public relations executive who once worked on *GE Theater,* loaned me his voluminous Reagan files.

I would like to thank Bob Woodward of the *Washington Post* for his help, as well as Robin Gradison. I would also like to thank Robert Redford, an honorary journalist, for his perceptions on Reagan as an actor/politician. I found Donnie Radcliffe's reporting in the *Washington Post* invaluable for understanding what was going on in the East Wing of the White House. Dr. David Gens took time out from his hectic schedule to guide the research and then to read the chapter on the assassination attempt for accuracy. Marsha Borie and David Ladd introduced me to Los Angeles.

Bill Campbell and the rest of my buddies at Radio Shack put up with my crazy questions about my TRS-80 Model II. Catherine Breslin, the novelist, was a constant source of encouragement. Barry Jagoda, Larry Kotlikoff, Lisa Berg and Carol Mann read the manuscript. Larry Ashmead, my editor, knew when to leave me alone and when to apply all his expertise. The term "photo editor" is hardly sufficient to describe the expertise and passion that Vincent Virga brings to his work. He has enriched this book immeasurably.

Make-Believe was not an easy book to research and write. But whenever I got discouraged, I looked forward to dedicating the book to the person who has done more for my career than anyone else: Carol Mann, my friend and agent.

MAKE-BELIEVE

The dawn of the inauguration of a president.
(Bill Fitz-Patrick, The White House)

— 1 —

A GILDED DAWN

On a gilded California day, Ronald and Nancy Reagan left their home for the last time. For all but four of their twenty-nine years in Pacific Palisades, the Reagans had lived in this house at 1669 San Onofre Drive, above and apart from most of Los Angeles. No more would they stand here looking westward to the blue Pacific Ocean, eternally promising. No longer would they worry about a brush fire sweeping down on them from the mountains to the east behind their house.

In five days, sixty-nine-year-old Ronnie would be inaugurated as fortieth president of the United States. He was the oldest president-elect in American history. This was as much Nancy's triumph as Ronnie's. She had begun dating him when he thought he would never love again. She had married him at the bottom of his career and she had nurtured him, bolstered him, protected him, even at times from his own children.

No one knew the cost of Ronnie's political success to the Reagan family better than Patti, their twenty-eight-year-old first born. She was here today to see her parents off, looking no more permanent than the luggage strewn through the rooms. She had written a song called "No Place Left to Hide" and as she kissed her parents goodbye in the doorway, a public moment in a public place, the cameras clicking away, she began to cry. Holding her hands over her eyes, Patti wept because "it's like your childhood . . . going out from beneath you." Escorted by police cars and motorcycles, the limousine carrying Nancy and Ronnie wended its way down Amalfi Drive. Neighbors waved goodbye to a man and a woman that many of them had never met and none of them knew very well.

As Nancy and Ronnie flew east across the continent in *Air Force One*, thousands of Americans were converging on Washington. The presidential inauguration was America's great symbolic testimony to the resilience of American democracy. Four years before, President-elect Jimmy Carter had walked down Pennsylvania Avenue after being sworn in, a gesture of humility that Thomas Jefferson first employed in 1801. For the Carter inauguration, no ticket cost more than a plebeian $25. There had been 200 free concerts, all sorts of open festivities and six $25 balls, a modern-day counterpart to Andrew Jackson's 1829 inauguration when he opened up the White House to a mob of thousands.

Ronald Reagan's inauguration would have nine balls with tickets going for up to $250, $500-a-plate formal dinners, a gala with seats $50 and up, and $75 for a good seat at the parade. To buy tickets for all the major events would cost at least $2,000 a person.

The country had a 7.4-percent rate of unemployment, but the suntanned, loyal Californians saw nothing wrong in flaunting wealth. They believed in all the pomp and flash and ceremony that money could buy. Ronnie himself felt that in America anyone who worked hard and struggled long could make money. Wealth was good, the loam soil from which more fortunes grew, good to be earned and good to be spent. And thus the inauguration was a time to enjoy the riches that were possible in a free capitalistic society.

Unlike many of his backers, Ronnie was no snob. He believed that everybody should have his shot at this great golden honeypot of American free enterprise. He wanted people everywhere to see his inauguration and appreciate what he considered the American miracle. Ronnie was a media populist. His longtime friend and a former producer, Charles Z. Wick, saw to it that the inauguration was structured for television, a gigantic show that would be seen everywhere, from penthouses on Manhattan's East Side to sharecroppers' cabins in the Mississippi delta, from condominiums on Maui to tract houses in Dearborn.

And so they came to Washington, those who had achieved what Ronnie and Nancy considered the American dream, to take part in the $16 million inauguration, by far the most expensive in history. At $750 a head, they came from Ohio in John Jacob Astor's private train with liveried porters at beck and call. They came from Indiana in a railroad car once owned by J. P. Morgan. They came from Texas with Governor William P. Clements, Jr., 380 strong in a chartered Boeing 747. They came by limousine from Scranton, New York and Chicago. They came as often as not by first-class plane or an estimated 400 corporate jets, row upon row of sleek planes lined up at National Airport. If they didn't have their own cars waiting for them, they rented limousines. And if they didn't want to shell out for a limousine, they rented cars, big American cars, Grand Prix, Cutlasses, LTDs with landau roofs.

They stayed at the best hotels. Everywhere they went, the Californians were courted. When Betsy Bloomingdale, Nancy's closest friend, arrived at the refined Fairfax Hotel on Massachusetts Avenue, John Coleman, the owner, had a gift waiting: a Steuben crystal elephant. And when Jerry Zipkin, Nancy's closest male friend, arrived in town, there was an elephant for him too. Marshall Coyne, owner of the Madison Hotel, also wooed the Californians. He gave a Friday night party honoring Frank Sinatra, chairman of the inaugural gala.

Ronnie would be the first president since John F. Kennedy to be sworn in wearing a formal morning coat, striped gray pants and a white pleated shirt, tailored by Frank Mariani of Beverly Hills for $1,250. In their new wardrobes, the ladies more than matched the president-elect's sartorial splendor. They arrived in the Capital with enough baggage for a siege. In an America where teen-agers know the labels on jeans the way a French worker knows his wines, the ladies were walking advertisements for leading designers: Adolfo, Blass, Saint Laurent, Galanos, de la Renta and Halston.

Gone was the "good Republican cloth coat" of which Richard Nixon had once been so proud. To the Reagan ladies, fur was the natural covering. At Edwards-Lowell on Rodeo Drive in Beverly Hills, some of Nancy's friends bought two or three new furs for the occasion before shopping in the boutiques for gowns, dresses and jewelry. One of Nancy's friends was said to have brought twenty-one fur coats to Washington with her. And if they had forgotten long white gloves, they were chauffeured to Neiman-Marcus on Wisconsin Avenue to pick up a pair for $175.

To the socialites and caterers, the party-goers and -givers of Washington, it was a joyous rebirth of taste and style after the gritty Carter years. Others saw the inauguration differently. "It was like falling into a batch of fudge," said Maryon Allen, widow of Democratic Senator James Allen of Alabama and a *Washington Post* columnist. "It made me sick—the racks of dresses and the fur coats they didn't even bother to pack, the lineup of private jets and the jeweled boots, the absolutely appalling overconsumerism, the insane jubilation."

Of all these rich, glamorous wives, Nancy was indeed the First Lady. For years she had struggled to be where she was today. As a teen-ager and a young woman, she had had her weight problems, but now at fifty-nine she was a perfect size six. Her high cheekbones, huge eyes, delicate features and extraordinary attention to appearance made her lovelier than she had ever been.

Nancy was already becoming a symbol that many middle-aged women gladly looked to and emulated. She wanted to be a standard for fashionable Americans as Jacqueline Kennedy had been twenty years before. In the Sixties when Nancy had shopped at Amelia Gray's, her favorite store in Beverly Hills, she had talked often about Jackie and the style and grace the young First Lady brought to the White House, affecting the way a whole generation of women would dress. Although Nancy denied it publicly, in her own way she intended to be an Eighties counterpart to Mrs. Kennedy, who had been twenty-nine years younger than Mrs. Reagan when she entered the White House.

Letitia Baldrige, Jackie's press secretary in the White House, was already in Washington working as a volunteer for Nancy, setting up the First Lady's office in the East Wing of the White House and introducing Nancy to Washington. Nancy even invited Baldrige to live in the White House for a while.

All her life Nancy had loved clothes and now finally she could have almost all that she wanted. For years she had bought dresses from James (Jimmy) Galanos in Los Angeles, one of the most expensive designers in America. Galanos was a proud, private man who at times appeared tired of Nancy's demands, but for the inaugural gala he donated a white gown embroidered with crystal and chalk beads in a delicate fern design. The gown was worth at least $10,000 and had taken the seamstresses weeks to complete.

In the month before the inauguration, Nancy had cut a swath through the stores of Rodeo Drive in Beverly Hills. At Gucci, Carlo Celoni, the manager, had taken her upstairs to a private room and feted her on chocolate-covered strawberries while she purchased a rich selection of goods. A few months earlier she had bought a fur-lined raincoat worth almost $1,000 at Edwards-Lowell Furs. And since for Christmas Ronnie had given her a Maximillian mink worth an estimated $10,000, she figured she could get by without any new furs. In these shops on Rodeo Drive and elsewhere, she did obtain an Adolfo coat and dress, a Bill Blass evening gown, David Evins shoes, on and on, collecting an estimated $25,000 wardrobe.

After their flight from California, the Reagans rested at Blair House across Pennsylvania Avenue from the White House. Nancy saw to it that their inaugural wardrobes were properly taken care of and hung. Then she explored the rooms in this mansion where foreign heads of state usually stay. Twin beds had been brought into one bedroom for Dr. and Mrs. Loyal Davis, Nancy's mother and stepfather. Patti would sleep in a four-poster bed, and Nancy scooped up a pack of cigarettes that might offend her nonsmoking daughter. There was a Victorian bedroom set in the room that Nancy's son, Ron, Jr., and his new bride, Doria, would occupy. Other rooms were ready for Ronnie's son by his first marriage, Michael Reagan, his wife Colleen, and son, Cameron, as well as for Maureen, his other daughter. And there was room for Julius Bengtsson, Nancy's hairdresser, and for Letitia Baldrige, who would be helping Nancy.

Ronnie left the unpacking chores to Nancy. From out of his wife's hatbox, he took his mother Nelle's old Bible, so worn with use that it was held together by Scotch tape. This was the Bible that he would hold when sworn in next week. "She wrote poetry," Ronnie said, and opened the book to a sonnet that his deceased mother had written, after a verse by Edwin Markham titled "The Dream."

> *When I consider how my life is spent*
> *The most that I can do will be to prove*
> *'Tis by His side, each day, I seek to move,*
> *To higher, noble things my mind is bent*
> *Thus giving of my strength, which God has lent,*
> *I strive some needy souls unrest, to soothe*
> *Lest they the paths of righteousness shall lose . . .*
> *In thought of mind, in word, and in each deed*
> *My life must prove the power of His grace*
> *By every action through my living days.*

By the time he finished, Ronnie had tears in his eyes.

While the Reagans settled in at Blair House, their friends and supporters took over the town. Peter Hannaford, the former public-relations partner of Ronnie's deputy chief of staff, Michael Deaver, displayed California's bear flag in his new town house the night the Hannafords hosted a "the Californians are coming" party to welcome the throng.

If you were a Californian close to Reagan, there was bound to be at least one party in your honor. Senator Mark Hatfield of Oregon and an old California Reagan friend, Nancy Reynolds, now a Bendix vice-president, had a Sunday brunch for Deaver and his wife, Carolyn. The VIP guests jammed into Hatfield's Georgetown home while others stood outside waiting to get in. Washington socialites weren't left out either. Nancy and Wyatt Dickerson gave a dinner at their estate, Merrywood, for the Armand Deutsches, old Reagan friends. The president-elect and the soon-to-be First Lady attended the elegant dinner at the childhood home of Jackie Kennedy.

Marion Jorgensen, one of Nancy's friends, gave a luncheon for her compatriots at the plush Jockey Club. She treated Jerry Zipkin, Betsy Bloomingdale, and Harriet Deutsch to what they considered a new culinary delight: Maryland crabcakes. Washington's best-known restaurants—

Dominique's, Lion d'Or and Watergate's Jean Louis—were scenes of private luncheons and dinners that caused non-Californians to strain for a better view. The menus took on a distinctly West Coast flavor with fresh fruit and California wine.

It was a time of festivity, celebration, celebrity. Indeed, the Reaganites seemed removed from the grease and sweat of mere politics. But even the anointed Reaganites had to pick up their tickets. Close to 40,000 celebrants fell upon Union Station where their inaugural tickets were supposed to be waiting for them. The Reaganites found themselves in the midst of a monumental snafu. Even longtime friends of the Reagans, like A. C. and Martha Lyles, discovered that their tickets had been lost.

The Reaganites had come to Washington thinking themselves part of a new elite, and here they were standing in line for hours on end, waiting for tickets that in many cases didn't exist. For this they could blame the inaugural cochairman, Wick, the new head of the International Communication Agency, and Robert Gray, a Republican public-relations executive who was as common at Washington parties as squares of quiche. When it was discovered that almost all events had been oversold, Wick and others pulled hundreds of tickets out of the computer system for their friends and special-interest groups, not thinking where their rashness might lead.

At least thirty-nine restaurants and nineteen wineries were serving free food and drinks. Here the Reaganites received a real "taste of America." The city's derelicts and bag ladies knew a soup kitchen when they saw one. With entrepreneurial zeal, they found their way into the Visitors' Center and stood sampling Florida lobster bisque, shrimp Merlin, *vitello alla gaetano* and escargots with the best of them.

Beyond the scheduled inaugural activities, there were over a hundred weekend parties for the anointed. There were parties within parties, before-the-party parties, after-the-party parties, state parties, cocktail parties, receptions. The only thing to do after the brunches and lunches was to head out in the late afternoon already formally dressed. At a party given by NBC, Senator Barry Goldwater, who had sired the movement that brought Ronnie to the White House, looked out on a sea of designer dresses and jewels. "Ostentatious," he said of the festivities. "I've seen seven of them. And I say when you've got to pay $2,000 for a limousine for four days, $7 to park, and $2.50 to check your coat, at a time when most people in this country can't hack it, that's ostentatious."

At the Saturday, January 17, afternoon reception for 500 top administration appointees, transition officials and Reagan supporters, the room was full of Nancy's and Ronnie's old friends. Waiting for the Reagans was Nancy's intimate, Jean Smith, the wife of William French Smith, Ronnie's personal attorney and the new attorney general. And next to her stood

Nancy's closest male friend, Jerome ("Jerry") Zipkin, the ubiquitous, rotund, witty one; Jerry, with a tongue as sharp as Sheffield steel; Jerry, social arbiter for Nancy and all her friends.

"Do I look all right?" Mrs. Smith asked. "Have I done anything wrong?"

Zipkin looked appraisingly at her black embroidered gown with purple sequined flowers and pronounced his approval, a blessing that gave his female circle confidence in their own grace, style and taste.

Ronnie and Nancy appeared. Ronnie was in a dark blue business suit, while Nancy wore a bright green wool chemise and heavy gold necklace that reminded some of the guests of the way Jackie Kennedy had dressed. Nancy looked out at the tanned California faces and said how much she was going to miss them.

The Reagans' days were as intricately choreographed as a Russian ballet, and they stayed for only ten minutes. While the drama of fifty-two hostages held in Iran was playing out at the White House, the president-elect was in a mood as buoyant as a helium balloon. He had the lilt in his step of a newlywed, and his sheer goodwill made even Washington's more cynical journalists write lyrical paeans to the president-elect.

That clear, frigid evening, the official inaugural program opened like Cecil B. De Mille's version of the Fourth of July. The evening was to end with a fourteen-minute laser and firework display orchestrated by Osmond Productions and a Disneyland creator, Tommy Walker. As Ronnie and Nancy stood on the steps of the Lincoln Memorial in 26-degree weather, the Mormon Tabernacle Choir sang "God Bless America" and the laser beams laced through the sky linking the Lincoln Memorial with the Washington Monument, the Capitol, the White House and the Jefferson Memorial.

"I've never been filled with such a surge of patriotism," Ronnie said later. "It was so hard not to cry during the whole thing." For forty-five minutes, the best show in town played before the 15,000 spectators and millions more watching on television. The close-to-a-million-dollar spectacular concluded in a final blaze of fireworks, illuminating the Washington skies with 12,000 rockets. Then for a moment it was quiet. One middle-aged man shouted: "That's a print!"

For four days Nancy and Ronnie moved through the events as evenly and sleekly as the limousine in which they traveled. Sunday evening the Reagans attended a performing-arts extravaganza in the three theaters of the Kennedy Center. To appease the exuberant crowd that chattered even during the performances, the Reagans made a twenty-minute appearance in each theater. As Nancy arrived in her full-skirted, pale lime Adolfo gown with jeweled bodice, she was a greater attraction than the performers on stage.

The Reagans shuttled from place to place, sometimes spending almost as much time in what the Secret Service called "holding rooms" as at the events themselves. They caught only snatches of each performance: the National Symphony playing the theme song from *King's Row,* Ronnie's finest film; Mikhail Baryshnikov in a modern ballet, *Push Comes to Shove;* and Lorin Maazel performing a Schubert sonata.

While waiting to go into the Eisenhower Theater, Nancy noticed that her daughter, Patti, was being interviewed on television. It was an old interview, but Nancy sat down in front of the battered black-and-white set to watch her child, totally oblivious to those around her.

Then it was time to go inside. The Reagans were already a world removed from their California friends who sat in nearby boxes. In the afternoon they had missed the concert given by another old friend, Fred Waring, and they asked that he sit in their box. But there was time only for a quick hello. They even had to miss the $500-a-plate candlelight dinners before and after the concert, which were hailed as the most elegant affair of the entire inauguration. The 2,500 guests entered the Atrium of the Kennedy Center through the Third U.S. Infantry's Old Guard Fife and Drum Corps dressed in Revolutionary uniforms. The cocktail area was decorated with pale green and white silk cloths and draped with garlands of smilax. The guests sat down to a lavish meal of bass, veal and fresh California raspberries served on place settings designed for the occasion by Boehm. The serving plates were themselves souvenirs of the evening, but some of the guests kept eyeing the centerpieces: chinoiserie cachepots holding rose trees. After dessert, many guests in their black tie and gowns overturned the rose trees, dumping gravel onto the green moiré tablecloths, and walked off with the green and white cachepots.

Both Reagans were alive with the sheer joy of the festivities, but Nancy was tiring. Monday morning, Nancy went back to the Kennedy Center to greet 7,000 women invited to the Distinguished Ladies Reception. Later that afternoon, Nancy went without Ronnie to a reception held in the State Department for disabled and senior citizens. With the release of the hostages in Iran rumored to be imminent, she had to walk through a gauntlet of reporters and cameramen staking out the building. On the eighth floor she was told apologetically that she would have to wait a few minutes before entering the gathering. Saying nothing, she took off one shoe, leaned against the chair rail and shut her eyes. She looked old and tired. But when her aides told her that it was time, she came alive and entered the room as if every camera in the world were upon her.

Most of his adult life Ronnie had been a Hollywood actor. He was proud of it. Both of his wives had been actresses. His eldest daughter,

Maureen, had been in show business for a while, and his other daughter, Patti, was still trying to make her way as an actress. Ron, Jr., his younger son, was a dancer. Thus there were few things he looked forward to as much as the gala performance in his honor Monday evening at the Capital Centre in suburban Maryland, a gigantic oyster-shaped sports arena, home to the Washington Bullets basketball team.

When the president-elect's helicopter swooped down near the entrance, the parking lot looked like a mating ground for limousines, and held by some estimates the largest number of limousines ever assembled in one place. The Reagans were already missing the greatest drama of the evening. The committee and staff had sold tickets to many of the seats twice, as well as double-booking some of the $2,000 boxes.

At the main entrances, bejeweled dowagers and distinguished executives begged to be let into the gala. Robert Gray was to have been there to deal with the scores of irate Reaganites. He lived by a Washington adage: Be there when the pictures are being taken and the credit is being given; but when the problems get too bad, beat hell for leather out of there. To deal with those turned away, Gray left two slim, handsome young men, one a photographer by trade, the other a magazine editor. In front of one of them, a matron knelt down in her gown and begged for one measly ticket, mascara running down her face. But her weeping did no good.

When the Inaugural Gala started, ten minutes late, there were still empty seats and celebrants pushing their way into the Capital Centre through ticket takers more accustomed to Bullet basketball and Cap hockey fans. To please the Reaganites, the standard fare of hot dogs, beer and peanuts had been royally augmented with oysters on the half shell, champagne and chilled crab claws.

Ronnie and Nancy sat in plush blue velour wing chairs. He wore black tie and she a black gown with a fitted velvet top and satin skirt designed by Bill Blass. With regally puffed sleeves, slim bodice and rich black fabric, the dress accentuated her tiny waist and white skin. Holding court from a raised flower-ringed platform, the Reagans looked indeed like American royalty.

"Well, this is the first inauguration to have a premiere," said Johnny Carson, the master of ceremonies, looking out on the spectators. At least half those sitting in the Capital Centre in black tie and long gowns could see Carson clearly only on the great hanging screens that enlarged the tiny figure so far below. But even that picture wasn't half as good as the one that millions at home saw watching ABC by tape delay.

"I have only been here three days and I have never seen so many lunches, receptions, parties and balls in all my life," Carson continued, elegant in his white tie and tails. "And they are not inexpensive. I went to the men's room at the Shoreham Hotel and found out it was by invitation only."

"Tomorrow . . . the president-elect will take the oath of office and . . . [an hour later] Ted Kennedy will be saying, 'Ask yourself, are you better off now than when Ronald Reagan first took the oath of office?' All those words will come back, you know."

Whether it was Carson's monologue, Bob Hope's quips, Rich Little's imitations, or the songs of half a dozen entertainers, almost everything focused on the president-elect. Ethel Merman had polished up her brassy voice for yet another rendering of "Everything's Comin' up Roses." "I had a dream, a dream about you, baby," she sang pointing at Ronnie. Donny Osmond took a classic rock-'n'-roll number and sang "Go, Ronnie, Go, Go, Ronnie, Go, Ronnie, Be Good."

By the momentarily bewildered look on Ronnie's face, he didn't appear to know just where Donny Osmond wanted him to go. But for Ronnie and Nancy and most of those in the audience, it was an extraordinary evening. As much as any man in public life, Ronnie appreciated the sheer emotion and theatrics of politics. He was profoundly moved when General Omar Bradley, the nation's only living five-star general, was wheeled in. Ronnie was touched, too, hearing his old colleague, Jimmy Stewart, pay tribute. ("Ron, I want to tell ya. You'll never know, you'll just never know how I feel about not being able to put into words, the wonderful feeling I have, [that] I'm going to be able to call you Mr. President.")

At the end of the evening, Frank Sinatra sang a medley. Sinatra was not just an entertainer tonight but the producer and director. For him this evening was vindication. In the early Sixties he had been a "big 'D' Democrat," as close to the Kennedys as anyone in Hollywood. He and Jack had even shared the same mistress. But he had subsequently been pushed aside, allegedly because of his unsavory connections with the underworld. Now, exactly twenty years later, Sinatra was a Republican's Republican, accepted in the White House and revered by Nancy.

"I should like to do something special for our new First Lady," Sinatra said, standing on stage in his dinner jacket wearing what appeared to be a Prince Valiant toupee and reading from index cards. "This is one of my favorite songs and we've had just a little change in the lyrics. And I hope you'll like this, Nancy."

> *. . . I'm so pleased that our First Lady's Nancy,*
> *Also pleased that I'm sort of a chum,*
> *Bet the eight years all will be fancy,*
> *As fancy as they come. . . .*
>
> *Nancy, Nancy, Nancy with the laughing face.*

As Sinatra sang, the television audience saw Nancy silhouetted in a

Johnny Carson at the Capital Center inaugural gala.
(Jim Nachturey, Black Star, © 1981)

cameo on the side of the screen appearing flushed and beautiful. During the last verse Nancy looked skyward; then, with tears in her eyes, blew the singer a kiss.

Sinatra's performance was supposed to end the evening. Before the gala, however, Ronnie had decided that he wanted to thank his show-business friends on stage. It was impossible. The Secret Service said so. The television people said so. But this evening nobody was going to tell the president-elect "no." And so in a few minutes of frenzy, the tightly scheduled gala was recast by Judy McLennan, vice-chairman of the gala, Reagan's advance men and the Secret Service.

To a thunderous ovation, Nancy and Ronnie walked down onto the stage. Few performers in America could work an audience as well as Carson, Hope or Sinatra, but Ronnie held the audience better than any of them. As he thanked the entertainers, he missed not a beat. Then he turned to another matter.

"I'm going to say something that I've dreamed of saying to an audience like this sometime, in the presence of these wonderful people," he said, looking at the entertainers. Ronnie had, in fact, recited the quotation that he was about to speak before, in 1950, when the Friars in Hollywood had honored him. But then his career as an actor was faltering; he was a divorced, unhappy man; and the words had a different kind of poignancy.

"'If it is true that when the curtain goes up on eternity all men must approach the gates bearing in their arms that which they have given to life, the people of show business will march in the procession carrying in their arms the pure pearl of tears, the gold of laughter, and the diamonds of stardust they spill on what otherwise might have been a rather dreary world. And when at last all reach the final stage I'm sure the keeper will say, "Let my children in."'

"God bless you."

As the applause continued to roll over him, Ronnie spoke again. "I'm going to quit with a God bless you. Almost every day for a long time now people have said to Nancy and myself, 'Has it really sunk in?' And we've looked at each other and said, 'Well, no, it really hasn't.' Well, tonight there was a part in the program when I leaned over to her and said, 'It's sunk in.'

"Thank you."

The next morning Ronnie lay in bed.

"It's time to get up, governor," said Mike Deaver, the president-elect's closest personal aide.

"Why do I have to get up?" asked Ronnie from his bed in Blair House.

Despite what he had said last night at the Capital Centre, both he and Nancy were having a hard time *feeling* the reality of what was about to happen to them. He hadn't felt what he called later "that moment of awesomeness."

When Ronnie looked out the window, he saw that the morning itself was a good omen. Washington had a cantankerous climate, but Ronnie was a Californian, and the day had dawned on what for January was as a close to a California day as the city had to offer. After a week so cold that the Potomac River had frozen over, Tuesday, January 20, 1981, dawned blessedly warm, a day to shuck overcoats and get outside. The political omens were just as good: After 444 days in captivity, it appeared that the fifty-two American hostages were about to be released—as fine an inaugural-day present as any new president had ever received. He and Nancy attended an early-morning service at St. John's Episcopal Church to give thanks.

Ronnie and Nancy were show-business folk, and they had a sense of theatrics to match the theatrics of history itself. For the first time the swearing-in would take place on the west side of the Capitol, facing the great expanses of the American continent.

Nancy was escorted to the first row of the platform, past the gray, subdued dress of the grandstand dignitaries. There were few furs to upstage her. She had specifically told the Republican ladies that good Republican cloth coats were the appropriate attire for the swearing-in. She was wearing a glorious red Adolfo coat, dress and halo hat ensemble worth $3,000, an outfit almost fluorescent against the drab surroundings. Nancy was stunning and had a fashionable and confident presence that had not been seen since Jackie's reign. NBC's Roger Mudd noted that Nancy's hat was "reminiscent of Jackie Kennedy's pillbox from twenty years ago."

Waiting for their father to appear on the banner-draped platform, Ronnie's four children talked softly, smiled, and scanned the crowd. Patti stood close to her brother, Ronald Prescott, who wrapped a protective arm around his bride, Doria. Maureen, who had campaigned so hard for her father, waved to friends and chatted with her brother Michael and his wife, Colleen. Ronnie's older brother, Neil, and his wife, Bess, were there among the prominent Republicans as were Nancy's parents, Dr. and Mrs. Loyal Davis.

Ronnie was waiting in Room EF100 in the Capitol, talking with Congressman John Rhodes, the House minority leader, and Senator Hatfield, chairman of the Joint Congressional Committee on Inaugural Ceremonies, while a pool camera captured his image for television across America. He was as comfortable with the cameras as with an ancient pair of boots, and he betrayed no more nervousness than an old actor opening in a new play.

Ronnie had a sense of stage presence unique among American polit···

figures. He walked out in front of the hundred thousand there below, and tens of millions at home, with a manner that was at once modest and presidential. After taking the oath of office, he gave a relatively short, twenty-minute address tailored to the television audience, complete with suggested camera shots. Much of the speech he had culled from campaign speeches, and he spoke in a voice that at times suggested Henry Fonda playing Abraham Lincoln. "Let us renew our faith and our hope," he said, a theme he had sounded a thousand times, a thousand ways. "We have every right to dream heroic dreams."

As her husband spoke, Nancy looked at Ronnie with the same devotion and concentration as she always did, whether she had heard his remarks a hundred times before or not. Today her eyes gleamed with tears.

The last page of the speech, the page his people called "the magic page," was a work of high rhetorical art crafted for the media age. "This is the first time in our history that this ceremony has been held, as you've been told, on this West Front of the Capitol," he said. "Standing here one faces a magnificent vista, opening up on this city's special beauty and history. At the end of this open mall are those shrines to the giants on whose shoulders we stand."

And then the new president pointed to the monuments that stood below him: in front, the Washington Memorial, a simple spire; to one side, the templelike monument to Jefferson; beyond the reflecting pool, the Lincoln Memorial; and across the river, the hills of Arlington National Cemetery, where lay the bodies of Americans killed in half a dozen wars.

Standing listening to the president that day, or better yet sitting at home watching, and seeing these memorials, Americans could not help but *feel* the history of their country, not as something that is done unto people but as something that people make themselves.

"The crisis we are facing today . . . does . . . require . . . our best effort and our willingness to believe in ourselves and to believe in our capacity to perform great deeds," he concluded. "To believe that, together with God's help, we can and will resolve the problems which now confront us.

"And, after all, why shouldn't we believe that? We are Americans."

By the time the new president and the First Lady entered the Capitol, the planes had taken off from Teheran Airport carrying the American hostages. It was a feast of a day, the end of one of the most humiliating diplomatic incidents in American history and the inauguration of a new president whose spirit and optimism were almost irresistible, at least for this day. The theme of Ronnie's inauguration was "A Great New Beginning," and so it seemed with the added blessing for the fifty-two Americans whom Ronnie now called openly "prisoners of war." He proudly announced their release at the Statuary Hall luncheon in the Capitol with members of Congress and Supreme Court justices.

After lunch, the parade started more than an hour late, but practically no one cared. Like everything else, the parade was tailored for television, cut to a palatable hour. When the parade did begin marching down Pennsylvania Avenue, spectators saw a jamboree of American symbols—regional floats with waving beauties; military units flashing their brass instruments; majorettes twirling their batons—all orchestrated by Terry Chambers, a professional showman who had organized Orange Bowl parades.

Ronnie had specified that he wanted to see "a sea of young faces." And so he did in the high-school bands that included his hometown of Dixon, Illinois. His penchant for horses was satisfied by twenty-six mounted units. And the finale, the "Battle Hymn of the Republic" sung by the Mormon Tabernacle choir, brought tears to his eyes. It was his people, his parade, and Ronnie enjoyed it as much as a five-year-old riding on his dad's shoulders.

Entering the White House for the first time as the new president, Ronnie walked into the Oval Office. The room was empty, bare of books, reports and documents, bare of any sign of life. The top of the ornate, carved desk was bare too, except for one paper clip.

Upstairs in the private quarters, Nancy saw that familiar belongings were already in place. As soon as Ronnie had been sworn in, Ted Graber, Nancy's decorator, had hurried into the White House to put the Reagans' furniture and possessions in their quarters.

Nancy was glad to see her things, but for her there was nothing so exciting as a great, glorious party, and tonight she would be going to ten of them. Her clothes were already laid out and waiting for her. For the whole week Julius Bengtsson, her California hairdresser, had been staying with the Reagans at Blair House. Weeks ago they had talked about doing a special style for this evening, and Julius combed Nancy's hair back, trying to get it to flatten down. When he got it right, he put in clips and sprayed the hair, ready to be further anchored by four pearl-and-diamond clasps. It was not an easy style to wear, but she had wanted something different, an almost regal coif to crown her night of triumph. It was different, so different that later some didn't recognize her small face without its crest of golden waves.

The gown Nancy put on was no easier to wear than her hair. It was daring for a woman in her late fifties to wear a one-shoulder dress displaying a frail arm. But Nancy loved to look youthful and, as Galanos knew, she favored one-shoulder and halter styles. The floor-length white satin gown with its silvery hand-beaded lace overlay looked exquisite. There was a stiffness to the dress that made it look far better than it felt, but the gown was indeed a standout, a one-of-a-kind in its Grecian lines. Her coat was of white flowing satin finished with an Elizabethan ruffed collar that framed her face.

Before leaving for the balls, the Reagan family gathered for an official portrait. In the center sat Nancy, elegant to a fault. Behind her chair stood Ronnie in white tie and tails, looking as if he were ready to conduct an orchestra. Two-year-old Cameron, the only grandchild, had stayed up to be in the picture. In his striped sweater, with long blond hair, he nestled in Michael Reagan's arms, mugging happily for the camera. Everyone else was dressed formally, even Patti, who preferred jeans. She didn't appear comfortable, though, and sat nervously, her knee exposed in the portrait.

When Peter Sorum, chairman for the balls, showed Mike Deaver and Joe Canzeri, Deaver's aide, the schedule that was to get the Reagans to the ten balls scattered all over town in four hours, they said flatly that it was impossible. But the Reagans knew that for any ball to have been a real part of the inauguration, they would have to make an appearance. And so they set out with an entourage like a great royal clan moving imperiously through the city: the motorcycle policemen, the Secret Service, the communications specialists, the aides, the press bus.

By Sorum's estimation, 56,000 to 60,000 people showed up with tickets when they were initially preparing for 42,000. At the Sheraton Hotel, hundreds of disgruntled celebrants couldn't even get into the ball, while a thousand or more others were shunted into a B room, *sans* entertainment, *sans* distinguished guests. At the Pension Building, temporary stairwells were set up next to the windows so that the fire marshals would allow more guests to enter.

Nancy and Ronnie saw none of this. For them the balls were a series of miniperformances: a stunning entrance, a few words from the president and a stunning exit. In Hollywood they had learned to wait for long periods, then suddenly perform. At each stop this evening, they had to wait until security was double-checked, the press was in place and the Ball Committee chairman had things ready. Their appearances were beamed to 100 satellite balls across the country.

At the Shoreham Hotel, they were about to go on stage when Mr. Carl Shipley, the ball cochairman, whispered to them that Ron, Jr., was there. So they quickly slipped back to private rooms and Nancy chattered effervescently about the evening's events with her son and daughter-in-law while the president stood quietly by. To Mrs. Shipley the new president looked "very relaxed, happy, genial, not really excited in that nervous way." After Ronnie and Nancy left, Ron, Jr., and Doria and their friends went downtown to have dinner and a separate celebration. As for Neil Reagan, he was having his troubles. "I'm the president's brother," he said, trying to enter the ballroom. "You're the tenth guy that's tried that today," the guard told him.

At the Kennedy Center, the ball of balls, the 10,000 revelers included

The Reagan family portrait, 1980. From left to right: Geoffrey and Anne Davis, Nancy Reagan's niece and nephew; Dennis Revell and his fiancée, Maureen Reagan, the president's daughter; Michael Reagan, the president's oldest son, with his wife, Colleen, and his son, Cameron; the president and the First Lady; Neil Reagan, the president's brother, and his wife, Bess; Dr. Richard Davis, Nancy Reagan's brother, and his wife, Patricia; Patti Davis, daughter of President and Mrs. Reagan (who uses her mother's maiden name); Ronald Prescott Reagan (often called Ron, Jr.) and his wife, Doria. *(UPI)*

the Californians, Hollywood entertainers and Nancy's closest friends. In the main hall downstairs, Ed McMahon's TV booth interrupted the flow of partygoers. Upstairs in the Atrium, mingling was easier. Guests could dance among the ficus trees surrounded by red tulips and white chrysanthemums. Here above the throng was the *crème de la crème*—the stars, the fashion designers, the biggest Republican contributors, and old Reagan friends. Jimmy and Gloria Stewart. The Armand Deutsches. Earle Jorgensen. Bill Blass. Estée Lauder. Roy Rogers and Dale Evans. Bob Hope. Rich Little. Henry Salvatori.

"Where's Jimmy?" Nancy asked as she kissed Betsy Bloomingdale on both cheeks. "Where's Jimmy?"

Galanos had been unable to push his way through the guests jammed into the room and had to settle for seeing his creation on a television monitor.

Nancy turned to kiss Jerry Zipkin. "Did you get the package?" Nancy asked, referring to a gift she had given her favorite male escort.

"I want to see you in that dress again before it goes to the Smithsonian," Betsy said as Nancy retreated holding Ronnie's hand.

The Reagans arrived at their final stop, the American History Museum, shortly after midnight, a good twenty minutes ahead of schedule. By then the floors were so jammed that the celebrants were more concerned with breathing space than dancing room.

"Do you mind if I have the last dance with my lady?" the president asked as the Tommy Dorsey band eased into "You'll Never Know Just How Much I Love You." For a minute and twenty seconds, Ronnie and Nancy danced intimately while thousands watched. Then at 12:30 they headed back to their new home, the White House. Their friends celebrated until morning light at a postball supper dance at the Fairfax Hotel and at other private dinners at the Georgetown Club and Pisces.

The next morning the president got up and put in his first full day in office, and Nancy began settling in. On their third evening in the White House, at about 7:15, Nancy was up on the third floor with Letitia Baldrige going through rooms that she felt had been left in appalling condition. Ronnie came bounding up the stairs. He hadn't seen Nancy since midafternoon, and his face lit up as he put his arm around her.

"What have you been up to?" he asked. Nancy led him through the rooms, showing him cubbyholes and nooks in their new castle. Holding hands, they moved through the rooms as if they were exploring a magical kingdom. Opening yet another door, they discovered a pool table.

"Hey, I haven't done this for years," the president said, picking up a stick and starting to play.

Nancy waited patiently, and then began tapping her foot. "Now, Ronnie, we have better things to do."

Watching them, Baldrige thought that they were still so much in love.

Those first days, Ronnie seemed to take to being president, but for Nancy it was different. She had vowed to "do something substantive," but she found it wasn't easy to get started. She had to sift through various interest groups wanting her attention and to pick a staff. There were so many decisions to be made quickly.

Nancy called Colleen Moore, her daughter's godmother and her mother's closest and oldest friend, in Paso Robles, California. Colleen could not believe that it was the First Lady calling.

"Nancy *who?*" she asked.

"It's me. *Nancy.*"

"Nancy! Why, it's you! Why . . ."

"Colleen, I'm so scared, so scared and lonely."

"Oh, Nancy, you aren't a movie star now, not the biggest movie star. You're the star of the whole world. The biggest star of all."

"Yes, I know, and it scares me to death."

Edith Luckett (Nancy's mother): the actress.

— 2 —
"NANCY ROBBINS, NANCY ROBBINS"

At the great house on Long Island, the guests wandered through the rooms talking about movies and the magical land of Hollywood. Richard Rowland, the host, had already made *The Four Horsemen of the Apocalypse,* a sensational Valentino picture, at Metro. Now he was the head of First National Studios, in charge of not one but dozens of pictures.

One of the guests, Colleen Moore, had the lead in First National's new film, *Flaming Youth.* With her pert *gamine* looks, bobbed hair and inquisitive, sparkling eyes, Colleen was the very image of the free young woman of the Twenties. Rowland was convinced that *Flaming Youth* would be a sensation.

Colleen stood talking to Rowland's wife and looking out on the scores of guests. She stared at a young blond woman with huge blue eyes. The woman was pretty, but what so intrigued Colleen was that she had a baby in her arms.

"Who is she?" Colleen asked.

"Oh, that's Edith Luckett," Mrs. Rowland said. "An actress. She's from Washington."

"And the baby?"

"Edith's just been divorced from a rich playboy who's not worth the powder to blow him up."

No one took a baby to a fancy New York party. But Edith had no place to put her daughter. As far as Edith was concerned, it was all her estranged husband's fault. She could see what Kenneth Robbins was now, but she had been bowled over by him. Ken had been a handsome stage-door johnny, bigger than life and twice as kind. Ken was a man of means, too, or so he had seemed, and from a far better family than Edith's. In the Robbins veins flowed the blood of colonial Yankees. Ken came from an old New England family with a big house, money in the woolen mills, and proud traditions.

Edith had been born in 1896 to Sarah Frances Whitlock and Charles Edward Luckett of Petersburg, Virginia. She was one of nine children. Her father worked in Washington, D.C., for the Adams Express Company, the predecessor of Railway Express. Edith's uncle Joe managed a theater in Richmond, the capital, the one place where she got away from the poverty of her home. The first time she had a chance to substitute on stage for a child actor, she headed out to the footlights. From then on, she hardly went to school any longer, becoming a full-time actress at the age of fifteen.

In contrast, Ken had enjoyed all the advantages position can give a person. He had gone to a military prep school and from there to Princeton. After that, he served as a sergeant in the army's quartermaster section during the world war. When Ken entered the service in 1917, he and Edith were newlyweds. But he had his duties and she had her career. Her first big break had come that year, a role in 'Ception Shoals' in New York City, which starred the legendary Alla Nazimova. It was a tiny role, but a role.

Ken had been released from the army in January 1919. Edith had tried to keep the marriage going with her twenty-three-year-old husband, but all she had to show for it was a baby, born on July 6, 1921, in New York City. Ken hadn't even been there.

The birth had not been easy. It was almost as if the child did not want to leave her mother's womb. The doctor stood over Edith, complaining about the heat, saying that he wanted to finish up and head out to the golf course. To deliver the baby, he used forceps. When Edith first saw her daughter, the child's right eye was closed, and the doctor said that she might be blind in that eye. Edith told him she had heard what he said about wanting to hurry to play golf. "If my daughter's eye doesn't open, I'll kill you," she said.

The eye opened up finally, and the infant's eyes were as big as her mother's. The baby was named Anne Frances Robbins, after a Robbins ancestor, Sister Anne Ayres, the first American Episcopal nun. But Edith decided to call her daughter Nancy, as if to make the child even more hers.

Edith loved Nancy, but without a husband it was difficult. She had to drag Nancy around from one theater and hotel to the next. After two years of using trunks as cradles, Edith decided she'd have to leave her child with her older sister, Virginia, in Bethesda, Maryland.

For Nancy, shunted off to the suburbs of Washington, ward of an aunt and uncle, the prospects were for a childhood that drew as much on *Oliver*

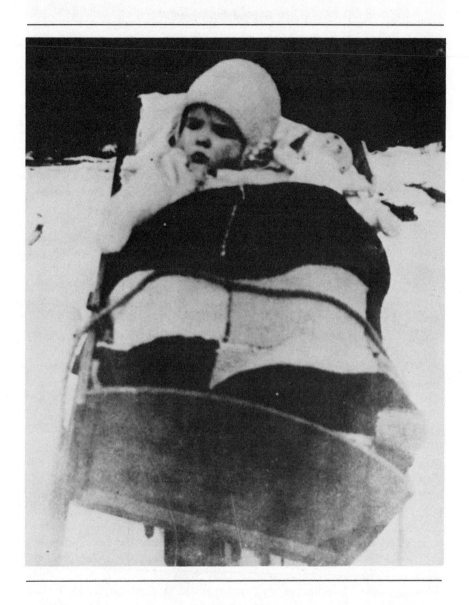

The baby, Anne Frances Robbins (Nancy).

Twist as on *Rebecca of Sunnybrook Farm.* But Virginia and Audley Galbraith looked after Nancy as they did their own child, Nancy's cousin Charlotte, and gave her a good and loving home. The Galbraiths lived in Battery Park, one of the first planned suburban communities in the area. The development had started as a place for active and retired army officers, and had the newly shorn look of a recruit's haircut. The houses were set down in neat rows on twisting gravel roadways, bare of trees. The development had its own small, unpretentious clubhouse with two tennis courts. The Galbraiths' white frame residence was the smallest model in Battery Park, but it was big enough to satisfy the fantasies of most middle-class Americans.

Just across Wilson Lane, a few hundred yards from the Galbraith house on Glenbrooke Road, lay an older community, Edgemoor, with woods and sprawling lawns, and houses set regally on two-acre lots. The promoter told the *Washington Post* that these were "millionaire's surroundings with a reasonable price," as well as "several estates . . . worthy of the attention of a multimillionaire, for finer sections can not be found around Washington." Here lived families to whom Europe was not a half-forgotten heritage but a watering place, with children who were chauffeured each morning to private schools.

On the other side of Battery Park, across Old Georgetown Road, lay a section known as Woodmont. This section was a scruffy warren of modest homes and tiny, unpainted houses, some with outhouses. Laborers and tradespeople lived here, up from West Virginia and rural Maryland in search of good wages.

Nancy knew that while it was fine to go across Wilson Lane to play with children in Edgemoor, she must not enter the disordered regions of Woodmont. She was hardly tempted. Just next door between the Galbraiths and their neighbors, the Greenes, was a vacant lot that the two fathers took turns mowing. Here the children of Battery Park came to play.

As Charlotte remembered years later, in the summer Nancy and the other little girls sat in the grass and made daisy chains. Sometimes they rummaged in someone's coalbin for a lump just right for marking up the driveways for hopscotch; roared down the walkway on roller skates along sidewalks bordered with freshly planted roses; or ventured across Wilson Lane to pick wildflowers. In the evenings when the fathers came home, the Galbraiths and their friends sometimes gathered in the vacant lot for a rousing game of catch as catch can, or, growing lethargic in the torpid air of a Washington summer, just sat and talked.

Mrs. Galbraith was a southern lady, with a lilt to her voice. She loved both girls. Nancy was a quiet little child, as plump as a jelly donut. She wore Mary Jane shoes and bobby socks. Her knees were so bruised from falling on the cinder driveway that she wore kneepads. Charlotte was tall and lanky. Almost three years Nancy's elder, she was like an older sister. Charlotte was outgoing as a carnival barker, a leader not only for Nancy but for most of the girls of Battery Park. Nancy usually went out only if Charlotte went along.

"Nancy Robbins, Nancy Robbins," the children yelled when they asked her out to play, using a last name that set her apart.

Only when her little boyfriend showed up did Nancy venture out alone. "Oh, it's *him*," she would say, and get up from the table ready to be pulled around the block in a red wagon.

Battery Park was a good place, a nurturing place, for Nancy to grow up. What she loved more than anything else, though, were her mother's visits. So far in her Broadway career, Edith was playing secondary roles—the heroine's girlfriend or a servant. She never rated a separate mention in the *New York Times* reviews. When she went on tour to Trenton, Pittsfield and Atlanta, she had bigger parts and a better reception. And when she came to Battery Park, she came as a star.

"Lucky," someone had nicknamed her, and lucky she seemed, rolling into Battery Park, a creature of glamour and glory, swathed in a raccoon coat. Everyone knew her. She had gifts for Charlotte and Nancy and wonderful tales of stars like Colleen Moore, Walter Huston and ZaSu Pitts, tales that the neighborhood kids told over and over. Sooner or later, Edith would take up a position in the center of the small living room and play all the parts in her newest play. In the evenings she sometimes went off dancing at the community club. One night she returned carrying her pumps in her hand, escorted by several of the neighborhood men, thoroughly scandalizing her older sister.

Whenever Edith appeared in New York, Nancy's aunt took her by train to visit her mother. Edith lived in a brownstone apartment, but her real life was in the theater and in the evening life of the city. Nancy sat in the darkened theaters watching her mother perform. It didn't matter if she had seen the play ten times; she would gladly see it ten times more.

Nancy took it all very seriously and thought it real. Watching one performance from a box, she saw her mother dying onstage. Nancy began to cry, wailing so loudly that Edith had to rise up from her deathbed and wave to her daughter. "You can't take this sort of thing seriously," Edith told her backstage. "It's not real. It's make-believe. It's a play and I'm playing a part."

Nancy wanted to be an actress. In Battery Park, she loved to go off by herself in the house and playact. She wanted to have long blond curls like Mary Pickford. When her mother bought her a wig, Nancy wore it everywhere. She wanted to be in movies, to be someone different.

As close as she was to Nancy, Charlotte never noticed that her cousin missed her mother. In the good times, Nancy had other things on her mind. But the bad times were different. Lying alone sick with scarlet fever, with a sheet tacked up across her bedroom doorway, she wished only for her mother. The time she had double pneumonia, she cried, "If I had a child and she got sick, I'd be with her."

Edith tried to make up for her absences. One visit, she brought a beautiful box of chocolates, not the block chocolate Nancy regularly ate. But Charlotte and Nancy both had already eaten their one piece of chocolate for the day. In the afternoon, Charlotte, her mother and Edith went downtown, leaving the box of candy high atop a cabinet. When they returned home, Nancy was sitting eating every candy in the box.

The Galbraiths, like Edith, wanted the best for Nancy as they did for Charlotte. When it came time for her to start school, the four-room public school in Bethesda wasn't good enough for Nancy. She would have to go to a private school with her cousin and get the kind of education that her mother never had. Thus in the fall of 1926 Nancy and Charlotte headed off together by trolley four miles down Wisconsin Avenue to Sidwell Friends School in Washington, one of the capital's most prestigious schools. For her first two years, the Galbraiths paid for Nancy themselves; the third year Edith took over.

At Sidwell Friends, Nancy sat with children whose fathers helped rule the country and the city or guided its commerce. When they came home in the afternoon, Nancy and Charlotte were different from the other children at Battery Park. At Christmas time, the Sidwell Friends children went across Wisconsin Avenue to a party at the great estate of Edward McLean, poker-playing friend of President Harding and owner of the *Washington Post*. The McLeans gave wonderful gifts: a carriage with a doll in it for the girls, and toy automobiles for the boys.

On visits to her father in New Jersey, Nancy saw a life not half as privileged as that of her new friends, or as romantic as her vision of Edith's life. Ken was five feet eight and a half, with blue eyes, brown wavy hair, a ruddy complexion. He was good-looking. But the story of his life was told in his small, uncertain eyes. They looked out on the world as if he couldn't quite believe what life had brought him.

Ken Robbins was a weak man, and if some called him a good man, it was a goodness that could not rise above the level of his weakness. He had New England bloodlines that went back to colonial times: a great-grandfather—Deacon Luke Francis—who helped found Pittsfield, Massachusetts; a grandfather—Captain Frederick Augustus Francis—who was a Civil War hero; and a father—John N. Robbins—who was the superintendent of the Tillotsons woolen mill at Silver Lake, Massachusetts.

Kenneth Robbins, Nancy's natural father.

But the Robbins blood had thinned out. Ken Robbins's father was dead. His mother lived on at the family estate in Verona, New Jersey. It was here that Nancy came most often to visit her father and "Nanee," the gray-haired grandmother who smelled of violet toilet water. Anne Robbins was Nancy's only living grandparent, and Nancy was Nanee's only grandchild. In the evenings they sat on the porch of the big old house, or walked around the tennis courts.

In the spring of 1929, Edith came to tell Nancy that on her recent sail to Europe she had met the "doctor she wanted to marry." Her mother was willing to give up her career and they would move to Chicago and live with Dr. Loyal Davis—but only if Nancy agreed.

Nancy had traveled to places most little girls never reached. She was a child of privilege who went to a private school and to theaters and restaurants. She was a child of divorce, full of the quiet cunning that comes from knowing the world is not the way *they* say it is. She had learned to act one way in Bethesda, another in New Jersey, yet another way at Sidwell Friends. Even at seven Nancy understood that she and her mother were speaking as one actress to another. Indeed, years later Nancy wrote in her autobiography that even if she had vehemently opposed the marriage, her mother would have talked her into it. More than anything, though, she wanted to live with her mother, even at the price of sharing her with a stranger.

In May 1929, two months before her eighth birthday, Nancy served as a flower girl at her mother's wedding in Chicago's Fourth Presbyterian Church. It was a second marriage for both bride and groom, and the ceremony received little publicity.

It would have taken almost any child a good while to develop a real relish for Loyal Davis. Born in 1896, the only son of an Illinois railroad engineer, Davis was regarded by many as a dour, humorless, pompous man. But he was also a very dedicated doctor. Trained by Boston's Harvey Cushing, the father of American neurosurgery, Dr. Davis was the first Chicagoan to specialize full-time in brain surgery. Davis became one of the leaders of American neurosurgery, a founder of the American Board of Surgery and president of the American Board of Surgeons. He was also the author of several medical books.

Devoted to improving what was a fledgling procedure, Davis fought for his medical principles. He was one of the first doctors to publicly denounce the practice of fee splitting between surgeons and referring physicians. He campaigned to tighten the restrictions on medical licenses, to prevent unqualified doctors from performing surgery in which they had not been trained. He spoke out against physicians who elevated their fees ac-

Loyal Davis, M.D., F.A.C.S. (Nancy's adoptive father).
(The American College of Surgeons)

cording to the amount of their patients' insurance. His crusades would have been controversial anyway, but his adamancy and self-righteousness made the kettle of controversy boil even more hotly.

Davis was a perfectionist, and that urge to reform inadequacies touched everything he saw. He believed that godliness was next to cleanliness. During the thirty-one years that he was chairman of surgery at Northwestern University, he was a martinet. When he entered the lecture room, he turned so that the best side of his Teutonic features might be appreciated. The first thing he told the new students was that they were supposed to dress like young doctors, in suits and ties. It didn't occur to him that a student might have only one suit and didn't like hanging it in a medical lab reeking of formaldehyde.

Davis became disgusted at the way some people didn't flush toilets. He rigged up a system in the new College of Surgeons headquarters so that whenever the stall doors were opened or shut, the toilet flushed automatically. One day, walking up the stairwell at the hospital, he noticed a cigarette butt lying there; picking it up, he raged as if the fag were evil incarnate. In the doctors' dressing room, he was forever swooping down to pick up gowns and throwing them in the hamper.

Dr. Davis was ultraconservative. Some of the medical residents were so appalled at Davis's racial attitudes that when they went out into the ghetto to deliver babies, they persuaded mothers to name their offspring "Loyal." But whatever was said or done against him, he had no illusions about equality. "It is a favorite saying that one citizen is as good as another," he wrote in his autobiography. "This must be recognized as a platitude, expounded vociferously and opportunistically by politicians and emotionally by do-gooders."

Dr. Davis believed that the rich and mighty were more virtuous. One time Dr. Davis thought a woman patient probably had a tumor. But two young doctors, Dick Sedlack and Arthur Norton, took a look at the well-to-do lady's rash and decided she might have syphilis. They did their own test, which confirmed the diagnosis. When they proudly told Dr. Davis of their discovery, he flashed: "My patients don't have syphilis."

The students and interns had no end of Loyal Davis stories. He terrified and angered generations of medical students. But his detailed concern and training stayed with his former students the rest of their professional lives.

For Nancy, though, this man was not merely the austere, formidable Dr. Davis. This man was her stepfather. The Davises lived in a spacious apartment on exclusive Lake Shore Drive overlooking Lake Michigan. Davis was as meticulous at home as he was at work; the place was as neat as an operating room. In the evenings he dictated notes from policy meetings at Passavant Memorial Hospital, so that even a year later he knew exactly what everyone had said.

Davis had been married before and had a son, Richard. But this new love between Davis and Edith was totally different from anything either had known. It was as if two disparate elements had come together, producing a new, marvelous compound. For Edith, her husband was the strength and security and status she had sought for so very long. For Davis, his wife was all the freedom, the frivolity, the gaiety, the joy he never could allow himself. Years later, at the Biltmore Hotel in Phoenix where the Davises wintered, the doctor sat outside a cabana watching Edith come dancing down the lawn like the heroine of a light opera. "Look at her," Davis said affectionately to Colleen Moore. "Look at her. I'd give anything in the world if I could be like that."

Edith and Loyal invited Nancy into their happiness. One evening little Nancy let herself out of the apartment and knocked on the door of a neighbor, a retired judge. The judge answered the door to find a very serious young lady standing there.

"Judge, I've come to see you on business."

"What is it, Nancy?" the jurist asked, peering down at her.

"I'd like to know how to adopt Dr. Davis."

"That's a little difficult," the judge said, nodding his head gently. "But I think it can be arranged."

When Nancy left, he called Dr. Davis and told him what she had said. "I've always wanted that," the doctor said. "But I didn't know how to approach Nancy or her mother."

At the age of fourteen when she had the legal right, Nancy took adoption papers with her on a trip to Verona to visit her father. Ken Robbins had come to visit his daughter in Chicago, and he still loved her and wanted her as his daughter. But when Nancy asked him to sign her away, he didn't let on how terrible he felt. Nancy's grandmother, gray-haired old Nanee, the one Robbins whom Nancy loved with pure and certain affection, could not hide how hurt she was. But Nancy left for Chicago with the papers all neatly signed, and proudly told her classmates at Girls Latin that they could call her Nancy Davis.

Her stepfather was always "Dr. Loyal" to Nancy. Sometimes she went to the hospital to see him. When she was old enough, Dr. Davis allowed Nancy to watch him operate and accompany him on house calls.

Nancy loved Dr. Davis in part because they were kindred souls. She, too, believed in order and neatness. She, too, sometimes couldn't make people understand her motives. As she grew older, she became so much like Dr. Davis that she did indeed seem to be his natural daughter.

Each morning Nancy headed off to the exclusive Girls Latin School, wearing a blue skirt, white blouse and blue blazer or sweater. Even for those days the discipline at Latin was harsh. The teachers were female, single and formidable. The girls stood when teachers or adults entered the classroom, and sat only when given the affirming nod. Rudeness was a sin. Any excesses, any smart-aleck remarks, and the perpetrator was rewarded with a trip to the headmistress's office. Some of the girls chafed under such severe discipline and couldn't wait to come bursting out of school in the afternoon. But Nancy was the perfect little miss.

Nancy's mother had always had remarkable vitality, but this marriage was a double tonic. She had given up her Broadway career to make Chicago her theater. It was her best performance: a largely uneducated, divorced actress who had married a divorced doctor, the son of a railway engineer, traveling at the heights of Chicago society.

A vivacious, unpretentious woman, Edith threw herself into social and charitable work and fund raising for the Republican party. Everyone seemed to know "Edie." The cops on the beat tipping their hats to her. The cabdrivers whizzing her between lunches, benefits and charity work. The medical students whom she directed in skits and told wonderful tales of her Broadway days. The grandes dames of Chicago society. Even Democratic Mayor Ed Kelly, whom Edith tutored in speech techniques.

Despite all her activities, Edie still had time for professional work. In "Betty and Bob," one of the first of the radio soap operas, she appeared not only as Bob's mother but as Gardenia, the black maid. "Sho is good to have you back, Mistah Bob," she would say in a voice bent over in subservience.

To both Davises, though, Nancy was the center of the universe. Vacations included not only Nancy but anyone dear to her. In the summer when cousin Charlotte came to visit, Edie took the two girls downtown to the studios of NBC's Blue Network, where they sat quietly while "Betty and Bob" was broadcast across the country. In the afternoon Nancy and Charlotte dressed up in Edie's old clothes and pretended they were princesses, queens and movie stars. Though Nancy was plump, Dr. Loyal thought the girls needed to be fattened up. He prescribed a regimen of "black cow" ice cream sodas, which he prepared nightly.

Out there beyond the elegant confines of Lake Shore Drive, it was not a world of chocolate sodas before bedtime. The Great Depression had fallen on the land, foreclosing farms, homes and human aspirations. Grown men in long coats and longer faces stood on the corners of State Street selling apples for a nickel. Hungry men and women rummaged through garbage cans in front of buildings like Nancy's, scavenging food from the wealthy.

Nancy's direct knowledge of the depression came only from Dr. Loyal's raging against President Roosevelt as a traitor to his class, and from lectures at Girls Latin. Poverty to her was indeed another country. The closest Nancy came to touching the bad times was during her visits to the Robbins home in New Jersey. Nanee, Nancy's grandmother, had lost a great deal in the stock-market crash. The family estate had become a place of fallen gentility. There were no servants any longer, and the tennis courts had been closed down.

But for Nancy, life was opening up. No longer living in the shadow of her more gregarious cousin in a home without parents to call her own, Nancy thrived. With only a dozen girls in her class at Girls Latin, friendships and involvement in school organizations—the hockey team, the glee club, the student government—came easily.

A group of her schoolmates who lived along the lake roller-skated down Astor Street and motored to the Riverview Amusement Park. Lela Ellis, Jane Beckwith, Ginny Skinner, the Stenson sisters and Nancy played together. Jean Wescott, Nancy's desk partner, became a special friend. The two girls gave each other nicknames based on the color of their underwear: "Whitey" for Jean and "Pinky" for Nancy. They were the perfect pair, pretty and demure. With her wavy yellow hair tied daintily with a colored ribbon, Whitey followed just behind Pinky.

Sometimes after school—and always on Saturday—they had time for a movie. Nancy loved sitting in the plush seats of the movie palaces. If she was watching one of her favorites, Bing Crosby or Jimmy Stewart, she got completely lost in the romance and adventure.

Until she was fourteen, Nancy spent eight weeks each summer at Camp Ketchuwa in Michigan. The three sisters who owned Camp Ketchuwa were graduates of Vassar College, ladies with a mission and a method. They mixed cold water and outdoor living with artistic endeavors and high culture. Nancy loved sleeping with the other girls in a tent on a wooden platform. She loved this pristine respite from the rigorous discipline of her Chicago life. She enjoyed the swimming, boating, sailing, the classes in archery, literature and theater.

During the school year, classmates often spent the night at the Davises' lovely apartment. They were drawn there as much by Edith's youthful humor as by their friendship with Nancy. Once, after the Davises had hosted a dinner party and Dr. Loyal was asleep, Edith slipped into Nancy's room. Nancy and her friend were still whispering happily. Edith winked in childlike conspiracy and motioned the girls to get up.

"Come and have your first champagne. There's still some in the refrigerator."

The girls jumped out of bed, flushed with excitement. "But be quiet," Edith cautioned. "We mustn't wake the doctor." While the two girls sipped

Nancy Davis: a mature young woman.

champagne, Edith listened carefully for rustling from her snoozing husband.

Another time, when a chilling wind blew off the lake into their apartment, Edith shocked the young girls by throwing her skirt above her head, revealing bright bloomers. "That's how I keep warm," the matronly-looking Edith said, then joined the giggling girls in a tumble of laughter.

Edith had left home to become an actress and had been divorced. Yet with her flamboyant style, the now fat and silver-haired Edith had been able to capture social Chicago. Despite all her joking and gaiety, Edith was grooming her daughter to maintain that position and legitimize it. Nancy would not have to flirt with stage-door johnnys and live out of a suitcase. All she would have to do was marry well.

Nancy had not inherited Edith's magical lightheartedness. To make her way, Nancy would have to depend on manners, grace, social connections and men.

In seventh grade, at the first fortnightly dance, Nancy and the other Latin School girls stood clumped together. As they chatted, they glanced at the thirteen-year-old boys far across the floor. The boys may have appeared sophisticated and world-weary to the young girls, but they were terrified to ask a girl to dance. As that moment of manly truth approached when they would *have* to ask someone to dance, a lone girl set out across the empty dance floor. Nancy spotted a likely prospect, walked up to him and started talking, her lilting laughter punctuating the conversation.

Before long, Nancy had begun to leave behind the comradeship and anonymity of her gang. She slipped easily across the bridge between adolescence and womanhood, never really suffering clumsy teen-age embarrassments. She seemed older, more serious, poised. She was the first to sport a gold bracelet with tiny diamonds flecking the charms, the first to wear a fur coat, which her mother loaned her.

During school hours Nancy was still shrouded in the blue uniform of Girls Latin, not allowed lipstick or nail polish, and wore only a ring and a watch as jewelry. But her mother bought her the finest clothes and took her to the finest places. One Easter her parents let Nancy bring her good friend Whitey Wescott along on a trip to Arizona, where the two teen-agers learned to ride.

In 1936, one of Nancy's paternal second cousins, Kathleen, and her mother stopped in Chicago. They had just come from visiting Nancy's grandmother, Nanee, and her father in New Jersey and had many stories to tell. Twelve-year-old Kathleen had spent most of her life in France. The Davises considered it jolly fun having Kathleen order in French restaurants. They bought new clothes for Kathleen and made her feel welcome. Kathleen trailed behind her older cousin, awed by sixteen-year-old Nancy's beauty and sophistication, and by her extraordinary wardrobe, all so neatly arranged, her angora socks drying in the bathroom.

Years later Kathleen Young remembered that she could hardly believe how many people Nancy knew. The Davises not only traveled at the top of Chicago's social world, but, thanks to Edith, they moved in the city's theatrical circles as well. In those years, Chicago was not merely a stop on national tours but a center of legitimate theater and national radio programming. Nancy not only knew Alla Nazimova, the movie legend; "Zim" was her godmother. Colleen Moore and ZaSu Pitts, the comedienne, were two other famous performers who had become close family friends.

Lake Arrowhead, outside Chicago, was a retreat for Hollywood, almost a midwestern Palm Springs. In the summer the Davises often motored out to spend the weekend. They knew Myron Selznick, the famous movie agent, who had a place on the lake, and Reginald Denny, the well-known actor. Walter Huston, with whom the Davises stayed, was not merely a famous actor to Nancy; he was "Uncle Walter," a beloved family friend, whose swimming pool and tennis court the Davises used as their own. In the main house hung a painting of "Alastair, duc de Crovenay." Visitors often thought that the duke was Huston's ancestor. The former song-and-dance man had, in fact, invented his relative. Nancy was in on the joke, but she considered movie stars and actors a natural aristocracy.

Nancy traveled in a world where the real and the unreal blended imperceptibly into one another. Jimmy Stewart was an image on the screen and a picture on the cover of her notebook. But the Jimmy Stewart on whom Nancy had a crush was a laughing, wisecracking young man whom she had met at "Uncle Walter's."

One summer she sat by the Hustons' pool listening as Josh Logan, a young producer, read a script to Uncle Walter. Logan was casting the play and he very much wanted Huston to star. At each laugh line, Nancy emitted a light, high-pitched chortle. Logan was sure that he had an encouraging booster in Nancy.

As soon as Logan left, however, Nancy turned toward Huston. "Oh, Uncle Walter, I don't think it's right for you," she said with all the confidence of inexperience. "I think it would be a big mistake for you to do it."

Huston went ahead anyway and starred in *Knickerbocker Holiday,* one of his biggest hits.

Nancy thought it would be swell if all her friends went to boarding school together. "I want to go off to school," Jean Wescott told her parents adamantly. The other girls were just as insistent. It was Nancy's idea, but when the others packed up and left, Nancy stayed in Chicago.

Nancy still wanted to travel. In her junior year, the Davises treated

Nancy with her first real sweetheart, Sangston Hettler, Jr.

her to an Easter trip to Bermuda. Since most teen-agers did not go off to Bermuda with their girlfriends, Nancy's vacation was unusual enough to merit her introduction to the readers of the *Chicago Tribune* on March 5, 1938. In her calf-length coat and her scarf, she looked like a young matron; only the black-and-white saddles shoes betrayed her age.

As Nancy began her last year at Girls Latin, a civil war raged in Spain and the statesmen of Europe were meeting in Munich to sign a pact giving Hitler the right to occupy the Sudetenland. The Chicago newspapers printed editorial cartoons showing Hitler's Germany devouring Eastern Europe. There were those who said that soon the world would be engulfed in a great world war. Nancy's stepfather was a prominent and outspoken isolationist, believing that America had to stay out of the trouble in Europe.

Nancy talked and wrote well enough about contemporary events to earn good grades, but she had other things on her mind. She loved parties and dances and good times. She had lots of crushes: Bobby Crane, Buddy Baird and others.

When she was sixteen, Sangston Hettler, Jr., was her first real sweetheart. A tall redhead, "Sock," the scion of a lumber fortune, was a student at Boys Latin. He took Nancy to the nightclub in the Sherman Hotel, where he introduced her to his friend Gene Krupa, the drummer. Sock gave her his signet ring, which some of Nancy's friends had worn before. Nancy and Sangston were enough of a duo to rate mention in the gossip column in the *Chicago Herald-American.* On their dates they often sat and talked earnestly about their future together. Much to the chagrin of Sock's mother, a photograph appeared in the newspaper with a caption insinuating their future engagement.

But Sock, parties and clothes weren't Nancy's only concerns. With Edith's prodding, Nancy traveled to the Martha Washington School for Crippled Children once a week to help amuse the children. She raised funds for the Seeing Eye Dog program and worked with the Service Club Follies.

In her senior year, Nancy was a school leader. Although she lost the election for the student body presidency, she became the student judge. Judge Nancy took the dress code and the rules about sloppy desks seriously. "Why did you do that?" she would ask offenders. She could not understand how a girl could possibly tolerate a sloppy desk, or go against the dress code by wearing lipstick to school.

On top of all her other work, Nancy had the title role in the senior play, *The First Lady,* by George S. Kaufman. As the First Lady, Nancy was busy during most of the rehearsals. When she wasn't needed, she sat on the gym floor, concentrating on her studies. It was Nancy's play, and on opening night she knew everyone's part. When other cast members forgot their lines, Nancy improvised.

Nancy felt that her years at Girls Latin had been good ones. In the fall, she and her friends would be going off to college or to finishing school. Nancy was sad to think that she would be seeing them only occasionally. She was particularly upset that she wouldn't be seeing Whitey, who had come back from boarding school. It wouldn't do, and Nancy talked Whitey into joining her at Smith.

Under the picture of Nancy in a gray sweater and a string of pearls, the 1939 Girls Latin yearbook reads: "Nancy's social perfection is a constant source of amazement. She is invariably becomingly and suitably dressed. She can talk, and even better listen intelligently, to anyone from her little kindergarten partner of the Halloween party, to the grandmother of one of her friends."

The "coming out" of Nancy Davis.

————3————

"LADIES ON THE LOOSE"

During their first months at Smith in the fall of 1939, Nancy and Jean Wescott kept much to themselves. The upperclasswomen on the Northampton, Massachusetts, campus seemed unapproachably sophisticated. Many of them were from New York and Boston and spoke in accents unlike the broad midwestern drawl, as flat as the cornfields of Illinois, that Nancy was used to hearing.

Though the school admitted many bright young women more interested in a cultured finish than a serious education, Smith had high standards. The school was one of the best colleges in America with a faculty that included world-renowned scholars. A woman could pursue as fine an education as her brothers at Princeton or Yale, or she could pursue a social life and a suitable husband.

Nancy appeared more interested in the latter. She loved glamour and glitter and glorious parties. During Christmas vacation she would make her debut, a ritual that signaled the beginning of her adult life. She had been interested in boys for years, but once she had "come out" she would be fully a woman. In July, *Townsfolk,* the toney Chicago magazine, had run Nancy's picture. With her silky dark dress and painted nails, she looked very much the socialite. "More than a score of young ladies in down east schools are watching the calendar feverishly these days awaiting the vacation hour when they can close their books and fly back home for a fortnight of gayety," the December *Townsfolk* reported.

A girl was a "bud" only once. "There never is any time in a girl's life when she is the center of everything the way she is when she is a debutante," said the *Chicago Tribune.* Nancy knew that for one magnificent fortnight the whole city would become a fairy tale: the fifty or so debutantes spinning from one party to the next, taxicabs and limousines dropping off their charges cloaked in sequined velvet capes and escorted by young men standing stiffly in white tie and tails. The papers and their society columns would become a chorus of adoring sighs.

It was always wonderful, but as Nancy could tell from all her invitations and letters, this year there would be more parties, more-extravagant parties, than ever. One deb's father had imported a New York designer who had worked on the World's Fair to transform the Blackstone Ballroom for his daughter's debut, at a cost of $3,000 for the decorations alone.

When Nancy arrived back in Chicago, her own debut on the twenty-eighth of December was a score of parties away. Some days there were four or more parties: luncheons, tea dances, dinners, supper dances and balls. And every occasion demanded a new outfit.

On Thursday, the twenty-first, for the first tea dance of the season, Nancy was one of ten buds assisting at Elizabeth ("Bubba") Stenson's debut at the Women's Athletic Club. Being an assistant was an honor akin to serving as a bridesmaid. Nancy took her turn presiding at a tea table graced with red roses. She still had plenty of time to be whirled around the floor, dancing with a beau past the green and red Christmas decorations.

After the dance, the Stensons had planned to take Bubba and her assistants downtown to the Balinese Room of the Blackstone Hotel for dinner. But there just wasn't enough room in the girls' schedule. They had scarcely enough time to change into their full-skirted, low-cut ball gowns before hurrying on to Barbara Bennett's dinner dance downtown in the Crystal Ballroom of the Blackstone.

Friday evening there was a dinner dance in honor of Whitey. And on Saturday, Nancy assisted at Barbara White's tea dance at the Fortnightly. Then most of the debs went on to Grace Shumway's dinner dance at the Casino, and from there to the ballroom of the Blackstone for Helen Dick's debut. Over 500 guests, two bands and resplendent decorations: feathered trees, silver-laced drapes, and fountains of flowers.

The buds and their beaux danced away the moonlit night. Women in gowns of satin, silk and velvet, swathed in feathers, fur, antique lace and sequin beading, swirled across the floor, creating a rainbow montage set off by the young men in black and white formal tails.

Nancy was everywhere. The season was just beginning and already the *Herald-American* had dubbed her "cute little Nancy Davis." Monday, Christmas day, was the craziest yet. First, Nancy assisted for her old schoolmate, Betty Gillespie, at her home. After the party, Mr. Gillespie took the assistants to the Balinese Room for dinner. Nancy's big event of the evening was Whitey's debut, a ball at the Casino Club. Whitey's gown was of frothy white tulle with a bodice embroidered in sequins and pearls.

She looked lovely. And the music? Newton Perry, Jr., and his Yale Orchestra. Who else? "Newtie" would be at Nancy's, too.

Nancy hardly slept before she was off again on Tuesday. The afternoon hours were filled with a tea dance at the Women's Athletic Club for Virginia ("Ginny") Skinner. Nancy had been there the week before for Bubba's debut, but the club had been completely transformed. Ginny's gold-and-silver decor, the gilded woodwardia masking the great pillars, created an entirely new wonderland, invented especially for Ginny's debut.

Taffeta rustled as girls embraced each other. It didn't matter that they had already seen each other that very day, sleepily lunching in someone's honor. Now they kissed and giggled, hastily checking to see if their friends' dresses were a touch more lavish, more enticing to the line of stags uncomfortably sipping the tea-dance punch. Many of the young gentlemen could hardly wait for the martinis that the evening balls would bring. They could have dispensed with these teatime conversations, preferring to sweep a girl onto the dance floor.

Then suddenly it was Thursday, Nancy's day. Nancy's parents were well-to-do. But, as Nancy knew, they weren't as well-to-do as many of her friends' families. Instead of an extravagant ball, the Davises had chosen the less expensive but more formal debut: an afternoon tea dance.

Edith made sure that Nancy's debut was very special. She saw to it that Nancy had a wealth of that most prized commodity of all: young men. "Today there are some 50 Princetonians in town to turn Nancy Davis' tea dance at the Casino and Priscilla Blackett's ball at the Blackstone into even gayer debuts than two such popular women would naturally have," the *Daily News* announced. Every Christmas the Princeton Triangle Club presented its show in Chicago. Thus Nancy would have a bonanza of beaux at her debut.

Nancy arrived early for the four o'clock tea dance at the Casino Club. As did all the debs for their formal coming out, Nancy wore white—not a sweet, maidenly white, but a stunning, sophisticated white. Her gown was of delicate *mousseline de soie,* the bodice twined with silver lace. Tight, long sleeves bound Nancy's arms, and the stiff skirt swished against the polished floor. She carried a nosegay of white carnations and white narcissus.

The decorations in the room complemented Nancy. At the center of the tea table covered with white linen stood a tree of white carnations set against the antique silver tea service. On eight of the ballroom's pillars were crossed silver canes bedecked with top hats and tied with ribbons, reflecting Edith's penchant for theater.

It was already four o'clock. Newtie and his band were playing a waltz. Nancy stood alongside Edith in the foyer. In her sky-blue silk dress, Edie looked very youthful. Everything was perfect. But practically no one had arrived. The Davises were always punctual. Nancy thought the dreaded thought: What if only a few people come? At least the Princeton men had arrived.

Nancy was terribly anxious. Waiting would have been even worse if it weren't for one Princeton boy. He could see how nervous she was. He kept coming down the receiving line, using a different name and a different accent. He was a whole crowd. He was just hysterically funny. He was handsome and thin. His name was Frank Birney. Suddenly, he wasn't there anymore. Suddenly, *everybody* was here.

Whitey, Bubba, Elizabeth, Virginia, Priscilla, Newtie's sister, Sally, and half a dozen other buds served as Nancy's assistants. Nancy danced and danced. Finally, she stepped in front of Newtie's orchestra. As everyone stood watching, she sang a popular song. She had sung at other parties at Latin, but tonight this was her audience, hers alone.

Nancy had no time to drink the last dregs of her own debut. She was off to the dinner party that a family friend, Mrs. Patricia Valentine, was giving in her honor. Then the guests had to rush over to the Civic Opera House to see the Triangle Club performance of *Any Moment Now*. The show was amusing, but it was only a prelude to her friend Priscilla Blackett's ball at the Blackstone.

Nancy loved to dance, and it was doubly exciting that Priscilla's father had hired Glenn Miller's band. Miller was all the rage, but there had been a storm back east and it was a wonder that the band had made it at all. Nancy swirled through a ballroom decorated with pink roses and mirrors. When Miller wasn't on the bandstand, the second band, Don Pedro, played Latin rhythms. Another day that ended with the dawn.

It was a hectic pace. As the *Daily News* pointed out, "anybody older [than eighteen] would collapse after one day of the program, let alone two weeks." Even the day after her own debut, Nancy couldn't rest. In the evening she attended a dinner party in her honor given by Mr. and Mrs. Robert J. Dunham. After that they went to a benefit performance of the Ballet Russe at the Auditorium Theater. And then most of the buds went to Sheila Cudahy's ball at the Blackstone with Duke Ellington's band as well as Newtie's.

Again Nancy couldn't sleep late. She had to be at the Casino for the luncheon that Mrs. Joseph G. Coleman and Mrs. Walter R. Kirk were hosting in her honor.

Nancy had other parties and New Year's Eve to celebrate, but it was all beginning to wind down, like a wonderful mechanical toy. It had been a magical world of youth and beauty, music and dance, elegance and grace. Nancy returned to Smith full of memories and shimmering silver dreams that had not been dreams at all.

Nancy had one souvenir from her debut that was not a pressed corsage or a newspaper clipping. Soon after she returned to Talbot House on the Smith campus, she began dating Frank Birney, the Princeton boy who had been so delightful the afternoon of her debut. Nancy and her Princeton beau had a great deal in common. Frank was from the Chicago area and had gone to exclusive Lake Forest Academy. He, too, had parents who were divorced. At Nancy's debut, Frank's humor had been the balm that soothed her. Frank was always funny. He kept Nancy in stitches. Frank was so theatrical that his friends predicted he would end up in show biz.

Princeton was full of rich boys like Frank who had read Fitzgerald too early and not very well, and poor boys who kept to their books and to their ambitions. Frank didn't put on fancy airs, but he liked to drink and dance, and go roaring off somewhere in a car. If Nancy didn't go down to Princeton for a Saturday football game, Frank drove up to Smith for a dance. Other weekends they met under the clock at the Biltmore Hotel in New York City.

Nancy and Frank were a gay and lovely couple. But to many of their contemporaries, they appeared innocent of the world outside. They didn't seem to see the ominous headlines about the Battle of Britain and Japanese moves in Manchuria. They didn't absorb their professors' tales of Nazi brutalities, often told in the thick accents of European refugees.

During Nancy's first year, the spirit of William Allan Neilson, the just retired president of Smith, was still very much alive on campus. In chapel he had talked passionately about the rise of Nazi Germany. He made room on the faculty for scholars who had fled Hitler's regime. In Nancy's sophomore year, some students were collecting clothes and funds for refugees and arguing about America's role in the conflict. Some faculty members took British children into their homes. The alumnae sent three mobile canteens to Britain for use during the blitz.

Nancy wasn't involved in any of this. At Girls Latin she had been a leader, but the world was growing beyond her and her interests. Rather than sitting in on some dreary discussion, she loved to go to one of the three movie theaters in Northampton. She often talked Whitey into bicycling downtown with her. She still liked Jimmy Stewart, but now she had a crush on Errol Flynn. There were new stars as well, including an actor named Ronald Reagan.

Nancy was not particularly popular at Smith, but she had a way with college boys. And not just Frank Birney. On Friday there might be an orchid at her table from her beau of the weekend. Nancy was five feet four inches tall and undeniably pretty though she weighed 130 pounds. None of the sixty women in Talbot House dressed any better. She wore what the more stylish women wore: matching Brooks Brothers skirts and Braemar sweaters and Spaulding brown saddle shoes or loafers. And when she went for her riding lessons, she wore jodhpurs.

Nancy was a drama major. In her entire class of 500, there were only eleven theater majors. That fact alone set her apart. Although Nancy was quiet, she had a theatrical flair. To some of her housemates she seemed glamorous; to others, sweetly demure. A few thought her a snob. To Mary Anne Guitar, a classmate who observed people with the interest of one hoping to become a writer, Nancy seemed "one of those attractive women who wait for something to happen, someone pushier, more dynamic, to start things for her."

Nancy had little to say to the more serious, contemplative students. And she had nothing in common with activist students such as Betty Friedan, who was a year ahead of Nancy.

Nancy loved to laugh, but she thought of herself as too mature to indulge in student pranks. The night some girls put honey on the toilet seats, Nancy was not involved. One weekend when she was going off to New York on a date, some of the girls put an alarm clock in her suitcase set to go off just as the train arrived in Grand Central Station.

"Nancy, what did you do when the alarm clock went off?" a housemate asked upon her return.

"Oh, I just ignored it," Nancy said airily, as if adolescent antics couldn't possibly bother *her*.

With her social life, Nancy was extremely busy. But she occasionally made time to see her real father. On a visit in 1941 to the Robbins home in Massachusetts, Nancy and her father had their picture taken together. Ken Robbins was doing fairly well in his automobile partnership. He had grown fat and stolid.

Nancy had originally planned to attend Smith for only two years. It had seemed almost preordained that she would head back to Chicago to marry one beau or another and start a family. But when she left Chicago, she had left Sangston, her old beau, for good. Now she was serious about Frank Birney, and had become interested in the theater.

Nancy wasn't making great strides as an actress. During her first two years, she had no roles in theater productions at Smith; she received most of her experience serving as an apprentice in summer stock. It wasn't until her junior year that Nancy had a role in a play at Smith, one done outside the theater department.

In the fall of 1941, a small group of Smith students began putting together what they hoped would be the first of several musical comedies. They called themselves "Bander-log," gleefully adopting the word from Kipling's monkey people who survived by mimicking. They intended to produce mirthful studies of their life-style, a grander version of the yearly Rally Day show.

Nancy Davis with Kenneth Robbins, her natural father, in 1941, years after she said she'd stopped seeing him.

It was an ambitious idea. *Ladies on the Loose* would be written, produced and directed by students, and would feature students from nearby Amherst in the male roles.

Two of the Bander-log founders, Mary Anne Guitar and Harriet Train, stayed up nights working on the script. Nancy was not involved in writing lyrics and satirical skits, in finding costumes or a hall, in the battles with Dean Laura Scales about charging admission. But she was a fledgling actress, and she was chosen for a role in the production.

Ladies on the Loose was nothing but a string of musical numbers basted together, but already during rehearsals it was clear that it was something special. The short skits were topical satires capturing a moment in time and place. The writers intuitively mimicked the films and ideas of their own era, and of their college life, living for the weekends and for their beaux. Even forty years later at the mention of the word "Bander-log," the cast and playwrights could recite lyrics verbatim and sing snatches of the tunes.

Nancy had a good part, and she was always on time for rehearsals. She was unfailingly polite and thoughtful, but she had few ideas about how she should act and sing. She constantly relied on the Bander-log directors to tell her where to stand and how to gesture. And though *Ladies on the Loose* was supposed to be satirical, when it came to comedy Nancy was flat-footed. She was the eternal ingenue, the perfect romantic lead.

As the evening of the first performance drew near, Nancy concentrated on the play. She was, however, having problems with Frank Birney. Frank was talented enough to be one of the authors of the Triangle Club production, but he was in danger of flunking out of Princeton. He wasn't much fun anymore. He was depressed and irritable. Nancy wasn't seeing him as often, and some of her housemates thought she had broken up with him.

For the two evenings of the Bander-log performance, the group rented the local high-school auditorium for $50. On opening night, December 5, an expectant crowd saw the curtain rise on a chorus of twenty dressed in traveling coats and sitting on their suitcases. They were eyed suspiciously by their professor at stage right. The female students sang:

> *We're not very subtle and never abstruse,*
> *Frankly, we're ladies just out on the loose,*
> *Beware of the smoothies of domicile fame,*
> *We're Dianas out for game!*

The audience thought this hysterically funny.

The next number was a spoof on the popular Carmen Miranda films, in which the actress's Latin accent was thicker than the plot. Nancy ap-

that weekend, not on her way to meet Frank in New York as she wrote later. Nancy took to her room and over the holidays spent time comforting Mrs. Birney, who in her distress clung to the pretty, quiet young woman.

Later Nancy retold the events of the death. "We were to meet in New York one weekend," Nancy wrote in her autobiography. "I was waiting for him when the telephone call came. He was late and had hurried to catch the train at Princeton Junction and had jumped the gate to run across the tracks ahead of the oncoming train."

Sometimes pain, remorse or guilt does to the truth what arthritis does to the hands, twisting and shriveling it until it is not itself any longer. This was the dark, dramatic tragedy of Nancy's young life. But it was easier for her to make it into a poignant ending to a bittersweet romance, a scene from a Victorian novel.

When Nancy got back to Smith after Christmas in January 1942, she began dating other men. The nickname "Cuddles" had stuck. In a time of war, the name seemed perfect. Nancy was like a kitten, an adorable pet that must never be allowed to cross the road alone.

The nervous urgency of the war had changed the sedate campus. The nation was going to war. Young men would be dying. Over the holidays many women had become engaged. Eleven students married men who would soon be full-time soldiers. Twenty-five women wanted to join the war effort so badly that they left college for good.

Each house at Smith had an air-raid warden. Some of the students worked several hours a week learning how to pack parachutes; the silk chutes were spread out in Scott Gymnasium. Others took special courses: motor ambulance, first aid, radio communications and flying. Wherever the students gathered, in class, at Wiggins Tavern, or in their houses, there were women knitting sweaters for the Red Cross. On weekends "Janies in jeans" went into the valley to help farmers harvest their crops.

A few of the students were almost hysterical in their demands to do something, *anything*. "I feel that a fire should be set and lit under the sleeping donkey that is college," one student wrote in *Scan,* a student magazine. "I feel that the college should be recessed for the duration of the war. . . . Not one of us is a complete idiot and this isolated college life, which is fine in time of peace, is an idiot's delight in time of war."

Nancy was not one of those wanting to exchange her penny loafers for work shoes. But even Nancy had to put up with changes the war brought. At Talbot House the heat was turned off in the evenings by a "heat monitor." In the dining room students started drinking their coffee black. They took turns clearing the tables and making beds. The day the rumor spread about shoe rationing, the stores downtown were mobbed. But the vital necessity that was in shortest supply was men. Nancy, however, was as popular as ever. She had plenty of beaux, including Jim White, a senior at nearby Amherst.

As Nancy had become more interested in theater, she had grown further and further apart from Whitey Wescott. They weren't even rooming together any longer. Nancy's new roommate, Frannie Greene, was as plain as a glass of milk, a far cry from Whitey. And Nancy, who thought that good-looks and style were the hardest currency a woman could have, sometimes treated Frannie as a princess did her lady-in-waiting.

In the fall of 1942, Nancy still had her education to complete. The new head of the drama department was Hallie Flanagan Davis. Mrs. Davis was the former head of the Federal Theater program. She was a formidable, fiery, controversial figure, not only a rabid New Dealer but decidedly a woman of the left.

The first day, Mrs. Davis strode into her seminar dressed in blue tweed from her dress to her hat to her cape, setting off her flaming red hair. She stood silently, flanked by her two assistants, and stared down at the twelve students seated around a long banquet table.

"I wish to say that this is a much warmer group than the last time I stood in front of a table like this," she said, her lessons in drama already beginning. "That was the Senate Investigating Committee for Un-American Activities."

The students had never had such an incredible character as a teacher. They sat dry-mouthed waiting to see what words would come spewing out of this redheaded whirlwind.

"I feel warmth," Mrs. Davis said suddenly. "Warmth!! I feel warmth."

For their first assignment, Mrs. Davis had the students prepare a dramatic presentation of the poem, "Wake Island" by Muriel Rukeyser. It was not the genre of theater in which Nancy felt most comfortable, but this dramatization of one of the first battles of the war in the Pacific became the first production of the new Department of Theater.

It was the beginning of what many drama students at Smith considered a time of great excitement. How often did students get to work with someone of Hallie Flanagan Davis's reputation? She brought in well-known theater and movie people. She had radical ideas about what and whom the arts should serve. At Smith she wanted to create dramas patterned after the Federal Theater's Living Newspapers that would play in factories and schools.

Mrs. Davis was working to create a highly political, socially conscious theater. Sometimes the students weren't sure just what they were supposed to do. Nancy didn't like this at all. To her, the theater department was not in a period of great energy and creativity but merely "in a transition period, not well organized."

Despite Nancy's qualms, she won a part in *Susan and God,* the first major production under the Davis tutelage. In the spring, just before she graduated, Nancy had her only other role while at Smith. This was in the musical *Make with the Maximum: A Factory Follies.* The musical was a morale-boosting, student-written production that played not only at Smith but at the Fisk Tire Plant in Chicopee. Nancy was chosen to play "The Glamour Girl," unhappy about wartime deprivations. She sang:

> *I miss my Nassau winters and Paris in the spring*
> *My butler's making nuts and bolts*
> *They've rationed everything*
> *And it's simply impossible to find an extra man*
> *The town car is in car storage*
> *The yacht is in disrepair*
> *And when I start complaining—*
> *"Sorry, madame, c'est la guerre."*

In the spring of 1943, Smith was a far different place from the college Nancy had entered four years before. Wiggins Tavern, where Nancy had loved to eat blueberry muffins, had been closed down to provide quarters for the first Officers Training Unit of the Women's Reserve. Every morning the 900 WAVES marched around campus. Many Smith students accelerated their classwork to graduate early. Some of Nancy's housemates were heading to Washington for mysterious work in intelligence and cryptography.

By now the war was touching women everywhere in America, from the workers at the Fisk Tire Plant to postdebs like Nancy. By the time the war ended, twenty-seven of those men who had danced in the youthful arms of Nancy and the other Chicago debs would die.

—4—

"NANCY, WHY DON'T YOU COME OUT AND MAKE A SCREEN TEST?"

As soon as Nancy graduated, in May 1943, she took the train back to Chicago to be with her mother. Dr. Loyal was serving in China as a lieutenant colonel in the Army Medical Corps. Nancy vowed to stay put until Dr. Loyal returned. Edith was pitching in, doing her part for the war effort. She even had a uniform of sorts that she wore at the servicemen's center, a blue smock over her portly frame. She tried to make the canteen a pleasant home away from home for the soldiers, complete with cakes, cookies and motherly companionship.

Edith's concern for enlisted men didn't stop at the exit to the canteen. Her friend Mayor Kelly had signed her up as an undercover policewoman, and she was doing her part to see to it that the soldiers were not led astray. The previous spring, there had been a series of raids on taverns. The saloons had been caught selling liquor to underage soldiers who wanted a few pops before being shipped out to the theaters of war. An eighteen-year-old sailor testified that just before the raids he and two other underage navy men had gone to Edith Luckett's apartment. There they had met three young women as escorts and several policemen and set out to visit the saloons.

Chicago's intrepid reporters were determined to track down the story of the alleged tavern-busting society matron. They discovered one "Edith Luckett" who lived at "199 Lake Shore Drive" had been a temporary police officer. This was hardly the kind of news coverage that the Davises were used to. On her visit to Chicago, a reporter had accosted Nancy to ask about the mysterious coincidence. "It must not be true," she said. When the reporter asked whether her mother was interested in preventing liquor sales to minors, Nancy said, "Not that I know of." And when the reporter had the considerable nerve to ask if her mother disapproved of drinking, she simply repeated herself: "Not that I know of."

Edith had already ended her short-lived career in law enforcement, and the controversy had died down. Edith and Nancy returned to the more routine pursuits of two society ladies. Nancy didn't have a clear place for herself in Chicago. Her respite became more tolerable because Jim White, one of her college beaux, was stationed in Chicago in the navy. Lieutenant White was a handsome figure dashing off his ship anchored in Lake Michigan for a rendezvous with Nancy.

Nancy was in love, but after three months, when White was transferred to the South Pacific, Nancy had to find something to do. The war was on and she couldn't just sit around waiting for Jim. She decided to take courses to become a nurse's aide. To earn some money and keep herself even more occupied, Nancy took a position at Marshall Field, the premier Chicago department store. With her long brown hair, subtle makeup, and wardrobe of cute junior dresses, Nancy was the perfect saleslady in the College Shop. She loved fashion, and the job was a graduate course in how to buy clothes well and wear them with distinction.

There were the occasional dramas. One time Nancy saw a shoplifter sneaking a piece of jewelry. She walked up to the thief. "Can I be of help to you?" she asked.

"No, I'm just looking," the woman said. "How much are these gloves?"

"Seven ninety-five," Nancy said, still staring at the woman.

The shoplifter started walking casually away. "Don't you think you, better give me back the jewelry before you go!" Nancy exclaimed.

The woman scurried for the elevator, Nancy in pursuit. Seeing the two women tearing through Marshall Field, the store detective made his pinch at the elevator. The thief reached out, grabbed the top of Nancy's stylish button-down dress and ripped it open.

That was a day to remember, for Marshall Field was hardly a kingdom of adventure. After a while, Nancy contented herself with her nurse's aide course and two days of volunteer work each week at the servicemen's center. When Jim White returned from the Pacific to California on leave, Nancy took the train out to visit him. They decided to get engaged. The Davises gave a party in their daughter's honor, inviting their friends and Jim White's parents as well. "The wedding will take place after the war," the *Chicago Tribune* announced, using a phrase that was common enough in engagement announcements.

The more Nancy thought about it, the more she realized that she wasn't ready for marriage, not with Jim, not with anybody. It was embarrassing, particularly after the announcement in the paper and the engage-

Above: Nancy Davis:
the stage actress. *(The
Lester Glassner
Collection)*

Right: ZaSu Pitts in
Hal Roach's *Broadway
Limited,* United Artists,
1941. *(The Eric Benson
Collection)*

ment party at her home, but during the war it was not that unusual a thing to have happen. Later, when Jim got back from the service, he came to visit Nancy, and the two remained friends for years afterward.

Nancy was still thinking of a career in the theater. She was shy and had never had to go out and seek for herself, but she really didn't have to— not with her mother's show-business connections. One day Edith's old friend ZaSu Pitts called to offer Nancy a small part in her first play, *Ramshackle Inn*. After almost thirty years as one of the screen's best-known comediennes, the doleful-looking Pitts was making her debut on Broadway. Nancy's role would be only three lines, but untried actresses would have done anything for a part in a play headed for New York.

Nancy joined the company in Detroit. One of the great joys of live theater, particularly on the road, is the camaraderie, the inspired buffoonery and mutual good cheer of the cast. Nancy, however, was the star's protégé, personally and professionally. She was a world and several dressing rooms away from the other young actors. Not only did she share ZaSu's dressing rooms, she shared her hotel rooms. The comedy-melodrama opened at Broadway's Royale Theater on January 5, 1944. Nancy searched the major reviews in vain for mention of her name. That was just as well. The reviews were as dreary as the New York weather. But to see the legendary ZaSu live, the audiences came anyway.

After the play closed, Nancy decided that she wanted to stay in New York and continue her career. In New York, Nancy was usually an out-of-work actress. Her greatest performance was in maintaining the illusion of affluence and success. Other fledgling actresses might live in Greenwich Village walk-ups; Nancy rarely even went below the pale of mid-Manhattan. Other fledgling actresses dated their struggling peers; Nancy went out with directors and producers, successful actors, and military officers. Other actresses chomped on deli sandwiches or made do at Nedick's; Nancy preferred the Stork Club and Sardi's.

For a while Nancy lived in the exclusive and elegant Plaza Hotel, right on Fifty-ninth Street and Fifth Avenue. She felt perfectly at home, but the rates were high. She decided to move into the nearby Barbizon Plaza Hotel.

At the Barbizon Plaza, Nancy was glad to have one of her Smith housemates living with her and sharing the rent. The young woman had quit her job and come to the city hoping to make it big in New York. Except for Nancy and one other Smithie, she had no friends. And instead of quickly finding a job, she discovered how lonely and tough New York can be. She was disappointed that Nancy had little time to introduce her to New York, and she finally decided to leave. As she was packing her bags to go to California, the telephone rang.

"Nancy?" a male voice asked, calling from the lobby.

"No, Nancy's in acting class."

It was one of Nancy's beaux, a navy doctor assigned to the Brooklyn Navy Yard.

"Gee, do you mind if I come up?" the doctor said. "I'd like to meet you."

As soon as the lieutenant looked at the young woman, he became even more curious. "Why are you leaving?" he asked.

"New York has not been kind to me. It hasn't worked out. I haven't had much fun, either."

"I wonder why Nancy didn't tell me," the lieutenant said, genuinely perplexed. "Why, I have all these doctor friends who are dying to have someone to go out with."

Nancy eventually moved into an East Side apartment. She loved being taken to the Stork Club, where Walter Winchell and the other gossip columnists had regular tables. As she admitted later in a radio interview, each time someone took her to dinner at the exclusive nightclub, she neatly filched two rolls and stuffed them into her evening bag. She was sure no one saw her. One evening, however, Sherman Billingsley, the owner of the Stork Club, sent over a pound of butter with a note: "I thought you might enjoy some butter on my rolls."

Maybe Nancy ate a pilfered roll for breakfast occasionally, but still she traveled with the *crème de la crème.* She could walk around the corner from her apartment on East Fifty-first Street to the Walter Hustons for dinner. Lillian Gish, the famous silent-film star and a family friend, lived nearby, too. Spencer Tracy was another star who knew her mother. "Spence" gave Nancy's phone number to Clark Gable, and in 1948 Nancy began dating the most famous movie star in America. "The King," they called him, and he *was* like a king. When they went to see *High Button Shoes,* the audience applauded and Clark had to take a bow. At the World Series, they never would have gotten in and out without the help of the police. Over dinner, even in the most exclusive restaurants (and that was the only kind Clark frequented), the two of them were bathed in attention.

For a while the gossip columns linked Nancy's name to Gable's, making her the envy of star-struck girls across America. "Has something at last happened to Clark Gable," a fan magazine asked, "something, to be exact, in the form of a slim, brown-eyed brown-haired beauty named Nancy Davis—that is changing the fitful pattern of his romantic life? Has he, in other words, finally found the Gable woman, for whom he is more than willing to give up the Gable women? The answer seems to be yes—even though, if it is a love at all, it is so far a love in hiding."

The love was in hiding because it didn't exist. Clark enjoyed Nancy's

Nancy on a date with Clark Gable. *(The Library of Congress)*

company, but she was not a major romance. Nonetheless, Nancy found it fun going out with Clark, fun being at the epicenter of glamour and attention, more fun than her career.

During this time of excitement and publicity, Nancy had a major family problem. Her natural father was in serious trouble. Ken Robbins had lost his partnership in the auto dealership, he was unemployed, and he turned to Nancy. But Dr. Loyal was her *real* father, as far as she was concerned. Ken had done little for her, and she refused to see him any longer.

Nancy could selflessly help another human being with a physical disability. Soon after his college graduation, Spencer Tracy's son came to visit. John Tracy was not the kind of young man with whom most young women would have spent much time. He had been born deaf. He had also been a polio victim, and had very poor eyesight as well. For a week, John slept on Nancy's sleep sofa in her living room. She led him around New York, taking the young man to museums, restaurants and Broadway shows, where he said that he sensed the music through the vibrations.

As much as John was enjoying his time with Nancy, he was particularly looking forward to a date with a young woman he had met in California. Nancy knew it would take a special kind of woman to understand John, and on the day of the date, when the woman telephoned to cancel, Nancy had her own brutal insight into social ambition. She was sure the woman had wanted to go out with John simply to meet Spence in Hollywood. With her back turned so that John couldn't possibly read her lips, she told the woman off. Then Nancy went out for dinner and dancing with John.

On the day that he was leaving for the airport, Nancy moved to help John with his bag. "Oh, no, you're my princess and I'm your slave," he said, taking the bag himself.

She kissed him and cried her goodbye.

Nancy finally got a part in another play. But during lunch at an early rehearsal, the director took her aside and led her through the stage door into the alley. "I hate to tell you this," the man said, "but it's just not working. You're just not right for the part. I have to let you go."

Nancy begged him to go back into the theater and bring her coat and purse. She was not a good enough actress to hide her embarrassment.

To earn extra money, Nancy worked as a model with the Conover agency. In the afternoons when she went in for assignments, she often saw an old Smith friend, Cathy Dugan, who had been one of the stars of the Bander-log production. Cathy was doing very well as a model. Nancy got some assignments modeling hats; but according to friends, her thick legs limited her career.

Not until 1946, two years after her fleeting Broadway debut, did Nancy get her next part in a Broadway show. While making the rounds of producers' offices, she walked into the offices of Michael Meyerberg, the producer of Thorton Wilder's *Skin of Our Teeth.*

"You look Chinese," Meyerberg said.

Nancy looked as Chinese as the king of England. Without an audition, Meyerberg gave her a secondary role in *Lute Song,* his new musical starring Mary Martin and Yul Brynner. That was doubly unusual. Although Nancy would never admit as much, she may well have owed the role as the princess's flower maiden as much to her formidable theatrical contacts as to her inscrutable Occidental looks.

Based on a classical Chinese work probably dating from the fourteenth century, *Lute Song* was a rather daring piece of work for a Broadway musical. The rehearsals were as intricate as a Chinese puzzle: the dancers on stage, the principals backstage, the chorus busy in the pit, the costume fittings in the dressing rooms.

John Houseman, the director, considered Nancy "a pink-cheeked, attractive but awkward and amateurish virgin." He spent little time with her. Nancy found it difficult catching on. In the meantime she dyed her brown hair black and in costume wore eyebrows set at an angle.

The cast of *Lute Song* headed to New England for tryouts in New Haven and Boston. This time Nancy wasn't under the tutelage of ZaSu Pitts, but was just another young actress. Once she caught on, she loved it and joined in with the fellowship of theater people.

During the first cast party in New York, Nancy had met Ron Fletcher, the lead dancer. Ron was stylish, effervescent and high-strung; he got bored around dancers, with their endless, tedious shoptalk. As soon as the cast hit New Haven, the two began spending much time together.

Nancy had difficulty making friends with other women. Ron was the first of a number of men who became her close friends, men who were not interested in dating her.

"There was a quality about her," Ron remembered years later, "something very appealing. She's got that vulnerability and a strength and control. I see that in a lot of marvelous performers. They are perfectly capable of taking care of themselves, but you want to say, 'That's all right.' She loved to laugh and had this amazing little chortle, and this touch of whimsy and fantasy."

After the performances they often went out ballroom dancing. Ron was a professional dancer and Nancy was the perfect partner. Looking at them gliding across the floor like Ginger Rogers and Fred Astaire, one might have thought they were lovers. But their dreams were as far apart as their bodies were close.

Nancy had a chameleonlike way of becoming whomever she was with;

for all Ron knew, Nancy was from a modest background like his. In Boston, Nancy and Ron pooled their money, $2.50 apiece, to join a rental library. A few days later they decided to go dancing, but they had no money. "If we could only get that deposit back," Nancy said. Nancy and Ron ran laughing through the streets of downtown Boston, chasing after their deposit.

Lute Song opened at Broadway's Plymouth Theatre on February 6, 1946, to an audience that included Nancy's mother and stepfather. The critics were highly respectful of the effort, if less than completely sanguine about the results of trying to mix a classical, simply told Chinese tale, elaborate sets and popular music. Nonetheless, *Lute Song* was unusual enough and Mary Martin a strong enough talent to allow the play to run for six months.

Nancy could have gone off on tour with *Lute Song*. Instead, she chose once again to take a role in one of ZaSu Pitts's plays. *Cordelia* was supposed to play Broadway, but it closed out of town. In the comedienne's next touring vehicle, the George Abbott production of *The Late Christopher Bean,* ZaSu made sure that Nancy had another chance.

In her tour for the play, ZaSu was doing what a lot of stars did later in dinner theater, heading a cast mainly comprised of local talent. The week before her arrival, an advance team was sent out to rehearse with the company.

One of the places in which ZaSu performed the play was Olney, Maryland, outside Washington. To semiprofessionals like these, with the emphasis decidedly on *semi,* it was an event performing alongside ZaSu Pitts.

As soon as ZaSu and Nancy arrived in Washington, a young actor, James Karen, walked up to the silent-screen star. "Miss Pitts, I think you're one of our great actresses."

ZaSu was quiet.

Karen tried again. "Miss Pitts, I'm a great fan of *Greed,*" referring to the controversial silent classic.

"That goddamn picture!" ZaSu exclaimed, turning away.

Opening night there was always a big party in the star's honor. The star inevitably invited the whole cast. To anyone knowing anything about theater, that was simply good manners. The star had to play alongside these people the following week and needed to be in their minimal good graces. Nonetheless, ZaSu insisted that it be just she and Nancy dining with the locals.

Whatever the cast thought of ZaSu, they didn't blame Nancy. If anything, they felt sorry for her. She was so completely under ZaSu's thumb, always at her side. They saw nothing of the laughing young woman who could dance till dawn and had a laugh that bubbled like champagne.

Returning to New York after the tour, Nancy was on familiar territory: unemployed. So far her career had been thin gruel. She had won only one role for herself—in *Lute Song*—and even that may have been because of connections. Other than that, her theater work had come through ZaSu Pitts.

Nancy had almost always played the ingenue, on stage as in life. She was darling little Nancy. She played it well to Clark Gable, to her navy lieutenant, to assorted suitors and dates. She was approaching her late twenties, though, in an era when women became matrons at thirty. Her days as an ingenue were numbered. She was in danger of becoming one of those well-brought up young ladies whom well-to-do gentlemen like to take on dates. Even with her acting lessons, beauty appointments, modeling assignments and theater calls, she had all kinds of time. When Benny Thau, a vice-president of Metro-Goldwyn-Mayer in Hollywood, was planning a trip to New York, a friend told him: "If you want to take somebody out to a show, call Nancy Davis. She's a nice girl who likes company."

Benny was no Clark Gable. He had a way with actresses, though, and there were cynics who thought it might have something to do with his role in casting M-G-M movies. M-G-M was a legend: the richest, the biggest, the greatest of the starmakers, creator of a whole firmament of legends. Joan Crawford, Ava Gardner, Eleanor Powell, Clark Gable, Robert Taylor, Fred Astaire, Judy Garland, Spencer Tracy, Elizabeth Taylor, George Raft, Ann Sothern, Lana Turner—the list went on and on, the fires of publicity constantly promoting new stars.

Nancy didn't usually go out on blind dates, but she said yes. They went to see a play starring Spencer Tracy. Afterward, as Thau remembered it, he said: "Nancy, why don't you come out and make a screen test?"

Nancy called her mother and told Edith that someone from M-G-M had seen her in a television play and wanted to give her a screen test. Edith was a far more aggressive woman than her daughter. She could hear opportunity's curt knock and set out to open the door for her daughter in Hollywood. Edith called Spencer Tracy. Spence persuaded George Cukor, the distinguished director, to direct Nancy's screen test.

In the spring of 1949, Nancy arrived at the great M-G-M studios, a city in itself. Benny Thau phoned the woman in charge of screen tests. "I'm going to bring down a girl for a test," he said.

For the test, a tall, highly regarded young actor, Howard Keel, played opposite her in a scene from a forthcoming production, *East Side, West Side*. For cameraman, Nancy had one of the best, George Folsey. From top to bottom, then, Nancy had as good a set of circumstances as could be imagined.

Envy is the highest emotion in Hollywood. Nancy's special screen test did not pass unnoticed. Other actresses thought that Clark Gable was behind it, not realizing that it was not M-G-M's greatest star who was responsible, but their boss, Benny Thau. "It was such a gilt-edge opeɪation all around, so well supervised artistically and technically to make sure nothing went wrong, that when the details got to be known, any number of aspiring starlets around Hollywood gulped their envy frankly to any and all who would listen," *Modern Screen* reported. "The sum of their remarks was, 'It should happen to me!' Or, as one girl, with a more direct mind, put it: 'He [Gable] should happen to me.'"

Whatever her fellow actresses thought, Nancy considered the screen test "the most terrifying experience I've ever had." What bothered her was "not only making it but then having to *see* it."

Soon afterward M-G-M signed Nancy to a standard seven-year contract. Nancy was joining M-G-M when Hollywood's contract system seemed as preordained as the Saturday matinee. The studio nurtured its talents, pruning their pasts, sprucing up their manners and wardrobes, gilding their personalities, then parading them past the public like floats in the Rose Bowl parade.

One of the first things Nancy had to do at M-G-M was to fill out a studio biography. This was the basic document that the publicity people used in their work, and newly signed actors and actresses usually took their time completing the four-page questionnaire. On the second line Nancy had to decide what to do about her age. She would be twenty-eight years old in July. She had never been married. She would be competing for roles with actresses who were five years younger, sometimes ten. She gave her birthdate as July 6, 1923, neatly shearing off two years.

Even with the euphoria of becoming a full-fledged starlet, Nancy was still thinking about marriage. In her bio she listed as her greatest ambition "to have a successful happy marriage."

M-G-M wanted to know if Nancy governed her life by any rule or rules. "Yes," Nancy wrote. "Do unto others as you would have them do unto you. I believe strongly in the law of retribution—you get back what you give."

Her phobias were moral as well. She wasn't perturbed by spiders, snakes and sundry monsters. Her phobias, she wrote, were "superficiality, vulgarity, esp. in women, untidiness of mind and person—and cigars!"

Alas, the Hollywood society that Nancy had just entered was one that was full of "superficiality, vulgarity, esp. in women, untidiness of mind and person—and cigars!" In 1950s America, the studios and their cigar-smoking executives were promoting many female movie stars who had seductive images that were essentially vulgar. The vulgarity did not end on the screen. When Dore Schary, a former screenwriter, took over as the head of production at RKO he discovered five "starlets" on the studio payroll whose main activity was servicing executives.

Around Elizabeth Taylor, Ann Sothern, Marilyn Monroe, Jane Russell, Lana Turner and their overt sexuality, Nancy was a modest flower indeed. Some at M-G-M considered Nancy a welcome relief. To Helen Rose, the M-G-M dress designer, Nancy "was completely different from most of the girls who came. She wasn't a sex goddess or glamorous, but was a delight to work with. Girls like Grace Kelly and Nancy, who came from good backgrounds, were very easy to work with. They weren't crude."

Nancy cultivated an image of the very proper young society lady come to make movies. She had what Leonard Spigelgass, the screenwriter, called "the respectable-lady look."

Nancy didn't fit the mold of M-G-M's red-lipped, full-bosomed sirens. Nor did she fit the other genre of Hollywood's 1950s starlet—the rosy-cheeked child-woman, the eternal girl-next-door. These roles were dominated by the likes of Jane Powell, Debbie Reynolds and June Allyson, still glowing with the vigor and innocence of their adolescence.

Nancy was carefully groomed into a dignified, quiet attractiveness. The studio publicity cameras captured a manicured prettiness, an allure that she had been unable fully to achieve herself. It was a look fashioned by the practical artists of the kingdom of fantasy.

"Nancy really looks very unlike the usual conception of an actress," wrote Louella Parsons, the Hollywood columnist, in introducing the new M-G-M starlet to her readers. "She might be the daughter of any town's leading citizen, or the competent secretary of a big official, but you would never label her an actress. 'Any one man in your life?' I asked her . . . 'Not yet,' Nancy said. 'I won't be trite and say I am married to my career, but that's pretty much the truth.' "

Nancy, in fact, was dating Benny Thau. Barbara, the pretty teen-age receptionist, saw Nancy frequently. Many years later she remembered that she had orders that on Saturday morning Nancy was to be sent directly into Benny Thau's suite. Barbara nodded to Miss Davis as she walked into the vice-president's office; nodded again when she left later.

Nancy's friendship with the M-G-M vice-president was hardly a handicap in her career. "You can say I helped her," Benny said thirty years later as he sat, an aged invalid, in a wheelchair at the Motion Picture and Television Hospital outside Los Angeles. "Stars like Norma Shearer, Elizabeth Taylor—she couldn't compete with that. She was attractive, but not what you'd call beautiful. She's a very nice behaved girl."

"Did you want to marry her?"

"I was friendly with her folks, and me being Jewish, I don't know."

"Did you think of marrying her?"
"I thought about it, but that's all I did."

Rarely had there been as ideal a marriage as that between southern California and the film industry. Along a sparse coastland and on brown hills, a great sprawling city had been born. Without water there would have been nothing except dust and sand and sun. But human beings had made an immense oasis of the land.

Here were immigrants of all kinds. Eucalyptus and acacia trees from Australia. The pepper tree from South America. Okies looking for a second chance. Texans in search of wages. Jews who brought their savvy to the film industry. Almost everything and everyone came from somewhere else.

Los Angeles was a city of endless tomorrows, a city where people were constantly rewriting their bios. Reality and illusion rode in tandem, harnessed to a million dreams. On reels of celluloid lay joy, sorrow, banality, wit, wonderment, glamour, fantasy, rude falsehoods and terrible truths.

If you thought you belonged in L.A., you belonged. And Nancy was soon as much a part of the city as anyone else. All her life, sitting in darkened movie theaters, she had dreamed of Hollywood. The movie stars, the kings and queens of the screen, were the conjurers of dreams. They rode down Sunset Boulevard in their long cars to premieres, parties and restaurants. It was a fairy tale come true—that she, Nancy Davis, now might become one of them: a star, a movie star.

In 1949, Nancy was immediately cast in her first film, *Shadow on the Wall,* a "B" picture starring Zachary Scott, Ann Sothern and Gigi Perreau. Nancy did not have a large part. Nonetheless, Pat Jackson, the director, helped her whenever he could. She was far from the center of attention, either on screen or off. Ann Sothern hardly considered her competition: "She was just a little girl under contract, a sweet, unassuming little person who didn't thrust herself forward."

Nancy was discovering that, like most public professions, being a movie actress was as much a matter of tedium as of glamour. On screen she had to look good, and she made sure she was always perfectly turned out. In her one-bedroom apartment in the suburb of Westwood, Nancy was up at 6:30, giving her plenty of time to groom herself before heading for the studio.

What set Nancy apart from most of her actress peers was her social acceptability. Dore Schary, the new head of M-G-M, was more literate and liberal than most of the old studio heads. He had been treated by Nancy's father for a back problem, and he was delighted to invite Dr. Davis's daughter to his great house. Nancy knew what fork to use, never got loaded, managed to be unfailingly polite whatever the inanity.

On Sundays, Frank McCarthy, a producer, occasionally saw Nancy at the beautiful Pasadena home of the Alfred Wrights. Wright, the attorney for the Motion Picture Association, was a friend of Nancy's father. Through Colleen Moore, Nancy was introduced to the Robert Stacks. Stack was an actor, but he came from a moneyed background. Here again Nancy felt perfectly at home. Stack considered her "well mannered, always in control, with a great sense of humor about herself." As she had in New York, Nancy fit in better among producers, lawyers and the socially prominent than she did with her acting brethren.

Well before her first film was ready to be released, Nancy had a small role in a second movie, *The Doctor and the Girl*, starring Glenn Ford. She was soon into her first big-budget film, *East Side, West Side*, the script that had been used for her screen tests. In the actual movie, Nancy had only a small part in one scene. She was nervous working with Barbara Stanwyck, but she got her long speech out well enough that the star congratulated her. Nancy was nervous about her career in general. She was now working on her third picture, and her first film had not even been released. She had no sense of how she would be received.

In the postwar years, M-G-M had not been doing well. The whole industry was nervous, especially about Communists. Nancy had begun to receive Communist propaganda in the mail, addressed to her, Nancy Davis. Her name had turned up on a list of Communist sympathizers. She knew what that could mean to her career, so she went to talk to the people at M-G-M. After that, Louella Parsons wrote in her column that there was another Nancy Davis. But she was still nervous.

One day at the studio, Nancy spoke to Mervyn LeRoy, the director of *East Side, West Side.* When LeRoy heard about Nancy's plight, he offered to introduce her to the president of the Screen Actors Guild, Ronald Reagan, who could clear her name once and for all.

For years Nancy had seen Reagan in pictures. Not only was he someone who could help her, he was handsome. She liked the gentle, easy manner that he projected on screen. That evening she sat in her apartment waiting for Reagan to call. But no call came.

First thing next morning, Nancy asked Mervyn LeRoy what had happened. The director told her that instead of calling her directly, Reagan had called him. The Guild president had explained that there were four other actresses called Nancy Davis and that the Guild would stand behind Nancy.

"Fine," Nancy said, her voice streaked with worry. "I'd feel better if the Guild president would call me and explain it all to me."

LeRoy was enough of a romantic to have produced the great M-G-M film *The Wizard of Oz.* As he listened he realized, as he said later, that Nancy had her heart set on meeting Reagan and not merely on clearing her name. The more he thought about it, the surer he became that they would make a great pair.

The Reagan family of Dixon, Illinois. From left to right: John "Jack" Edward Reagan, Neil "Moon" Reagan, Ronald "Dutch" Wilson Reagan, Nelle Wilson Reagan. *(WH)*

5

"A LITTLE BIT
OF A FAT DUTCHMAN"

W hen Ronald Wilson Reagan was three years old, he often went to his room and took out his lead soldiers. Sitting on the floor, he was a sturdy, square-shouldered little lad, built like a box of Kellogg's Corn Flakes. With his vivid imagination, he needed no one and nothing beyond these bits of metal. For hours vast armies marched across the floorboards. Kings and kingdoms rose and fell. Great armadas sailed beneath his bed. Cowboys and Indians engaged in mortal combat below the window shade.

"Dutch! Dutch!" his mother called, using the nickname his father gave him the day he was born, February 6, 1911, in Tampico, Illinois. He had come screaming from the womb, all ten pounds of him, like "a little bit of a fat Dutchman [who] . . . makes a hell of a lot of noise."

Dutch was so lost in his own universe that sometimes he didn't even hear his mother. But when he did, he immediately put his soldiers away. Dutch was good as gold: good to Jack, his father; good to Nelle, his mother; good to Neil, his older brother.

Dutch was the second son of John ("Jack") Edward Reagan and Nelle Wilson Reagan. He was born in a five-room apartment above a bakery on a wide, unpaved Main Street. With its carriages, horses and frame buildings, it could have been in Montana as easily as Illinois. Tampico was a little burg of a thousand, but it was a stop on the Burlington line and had a seventeen-foot-tall Spanish-American and Civil War memorial that was fit for a town ten times its size.

Jack was a big, brawny black Irishman, scion of a race known for soddenness and song. He had a rude, sardonic wit that he laced with profanity. He was a Democrat living in towns that were as Republican as

Rome is Catholic. He left a hotel once because the manager bragged that he didn't admit Jews. And he didn't let his two boys see the famous film *Birth of a Nation* because it glorified the Ku Klux Klan. He didn't care that every other kid in town saw the film, and most of their parents as well. That didn't make it right.

Jack was handsome enough to win admiring glances from ladies in the dry-goods store where he worked, but he was a loyal husband, and a caring father, too. One of Dutch's first Christmases, he and his brother wanted a windup train from Santa Claus. They didn't know that money was short and that a train was a costly present. On Christmas Eve when the two little boys were supposed to be in bed, they crept down the stairs. Under the tree sat Jack, playing with the windup train he had purchased with a good share of his weekly wages.

Jack Reagan had good children, a good wife and a steady job. Yet there was a darkness within the man. Often he got tanked up and roared home late at night acting as if only a drunken Irishman could understand the world. He didn't drink all the time; but when he drank, he couldn't stop. It cost him a fair measure of his reputation and a number of jobs. "It wasn't a case of bad times bringing on the drinking," Neil Reagan remembered years later. "It was the drinking bringing on the bad times."

No matter how late Jack staggered home, Nelle Reagan was waiting for her husband. She was of Scotch-Irish descent and had the lean, strong face of a prairie woman. She was a Christian lady, ministering to the sick and needy wherever the Reagans happened to be. She also visited the prisoners in the county jail, making that part of her calling.

During Dutch's first years, the Reagans lived what was for that time an almost itinerant life. From town to town they traveled across the plains of Illinois; first Tampico, then to the south side of Chicago where Jack had a short-lived job at the Fair Store, to Galesburg, to Monmouth, and back to Tampico.

Dutch made the best of it. He didn't need a big gang of friends—he had had many of his best times alone. In Galesburg he went up into the attic one day. There among the landlord's hidden troves he found an immense collection of butterflies and birds' eggs. To Dutch these weren't mere dead *things;* they were "gateways to the mysterious." He looked at the colors and touched the shells and fragile wings. He felt the "scent of wind on peaks, pine needles in the rain, and visions of sunrise on the desert."

Dutch was a dreamer. In Monmouth he liked nothing better than to visit the next-door neighbor's strange, wondrous house. They were an old childless couple and their living room was a treasure of Victoriana. They had horsehair sofas and chairs that in the shadows became animals; stuffed birds resting under glass globes. The musty, leathery scent of old books filled the air. Sitting in that living room, Dutch created his own universe.

Dutch was born in a time and place where the common culture of nineteenth-century America was still alive. Carriages, horses, church socials, steam engines, the Klan, Chautauqua, six-day workweeks, corsets, waltzes were still part of life. Men still lived who had seen Abe Lincoln and heard him talk. Old geezers sat in the town square and told tales of Shiloh and Bull Run. The popular Christmas songs about sleigh bells and Santa dashing through the snow were about things that were real to Dutch. One Christmas he got off the train at his uncle's farm and rode in a sleigh, his feet warmed by hot bricks and a buffalo rug.

To Dutch the radio was not something to be clicked on and off; it was a miraculous, half-heard voice on a crystal set saying, "This is KDKA, Pittsburgh, KDKA, Pittsburgh." Nor did he slap his dime down for a movie each Saturday afternoon and think nothing of it; he knew that films were a marvelous new invention.

In 1920 the Reagans moved once again. Jack's old boss, H. C. Pitney, set him up in business at the Fashion Boot Store in Dixon, Illinois. This time he had a real opportunity. Nine-year-old Dutch set his roots deep and strong.

Dixon (pop. 10,000) lies on the banks of the Rock River, 100 miles due west of Chicago. The town had been founded in 1828 as a ferry crossing with a tavern. Since then, there had been no great events; no dramatic growth; no tales of glory to sing in Kankakee, Rockford or Dubuque; no cataclysms to etch the town's name in the minds of sophisticates in Chicago and points east. The biggest event had been when the men returned from the wars. The year before the Reagans arrived, Dixon had constructed its proudest civic structure: a beaverboard arch over Galena Avenue to celebrate the homecoming of the soldiers from the Great War.

In the thousands of small towns like Dixon across America, there were many houses like the old frame dwelling Jack Reagan rented on South Hennepin Avenue. The two-story structure had a porch and a peaked roof and enough crannies to please any nine-year-old boy. Dutch was a gentle boy, so well mannered and quiet that his fifth-grade teacher, Esther Barton, could hardly remember him in her class. That's the way he was in all his grade-school classes, a little lad who caused no trouble and left few memories.

From an early age, Dutch knew that there was a dark, inexplicable area in life that he wanted to avoid. As a seven-year-old, he had stood watching the Armistice parade: the torches, the soldiers, the burning of the Kaiser in effigy. He felt not excitement but unease about this strange, violent world that existed beyond his own. When he played football, he had a horror of getting caught at the bottom of a pile of writhing, screaming bodies.

In his own house, Dutch lay in bed pretending he was asleep while he

The young Dutch. *(WH)*

heard loud shouts in the parlor below. He realized that Neil, his brother, knew things about his father that he did not know. But he shut that out.

One winter day, eleven-year-old Dutch came home and found his father lying drunk on the front porch. Jack lay there on his back, snoring, his arms spread, his hair crowned with melting snow. Dutch knew that he must flee his father, flee this knowledge. He must go into the house and up to his room and get in bed and make it never have happened. But it was Jack, his father, at his feet, snoring peacefully. Dutch took hold of his father's overcoat. He pulled Jack up, got him inside and put him to bed. And from that day on, he could not think of his father the same way.

Their mother sat Dutch and Neil down and told them a great deal about their father's alcoholism. Nelle said that Jack had a sickness, like the grippe or measles. Nelle only had a grade-school education, but she was a wise woman. Dutch grew up believing that fancy degrees couldn't compare with Nelle's deep and simple truths. Years later when Dutch talked of the common American people and their wisdom, he was talking in good measure about Nelle.

Neil and Dutch both loved their mother, but the two sons were as different as beer and milk. Neil was his father's son, a boisterous, outgoing, devil-take-the-best-of-me Peck's bad boy. Jack was a Catholic and Neil was raised as a Catholic. The two of them went to mass, a big Irishman next to a little Irishman.

Nelle Reagan was a pious, God-fearing Protestant, and little Dutch was very much her son. It *was* "little" Dutch, too—not only two years younger than Neil but small for his age, always wearing Neil's hand-me-downs. When Jack and his father went off to mass, Dutch and his mother walked over to the First Christian Church.

Often in the evenings Jack sat at the kitchen table looking at his newspaper while Nelle read aloud to her two sons. Dutch and Neil listened closely, munching from a pan of buttered popcorn in the middle of the table. The big nights for the Reagan family, as for most Dixon families, were when they went downtown to see a double feature.

In the summers Nelle took her sons to the old Chautauqua grounds to hear the speakers. The Chautauqua summers were not what they had been a quarter-century before, when the movement had brought culture and ideas to the rural areas of America. Then hundreds of families had camped by the river to hear such orators as William Jennings Bryan and Billy Sunday. There were no longer such famous speakers but sitting in the amphitheater, Dutch heard what a man could do with words. The best of the lecturers were conjurers. Stringing words together in silvery phrases, they took the audiences on journeys that made them forget that they were sitting on hard chairs sweating in the torpid August night.

Nelle had her own way with words, which Dutch inherited by blood and emulation. Nelle was often called upon to give dramatic readings at church meetings and sewing circles.

When Dutch entered high school, the family moved to a rented rock-dash house on West Everett Street on the north side of the Rock River. The north side was the better side of town, but Neil had already gone to South Dixon High School for two years and he refused to study with what he considered the snooty, stuck-up bunch at North Dixon High School.

"I won't go," he told his parents. "They're a bunch of sissies over there." And thus each day Neil walked alone clear to the other side of town. On winter days he shivered as he scurried across the windswept, snowblown reaches of the bridge. After school, he and his buddies sometimes played pool in a basement pool hall that parents and random squealers couldn't see into from the street. Dutch was not invited to play with his older brother or to share in the adventures of the boys who hung around Neil.

Neil was an end on the football team, and a good one at that. Freshman year, Dutch decided to go out for football, too. The problem was that at only five feet three inches and 108 pounds, there wasn't even a pair of pants small enough to fit him. And that said nothing about the problems he met on the football field. He was too small even to scrimmage. He kept at it, though, standing on the sidelines watching the bigger, stronger boys. And in the middle of his junior year, when he had grown, he was made starting guard. As a senior he was switched to tackle.

Dutch wasn't much of a football player. Dixon didn't have much of a team. Moreover, as a lineman he was one of the anonymous grunts of the team. But he was still the dreamer. Years later a townsman remembered seeing young Dutch alone one day running as if he had caught a thirty-yard pass. His face a grimace of determination, Dutch spurted by the last defender, and scored a touchdown, his face flushing with ecstasy.

One afternoon when riding with his family, Dutch realized that while his brother could read the highway signs, all he saw were vague forms. Putting on his mother's glasses, he saw that trees had individual leaves, that houses had clear shapes, and that hills stood stark against the sky. As much as he detested the thick glasses his parents got for him, at least he saw the world anew.

Dutch went out for all kinds of sports, but most of what athletic fame he won came from his years as lifeguard out at Lowell Park. Ed Granwell, the owner of the concession at the park, first thought that Dutch was too small to be hauling water-soaked people out of the Rock River. But Jack Reagan stood behind his boy. "Give 'im a chance," he said.

Fifteen dollars a week was not bad wages for strutting up and down the bank watching over matrons, youngsters, families and assorted young lovelies. Lowell Park was the center of Dixon's summer social life. Dutch loved the river and the wooded limestone hills and the people that he met. His height had stretched to a good six feet, and with his lanky build and his father's full features tempered by his mother's more austere looks, he was a handsome lifeguard indeed. Dutch had a second sense about his work. The Rock River flowed as slowly as the summer days, but when the sluices were opened on the dam downstream, the water quickened. Every time Dutch had to pull someone in, he added a notch to a log. In seven seasons of lifeguarding, he made seventy-seven notches.

Dutch wasn't much of a student, but he was an immensely likable young man who took joy in the daily business of living. Like his mother, he was interested in performing. He was a good enough actor that Esther Barton, his old fifth-grade teacher, made a point of attending any of the high-school plays in which he was featured.

B. J. Frazer, the drama coach at North Dixon, took a special liking to his star performer. The young teacher got Dutch interested not only in performing but in writing, giving him full rein to write essays on sports and anything else that interested him.

In the summer, Frazer often walked out to Lowell Park to chat with Dutch.

"I like this job because it gives me spending money," Dutch told him late one afternoon as dusk settled on the Rock River. It had been a long day. Almost everyone was gone. Only one group was frolicking in the water, diving off the float into the darkening waters.

"What I don't like is these people who stay after dark."

Dutch got up, jumped into the river and started swimming out to the float. "You know there's a rule that you can't swim after dark," he yelled.

"Yeah, but we *like* to swim after dark," said a distinctly masculine voice.

Dutch thought a moment. He reached down and picked up a stone from the riverbed. "That's fine," he said calmly, "just as long as the river rats don't get you."

Dutch set the flat stone skimming across the water. The group jumped into the river and made a desperate dash for shore.

The best education many young men and women received in Dixon was the one that took place immediately after they graduated. They had been classmates for four years, sharing the good times and the bad. There were football heroes, prom queens, cheerleaders and greasy grinds among them, but they were all members of a class together. A few went off to college, while most settled into jobs and marriages with high-school sweethearts.

Dutch's brother, Neil, or "Moon" as he had been nicknamed in high school, was more likely to be found hanging around a speakeasy than a football game. Neil had never been much of a student. After graduating he took a job in a cement factory. In the evenings he arrived home in clothes streaked with white dust. "I never gave a thought of going to college," Neil said. "I just figured I was so smart I already knew everything."

Dutch shared neither his brother's rash pride nor his working-class friends. Dutch was a north-side boy and he traveled with a better set. One of his close friends was Carl Buchner, whose sister he had saved from drowning. Carl's uncle owned the cement factory. His father was the distributor. Carl's dad had two cars, so the boys could drive their dates in either a LaSalle or a Packard.

Dutch always took one girl with him, Margaret Cleaver, daughter of the minister at the First Christian Church. To Dutch, Margaret was a "sparkling brunette." She had dark brown eyes and a way about her that inspired the yearbook staff to name her "our popular all-around everything." What could be better than cruising up Route 51 to see a show in Rockford, or heading east to Chicago for an evening's fun? With his arm around Margaret, the wind tousling his sun-bleached hair, he had not a care in the world.

In their junior year, Dutch and Margaret had been the romantic leads in the junior class's production of Philip Barry's *You and I*. It never occurred to Dutch that things might not work out with Margaret. He had that same feeling about everything. His parents had only grade-school educations, but he was sure he'd find a way to go to college. He'd been saving for it since he started working in the summers. He had $400 in all.

It wasn't that Dutch wanted to become a doctor or lawyer. He wasn't much of a student, but he just assumed that he would be one of those going on to college. He was a big man in high school, president of the student body and of the Drama Club, and second-semester vice-president of Hi-Y. The organization was supposed "to create, maintain and extend throughout the school and community, the highest standards of Christian character" and to promote "Clean Speech, Clean Sports, Clean Living and Clean Scholarship."

He viewed the era as one of "raccoon coats and things called collegiate" and he wanted to be part of it, of football games and fraternity parties and good cheer. From his days in grade school, Dutch had known where he wanted to go to school: Eureka College. He had never seen the school, but his idol, Garland Waggoner, a Dixon football star, had gone to Eureka. Dutch could think of nothing finer than to follow in his footsteps. What made it all the sweeter was that Eureka was affiliated with the Christian church. Margaret would be entering Eureka as well.

Dutch knew he would miss Dixon. He had a deeply felt, lyric sense of the town and his place in it. In his senior year Dutch wrote an essay for the yearbook about his experience as a lifeguard, a loving meditation about the people of the town. ("On they come, hordes of swimmers, bathers, sleepers, or what have you! A mob of water seeking humans intent on giving the beach guard something to worry about.")

Dutch remembered tiny details about his home, all the details that exemplified an American small town at its best. Dutch's Dixon was not a place like Sherwood Anderson's Winesburg, Ohio, or Sinclair Lewis's Main Street, places with their full measure of darkness and morbidity, places ready to be brushed with satire. Dutch embraced Dixon like a first lover. He loved sitting in church on Sunday morning looking over his hymnal at Margaret. He loved B. J. Frazer and the hours he spent with him. He loved the football games and the winter snows, the merchants who knew his name, and his buddies in the neighborhood. He loved being a star in *his* town. When he left for college that September day in 1928, he carried with him rich, deep memories that were like a well of sweet, pure water from which he could always draw.

The fields on the highway to Eureka were heavy with the bounty of the harvest. By nature's measure, this was a good year; but for the farmers of the Great Plains, it was yet another season of poor prices, high costs and more foreclosures. Life didn't make sense anymore; a man and a woman had nothing but more debts to show for a year's honest toil.

Dutch could see that things weren't the way they'd been. When the farmers didn't get a decent price for their corn, they didn't have cash; and when they didn't have cash, they didn't buy shoes; and when they didn't buy shoes, Jack Reagan didn't have money for the family. But Dutch felt that somehow things would work out.

From the moment he first saw Eureka, Dutch knew that he had chosen well. With its five red buildings in a semicircle that rose above the flat Illinois turf and its 220 students, Eureka was a collegiate version of Dixon. It was a small, comfortable place where a young man could make his mark, especially one who admitted later, "I just liked showing off."

Eureka was a Christian college in the Protestant heartland of America, as wholesome as a square dance. Dancing hadn't even been allowed until the previous year. Virginity was considered a virtue, not a euphemism for a lack of opportunity. Students had to be in their rooms at 10:00 P.M. on Fridays, 11:00 P.M. on Saturdays. They attended compulsory chapel.

Dutch arrived on campus with $400 in his pocket. The scholarship office cut his $180 tuition bill in half. To pay for his board, he washed dishes in a fraternity house. That was by far the most onerous of his duties.

Other than that, he spent his freshman year living the good college life. He proudly strutted across the small campus, a green freshman beanie on his head, one arm around Margaret, the other full of books.

Dutch immediately set out to become as much a part of Eureka as he had been of Dixon High School. He joined the other twenty-five males trying out for the football team. Eureka was a small school, playing universities with as many as 2,000 students. Coach Ralph McKinzie needed all the players he could get. Of the twenty-six who had gone out, Dutch was the only one not to make the cut. The 1928 team photograph shows twenty-six gruff midwestern football players. Twenty-five were wearing the school's varsity jersey; Dutch was wearing a white sweat shirt. A player behind Ronnie held up two fingers behind Ronnie's head, giving him rabbit ears.

"Everyone else who went out for football that year, made it," remembered Howard Short, a senior who was manager of the team. "Even the other freshmen were starters. He didn't get to travel with the team, but he'd still come out for every practice. He'd stand on the sidelines during the game and yell and pat people on the back. I really admired his perseverance. It took guts. The snottyness of a small school is often far worse than at a big one. Everyone knew that he kept going out for the team and not making it."

Dutch had better luck with other groups. He became a reporter for the school paper, the *Pegasus,* and a member of the winning freshman debate team. He pledged Tau Kappa Epsilon, one of three fraternities on campus. Margaret also helped ease the humiliation of not making the football team. She was a steady, pretty companion who gave Dutch a badge of success that most other freshmen didn't have. She pledged the Delta Theta sorority. When she wasn't studying, she was with Dutch. They attended weekly dances at the Teke House and went to church together each Sunday.

When Dutch took Margaret out in the evening to the cemetery, carrying a blanket over his arm, he didn't receive sly, knowing glances from his fraternity brothers. After all, the innocent tradition of "kegging" was a favorite with his fraternity brothers and they might be out later themselves to smooch with their girlfriends. Sometimes when he was out walking with his girl, Dutch had what he called later "repressed heartburnings of a different sort." Sex, though, wasn't anything he felt he had to do to prove himself a man.

The biggest excitement of Dutch's freshman year, however, was the school's financial crisis. There was scarcely a student in the college who hadn't sat in church hearing the minister pleading for one special offering or another: for a new Sunday School building, a rectory, missions overseas, or for the church-affiliated colleges. There was always a crisis and the students could be forgiven for not listening too closely to Eureka College's tale of woe. But they took it seriously indeed when right before Thanksgiving the college president, Bert Wilson, announced a money-saving austerity plan that would dramatically curtail the academic program and dismiss many of the teachers. On November 16, 1928, the board of trustees adopted the cutback proposal.

The faculty was as upset as the students, and together they circulated a petition demanding Wilson's resignation. This was not the thing that was done in college in the 1920s, particularly in the Midwest, and reporters from Chicago and even the *New York Times* showed up to write the biggest story of which Eureka had ever been a part.

On the evening before the students were to leave for Thanksgiving, the board of trustees met to vote on Wilson's submitted resignation. Dutch waited for their decision with the rest of the student committee, which was composed of three seniors, three juniors, two sophomores, and one freshman, Dutch. At midnight, an hour fit for chicanery, the board meeting broke up. Dutch and the others learned the bad news: Not only would the president be retained but his program would be implemented as well.

The college bell began to toll. The students and faculty knew what the signal meant. Dormitories and fraternity houses emptied out. Students wearing coats over pajamas and nightgowns hurried through the November night. Faculty members walked over from their homes. Before long, the chapel was filled.

The committee had decided to ask the student body to strike, staying away from classes until Wilson resigned. Dutch was one of the committee members chosen to speak. He had debated, he had acted, but never before had he incited a crowd to action. Never before had he woven emotion and fact together so dramatically or effectively. It intoxicated him. Dutch would remember the magic of that evening as one of the most exhilarating moments of his life. He wrote later in his autobiography: "I discovered that night that an audience has a feel to it and, in the parlance of theater, that audience and I were together. When I came to actually presenting the motion there was no need for parliamentary procedure; they came to their feet with a roar—even the faculty members present voted by acclamation. It was heady wine. Hell, with two more lines I could have had them riding through 'every Middlesex village and farm'—without horses yet."

Many of his Eureka contemporaries barely remember Dutch speaking, and the newspaper accounts didn't include his name on the roster of students leading the strike. "He was involved all right," said Short, who was senior-class president and chairman of the strike committee, "but at our invitation. Andy Paine, another senior and a star basketball player, was to speak, then me, then Dutch. We asked him to speak because even then he was full of baloney. He made a good rabble-rousing speech, but all three of us had them eating out of our hands."

The strike succeeded. All but twelve of the 220 students refrained from attending classes for a week. Under such pressure, Wilson resigned and his attrition program was dropped.

The rest of Dutch's freshman year proceeded without further drama. That summer, back at Lowell Park as lifeguard, he had so little sense of destiny or simple ambition that he was thinking about dropping out and working as a surveyor. A talk with Margaret and a quick look at Eureka's new football uniforms while on a visit to the campus cured him of that idea. He called home. "I'm staying, Nelle," he told his mother.

"That's what Moon said you'd do," Nelle said. "Wishes he could join you."

"No kidding! Tell him to hold everything, and I'll call back."

Dutch was never one to come out and say something negative about another human being, especially his brother. That didn't mean that he was totally without such thoughts. He had been brought up wearing Neil's hand-me-downs, and he wasn't wearing hand-me-downs any longer. He didn't think that Neil would fit in. Neil never paid back any of the small loans Dutch had made to him. He was too worldly, too cynical, too much the devotee of speakeasys.

But Neil was his brother, and Dutch went over to see Coach McKinzie. By the time he called his mother again, not only had he gotten Neil a job in the Teke kitchen but the college had agreed to defer his tuition. Dutch returned to Dixon to fetch his older brother, bringing for Neil's use his most cherished and expensive possession: a new steamer trunk.

"I've got a football scholarship for you, Moon, and a job as well," Dutch said proudly. "All you'll need's about ten dollars a month."

"I'm not going," Neil said blankly. Despite what their mother had said, Neil hadn't the slightest interest in going off to Eureka College. Life had enough ironies without having to follow in the footsteps of a younger brother who Neil felt looked down upon him.

The day Dutch was supposed to head back to Eureka College, Neil went to work at the cement factory. That evening when he returned home, Dutch's trunk was still sitting there.

"Nelle, I thought Dutch was going back to school today," Neil said, puzzled.

"He did," his mother said angrily. "And you ought to be ashamed of yourself. He left his trunk for you."

That did it. Neil filled up the trunk and headed off to Eureka. Neil loved his brother, despite what he considered Dutch's occasional self-righteousness. Dutch had found him a school, a job, even provided him with

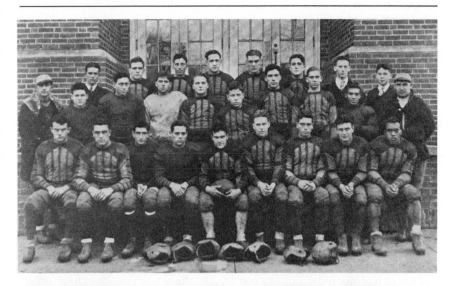

At Eureka College during his junior year, in 1930, Dutch was a right guard on the football team (middle row, white jersey); and played the role of a Greek shepherd in Edna St. Vincent Millay's *Aria da Capo*. *(Eureka College; UPI)*

many of the well-to-do families from Chicago and elsewhere who vacationed in the lodge at wooded Lowell Park. The wealthy men took great pleasure in lecturing promising young men on the subject of success and they were delighted to have Dutch listening to their talk.

Like a lot of ski instructors and tennis pros, Dutch had a seemingly guileless way of ingratiating himself with the wealthy. He chatted and joked, but he knew the limits of his position and never overstepped them. The men offered him all kinds of help when he would graduate that spring with a bachelor's degree in social studies and economics. He noticed, however, that as the depression deepened, their offers dried up. They were as frightened as anyone.

Dutch couldn't avoid the realities of the depression any longer. Jack had lost his partnership in the Fashion Shoe Store in Dixon. Nelle had gone to work in a dress shop for a dollar less a week than Dutch earned as a lifeguard. After a stint selling shoes on the road, Jack had ended up managing a chain shoe store in Springfield, 200 miles to the north.

Jack had poured all of his pride and know-how into the Dixon store, turning it into a sedate establishment with good shoes. Dutch had visited the Springfield store and had cringed. The chain store was a cheap, grungy place with crude orange ads pasted on the windows and one bench with iron armrests.

Christmas 1931 was the worst Christmas that a lot of people had ever had. Millions of Americans were out of work. Hundreds of banks had closed down. Jack and his family had had to move out of their house into an apartment. But stacked up against all that other people were suffering, the Reagans had a good deal about which to be thankful. The two Reagan boys were still in college, and Jack and Nelle had work. For the holidays Nelle had time off from the dress shop. Jack had come home from Springfield for a few days. Dutch and Neil had driven up from Eureka in Neil's rattly old car. This was Dutch's last Christmas as a college student. It was possible he would not even be in Dixon next December.

The Reagans had little on their minds but enjoying the holiday, forgetting the world and all its uncertainties. On Christmas Eve, Dutch and Moon were getting slicked up to go out on dates when a mailman appeared at the apartment door. Jack opened the envelope and held the blue paper in his hand.

"Well, it's a hell of a Christmas present," Jack said quietly. The shoe chain had let him go.

6

"YE DID GREAT, YE BIG S.O.B."

In the summer of 1932, Dutch put in another season at Lowell Park. He was a twenty-one-year-old college graduate working as a lifeguard, but in those lean times a job was a job. Soon he would have to look for a full-time position, and the prospects were lean indeed.

Dutch didn't see it that way. He was a person who woke up feeling good about life, a sentiment from which no philosopher, no worldly cynic, no small-town naysayer could dissuade him. If Dutch could have bottled that feeling and peddled it on the street corners, he would have been a rich man right then.

Dutch sometimes sounded like a Dixon businessman thumping away at the weekly Rotary luncheon about how things had to get better, by golly, because this was America. But his optimism went far beyond small-town boosterism; it colored everything he felt about family, friends, life or politics. A poem he had written while still in high school expressed his feelings exactly:

> *I wonder what it's all about, and why*
> *We suffer so, when little things go wrong?*
> *We make our life a struggle,*
> *When life should be a song. . . .*
>
> *Millions have gone before us,*
> *And millions will come behind.*
> *So why do we curse and fight*
> *At a fate both wise and kind.*

One evening at Lowell Park, Dutch sat listening to Sid Altschuler, a Kansas City businessman whose daughters he had taught to swim. "When

The twenty-one-year-old lifeguard. *(WH)*

you determine what line of work you want to get in, let me know—and if it's in one of those areas where I can help, I'll get you a job."

Other wealthy businessmen had made promises to Dutch, and they had been like the sun setting over Rock River, golden and short-lived. But Dutch took Sid's words seriously. Several days later he told Sid excitedly of his desire to become a sports broadcaster on the radio.

"Well, you've picked a line in which I have no connections," the businessman said. This was hardly the bolstering Dutch was looking for. Sid tried again. "You've picked a sound industry and one that should have hundreds of undreamed directions. . . . So start knocking on doors, tell anyone who'll listen that you believe you have a future in the business, and you'll take any kind of job, even sweeping floors, just to get in."

As soon as the swimming season ended, Dutch intended to pack his bags and set out to find his first job in radio, even sweeping the floors. Jack, however, thought that such youthful idealism was something to be discarded when you graduated from college, if you hadn't had it beaten out of you before. *He* knew what the world was like, and the depression was no time for wet-behind-the-ears kids to be bouncing about looking for pie in the sky. "Quit chasing rainbows and piddling your dough away," he told his son. "Dixon has jobs."

Dutch listened politely and then told his parents that he wanted to visit Neil at Eureka before starting his job search. It was true that he wanted to visit Neil, but that was only the beginning of his intended trip. From there he planned to hitchhike to Chicago.

As soon as the swimming season ended, Dutch headed out. At the Teke house at Eureka, he swaggered in and told his brothers: "If I'm not making five thousand a year when I'm five years out of college, I'll consider these four years here were wasted." This bold statement was met with more laughter than many of Dutch's jokes had received. His ambitions received a happier hearing at the home of Margaret Cleaver, whose father was now a minister in town. They had a bittersweet parting, though— Dutch off to the Windy City and whatever great adventures met him there; Margaret off to teach in a small high school.

Dutch could boast to Margaret and his fraternity brothers, but when he saw the big buildings of downtown Chicago and walked among those thousands of ambitious, determined people, he was scared. He didn't even know how to find a bathroom.

That evening Dutch stayed at a medical fraternity house with an old Eureka brother. He did what he often did when he was scared: bragged and exaggerated. He told the medical students that he had an appointment at NBC on Thursday. The fact was that he had merely gone to NBC and learned that the program director interviewed on Thursday. But it sounded impressive. For the next few days he couldn't even get any interviews. Radio executives weren't interested in hearing the noble sentiments of a young man willing to start not with a microphone but with a broom.

Thursday's "appointment" at NBC became more and more important. Dutch walked into the offices more resolute than ever. The program director did not make an appearance, but a young woman spent a few minutes with Dutch. She did not tell him her title, leading him to conclude later that she might have been merely a secretary. But at that moment she *was* NBC.

The woman listened to Dutch's story. When he finished, she said, "This is the big time. No one in the city wants to take a chance on inexperience. Go out in what we call the sticks and try some of the smaller stations."

This advice was a winter tonic, bitter to swallow. She ended by sweetening her sour words: "I think you will make it—come back and see me after you have some experience."

Dutch panned through the muck of his days in Chicago looking for at least one fleck of gold. All he could come up with was the advice at NBC. The more he thought about the meeting, the better the idea sounded. By the time he hitchhiked back to Dixon and sat down over supper with Jack and Nelle, he was talking as if he had struck it rich in Chicago.

Jack had once been full of dreams himself. Now his one hope was that if Franklin Roosevelt won the election in November, he would be remembered for his campaign work and get a job. Whether he quite believed Dutch or not, he decided that he wanted his boy to have a chance to play out his aspirations. Why didn't Dutch take the Oldsmobile and make the rounds of all the radio stations he could reach in a day? With that, Dutch's rejection in Chicago was all forgotten. He was soon looking over a map, figuring just where he could get to on Monday.

For his first stop, Dutch drove seventy miles west to Davenport, Iowa, home of mighty WOC, the World of Chiropractic. Owned by the Palmer School of Chiropractic, WOC beamed its signal throughout the Midwest.

Radio stations were one of the wonders of the time, gigantic, marvelous worlds coming from a microphone in a tiny room. Peter MacArthur, the station manager, could have been the Wizard of Oz. Anyone hearing his strong voice on the radio ("WOC, Davenport—where the West begins, in the state where the tall corn grows") would never imagine that he was a cripple. An old Scottish vaudevillian, MacArthur had ended up in Davenport needing treatment for arthritis. He had to be lifted out of his chair and stood only with the aid of two canes.

Dutch sold MacArthur the only product he ever wanted to sell: Dutch

Reagan. He was a persuasive salesman and the station manager seemed impressed.

"Where the hell have ye been?" MacArthur yelled. He usually laced his conversation with profanity that would make a Quaker blush. "Don't ye ever listen to the radio?"

For a month WOC had been advertising for a new announcer. Out of the ninety-four applicants, MacArthur had already made his choice.

Dutch's heart fell. "How in hell does a guy ever get to be a sports announcer if he can't get inside a station?" he asked, spitting out the words like watermelon seeds.

Dutch stood at the elevator waiting to leave, reading the homilies and aphorisms on the wall. He was struck on the leg by a cane. "Not so fast, ye big bastard. Didn't ye hear me callin' ye? Now what was it ye said about sports?"

Good, gruff old Pete MacArthur took Dutch into the velvet-draped studio, set him down before the microphone and told him to announce an imaginary football game.

"When that goes on, ye start talkin'," the station manager said, pointing to the red light. "Tell us about a game and make me see it. That's the mike in front of ye—ye won't be able to see me, but I'll be listening. Good luck."

Dutch was more a novice performer than a fledgling journalist anyway. He'd had years of practice before captive audiences at Eureka. He chose the fourth quarter of a game between his alma mater and Western State University.

Twenty minutes later, MacArthur walked back into the studio. Dutch sat drenched in sweat. "Ye did great, ye big s.o.b. Now look, we have a sponsor for four University of Iowa games. Ye be here a week from Saturday and I'll give ye five dollars and bus fare. If ye do all right on that one, ye'll do the other three."

Dutch's life was unreeling like an inspirational "B" movie. No wonder he was a sucker for the happy endings that film critics dismissed disdainfully for their improbability. Dutch was a natural, and if he had to wait a few months for a full-time job, that only made the script more interesting.

There was even a scene of romantic tragedy in his young life. Trouble with Margaret had started when she and Dutch were still at Eureka. She had spent her senior year at the University of Illinois and had dated other fellows. "Dutch and Margaret just grew apart," remembered Lois Binkley. "They were in different worlds. She went on to get her master's degree and was teaching in high school. Then she and her sister had gone to Europe. She met the man she later married on the boat going over. I don't believe Dutch was ever in contact with her again. He had loved her very much and it was very hard on him."

For a while Dutch was distraught. According to B. J. Frazer's widow, he wrote a letter to his drama coach saying that he didn't care whether he lived or died. But by then his career was on its way.

By early 1933 he had a regular announcer's job at the munificent salary of $100 a month. He had entered radio at an auspicious time. The industry stood at the frontiers of technology. Before long, WOC's newest announcer advanced to being a sportscaster for WHO in Des Moines. This was the big time. The owners of WHO were so confident of the future of radio that they had built one of only a dozen fifty-kilowatt stations in the United States.

Dutch's voice was beamed across the Midwest. Iowa University football games. Chicago Cubs baseball games. White Sox baseball games. Chicago Cubs baseball games. White Sox baseball games. As a sports broadcaster, Dutch had a telling eye for detail. He couldn't work like a print journalist and try half a dozen leads. He was always on. For the sports fans of the Midwest, he created a reality that was as vivid as a television picture would be to a later generation.

Dutch was a storyteller. While other radio stations sent their announcers to Chicago's Wrigley Park to broadcast the Cub games, Dutch sat in the WHO studios in Des Moines. In the press box at the Chicago stadium, a telegraph operator tapped out Morse code to another telegraph operator at the WHO studios. All Dutch had were the barest statistics—the strikes, the pitches, the outs—from which to paint his word picture.

Dutch's games were less accurate but more lively than those of his competitors. One memorable day the wire went dead. Dutch had the batter foul the ball off again and again for at least seven minutes before the telegraph started working again.

It was good doing something that difficult so well. Before long, Dutch was earning $75 a week from the station, a princely sum, especially at age twenty-five. And that wasn't all of it. In Des Moines, Dutch was a celebrity, and he made the most of it. There was money for touring, money for talking at banquets, money for writing an occasional column, money for public relations, money for introducing sporting events. Fifty dollars just to talk about football at a high-school banquet. It just came rolling in.

Over the air, Dutch read news about the depression. He saw the panhandlers in the street, but that didn't affect him. The worst news he received was that Jack had suffered a heart attack. But at least Dutch could help out now, and his father would never have to work again. Even after he sent money to Neil at Eureka, and a substantial check to his parents, he was flush as could be.

Like many young men about town, Dutch started frequenting Si's Moonlight Inn. He had been heartsick about losing Margaret, but there

Dutch Reagan, sportscaster, WHO Radio, Des Moines, Iowa, 1933. *(WH)*

were plenty of young ladies to assuage those wounds. When he wasn't at the old speakeasy tippling Si's notorious combination of near bear spiked with alcohol (or was it alcohol spiked with near beer?), Dutch was often out riding horses. To get the best training possible, he signed on as an officer candidate with the Fourteenth Calvary Regiment.

It was a good life, a good life indeed. He had been able to help get Neil a job in broadcasting as well in Des Moines. The worst thing he had to complain about was the Iowa winters, and he even finessed a way out of that. He had convinced WHO that the station needed a broadcaster—namely Dutch Reagan—to go to Catalina Island, California, and get the local color at the Cubs' spring training. The main local color Dutch was interested in was a suntan. Moreover, he was the man who broadcast the Cub games without even being there. But he was persuasive, and each winter the station sent its star broadcaster to California.

California felt like the future. Compared to much of the rest of the United States, southern California was booming. But the state had its woes. There were the poor and unemployed, over 200,000 of them in L.A. alone. Farmers dumped tons of oranges and vegetables into the bed of the Los Angeles River while thousands went to bed with the gnawing ache of hunger.

Somehow, though, a beggar on a beach, a family of red-faced Okies clunking up the highway in an old truck, wasn't as tragic as homeless men huddled over a barrel on a cold Chicago street corner, or an old Iowa family at a foreclosure sale. And people were still making it out here, making it big.

Dutch felt comfortable in southern California, the way he hadn't on his trip looking for a job in Chicago. He was a success himself now, and that mattered in Los Angeles—not your bloodlines, not your alma mater, but how you were doing today.

Dutch could see what was happening in the film industry. Just thirty years ago the movie pioneers had come west by train and car, cradling contraptions called "cameras" in their arms, plopping themselves and their equipment down in the streets of Los Angeles, on the beaches and in the residential neighborhoods. They had churned out one-reelers, spending a few minutes plotting their next film, and days plotting how they were going to finance it. Now Warners, M-G-M, Paramount, Universal, RKO, 20th Century-Fox and Columbia were great fiefdoms, empires with their own theaters and distribution systems.

Dutch knew it was possible to make it big in films. It had already happened to WHO's barn-dance band, the Oklahoma Outlaws. In the winter of 1937, on his way to Catalina Island, Dutch stopped off to visit the Oklahoma Outlaws. The former WHO band had been picked up by Gene

Autry to be featured in one of the Singing Cowboy's movies. If the Oklahoma Outlaws could make it in movies, then why not Dutch Reagan? All he had to do was meet their agent and strut his stuff.

The agent introduced Dutch to a casting director. Movie people have scores of ways to say no, one of them being by saying yes. The casting director agreed to give Dutch a tryout and sent him off with a couple of worn scripts, but Dutch could tell that the man didn't think he had a great talent on his hands.

The Oklahoma Outlaws weren't the only folks from Des Moines making it in Hollywood. Dutch went to visit Joy Hodges, a pretty singer who had appeared on WHO. Now she was in films and the featured singer with Jimmy Grier's orchestra at the Biltmore Bowl. Between shows, Dutch told Joy about his hopes of becoming an actor.

"I know an agent who will be honest with you," the singer said. "If you're wrong, and you should forget this idea, he'll tell you." She set up an appointment the next morning with an agent named Bill Meiklejohn.

This meeting with Meiklejohn was Dutch's big moment. Dutch had been brought up to tell the truth; but to him, facts had become flat little balloons that had to be blown up if they were to be seen and sufficiently appreciated. The Eureka Dramatic Club had been a bunch of college kids, but they were darned good, and Dutch puffed them up into a full professional company in which he'd had a stellar role. In radio he was taking home a base salary of $75 a week plus a lot of extras, far more than most people in the heartland ever dreamed of earning. To show Meiklejohn, what a successful fellow he was talking to, Dutch gave himself a raise, doubling his salary.

Dutch had pretty much run out of things to exaggerate. "Look," he said finally, "Joy told me that you would level with me. Should I go back to Des Moines and forget this, or what do I do?"

Meiklejohn picked up the phone and called Max Arnow, the casting director at Warner Brothers. "Max, I have another Robert Taylor sitting in the office."

If God had decided to strike down white liars that morning, he could have killed two birds with one stone. Even Dutch knew that in comparing him to the newest box-office sensation, Meiklejohn was exaggerating.

"God made only one Robert Taylor!" Arnow yelled.

God may have made only one Robert Taylor, but he made an awful lot of secondary actors and actresses who peopled the hundreds of movies that were churned out each year. Arnow gave Dutch a screen test with a scene from Philip Barry's play *Holiday;* Arnow was impressed by "his warmth and his voice."

Soon afterward, Carl Schaeffer, director of international advertising and publicity at Warners, received a call. Jack Warner, the head of the studio, wanted to see him in the projection room.

"I want you to see a new guy," Warner said, motioning to the projectionist to start the film.

"This is Dutch Reagan," Warner said, pronouncing it Ree-gun. Dutch appeared on the screen answering questions thrown at him off-camera. "The guy might have something."

It was no small matter for the man who had made stars of James Cagney, Bette Davis and Errol Flynn to utter such words.

On Dutch's first day back in Des Moines, a telegram arrived:

WARNER'S OFFER CONTRACT SEVEN YEARS, ONE YEAR'S OPTIONS, STARTING AT $200 A WEEK. WHAT SHALL I DO? BILL MEIKLEJOHN

At the end of May 1937, twenty-six-year-old Dutch set out for California. Life for him was whatever was in front of him, on his own plate. Cruising westward in his new convertible, Dutch felt right with the world. For years he had listened to Jack going on about the New Deal. He figured Roosevelt was doing about the best that could be done. He read the headlines, too—all about civil war in Spain, and Hitler's rantings. Sure, it was a mess over there. But it wasn't his problem. He had an exciting future to think about.

Dutch sped across the California desert, chasing the sun through the long day. By late afternoon he reached the cooler breezes of San Bernardino. As night fell, he drove toward the sea along a road graced by orange trees. Suddenly, the lights of Los Angeles appeared below, like a thousand torches. Soon Dutch Reagan was entering Hollywood, not as an interloper but as an invitee.

══7══

LOVE IS ON THE AIR

Ronnie drove his Nash convertible past the white-columned gates of the Warner Brothers Studio near Bronson and Sunset in Hollywood. For a newcomer the lot was a bewildering array of buildings and people, frantic activity and endless waiting. Sound stages. Recording studios. Producers' offices. Writers' cubbyholes. Warehouses. Wardrobe rooms. Commissaries.

Just two decades before, Jack, Harry and Sam Warner had bought this land on which a ranch had stood. Here they built a great film studio. The three brothers were the sons of a Polish cobbler. They were rude, largely uneducated men with a shrewd sense of the American public. Harry had died in 1927. Sam still handled business matters, while Jack, the producer, was the creative boss of the studio. A brash, irrepressible man, Jack Warner had the quick humor of a borscht-belt comedian and a temper to match.

More than any other studio, the Warner films captured the populist pulse of the Thirties. Brutal gangster films: *Little Caesar* and *Public Enemy*. Socially conscious films: *I Am a Fugitive from a Chain Gang* and *They Won't Forget*. Flashy fantasy musicals: *The Gold Diggers of 1933* and *Forty-Second Street*. Adventure films: *The Charge of the Light Brigade* and *Captain Blood*.

To accomplish this, the Warners had created a gigantic human machine out of creative individuals. The writers sat in their cubbyholes producing pages of crisp, fast-paced dialogue, their scripts detailing camera movement. The producers took the approved scripts and budgets and cast the main players. The director took the script and the players and set to work within rigidly defined limits of time and money. The top actors were

Ronald Wilson Reagan at the age of twenty-three.

called "stars," but they were merely another part of the machine, retooled, rehoned until they fit the way they were supposed to fit.

Ronnie had his nickname burnished away even before Warners had begun to work on the rest of his image. He didn't care. He was ecstatic. "I came to Hollywood, a sports announcer by trade," Ronnie wrote Charles Martin, the journalist, in a 1971 letter after his career as an actor had ended, "filled with all the star-struck awe of one who had from childhood been entertained in the house of illusion—the neighborhood theatre. I never did get over being awe-struck at finding myself working with and among those familiar faces."

Hollywood was America's capital of dreams, its peddler of illusion. People didn't go to the movies to see the mirror reflection of their own hard lives. During the depression, movies were the drug of choice. For a dime or a quarter you could sit for three hours or more and watch two films, a cartoon and a newsreel.

The big Warners features drew the crowds, but the audience sat through a second "B" picture as well. The studio churned out these films cheaply and quickly, usually in about three weeks. The "B's" were the farm team of stardom where most actors got their start. To an innocent like Ronnie, though, a movie was a movie.

Whatever doubts Ronnie may have had about talking his way into a field in which he was a rank amateur, he didn't have any time to sit around worrying. Three days after his arrival he was starring in his first "B" picture, *Love Is on the Air.* Bryan ("Brynie") Foy, the producer, had been the youngest member of a famous vaudeville act, The Seven Little Foys. Now as Warners' "Keeper of the B's" he had gone into recycling long before the environmental movement. The film was a new version of a 1934 trifle, *Hi, Nellie,* which had starred the fine actor Paul Muni.

Ronnie's luck was holding out. In *Love Is on the Air,* he played Andy McLeod, a brash young radio announcer, a role that helped to hide his clumsy acting. At the first rehearsal, Ronnie read the script as if it were the Los Angeles phone directory. The next morning he performed before the camera with gestures that were wooden and broad. But it was for "his warmth and his voice" that Max Arnow, Warners' casting director, had hired Ronnie, and there was something immensely likable about him on the screen.

Unfortunately, though, Ronnie was no new Robert Taylor, James Cagney, or even Errol Flynn, the rakish hero of swashbuckling epics. Ronnie didn't project the magnetism that made a great star. Two years before, when Robert Taylor had a small part in *Society Doctor,* the studio had been deluged with thousands of letters each week from women across America. By the time his next film appeared, *Magnificent Obsession,* he was in the top five of every popularity poll in the country. Ronnie was more the nice, good-looking guy down the street whom you could trust with your wife or girlfriend. Women were attracted to him, but he wasn't the kind of man they swooned over at the Bijou on Friday nights, or to whom they wrote scented letters.

Ronnie was, nonetheless, an American archetype, a man with whom people could identify. He radiated a uniquely American kind of "niceness." Warners knew just how to use him. Max Arnow saw to it that Ronnie didn't have to take acting lessons—he didn't want anything to spoil Ronnie's natural charm. The studio got rid of his crew cut, which had made his head seem an extension of the Great Plains and had earned it the nickname "Bowl Number 5." Before long he had a snazzy-looking pompadour. The other improvement the studio suggested was that Ronnie throw out his suits with padded shoulders that made him look as if he were still on the football field. But he said that those were his real shoulders.

"I was the Errol Flynn of the B's," Ronnie wrote in the *Saturday Evening Post* years later. And so he was, playing the hero in one low-budget epic after another. In his first year in Hollywood, he acted in nine pictures. In four of his first seven movies, he was typecast as a radio announcer. In one of them, *Hollywood Hotel,* he broadcast the premiere of an Errol Flynn movie.

Keenan Wynn, a longtime colleague, says Ronnie was not so much an actor as a performer who played versions of himself. "He wouldn't move you emotionally," Wynn said. "The situation would." Ronnie wasn't an outstanding lead actor. Nor did he have the potential to become a brilliant character actor like Paul Muni, who *became* his roles, so that the audiences remembered not Muni but Louis Pasteur, Émile Zola or Al Capone. Ronnie didn't feel his way so far into the depths of his roles that it seemed he might never come out. He didn't have that profound, visceral interest in his craft that was the essence of a fine actor.

None of that mattered to Brynie Foy at Warners. He always had eight pictures in production, eight on hold right behind them, twenty writers, eight directors and five producers. He needed all the actors like Ronnie he could get: serviceable, reliable, likable. What impressed Foy about Ronnie? "He showed up in the morning. Sober."

In Hollywood in the Thirties, the machines of publicity whirled as rapidly as the movie cameras. The film journalists weren't clamoring for a chance to interview Ronnie, but as a contract player the studio saw to it that he got his share of publicity. "We started to work," remembered Carl Schaeffer. "For my part, I'd have foreign correspondents meeting him. They wanted to meet the stars. I'd say I'd be glad to introduce you but I'd like to introduce you to Ronald Reagan as well. He was always very cooperative."

At openings, the stars, starlets and hopefuls were paraded past an adoring public in scenes that made many actors cringe. Ronnie often took starlets out on studio orders to premieres, fancy restaurants, wherever there would be flashbulbs popping. "Do we have to go?" a newly signed actor asked Ronnie about a Warner premiere.

"No, but you'll be around longer if you do," Ronnie said. That very evening he and a beautiful blond sweater girl, both in evening clothes borrowed from the studio, pulled up at the premiere in a taxicab. That was Ronnie's first and last date with Lana Turner.

Ronnie did whatever he was supposed to do for publicity—put on clothes or take them off. It was part of Ronnie's studio legend that one day a publicity man saw him emerging from the sea around Santa Monica like an Adonis of the deep. Zappo! A new image was created. From then on, the studio often posed him in swim suits or shirtless.

"I didn't know what that fellow was talking about that day down on the beach," Ronnie told *Modern Screen.* "I'd just come down for a swim, and he kept telling me that I should have told him I had a body. Well, what did he think I had anyway? I used to be a four-letter man at college, but I didn't think that that gave me an excuse to stick out my chest and expand my biceps publicly every time some one mentioned the word health."

Ronnie didn't like many of the roles he was getting, but he loved Warner Brothers. He was a small-town boy, and once inside the gates, the studio was like a small town. Ronnie had a way with people, no matter who they were. He had a small part in *Hollywood Hotel,* a major picture starring Dick Powell, one of the biggest stars of the day. He and Powell hit it off like equals. The same happened with Pat O'Brien when Ronnie played opposite him in *Cowboy from Brooklyn.*

What made Ronnie proudest of all was that he was welcome at one special table at the Warner commissary for lunch. In those days the stars all came to lunch at the studio; they didn't sit cloistered in dressing rooms. The Warner Green Room was as good a place to stargaze as anywhere in Hollywood. The stars had their own tables—Bette Davis here, Edward G. Robinson in a corner, Fredric March sitting right here. But for most men, the only place to be was the table where Brick Enright, a director, and Mushy Callahan, the physical-education instructor and former junior welterweight champion, held court. Enright and Callahan weren't big shots, but they were real men. Joining them for lunch on a given day might be Pat O'Brien, Dick Powell, Humphrey Bogart, Ronnie and a few others. It was an hour of joshing, and manly talk. Ronnie loved it and was glad to be accepted.

Genial as he might appear at the studio, Ronnie spent little time with his actor buddies in the evenings. He was still a boy from Dixon, Illinois. He was more comfortable chewing the fat with Peewee, Willi, Butch, and Little Man, with whom he had caroused at the Moonlight Inn outside Des

Moines. His friends had come to Los Angeles to get jobs with a future, and Ronnie was grubstaking them. They often went to Barney's Beanery on Santa Monica Boulevard, sang some barbershop harmony and had a drink or two.

Ronnie had not forgotten his parents, either. Jack's heart attack had ended the possibility of his working again, and Ronnie was supporting them. From the moment he got his first $200 paycheck, he kept wondering when he would be able to bring Jack and Nelle to Los Angeles.

Scarcely three months later, he felt secure enough to send for them. "Come whenever you're ready, but don't travel in a hurry," Ronnie wrote in a letter quoted in *Modern Screen*. "Take in the Grand Canyon and all the little canyons, because once you're out here, you won't want to budge."

"Nelle told me that Ronnie had called and told them he wanted them to move out there," remembered Helen Lawton, a Dixon friend. "She said, 'Oh, you don't want your old mother out there.' And he said, 'I need you.' She said that's all she needed was to be needed."

Ronnie put his parents up in a hotel in Hollywood while he found an apartment for them just around the corner from his place on Sunset. As often as not, Ronnie showed up at LaRue's on Sunday evening for spaghetti and meatballs not with a gorgeous starlet but with his parents. It was an anomaly in Hollywood: a handsome young bachelor who spent so much time with his parents.

Nelle knew that in her two sons she had been double blessed. This thin, angular, austere-looking woman was especially happy when Neil moved to L.A. to work in radio. She was a familiar figure at Warner Brothers, no stage-door mother shepherding her son's career but a kindly lady with a good word for everyone. She was not happy unless she was helping someone else, and she was soon doing volunteer work at Good Samaritan Hospital.

Ronnie put his father to work answering his fan mail, as much to have Jack occupied as anything else. Ronnie had given his father a precious gift: the monetary resources to live the last years of his life with security. Jack was no longer an angry Irishman raging against the injustices of the world. He was an old man who loved the California sun and went for long walks. "I never knew there were birds before," he told Nelle. "I never knew there was anything so pretty as a flower."

In 1938, in his ninth film, Ronnie was moved up to a featured role in *Brother Rat,* a major film about three cadets at the Virginia Military Academy (VMI). Wayne Morris had the lead, with Eddie Albert and Ronnie as his sidekicks. In the film, Ronnie had a girlfriend played by Jane Wyman, a former dancer. Like Ronnie, she was typecast in her usual role: the lead-

Jane Wyman and Ronald Reagan in their first movie together: *Brother Rat,*
Warner Brothers, 1938. *(The Memory Shop)*

ing lady's adviser and chum, a pert, wisecracking comedienne who still had moments of sensual allure. In *Brother Rat,* she made eyeglasses appear as sexy as a wet bikini. In the one romantic scene, she was the one who smoothed out the sofa and suggested that they sit down. When Ronnie finally kissed her after a walk in the garden, he said, "Just something I forgot to do in the rose garden." He was so passionless that he could have been talking about pruning roses.

Ronnie found the blond actress terribly attractive, but she was going through a divorce and he didn't try to date her. At the end of the filming, Ronnie and Janie were scheduled to have publicity photographs taken together. When they arrived at the photo studio, they discovered another actor in their place. Janie exploded about "people pushing us around."

"It's just a mistake," Ronnie said gently, soothing her. "It's no one's fault. No one would inconvenience us on purpose."

Ronnie's attitude relaxed Janie. She began wondering about this actor whom she knew so slightly.

The cast was young, upcoming and carefree. The filming of *Brother Rat* at Warners' Burbank studio was a romp. The good humor and fun of the film spilled over into the evenings. Eddie Albert; Frank McCarthy, the technical director, who later produced *Patton;* and some of the other cast members lived together at the Hollywood Athletic Club on Sunset Boulevard. They had a secondhand car and they tooled around Los Angeles together, eating, drinking, and going out with the ladies.

Ronnie was the exception. When the day's shooting was over, he didn't join the other players. "Ronnie moved in other directions," Frank McCarthy said. "He was serious about his work, serious about everything."

Ronnie wasn't completely serious. He had his own interest in the opposite sex. Indeed, the best singles meeting place Ronnie had discovered was the set itself. Speaking witty lines supplied by the screenwriter, and taking a girl in your arms on cue, took away the apprehension. The transition from staged romance to romantic meetings was easy. He had dated June Travis, his first costar in *Love Is on the Air,* and other young actresses. But none of the interludes had much more substance than the plots of the movies that had inspired him.

Then Ronnie asked out Jane Wyman. Janie had adopted the Thirties glamour-girl image—bleached her brown hair blond, pasted on false eyelashes, and assumed a sultry come-hither look for promo photographs. On their first date, Ronnie talked sports and ordered beer. Janie couldn't stand beer and only tolerated sports, but she choked down the brew and listened for all she was worth. Ronnie was an incredible talker. Even when he went out with a beautiful young woman like Janie, he didn't converse so much as broadcast.

Ronald Reagan and Jane Wyman,
dating; and Jane Wyman, the star.
(LC; LGC)

Instead of asking directly for another date, Ronnie offered to help Janie with her golf game. This in turn led to tennis dates, swimming dates, even ice-skating dates. From a distance it was hard to tell whether they were dating or in training together.

"I used to be the kind of person who sat in swank nightclubs with a big hat on my head and a long cigarette holder sticking out of my face," Janie said later. "Athletics had no charm for me. . . . Till along came Reagan and all I heard was football and swimming and golf. The only place I could get to see him was out on the golf course. So where do you think I went? Out on a golf course."

"She's a good scout," Ronnie told his mother after one date. Despite her girlish appearance, at the age of twenty-four Janie had already been married once, to Myron Futterman, a New Orleans dress manufacturer. On their wedding day, June 29, 1937, Futterman had vowed to show Janie the good life. Little more than a year later, on November 11, 1938, Janie won a divorce on grounds of mental anguish.

This was a first for Ronnie. Back in Dixon there weren't that many divorced women. But Ronnie thought himself a man of the world. He could handle the fact that he wasn't the first to be nestling Janie in his arms.

Like Ronnie, Janie was a small-town, midwestern girl. She was born Sarah Jane Fulks on January 4, 1914, in St. Joseph, Missouri. Her father was chief of police detectives, and when she was young she had an easier life than Ronnie. Then her father died, the depression struck, and, like so many Americans, the Fulks family headed west to Los Angeles. In high school Janie was a mediocre student. After graduation, she got a job as a waitress at Manning's Coffee Shop.

If she didn't want to measure out her life in coffee cups and slices of blueberry pie, Janie knew that she had to find something else. The one thing she could do was dance. The musical was just coming into its own, and Janie was taken on at Paramount. *Anything Goes. College Rhythm. Rhumba. Stolen Harmony.* If it hadn't been for an agent named Bill Demarest, Janie's career might have been a matter simply of "third girl from the left, second row" and "blonde on the end." Demarest convinced her that she could act, and in 1936 she was picked up by Warner Brothers.

The studio didn't think they had a new Bette Davis on their hands. They gave her secondary roles in secondary films, almost always playing one version or another of a feisty, wisecracking blonde. *Smart Blonde. Fools for Scandal. Mr. Dodd Takes the Air.*

Small parts. A bad marriage. Janie wore her chips on her shoulder like epaulets. If Ronnie had learned to trust people too easily, Janie's problem was that she did not trust people at all. "This was a terrible thing for me, all this distrust," Janie wrote in *Movieland* in July 1944. "I was so afraid that I should make a wrong move or jeopardize my opportunity in some way! I guarded my budding career so fiercely and with such terrible suspicion of everyone that I made it extremely difficult for anyone to help me. . . . Then, of course, Ronnie *really* came into my life. It was *his* easy friendliness which attracted me to him first. Everyone liked him and it seemed to me that he liked nearly everyone. I began to try to analyze what it was in *me* that he liked . . . and to try to have more of it! I began to analyze whatever there was in me that anyone else could like, too, and to wonder what traits I could acquire which would attract people."

Janie sometimes thought that Ronnie's feelings about his fellow man were a bit naïve and sentimental. "I'd like to hear you knock someone, just for a change," she said, naming a man she knew to be a complete scoundrel.

"Oh, he's okay," Ronnie said. "Always been swell to me. Don't believe everything you hear."

"But I didn't hear it, I know it."

"Well, maybe somebody conked him as a babe and he never got over it. Anyway, what's it to us?"

"Ronnie, you really believe all that stuff, don't you? About people being decent and they'd rather boost you than knife you."

"Hell, yes. How could you go on living if you didn't?"

Despite the occasional rebuff, Ronnie was doing well with Janie. One evening he was heading off by rail for a publicity tour. As he stood saying goodbye to Janie, Rosella Towne, his costar in two of Warner's films about the Secret Service, watched from the train. Silhouetted in the lights, Ronnie embraced Janie passionately. Rosella thought that it was almost perfect, a scene from a movie.

Ronnie and Janie had romantic moments, but theirs was a kidding, almost comradely love. Janie was a funny, funny lady. Her laughter and wit neatly counterpointed Ronnie's own storytelling. She unsheathed her wit carefully, though. She wanted Ronnie, and to win him she put up with his constant jabbering, his endless sports stories, his buddies from Des Moines.

Janie was a complex, mercurial woman. Her laughter halted abruptly when clouded by darker thoughts. She was lighthearted yet sensitive, sensuous yet girlish. Her huge brown eyes spoke of a maturity beyond her years, yet they were set in a rounded childlike face with a button nose. It was a pliable face that easily registered her shifts in moods, and it fascinated Ronnie.

He didn't realize just how he needed her until the spring of 1938 when Janie was sick and hospitalized with a spastic stomach. Even then he could not express his feelings overtly. His roses carried the sterile message "Get well soon, Ronald Reagan." To Jane it was like a greeting from a fan in Kansas City.

When Ronnie showed up at the hospital, he was met at the door by

Janie's sister. "Janie doesn't want to see you," the sister said boldly, blocking the entrance.

"But that's crazy. Why not?" Ronnie asked, plainly bewildered.

"If you don't know, Ronnie, it's most certainly not up to me to tell you."

That evening Ronnie paced back and forth at his parents' home. "I didn't know I loved Jane," he told Nelle. "But I just can't see myself going on without her. Do you think that's love?"

"I don't know what else it would be, son."

Ronnie told Janie of his feelings, and in the next months they grew closer and closer, until it seemed inevitable that they would marry.

In the fall, Janie and Ronnie worked together in another film, an uninspired sequel to *Brother Rat* called *Brother Rat and a Baby*. In late November, a reporter for *Photoplay* sat in Janie's petite portable dressing room with the twosome. He had been promised the exclusive story of their romance, but they seemed reluctant to come right out with it. He was bold enough to ask whether Ronnie Reagan's appeal would diminish if he married.

"You see? You see what I'm giving up?" Ronnie said pointedly.

"But look what you're getting," Jane countered.

"That sentiment, alas and alack, has led us to where we are," Ronnie said, as always getting the last word.

Soon after, late in 1939, Ronnie and Janie joined a nine-week vaudeville tour for the "Stars of Tomorrow," put together by Louella Parsons, the famous Hollywood gossip columnist. Louella was a shrewd, calculating lady, a small-town girl made good, from Dixon, Illinois, no less. She took great pride in the fact the her biggest name on the tour was a Dixon boy. More than that, Ronnie personified the all-American values she promoted.

On the tour Louella talked sweetly to Janie, all the while watching her woo Ronnie. To Louella, Janie was nothing, a bit player earning $75 a week. She took Janie's measure—the bleached hair, the rattling costume jewelry, inexpensive clothes that Louella cattily called "not really in bad taste." She noted how Janie squeezed in next to Ronnie at dinner. One afternoon before the matinee, Louella came out of her dressing room and practically bumped into Ronnie and Janie embracing more passionately than they ever had on the screen.

Ronnie was in love. They announced their engagement on tour. It was all the sweeter since Ronnie was beginning to feel like a movie star. The fans shouted his name and mobbed him in Philadelphia. In Hollywood, nobody made much of a fuss over him. Acting in one "B" movie after another, seventeen of them in all, on the same lot as stars like Dick Powell, Bette Davis and Olivia de Havilland, he had felt almost anonymous. Now

Louella Parsons (another Dixon, Illinois, native), Ronnie and Janie, *The Stars of Tomorrow* vaudeville tour, 1939. *(EBC)*

he understood the power of the movies, the way the camera anointed the chosen with glory and celebrity. Suddenly, the drudgery of the "B's" didn't seem so bad any longer.

If Ronnie was going to take Janie as his bride, they had to tell his family. Nelle was sitting in her bedroom when Jane burst in. "Oh, Nelly, Nelly, I love him so much," she said. "I think I've been waiting for him all my life."

"That's all I wanted to know," Nelle said.

Ronnie and Janie were married on January 26, 1940, at Wee Kirk o' the Heather, one of three chapels at Forest Lawn Memorial Park in Glendale. The ceremony was followed by a reception at Louella Parsons's home. Both Forest Lawn and Louella were perfect products of Hollywood. Forest Lawn had been founded on the idea of making death as painless for the survivors as possible, with "peaceful slumber rooms" and "no long funeral processions." When the chapels were not being used for funerals, they were used for wedding ceremonies.

For the wedding, Janie wore a stunning, tight-bodiced, ice-blue satin dress. She carried a fur muff and wore a fur hat that accentuated her dark eyes. Ronnie may have been the Errol Flynn of the "B's" but he had the same problem on his wedding day that he had in getting roles. Wearing his best dark suit, neatly shorn, pink-cheeked and boyish, he looked positively virginal.

"Don't take Dutch away from us," Jack said as he kissed the bride.

"Everything's going to be the same," Janie answered.

It had been no mean coup having Louella give them their wedding reception at her house. The gossip columnist was sure that she was siring the perfect Hollywood marriage. "But the sweetest moment of all to me was just before my 'kids' slipped away," she wrote later. "They called me into the library and whispered they were leaving. And, then, with tears streaming down all our faces, they threw their arms around me. They said 'There is no one in the world who could have given us such a perfect day. We love you very much—and you will always be part of our happiness.'"

If Ronnie and Janie were to be big movie stars, Louella would indeed always be part of their happiness. The studio itself thought that this new marriage was something that could be promoted. Warners immediately cast Janie and Ronnie as husband and wife in *An Angel from Texas*. But even then the Reagans didn't rate star billing, playing in a cast headed by their old friends from *Brother Rat,* Wayne Morris and Eddie Albert. It was just as well since *An Angel from Texas* was a weak show-business comedy.

Ronnie loved his wife and enjoyed playing opposite her, but both their careers seemed static and tired. Janie didn't make so much of it, but Ronnie

The wedding, from left to right: Nelle, Ronnie's mother; the groom; the bride in her ice-blue satin dress; Jack, Ronnie's father (January 26, 1940). *(EBC)*

was sick of playing in low-budget films as a lowbrow hero. Eddie Albert had gone on from *Brother Rat* to become a star. But after his one "A" picture, Ronnie was saddled with the role of Lieutenant Brass Bancroft of the Secret Service, the intrepid hero of a series of adventure films fit only for the tastes of kids at Saturday matinees. Ronnie usually had the cool, even temper of Brass Bancroft, but even he began to feel the whole business demeaning.

"This is another lousy Warner Brothers 'B' movie!" he exclaimed one day in disgust. To the other cast members, this was self-evident, but it was work. Even when you were under contract at Warners, if you didn't work you didn't get paid.

One day in 1939, though, Ronnie had had enough. In the midst of filming yet another cheapie, *Code of the Secret Service,* he went to Foy, the producer, to complain.

"Brynie, take me off the picture," Ronnie begged. "It will ruin me!"

If a bad picture could ruin an actor or actress, Foy would have been a major criminal. After all, he produced thirty-five "B" pictures a year at Warners. "Ronnie, I tell you this picture cannot hurt you," Foy said blithely.

"But, Brynie, how can you say that?" Ronnie asked earnestly.

"Because, my boy, nobody goes to see a bad picture. Nobody."

But in the unlikely event that anyone in Hollywood might stumble into the film, Foy saw to it that *Code of the Secret Service* was never shown in Los Angeles.

By early 1940, Ronnie had made twenty films, but the one role he wanted more than any other was that of George Gipp, "the Gipper," in the "A" movie *Knute Rockne—All American.* Gipp would appear in only one reel of the film, but Ronnie knew what that role could mean to him. Gipp had starred at Notre Dame when Ronnie was growing up, and had been one of his many athletic heroes.

Ronnie thought of sports events as arenas for heroism both moral and physical. In high school he had written a passionately felt story about "the quitter . . . the greatest halfback the school had ever produced." In the team's next to last game against a superior opponent, the quitter had "refused to risk his brilliant reputation by being flopped for losses." After the game, "great sobs shook him and he writhed before the pitiless conscience that drove him on in his agony of self punishment." At half time of the team's final game, "the quitter rose and spoke . . . and eleven boys were wiping tears from their eyes as the quitter took his place by the fullback. To finish the story right, perhaps they ought to win the game, but this is a story of football, of football when the score stands thirteen to nothing against you. Time and time again the quitter pounded around right end in a beautiful gaining stride that made the coach want to recite poetry, the rhythm was so even. . . . The game ended a tie. . . . As they carried him off the field he received the perfect tribute; with rooters for both sides standing while the waves of sound broke on the gray cloudy sky, broke and seemed to shriek in the eyes of the quitter."

The man who wrote those words was not going to sit idly by while he had a chance to play the "Gipper," who personified the ideals in which Ronnie believed. By Knute Rockne's estimate, the Gipper was not only "the greatest football player Notre Dame ever produced, he was the genuine thing: a hero. At the age of 23 he died as he had lived, with his chin up, charging forward."

When Ronnie went in to see Brynie Foy, the executive producer had a hard time envisioning Ronnie as a football player. But after looking at some photographs of Ronnie back at Eureka, he agreed to test him for the role.

Pat O'Brien had already been cast as Knute Rockne. O'Brien was an Irishman from Wisconsin who to many Americans represented Catholicism as much as the church itself. O'Brien liked Ronnie as a human being. O'Brien did not try to appear terribly sophisticated or urbane. Neither did Ronnie. "You couldn't ask for better qualities in a young man," O'Brien said.

Much to Ronnie's surprise, when he showed up for his screen test, O'Brien was already there, ready to play opposite him. "I got him the role of the Gipper," O'Brien said. "I made the pitch for him. I put on the uniform and played the whole scene."

Out at Loyola University, Ronnie had a joyous time playing Gipp. He was with real football players from UCLA and USC, and he charged through them eighty yards for a touchdown just as he had so many times in his daydreams. *Knute Rockne—All American* was a sentimental story that Ronnie played for all it was worth, squeezing every drop of emotion out of his part.

In America people *believed* in movies, finding in them not only glamour but moral verities and hope that they sometimes did not find in religion, or politics, or the mundane realities of their lives.

Knute Rockne—All American was not so much a movie as a hymn to American values. When the movie opened, eighteen states declared the first week of October 1940 "Knute Rockne Week." The premiere at South Bend, Indiana, was one of the most spectacular openings a film had ever had. A few days before the premiere, people began camping out on the Union Station plaza in order to see the stars.

It wasn't just strangers who wanted to make this pilgrimage to Notre Dame, but Ronnie's own father. Jack was as Irish as a Dublin pub. To him Notre Dame was Harvard and the Vatican all wrapped up into one ivy-covered package. Ronnie was all for his father making a sentimental sojourn, particularly because Jack's heart condition threatened to end his life soon. But he had the same worries he'd always had about Jack. Despite his new life, Jack still had his problems with liquor.

When the Super Chief pulled out of the Los Angeles Station with two special cars for the stars, it carried not just Ronnie but Janie and Jack. Pat O'Brien knew a fellow Irishman when he saw one, and he and Jack toasted their new friendship through the long trip.

Ronnie was arriving home a star, the kind of star he had wanted to be, playing in a movie in which he believed, in which America believed. Over a quarter of a million people lined the streets of South Bend to see the arrival of O'Brien, Ronnie and the other actors. Even President Franklin D. Roosevelt, in the midst of his unprecedented campaign for a third presidential term, knew the importance of the premiere. He had sent his son and namesake, F.D.R., Jr., to represent him. On that evening in October 1940, Ronnie spoke not only to the thousand people gathered in the Notre Dame dining hall but to millions listening to the Kate Smith program broadcast nationwide on the Mutual radio network. What struck O'Brien about Ronnie was that "he took it all in stride. He was steeped in humility, not an element of braggadocio."

Jack went out afterward and got drunk with Pat O'Brien, but even that could not ruin Ronnie's success. When Jack got back to Los Angeles, he told Nelle: "I've had everything now. I've seen Dutch get to be a star. Oh, I know the studio hasn't made him one yet, but the folks back there did. I wish you could have heard the welcome they gave him, Nelle. Far as I'm concerned, nothing'll ever top it. I'm ready to go any time now."

Ronnie had bought a small two-bedroom house for Nelle and Jack, the first house his parents had ever owned. On a clear day they could see the Pacific. Jack loved puttering in the garden, building a trellis, fertilizing the plants, pruning the roses. He did more than he was supposed to do, but he seemed so happy that Ronnie and Nelle said nothing. "If you're going to make me twiddle my thumbs," he told them, "I'd as lief be dead. While I've got my breath, let me know I'm alive."

In April 1941, Ronnie and Janie stopped by the house to say goodbye before catching a train for the East Coast. As Ronnie got into the car, Nelle and Jack waved goodbye from the doorstep. Then, as if he had a premonition, Ronnie turned back up the front walk, kissed his mother and shook Jack's hand.

A few days later, Jack died.

After his success in *Knute Rockne*, "the Errol Flynn of the B's" got a chance to costar with the *real* Errol Flynn in *Santa Fe Trail*. On screen

Flynn was always the devil-may-care hero. On the set he was a relentless, petty scene-stealer, always maneuvering himself for the best angles. In *Santa Fe Trail,* Flynn and Ronnie courted the same woman, Olivia de Havilland, but Ronnie was as persistently outmaneuvered here as everywhere else in the film.

In comparison to Flynn and some of his friends, Ronnie was an innocent, left out of the bawdy horseplay. The director of the film, Mike Curtiz, had a rigorous luncheon schedule from which he rarely deviated. According to journalist James Bacon, Curtiz always had a lunchtime dalliance with a gorgeous extra whose career consisted largely of servicing the Hungarian-born director. There were plenty of interior sets around the sound stage so that Curtiz could take his pleasures in the Old West, or the Twenties, among the rich or poor. Alas, such sets are built without roofs. And one day at his moment of ecstasy, Curtiz looked up to see the crew looking down at him with more than academic interest. "What are you doing down there?" he yelled at the extra, hitting her on the head. "Get out and let me work."

In such a league, Ronnie wasn't considered much fun. He talked too much and too seriously for Flynn and his cohorts. One day while filming a scene, Ronnie jumped on his horse to gallop off—except that the other actors had uncinched his saddle so that he toppled off into the dirt.

In *Desperate Hours,* a later film in which Ronnie costarred with Flynn, the two actors again had their troubles. Flynn was so irritated at the Saturday shooting schedule that he got everyone liquored up on bourbon— everyone but Ronnie.

When the cameras started rolling, Ronnie spoke his line to Flynn with his usual professionalism.

"Why don't you go fuck yourself?" Flynn said.

After his days at the studio, Ronnie almost always headed directly home to Janie and their house in West Hollywood. Sometimes they attended meetings at the Screen Actors Guild, the union on whose board both of them sat, alongside Jimmy Cagney and Robert Montgomery. Ronnie had joined the board of the five-year-old Screen Actors Guild (SAG) in 1938. Some actors avoided getting too involved with politics, thinking it might hurt their careers. But the moment he walked into the SAG boardroom and saw the famous faces gathered there, he figured that this was where he belonged. He came to believe in the union movement and what organized groups could do for people. Ronnie was articulate and serious, and loved being part of an organization helping his fellow actors.

At home Ronnie was a calming influence on Janie, cutting down on her shopping sprees, managing their budget, planning for a new house and children. Janie's exuberant spirit cheered Ronnie up. With her guidance he

Ronald and Jane with their baby daughter, Maureen Elizabeth, making her first appearance before the cameras, March 23, 1941. *(UPI)*

even began to buy new shoes and suits. In the spring of 1940 when Janie became pregnant, Ronnie couldn't have been happier. That was the one thing he wanted: a baby, a son, whom he could teach baseball and golf and take horseback riding. The pregnancy itself went well and Janie was able to continue working for several months. In January 1941 the doctor himself drove Janie to the hospital, a good month before her due date. That evening Ronnie arrived from the studio and plunked himself down next to Janie's bed.

"It made all this cartoon stuff about prospective fathers seem cheap," Ronnie told *Photoplay*. "I was with Janie. I was busy. It kept my mind off things. It gave me a kind of cooperative feeling. It was good for me, and for her too, I think. She didn't seem conscious of what she was doing, she never once opened her eyes, yet she'd throw aside the nurse's hand and the doctor's hand and grab mine and hang on to it for dear life . . . that gave me such a thrill as I can't believe."

A few hours after the birth of a baby girl on January 4, 1941, Janie's birthday, John Flinn, the Reagans' publicist, showed up at the hospital with a photographer in tow. As Janie held the baby in her arms, the photographer's flashbulb exploded. If he hadn't been using cellophane over the bulb, the baby might have been hurt.

Ronnie dubbed Maureen Elizabeth Reagan "Button Nose No. 2," a junior version of his pet name for Jane. "Button Nose No. 2" became a public figure. Movie fans heard about her first spanking; her broken leg; her two dogs, Scotch and Soda; even her calling a kindly old woman "you old goat."

Like politicians of a later generation, Ronnie and Janie cooperated with the studio in using their private lives to sell their public careers. At a time of endless Hollywood scandals, they were proof that Hollywood had "just folks," good people who got married and lived by the moral standards of small-town America. In a country without royalty or aristocracy, Americans wanted their movie stars to inhabit a magical other world and yet to be like themselves. In those years, Janie and Ronnie were bigger and better in the fan magazines than they were in their own careers. They had a good and loving relationship, and the magazines ran numerous splashy stories of their marriage, its glories and nuances.

Janie's cynicism had been tempered by Ronnie, but she kept a certain perspective on their marriage. After all, she had been married before and, as a waitress and chorus girl, had seen the world as Ronnie had never seen it. She had her dark, melancholy side that her husband did not like or understand. Whenever Janie seemed down, he tried to turn off her dark mood like shutting off a spigot. "We'll lead an ideal life if you'll just avoid doing one thing: Don't think," Ronnie told her once.

The climax of *King's Row*, Warner Brothers, 1941. After having his legs amputated by a sadistic doctor, Drake McHugh (Ronnie) asks his girlfriend (Ann Sheridan), "Where's the rest of me?" This legendary comment would become the title of his autobiography some years later. *(LGC)*

8

"THIS TIME WILL BE
THE LAST TIME"

W here's the rest of me?"
In the summer of 1941, the line kept running through Ronnie's head.

For the first time in his career, Ronnie had a role in a movie which explored so many of the dark shadows of human existence that what was good and noble stood out with the richness of fine ivory. In *King's Row*, Ronnie played Drake McHugh, a rakish, charming, good-humored young man, a spicier version of a character Ronnie had played a score of times before. With his roguish bravado and zest for excitement, the character was not unlike Ronnie's brother, Neil.

Drake came from the right side of King's Row. In the opening of the film, it appeared an idyllic town that could easily have been the Dixon, Illinois, of Ronnie's memory. Drake had the prospect of an inheritance to allow him to continue his gay, carefree life without the encumbrance of work.

But the world was not what it seemed any longer. *King's Row* took place at the turn of the century. The film was in part a parable about the changes facing a nation moving from the provincial nineteenth century to the ambivalent, difficult realities of the twentieth century. Small towns were not clean places any longer. Banks were not safe. Society was not good. Evil could wear even the white coat of medicine. Goodness held court not in high places but in the sweaty recesses of the poor.

Drake's inheritance was embezzled, and then a sadistic doctor cut off his legs. The climactic scene, and the greatest scene Ronnie ever played, took place when Drake woke up legless.

For days Ronnie thought about it. Losing one's legs meant everything.

Ronnie was not a man of the mind. He had a strong, young body. "Where's the rest of me?" He asked psychologists what they thought. He talked to disabled people. "Where's the rest of me?" The image of the scene came to him as he stood in the men's room in restaurants. At night he lay looking at the ceiling, muttering the line. "Where's the rest of me?"

He was Drake McHugh as he had been no one else in his film career. The night before, he couldn't sleep. He appeared on the set the next morning with the exhausted look of a man who had gone through a brutal operation.

"Where's the rest of me?" He had said it so many times that he didn't have any idea how he should say it. The words had lost their meaning. After he put on a nightshirt and was made up, he walked over to a set of a modest bedroom. Underneath the bright quilt, the propmen had cut a hole in the mattress and set a supporting box beneath. He looked at it for a while.

He felt compelled to get into the bed, and sink his legs down into the hole. Ten minutes. He lay there looking at his truncated legs. Twenty minutes. It looked so real. Thirty minutes. It almost felt as if his legs were gone. Forty minutes. He was afraid. He was terrified. Fifty minutes. He filled with horror.

He looked up. The crew had appeared.

"Want to shoot it?" Sam Wood, the director, asked in a low voice.

"No rehearsal?"

"Let's make it."

The set grew quiet. Ann Sheridan, playing his girlfriend, was scheduled to be off-camera during the scene. However, to give Ronnie someone to play to, she was there in the background. The only sound was the whirring of the cameras.

"*Randy!*" Ronnie screamed. Sheridan ran from behind the cameras toward him.

"*Randy!*" His hands reached down, grasping his thighs.

"*Randy!*" He quivered like an animal in its death throes.

"*Where's the rest of me!*"

It was a cry that rose out of an emotional reservoir that few imagined Ronnie Reagan had. Men on the set who had lived their lives in the make-believe of Hollywood were close to tears.

The rumor around the studio was that *King's Row* was a good film, maybe even a great film. Ronnie's just-released movie, *International Squadron,* was neither; but this story of a group of gutsy Americans flying with English pilots against the Nazis caught the public imagination.

Ronnie was great giving heroic speeches and running off to fight the

Germans on film, but he still was no sex symbol. In October 1941, he had given a luncheon interview to a reporter from *Motion Picture* and brought up his image problem. "I'll read all those ads and I'll do everything they tell you to do," he joked. "I'll go in for those open-throat polo-shirts. I'll buy a sun-lamp. . . . What more can I do to make the little ladies' hearts flutter? Besides—think how awful it will be if in a few years my daughter were to come to me and say, 'Daddy, what is it that Errol Flynn has that *you* haven't got?'"

But despite his reputed lack of sex appeal, Ronnie was popular with the fans. On December 2, Warners announced that in 1941 he had received more fan mail than any other male star at the studio except Errol Flynn. James Cagney was just behind Ronnie. "His case is very typical of the skyrocketing that happens when a star begins to hit," the *Los Angeles Times* reported, "and it will behoove Warners to set about getting good roles for Mr. Reagan from this point on." The early public and critical reaction to *King's Row* was strong enough to clearly indicate that Ronnie was on the verge of major stardom. Warners renegotiated his contract for three times what it had been.

But on December 7, 1941, the Japanese attacked Pearl Harbor, signaling the beginning of World War II. Four months later, on April 4, Ronnie received an induction notice ordering him into the U.S. Calvary as a second lieutenant. Because of his nearsightedness, he had been ticketed for "limited service." He wouldn't be fighting his way through German lines as he was in the movie he was filming, *Desperate Journey,* or fighting Nazi planes as in the previous *International Squadron.* His duties would be more sedate.

Ronnie had only two weeks to finish up work on *Desperate Journey* before he had to report for duty. He and Janie had just moved into their new seven-room, $15,000 house in the hills above Hollywood. For two years they had plotted and planned and waited for an FHA twenty-year mortgage to come through with a nearly manageable $125-a-month payment. Their dream house had a big living room to accommodate all their friends, and two big dressing room/bathrooms where they could dress without getting in each other's way.

More than anything, Janie wanted to give Ronnie a feel for what their house would be like when he returned from the war. As reported in *Modern Screen,* after telling him she had to work Saturday afternoon, April 18, she and her decorator, Connie Rennick, managed to get all the new furniture delivered and set up. That evening when Ronnie returned from the ball game with his friends, Bob Cobb and Irving and Betty Kaplan, he noticed that the area around the outside of the house looked like a parking lot.

"What's all this about?" he asked.

"Oh, I guess Rennick's with Jane."

"Rennick and sixteen Cadillacs, that's fine."

Suddenly, Pat O'Brien pulled the door open. There stood all the Reagan friends—Barbara Stanwyck, Robert Taylor, Jack Benny, and Ann Sheridan, and a number of others. Inside, there wasn't an unfurnished room. Ronnie found a warm living room with English hunting prints and drapes and gracious sofas and straight-backed chairs.

The next evening, after Ronnie kissed "Button Nose No. 2" goodbye, he and Janie had dinner at the Brown Derby and then drove to the Glendale station. At 9:46 the northbound express stopped for four minutes. He kissed his wife and boarded the train for San Francisco.

Ronnie was stationed at Fort Mason in the Bay Area. Since he was a star, the army used him as a glorified public-relations man. In less than two months, on June 10, Ronnie was transferred to the army air force and sent back to the Los Angeles area. It was here that Ronnie spent the rest of the war.

No great city in America was so affected by the war as Los Angeles. On February 26, when Ronnie was still a civilian, Japanese planes had been sighted over the city. The night sky was slashed by scores of searchlights as gun crews poured 1,433 rounds of ack-ack fire into the sky. The planes had been mythical, the worst casualty a valiant warden who broke his left arm falling down his own front steps.

The war, however, was no joke. Everywhere Ronnie went now, he felt the tempo and energy of wartime. Barrage balloons floated above the city. Posters cautioned about speaking too freely. Citizens of Japanese ancestry were herded into camps. As Ronnie drove his 1938 LaSalle convertible through the streets, he saw people lined up at grocery stores, waiting for tables in restaurants, the buses and trolleys jammed. Between 1939 and 1943, the number of workers in the country's aircraft factories alone had grown from 20,000 to 243,000. And with all its factories in full production, Los Angeles developed its first real smog, the fumes casting their own gray pall over progress.

One of Ronnie's first duties was as liaison officer at the Los Angeles Port of Embarkation. From here thousands of soldiers were shipped overseas.

"I have a husband who's in the air force," Janie told an audience on a bond tour to raise money for war relief. "He was stationed at a point of embarkation. I was allowed to visit him, and one day I stood with him on the docks and watched the boys go off. Soon I noticed something. As they reached the top of the gangplank, each of them turned to take a long look at the skyline. You didn't have to be smart to know what they were thinking:

A bedroom fit for the heroic pilot of *International Squadron*,
Warner Brothers, 1941.

When would they see an American skyline again?

"I said to my husband: 'I can't stand it—'

"His face was a little grim. 'You've got to stand it,' he said. 'They're well trained for their job. They know what they have to do.'"

The film industry was the Allies' greatest and loudest cheerleader. The stars raised millions of dollars for the boys overseas. The studios churned out patriotic films by the score. Yet another largely Hollywood contribution to the war effort was the First Motion Picture Unit of the Army Air Corps. It was here Ronnie was assigned for his major duties of the war. For most of the time the unit was stationed in Culver City at the nine-acre studio once operated by Hal Roach.

Some of the zaniest of film comedies had been made here. There were some who claimed that the studio—nicknamed "Fort Roach" or "Fort Wacky"—was still a place of madcap comic relief. The 1,500-man unit consisted primarily of men who were too old or unfit for more rigorous duty. It did seem to many Americans that Hollywood was full of robust-looking men whose afflictions, though not visible to the naked eye, were enough to get them disqualified. But Hollywood had no more shirkers than anywhere else.

Ronnie regretted remaining safe from combat and losing the chance to be a hero. As it was, the pomp, uniforms and lingo of the military were like a movie and he loved it. Unfortunately, his new Hollywood unit was as unmilitary as "M*A*S*H," a bunch of movie people who thought that a "pup tent" was a place to keep your dog, and that "mess" was what the critics called your last movie.

The afternoon Ronnie made his first dramatic appearance at his unit, he pulled up in a jeep, smartly dressed in military breeches and shiny black boots. He was assigned to oversee basic training, and he had arrived just in time to see the ragtag unit parading around the grounds. He immediately set out to turn them into a unit every bit as smart as the boys in *Brother Rat*. Like Ronnie, many of these soldiers were rejects from more strenuous service who thought that by making movies they could fight Hitler. But they hadn't expected to be run up and down the field like Boy Scouts by a youthful-looking martinet in big boots.

After Ronnie had put his troops through their paces, a group came up to him. "We ain't gonna do this, Ronnie."

"What do you mean?" he asked, totally nonplussed.

"Look, you're the officer and we're the enlisted men. Right?"

"Right."

"You're an actor, and a lot of us are producers and directors. Right?"

"Right."

"And after the war you're gonna be an actor again and we're gonna be producers and directors. Right?"

"Right."

"So knock off with the marching around."

That was the end of basic training at Fort Roach.

On duty one night, Ronnie filed a report to the commanding officer, Paul Mantz, a former stunt pilot. "Very poor place to make pictures," he wrote in the duty book. "Recommend entire post be transferred as near to 42nd Street and Broadway as possible. Also suggest several Westerns be made to round out the program." As for any irregularities and disturbances during the night, he noted: "3 A.M.—post attacked by three regiments of Japanese infantry. Led cavalry charge and repulsed enemy. Quiet resumed."

Fort Roach was a bizarre, eerie juxtaposition of the real and unreal. The men had made their livings creating myths and fantasies—writing, directing, producing, editing and selling them. Now they were creating training films about how to survive combat. The films were not much different from scenes in "B" movies.

This Is the Army, the feature film that Ronnie made in the spring of 1943, was even further removed from the realities of war. Ronnie was temporarily assigned to the film because Irving Berlin, the composer, had talked the War Department into lending him 300 servicemen to make a musical that would earn money for Army Relief. For the finale, Ronnie and the other soldiers stood on stage with fixed bayonets. Then, singing "This time we will all make certain that this time will be the last time," they headed out to war through the audience.

Marines fighting their way across stinking jungles in the Pacific and GIs lying pinned down on the Normandy beachhead would have had choice words about such a piece of propaganda. But Ronnie hadn't gone overseas and he didn't have any of the combat soldier's cynicism that Bill Mauldin was capturing so brilliantly in his "Willie and Joe" cartoons. He smilingly would have marched out of the theater into the hell throes of battle.

During the war, Warners kept the klieg lights of publicity fully upon the new Captain Reagan. Many Hollywood people had entered the service. Indeed, in May 1944 *Movieland* listed 72 actors, 38 producers and executives, 132 directors and unit managers, and 215 writers and publicists in uniform. Some of these were stationed no farther away than Fort Roach, but others were as far from Hollywood as the farthest battlefield. Craig Reynolds was the first actor to be wounded in action, in one of the first

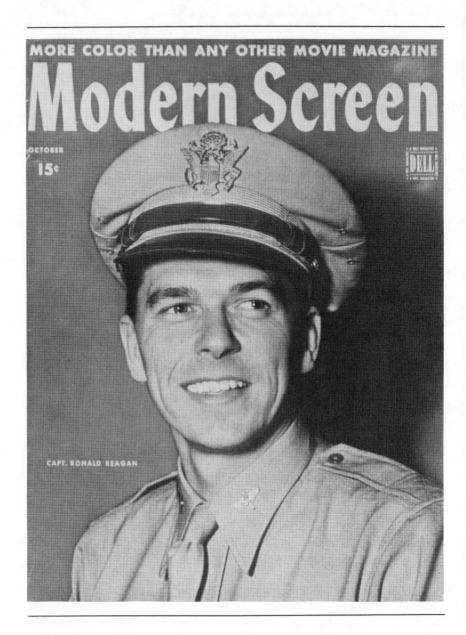

Captain Reagan of the First Motion Picture Unit of the Army Air Corps at the Hal Roach Studios in Culver City, California, 1944. *(LGC)*

barges landing on Tulagi Island. Sterling Hayden was dropped behind enemy lines to fight with the Yugoslav partisans. Jimmy Stewart was flying
bombers over Europe.

While others were fighting overseas, Captain Reagan was adjunct at
Fort Roach in charge of administering the 1,500-member unit and narrat-
ing films. He was living in Los Angeles near his wife and daughter under
conditions that most Americans would not have dreamed possible for themselves, in peace no less than war. Moreover, while he was still in uniform,
his agent, Lew Wasserman, renegotiated his contract once again: a million
dollars for seven years' work.

In the movie magazines, Captain Reagan was portrayed as something
of a hero. "I remember that during the war when he was stationed right
here in town, we would run articles as if he were three thousand miles
away," said Silvia Wallace, then an editor for *Modern Screen.* "It was all
done with the cooperation of the studio and it helped keep the screen romance alive."

"So Long, Button-Nose," the July 1942 issue of *Modern Screen* head-
lined. "He said it with a grin, she smiled in reply. But when Ronnie went
riding off to battle, he left his heart behind him!"

By then Ronnie was already back in L.A. from his two-month service
in San Francisco. Yet in the August 1942 *Photoplay,* his by-lined article
said: "I've just been told, here at the studio, of two very important parts
that were to be mine. . . . But I won't be doing these pictures. Uncle Sam
has called me, a Reserve officer in the Cavalry and I'm off to the war."

In October 1944, a beaming picture of Captain Ronald Reagan appeared on the cover of *Modern Screen.* The article made it clear that Ronnie's military duties were in the Los Angeles area.

The first authentic Hollywood hero of the war was not a soldier at all
but an actress, Carole Lombard, killed in a plane crash in 1942 while on a
tour selling war bonds. On the home front, the lives of women were changing more than those of men. Women were having to cope with rationing
and food shortages. They were exchanging dresses for overalls and bandan-
nas, filling in for and working beside men in the factories.

During the war, Janie was a more authentic figure of her time than
her husband. She was still cast in one fluffy, mindless part after another,
but she took time to help in the war effort and boost morale. Soldiers going
overseas dreamed of women like Janie, Betty Grable and Lana Turner. To
most GIs, a pinup was not a Forties version of a centerfold but a symbol of
what they hoped might be waiting for them on their return to America. As
her parting gift to those leaving Los Angeles, Janie had gone to the embarkation station and stood singing to the soldiers: "Tangerine," "He's 1-A

in the Army," "Not Mine," "I Said No."

Photoplay credited Janie with beginning the fad of ending letters to servicemen with a lipstick kiss, not just a series of xxx's. She shared the first Thanksgiving of the war not only with Ronnie but with a soldier who she had learned had bet his buddies he could meet Jane Wyman. The pictures and story made papers across America. She talked on shortwave radio to the troops overseas. In September 1942, just after completing *Princess O'Rourke,* she went on a month-long bond tour, raising thousands of dollars. She lost fourteen pounds in the process.

Despite her frivolous films, Janie's public persona was increasingly that of a serious wife and mother concerned about the world in which she lived. The fan magazines painted her as a soldier's wife like millions of others, struggling to be a good mother and to do her part. She did a monthly personal-advice column for *Movieland* called "Your Problem and Mine," which again stressed that Janie was like any other woman. She had a by-lined article in *Photoplay* in May 1944 called "Our Child Must Not Hate."

The publicists at Warners had a lot to do with all Janie's and Ronnie's public exposure. Not only did they write material under their by-lines, but they sat in on their interviews. "They were very cooperative," John Flinn, their Warners publicist, remembered. "But any push would come from me or the studio. They did a lot of nice things for us. On Christmas Day they brought flowers around to the house and left them at the door."

It would have been easier by far to play an aloof, cloistered movie-star couple than the home-loving, all-American Reagans. After all, Janie and Ronnie were hardly the typical young couple, and Janie was far from the average working wife. Women identified with Janie, but their worlds were totally different. Down at the Douglas plant during their lunch break, Rosie the Riveter and her friends didn't spend much time discussing servant problems.

During the war, Janie went through several servants. A new couple— a butler and maid—made their appearance shortly after Ronnie left for the service. "Madame, your nap is all wrong," the man said.

"Hmm?"

"The nap on the rug, madame. It should all go in one direction."

"Oh. Oh, well, that's fine. We'll have it go in one direction in the future."

The couple were far too formal for the Reagans, and they left. At least Barbara Stanwyck had been nice enough to will them her son Skip's nanny so they had someone to count on for Maureen.

Ronnie and Janie adored their daughter, but they saw far less of her than most parents saw of their children. Few mothers would have left a two-year-old for a month, even for such a noble cause as raising bonds. They were loving, caring parents, but it was not Janie who usually bathed, fed, and put the child to bed, but a nanny.

The one parental duty left to Janie and Ronnie was discipline. Over the Christmas holidays in 1943, *Modern Screen* reported that the nearly two-year-old Maureen had decided to wage a struggle over a bowl of soup.

"If you don't eat it now, you'll get it for breakfast, then lunch, then dinner, till you *do* eat it," Janie said, looking at Maureen down the fifteen-foot dining-room table.

"I won't."

Janie ordered her daughter into the corner. But Maureen had inherited not only her mother's looks but her stubbornness.

"Ronnie, will you discipline her for me tonight? I just haven't time."

Ronnie proceeded to lecture Maureen on the myriad merits of soup, seeking to lead her with sweet reason to down her bowl of the now tepid liquid. Losing patience with Ronnie's endless philosophizing, Janie grabbed Maureen and initiated her daughter into one of the rough realities of childhood: spankings.

Ronnie and Janie didn't have many nights out, but when they did, they made the obligatory appearance at Ciro's or the Brown Derby, where it was important to be seen. Peggy Cobb, whose father owned the Brown Derby, met the Reagans at a party during the war when she was a little girl. "Then when stars went out, they didn't go out in jogging outfits," she said. "Ronnie was a handsome man in his army uniform, and Janie was a ballsy broad. She loved to sing. Bing Crosby and Janie and a couple others would sit around and do barbershop quartets."

Janie and Ronnie often went out with Neil Reagan and his wife. Neil was working in advertising. Ronnie was still close to his brother, though listening to them, it was hard to tell. Neil was as conservative as Ronnie was liberal, and they argued politics until Janie couldn't hear herself think.

Modern Screen reported that one Saturday night at a crowded restaurant, Ronnie was mobbed by fans. He gave autographs and talked and talked and talked. By the time he finished, the restaurant's limited quota of food was gone.

"That's my brother!" Neil stormed.

"Listen, if I wasn't wearing a uniform, I'd sock you one!"

"You and who else?" Neil said.

Such was the brotherly love of the Reagan boys.

At Fort Roach, Ronnie became increasingly interested in politics. He had grown up in a household where the name Franklin Delano Roosevelt was sacrosanct; and like most younger Hollywood actors, Ronnie was a man of the Left, a strong liberal. Progressive groups, including everyone from New Deal liberals to Communist party members, sat around discussing Marx and Lenin with the same energy and excitement that they talked about that week's grosses.

Before the war, Reagan hadn't frequented the fashionable salons of the Left. He loved to talk politics, but he would have been hard put to hold his own at such gatherings. He was a small-town midwestern boy, hardly able to keep up with the likes of John Howard Lawson, the formidable leader of Hollywood's Communists, snapping ideology like a whip. Ronnie wouldn't have fit in at parties where sharp-witted refugees from New York discussed world events while money was collected for the Salinas lettuce strikers, the Spanish loyalists, or coal miners striking in Harlan County. He got most of his ideas, if not his politics, from the *Reader's Digest*. He couldn't wait to get his copy each month.

"I remember that somehow he managed to get his copy of *Reader's Digest* earlier than everyone else on the post," remembered Irving Wallace, the novelist. "He would read it cover-to-cover overnight and come in the next day and tell everyone about everything he'd read. When we finally got our copies, we'd already heard the whole damn issue from Reagan."

Ronnie was a strong booster of FDR's bid for a third term, and as such supported the unions and militant veteran groups. "You got to join the American Veterans Committee," he told Howard Koppleman, his colleague at Fort Roach. "When you get out of the army, nobody's gonna give a shit about you. You got to have a group that will get in there and fight for you."

Koppleman never joined anything, but because of Ronnie he joined the Americans Veterans Committee. Ronnie ended up on the executive board. Some of the soldiers at Fort Roach didn't join because the organization was said to be full of Communists. Philip Dunne, the screenwriter and as committed a liberal as there was in Hollywood, was one of those who refused to join. Before the war, the House Un-American Activities Committee had tried to paint him pink. He had vowed to stay out of any organization whose roster was heavy with Communists.

During the war years, Ronnie worked hard. Occupied with a man's pursuits in a man's world, he hardly noticed how Janie was changing. She played the devoted wife as she had always played it, but she had let her hair turn its natural brunette, and she was more independent and confident than she had been. When *King's Row* came out, Ronnie was touched for a moment by stardom. He exuded a reassuring warmth and attractiveness that charmed audiences, a quality so strong that Warners had quickly tied him into a new seven-year contract. Now it was Janie's turn.

"Things have been happening to Captain Ronald Reagan's women," wrote Ida Zeitlin, one of the "sob sisters" of the fan magazines, in the April 1944 *Modern Screen*. "Button-Nose Senior—Jane Wyman to Warner Brothers—has burst into stardom. Button-Nose Junior has slipped out of babyhood. . . . As for Ronnie, the Army's got him, body and soul. For him the movies have ceased to exist."

Janie's new movies weren't necessarily noteworthy—*Crime by Night, Animal Kingdom, Make Your Own Bed, The Doughboys*—but the studio was using her almost constantly. Day after day, month after month, she was up at 5:30 A.M. and off to Warners. When she came home, she brought her problems with her.

"You don't know what things are like," she accused Ronnie. "You've been away too long."

"Things like that don't change," he answered calmly. "It's just a question of diplomacy."

Ever the perfectionist, at home or at the studio, Janie's diligence was beginning to bring its rewards. Billy Wilder, the director, had been impressed by her one straight scene in *Princess O'Rourke*. Out of that he had cast her as the fiancée of Don Birnam, the alcoholic played by Ray Milland in *The Lost Weekend*. Her performance in the 1945 film was stunning, and anyone who had questioned Janie's abilities as an actress questioned them no longer. She was becoming a greater star than Ronnie had ever been.

Janie and Ronnie loved one another, and they wanted everything. They wanted fame and they wanted privacy. They wanted great careers and a strong marriage. They wanted to go off on location or promotion tours and still have a good and rich family life. And they tried to set up their lives so they could have it all.

They had a nanny and maids to manage their house and family. They had public-relations people to write what they would have written had they had the time, and to affix their names to it. They wanted a second child, the boy they had hoped for the first time, but Janie's career was soaring and she had no time. "I was too busy to take off time and have a baby," she said later. And so in 1945 they adopted little Michael, a newborn who seemed like their own blood child.

"I wanted a baby brother so badly that I went to the toy department at Saks Fifth Avenue and asked if they had baby brothers—to the surprise and chagrin of my poor father, who had to stand there and listen to this," remembered Maureen. "I wanted two things in this world—a baby brother and a red scooter. And they kept telling me that if I wanted a baby brother, I would have to save up. And one day they said I was going to get what I wanted that night. I was sort of looking for a red scooter. But sure enough, it was a baby brother, a four-day-old baby brother. And my father said, 'Where is it?' And I went up the stairs. I had ninety-seven cents. So I gave the lady from the adoption agency my piggy bank."

Despite appearances, Ronnie and Janie did not have it all, and could not have it all. Their daughter was spoiled. Their two terriers, Scotch and Soda, were spoiled. And their marriage was on the verge of spoiling as well.

Ronnie wasn't jealous of his wife—or, if he was, he would never have admitted it. He had a sensitized vanity common to politicians and actors. When the Reagans went out to a restaurant, it was Janie who caused murmurs and stares, not Ronnie. With Janie becoming so successful, it was taken for granted that the Reagans' marriage was in trouble.

One evening in 1945, Ronnie left Ciro's, the exclusive Hollywood restaurant, an hour before Janie. She stayed on and danced with Van Johnson, another star and a family friend. The next day an item appeared in the paper about her "looking into Van's eyes." Another day the Reagans opened the paper to read an even more ominous item: "The Ronald Reagans are readying an unfortunate announcement any minute."

Janie told Louella Parsons that a woman called to say that she had heard the Reagans' house was for sale or rent. Another came up to Janie and gushed; "Oh, Janie, dear, you're doing so well now. Is it true that when you went to a restaurant the other night the waiter said, 'What does Captain Wyman want?'"

Ronnie was not quite Ronald Wyman yet. At Fort Roach, however, he had heard the teen-age stenographers swooning over movie stars like Robert Mitchum, Gene Kelly and Van Johnson, not Ronnie Reagan, Robert Taylor or Jimmy Stewart. These young women were the ones who bought the movie tickets, and they had new heroes.

When he got out of the service on September 12, 1945, he wasn't the Ronald Reagan he had been before and he knew it. He was pocketing a $3,500-a-week salary and unlike most veterans he didn't have to face the realities of looking for a job. But the studio wasn't rushing to find roles for him, and he had a lot of things he wanted to sort out.

Janie was going from one success to another. Many serious actresses in Hollywood had coveted the role of Ma Baxter in the M-G-M production of the best-selling novel *The Yearling,* but M-G-M had chosen Janie to play the Florida backwoods mother. When the movie went on location at Lake Arrowhead, two hours east of Los Angeles, Ronnie and Maureen joined Janie. Maureen fell in love with nine-year-old Claude Jarman, Jr., who played Janie's son, Jody, and followed him around the set. But Ronnie wanted to be by himself. Years later in his autobiography he would write that he had gone up to the lake all by himself. He was indeed alone, a stranger to the studio for whom he had not worked for three and a half years, a stranger to the crew and cast of *The Yearling,* who were like a family unto themselves.

Ronnie rented a speedboat and for hours zoomed up and down the glassy blue waters trying to clear his head. The owner of the boat-rental shop thought Ronnie was crazy to rent the boat twenty-four hours a day just to have it ready when he wanted it. For all the money he spent renting the boat, he could have bought it. But Ronnie was earning more in a week than most Americans made in a year.

Ronnie didn't like the looks of the civilian society of which he was now a part. As his marriage began to suffer strains, the world that had seemed such a familiar and welcoming haven turned threatening and corrupt. A touch of cynicism crept into his usually optimistic conversation. As he saw it, "During the war the rich had gotten just a little richer and a lot of the poor had done a pretty good job of grabbing a quick buck."

The stratagems of the war, which had dominated his casual conversation at Fort Roach, no longer needed his or anyone else's analysis. The war had been won without his flying missions over Pacific Islands or slogging his way toward Berlin. Now Ronnie believed that a real peace had to be won in which workers and veterans received their just share of America's bounty. And Ronnie had to win back the peace that once had been within himself.

Jane Wyman as Ma Baxter in *The Yearling*, 1946. *(EBC)*

—9—
"HEY, I GOTTA GET A GRIP HERE"

Over the slate fireplace in the Reagans' home hung a portrait of Janie. The artist, Paul Clemens, had painted her as Ma Baxter in *The Yearling,* a simple, strong woman, without makeup or pretense. Ma Baxter was Janie's first dramatic role where she played such a strong, positive part, a good woman living with her family in a remote cabin in the Florida Everglades.

Janie and Ronnie would have liked their married life to have been like the Baxters' in the film: a courageous, determined father; a loving, caring, wise mother; children exploring the wonders and fears of growing up, with the protection of their parents; problems no more complicated than an occasional rampaging bear. But ordinary life in postwar America was not like that, not even for the Reagans.

On the weekends Ronnie could put on his boots and jeans and head out into the hills like a western hero. But he wasn't like Pa Baxter, who could feed his family by shooting a deer or two. Instead, he had a whole entourage feeding off him: accountants, maids, cooks, agents, advisers. He had grown up in a town where a good day's work deserved a good day's pay, and no work brought no pay. Now, for months Ronnie had been earning $3,500 a week for doing nothing more strenuous than signing a contract.

At first it hadn't been all that bad. He had built some boat models, shoveled tons of dirt for shrubbery, constructed a patio and paved the service porch, worked on union activities for SAG, and given a series of rip-roaring speeches about veterans' rights and liberal causes. But he was often already home when Janie arrived from her day at the studio.

For two weeks in a row during the filming of *The Yearling,* Janie had

Ronnie and Janie with Maureen (five and a half) and Michael (sixteen months) interviewed by ABC Radio's human interest commentator Ted Malone for a coast-to-coast broadcast from their home in 1946. *(UPI)*

had to cry on cue. "In order to give a performance, I had to work myself to such a pitch that I could feel the scene and deliver to it the proper emotional impact," she said later. "Naturally, when I came home at night I was totally exhausted in mind and spirit. Children can be exasperating, no matter how dearly one loves them. Maureen got on my nerves and I snapped at her."

Janie needed to feel free of the routine and ritual of career and marriage, free to do whatever she wanted to do. One day in February 1946, at the end of her work on *The Yearling,* she told *Photoplay,* she came waltzing into the house. "Hi, Uncle Ronnie," she said, using one of her pet expressions, "how'd you like a drink?"

Ronnie knew there was no figuring Janie's moods, but he did want to know why they were drinking.

"On account of we're celebrating," Janie said. "On account of I finish tomorrow and we're going to New York."

"Oh, we can't do that!" said Ronnie. He was a liberal outside of the house, but in his living room he was the great conservative.

"Give me one good reason—come on, just one," Janie said, knowing that there was no good reason. "See? What did I tell you? You can't think of a single reason."

By this time Janie was dialing the travel agent. "But we've never been to New York together, Ronnie. How can you not get excited?"

"I'll work up to it, honey."

Ronnie never traveled by plane, and he enjoyed their train trip to New York. But he still had his career to worry about. Warners kept telling him that they were looking for the right role in the right movie. The studio was no longer cranking out so many "B's." An actor might make only two movies a year, his career rising or falling on each role.

It wasn't until March 1946, a full nine months after he had left the service, that Warners found a part for its aging, expensive prewar star. *Stallion Road,* a film about life on a horse ranch, originally was to feature Ronnie alongside Humphrey Bogart and Lauren Bacall. Bogey and Bacall were as bankable as any couple in the business, and Ronnie knew that his debut would be the success that he so badly needed. But the Bogarts backed out because *Stallion Road* did not fit their image of a sophisticated, urban couple. Though Warners went ahead with the project, they decided to film in black-and-white, making the magnificent panorama of California's Sierra Nevadas look as washed out as a studio backdrop.

Ronnie was not a carper. He was happy to be out in the mountains again, riding horses and working alongside Zachary Scott and Alexis Smith. Up here he was away from the difficulties of his marriage and the demands of his political life. He was so happy working the horses that he decided to go into partnership with Nino Pepitone, his riding coach on the film, in an eight-acre horse-breeding farm in Northridge, just outside Los Angeles.

Ronnie had become politically active again. He was serving on the SAG board as well as on the boards of the American Veterans Committee (AVC) and the Hollywood Independent Citizens Committee of Arts, Sciences and Professions (HICCASP)—both liberal, progressive organizations. Ronnie was an articulate and passionate supporter of the new veterans organization, working to build it into a prominent national force.

Like most Hollywood liberals, Ronnie was sympathetic to the insurgent Conference on Studio Unions (CSU) and to Herbert Sorrell, its fiery, leftist leader. He had seen how corrupt the older, more conservative International Alliance of Theatrical Stage Employees (IATSE) had been in the late Thirties, but he was learning that political life was more complicated than he had thought. The year before, just as Ronnie was getting out of the service, CSU had staged a jurisdictional strike against Warners. The studio had made a giant barricade of cars, a scene out of a Warner film of the Thirties. It was hard to tell who started the trouble, but an ex-marine was beaten unconscious when he tried to cross the picket line, and another worker was stabbed in the nose before the police came in swinging their clubs.

Though Ronnie had at first been sympathetic to the CSU, he had become less and less so. As a leader of SAG, he simply wanted to get actors back to work. For the 1946 strike, Ronnie was no longer even neutral toward the CSU in its militant struggle for broad recognition. He was a marked man. "I was out on location in the country," he testified in a 1954 libel trial brought by Mike Jeffers, an actor, against the Screen Extras Guild, "when I was told that if I made the report [about the nature of the strike] a squad was ready to take care of me and fix my face so that I would never be in pictures again."

At times, Janie wished that Ronnie would spend more time with her and the kids. But he was forever off to one meeting or another. She was now the star of the family, nominated for an Academy Award for *The Yearling,* offered parts by all the studios. But she still wanted uninterrupted time with her family.

On Sundays when the servants were off, she would get into the swimming pool. The phone would ring and ring and ring, making her feel, she said, as if there were "an underground plot to get me out of that pool." As soon as new equipment was available, she installed an extension phone. That Sunday, Ronnie was off to a meeting, and Janie, Michael and Maureen spent the afternoon in the pool. "Hours went by," she said. "Not *one* single call. Finally, at four o'clock the phone rang. Is Mr. Reagan available

Jane Wyman, Henry Fonda, Ronald Reagan, Boris Karloff and Gene Kelly are just a few of the hundreds of screen stars discussing the actors' strike at an emergency meeting of the Screen Actors' Guild, October 3, 1946. *(UPI)*

for speeches, someone wanted to know! 'I wouldn't be knowing,' I answered. 'I haven't seen him for days!'"

Ronnie preferred his tiny Northridge horse ranch to the pool. He loved to do the work himself and built a jumping course for the horses. One weekend, as *Silver Screen* reported, he stood beside Janie proudly surveying the neatly laid-out obstacles of stacked redwood logs.

"It isn't Aintree by a long shot," he said, 'but it will give us something to test our mettle."

"Mettle?" Janie laughed. "You mean that stuff out of which they build the pins used to fasten broken bones together?"

One evening at the house when the servants were on vacation, Janie decided to cook dinner. That was an event. It had to be celebrated with wine, song and good friends. The Reagans invited June Allyson and Dick Powell.

Janie took to the kitchen and went through momentous preparations. As the threesome sat at the table, Janie brought in the barbecued steak and vegetables. Like any great actress, Janie knew to give no hint of her stunning climax, an ice-cream pie, until the audience had savored her full performance. She sat waiting for their verdict on the main course as apprehensively as she ever had her movie reviews.

"How is it?" she demanded finally, unable to contain herself.

"Great!" they shouted, sounding like three Soviet critics reviewing Stalin's autobiography. The only problem was that they hadn't tasted even a morsel.

"Then why don't you *eat* it?" Janie asked in bewilderment.

They laughed, and told her that they had agreed not to eat anything but simply to stare at her.

On these simple occasions, Ronnie and Janie still seemed so in love. Rhonda Fleming, another star of the period, remembered seeing them "looking like the perfect couple sitting in the movies sharing a box of popcorn."

But more and more their evenings out were cut to a stiffer pattern. Once Ronnie got the obligatory pleasantries out of the way, he would be off in a corner talking politics. Janie loved her husband and she tolerated his endless political talk, but she got tired of being alone.

"Okay, Reagan," she said at one party late in 1946. "Break it up. Come on over and talk to the girls. They love you too!"

To one reporter, Jerry Asher of *Photoplay*, Ronnie looked like "an injured, coerced husband." Taking his pipe from his lips, he proceeded to play the good husband, a role that he played less convincingly than any he had played on the screen.

"You win," Janie said finally. "Go back and save the people."

Janie knew that she was not the easiest person to live with, and she forgave Ronnie his excesses as he forgave hers. She had quipped once: "If you ask Ronnie what time it is, he tells you how to make the watch." At first the remark had been a harmless little joke; but as time went on, Janie's voice had a more bitter tone. She was growing tired of his talk, and like anyone who didn't care about the CSU, the IATSE, SAG, and AVC, she thought it all a God-awful bore.

More than ever Janie wanted to be a great actress playing great roles. On March 13, 1947, she sat next to Ronnie at the Shrine Auditorium as their friend Jack Benny emceed the Academy Awards. Many people felt she should have been nominated three years before when *The Lost Weekend* won for best picture and Ray Milland, her costar, took home best-actor honors. But this time she could not be ignored. She was immensely proud of her nomination as best actress of the year for playing Ma Baxter in *The Yearling*. This evening Claude Jarman, Jr., who had played her son, had already won for outstanding child actor. Then came the best-actress award. Janie sat applauding as another Warner actress walked to the stage: Olivia de Havilland for her role in *To Each His Own*.

Janie knew that awards were only awards. She wanted to be a fine mother and wife as well. As she sat there that evening, she was carrying within her womb the most positive evidence of that: a new baby. For Ronnie and Janie, the new child would be an affirmation of their marriage to Hollywood's cynical detractors so full of petty, mean gossip, waiting for their marriage to fall.

As she had when carrying Maureen, Janie continued working during the first months of her pregnancy. But now that she was a major star, the stakes were infinitely higher. She was starring alongside Jimmy Stewart in *Magic Town*. William Wellman, the director, said that he had never seen an actress work any harder. "She was letter-perfect," he said. "She was painstaking, she insisted upon perfection," he said. But a movie is not a work of needlepoint, where meticulous concern is enough to create a thing of beauty. The movie wasn't up to the standards Janie had set for herself.

As for Ronnie, he didn't have his sights set on any Academy Award but merely a decent part or two. After *Stallion Road,* he had suffered through *Night Unto Night,* in which he played a doomed epileptic biochemist, a bit of miscasting on a par with Doris Day playing Mary, Queen of Scots. He had tried to turn down his next film, *The Voice of the Turtle,* with Eleanor Parker and Eve Arden. But as Sergeant Bill Page, he had a worthy comic role, the poor man's Cary Grant.

In the spring of 1947, when Janie was having her problems with *Magic Town,* Ronnie was playing in *That Hagen Girl* opposite a teen-age former child star, Shirley Temple, in her first adult role. Ronnie believed in movies that were a positive moral force. It appalled him to be romancing a young woman who could have been his daughter. When he arrived home in the evening, he was often in no better a mood than Janie.

Ronnie was no less ambitious than Janie, though his goals were far more nebulous. He had become a strongly anti-Communist liberal, repudiating AVC, HICCASP, and the CSU, organizations whose goals he had once so articulately supported and that now he decided were full of Communists. He had not been a hero in the war; but on this great public stage, he played what in his mind was a heroic role, standing up to the Communists and fellow travelers in public meetings and private gatherings, baiting them as they baited him, while conspiring with his friends to defeat what he considered the Communist conspiracy. It was exhilarating stuff, better than making the second-rate movies he was making, better than listening to Janie and her friends discuss movies or kids.

Ronnie was busy day and night. As *That Hagen Girl* neared completion, he tried to rescue some dignity from the production. In later years he would state defiantly that he almost always did get the girls in his movies. But Shirley Temple was one girl he didn't want to get. "You know, people sort of frown on men marrying girls young enough to be their daughters," he told Peter Godfrey, the director.

"I'm old enough to be my wife's father," Godfrey responded.

The audience at the sneak preview moaned "Oh, no" when Ronnie kissed Shirley Temple. Ronnie crouched down in his seat and sneaked out of the theater, not wanting them to see the lecherous Ronald Reagan in the flesh. But the reaction was enough to convince Warners to cut out the kiss, leaving an ambiguous ending.

One hot June evening soon afterward, Ronnie attended a premiere at the Carthay Circle Theater. As he and Janie walked out into the torpid air, he felt wheezy. He coughed, but he figured it was nothing. During the night he became sicker and sicker. In the morning Janie had to call an ambulance to take him on a stretcher to Cedars of Lebanon Hospital.

Janie came to the hospital and watched over Ronnie, who lay in a private room sweating and shivering with viral pneumonia. He made the nurses wrap him in a cocoon of blankets and feed him tea through a glass tube—memories of Nelle's sweet care. He dreamed he was playing opposite Humphrey Bogart in a trench coat. He was lost in a miasma of memories and dreams. He burned with fever as if his whole body would burst into flame. He decided he wouldn't breathe anymore. Then a nurse in white came to him and told him to inhale. "Now let it out," she said. "Come on now, breathe in one more time." The sweat came finally and he knew that he would survive.

Janie had been distraught when they had wheeled Ronnie away. Whether for this reason or some other, her labor pains started three months early. "Miss Wyman was at his bedside almost to the time she was rushed to the hospital," the *Los Angeles Times* reported. On June 26, 1947, at Queen of Angels Hospital, Dr. Robert L. Blackmun delivered a baby girl. The next day the newspaper reported that the mother's condition was "satisfactory" and that the baby had "a good chance of survival." But by the time that account appeared in the Los Angeles papers, the baby was already dead.

Like many troubled couples, Janie and Ronnie may well have thought that the birth of a child might rekindle their own romance. But what did the death of their child mean? Janie had been proud to work full-time while she carried the child, but in the folklore of her time—and it was no more than folklore—women were supposed to stay home during pregnancies. And what of Ronnie and his sudden illness that seemed to have been enough to trigger the birth? What kind of an omen was that? What commentary on the frenetic life he was leading?

Janie and Ronnie did not like to talk publicly or think about the death. They sought to avoid the subject. Years later in his autobiography, Ronnie gave no indication that Janie had even been at his bedside in the hospital. Moreover, Ronnie called the birth "a miscarriage," as if there had been no live birth at all.

Ronnie and Janie quickly put their lives back in gear. But in so doing they once again began living at the pace that had made them unhappy. Ronnie was not pleased with the way his career was going and he didn't talk much about his current roles. He was proudest of his work in *King's Row*. Often when the Reagans had guests, he insisted on screening the film. It was as if in *King's Row* he caught a glimpse of the actor he could have been.

Ronnie became even more involved with SAG. In October 1947, he went with a group from Hollywood to testify before the House Un-American Activities Committee (HUAC). In the next few years, scores of Americans were summoned before a HUAC that was not so much a congressional committee as a tribunal. Ronnie told about his bitter experiences with Communist-front organizations in Hollywood, but named no names. Then he made sure that the committee understood his position on communism in America.

"I detest, I abhor their philosophy, but I detest more than that their tactics, which are those of a fifth column, and are dishonest," he said, sitting bolt upright in a tan suit and blue tie. "But at the same time I never as a citizen want to see our country become urged, by either fear or resent-

Jane Wyman as a deaf-mute who is raped, gives birth to a child, and is then put on trial for the murder of the rapist (who tries stealing the baby away from her) in the Oscar-winning performance of *Johnny Belinda*, 1946. *(EBC)*

ment of this group, that we ever compromise with any of our democratic principles through that fear or resentment. I still think that democracy can do it."

Ronnie's testimony impressed many people, liberals and conservatives alike, for its fairness and lack of name-calling. The following month he was elected president of SAG, a nonpaying position that during those difficult, traumatic years was almost like a second full-time job.

Janie was just as busy as her husband. A few weeks after the death of her child, she received a phone call from Jerry Wald, the producer of her new movie. "Let's start to work on *Johnny Belinda*," he said, as much to help Janie as to help himself and his movie.

Janie had had roles that tapped the depths of her emotions before, but *Johnny Belinda* went beyond all that. As Belinda, she would be a deaf-mute girl capable of making only grunting sounds. Raped by a town bully, she gives birth to a son, Johnny Belinda, who is almost taken away from her by her rapist, whom she eventually kills. In a script that went from one emotional scene to another, Belinda was the part of a lifetime.

Janie went to a school for deaf-mutes. She learned to read lips. She talked to psychologists. She even wore earplugs on the set to *feel* deaf. At first she almost gave up. She couldn't do it. She couldn't get it. "Why don't you get someone else to do it?" she told Wald.

But eventually she entered deep into the psyche of the deaf-mute girl. She began losing weight. Five pounds. Ten pounds. In her crying scenes she cried and she cried, and when Jean Negulesco, the director, shouted "Cut," she kept crying. Others on the set began to worry about her very sanity. She seemed not to be acting a part but to be possessed by it. When she nestled in her arms the baby that the town wanted to wrench from her, Wald thought that "the role itself brought memories that were almost too much to bear."

Ronnie knew what had happened to Janie when she had been filming *The Lost Weekend* and *The Yearling*. He understood as best he could, but he was an outsider to her now, both as a husband and as an actor who did not immerse himself so deeply into a role. He spent time on the set. He brought Maureen and Michael to the studio. He even went on location with the film crew for several weeks on the coast above San Francisco.

Janie and Ronnie never argued in public, but even the crew noticed how rude Janie was to her husband. Another evening, outside the Beverly Club in Los Angeles, a doorman overheard the Reagans arguing. "I got along pretty well without you before, and I can get along without you now," Janie was reported to have said.

By December, Janie's epic performance was complete. She decided that she wanted to go to New York City to visit friends. Twenty-two

months before, when Janie had finished *The Yearling,* she had come dancing into the house talking Ronnie into taking off with her. This time she
wanted to go alone.

In New York she was away from the paternal care of the Warner
public-relations people, away from the constraints of home and friends.
When she was asked about her marriage, she told the truth. And telling the
truth, feeling the truth, she changed Ronnie and her life forever. "There is
no use in lying," she told Hollywood reporter Harrison Carroll. "I am not
the happiest girl in the world. It's nothing that has happened recently, it's
an accumulation of things that have been coming on for a long time. . . . We
will talk things over and I hope and believe that we will solve our problems
and avoid a separation."

Ronnie knew that there were problems in his marriage, but he had no
idea how serious they had become. On December 4, he was returning to his
house from a shopping trip to buy Janie a Christmas present when he
learned what his wife had said. He had been brought up to keep private
feelings private. The idea that he should have to find out about his wife's
feelings from the newspapers appalled him. He turned immediately to
Hedda Hopper, who along with Louella Parsons had championed the Reagans' marriage as Hollywood's ideal. "We had a tiff," he told her. "That's
right. But we've had tiffs before, as what couple married eight years hasn't.
But I expect when Jane gets back from New York we'll get back together
all right . . . The bad part of Hollywood is that you have to live your life in a
goldfish bowl—and what you see in a goldfish bowl is too often distorted."

When their marriage was a happy one, Ronnie had been only too glad
to let observers peer into it, then write about it as if it were made of pure
gold, not flesh, blood and travail. Now he was sickened that their private
agonies should become a public spectacle. The gossip columnists hovered
over them when Janie returned the following Friday.

It had never occurred to Ronnie that he, Dutch Reagan from Dixon,
Illinois, might one day end up a middle-aged divorced man, thrown out of
his house, pushed away from his children, forced to assume a role that he
considered a mark of shame and moral failure. But there was agony beyond
the public humiliation. He still loved Janie.

Janie wanted a divorce. On December 14, 1947, according to court
documents, she and Ronnie separated for the first time. Two-and-a-half
weeks later, Ronnie went to a New Year's Eve party by himself. As the
hour of the New Year approached, he grew more and more depressed. Just
before midnight, Patricia Neal, a young actress from New York, noticed
Ronnie and an older woman walking out into the backyard. As the celebrants sang "Auld Lang Syne," tooted horns, kissed and made merry, Ron-

nie laid his head on the woman's shoulder and cried.

Janie and Ronnie tried to work it out. "A few of their pals went so far as to retain a West Los Angeles psychiatrist to talk to them and try to straighten things out," reported *Motion Picture,* "but he was unable to get to first base." Janie had a catalog of grievances, and Ronnie simply could not understand his wife. He kept thinking that she would get over her irritation and come back to him.

Seven-year-old Maureen and even three-year-old Michael knew that something terrible had happened. "I remember sitting in the car crying hysterically, with my father trying to explain it," said Maureen. "He said the same things that parents always do at a time like that. They're still my parents and you're still their kid. We'll all learn to adjust to this. There's an age-old speech that goes with it, though in those days you didn't do it so often."

Janie could see how the children were suffering, and for Ronnie's birthday, February 6, she planned a special surprise. Ronnie was called off the set of his new movie, *John Loves Mary,* and asked to go outside. There sat a Cadillac convertible with a birthday card from Maureen and Michael.

The evening of Ronnie's birthday, the children wanted their daddy to come out to the house for dinner and birthday cake. For the children, the party was a symbol of hope that their life would be what it once had been. To Ronnie, the evening was a symbol of the end. "The latest attempt at a reconciliation has failed," he told a reporter on his thirty-seventh birthday. "I'm going out to the house tonight but it may be our last domestic scene together. From now on it will be out of my hands."

On February 17, the Reagans agreed on a property settlement. Janie journeyed to Las Vegas and checked into the Flamingo Hotel. Other than talking to John Cope, an attorney, about establishing legal residency for a quick divorce, she kept to herself, away from the gaming tables and the prying reporters. Friends who talked to her said that she seemed depressed, lonesome for her children. Then, early one morning a few days later, just as suddenly as she had arrived, she checked out of the Flamingo and headed back to L.A. But the reconciliation lasted no more than a week, and Ronnie was out of the house again.

The death throes of their marriage had become a public spectacle. Louella Parsons reported that "no marital separation since I broke the story that Mary Pickford, America's sweetheart, was leaving Douglas Fairbanks, has had the effect of the parting of the Reagans."

To the public moralists, Janie was to blame. "Hollywood sympathy in this case is one hundred percent with Ronnie, who is a prince," *Silver Screen* reported. "Jane is a moody person, temperamental, ambitious, restless and seeking, and furthermore, she is not now and hasn't been well for some time. It is to be hoped that, as her health improves, Jane's other problems will vanish, and two of the town's favorite people will resume their marriage."

At Joan Crawford's party for Noël Coward, Janie arrived by herself. She scanned the room; listened a moment to the gay, convivial chatter; and broke into tears. Soon afterward, she left.

Ronnie couldn't stand having the pulse of his marriage taken every day by the journalists. At Warners he flared up at a gossip columnist who had sought him out to hear the latest. He wanted to be alone with his unhappiness. One evening, two stars happened to drive by the Reagans' house. Outside on the road, Ronnie sat in his car looking up at the brightly lit windows.

In May, Janie filed for divorce in Los Angeles, charging that it was "impossible" to live together happily. On June 28, 1948, Janie and her attorney, Charles E. Millikan, appeared before Superior Court Judge Thurmond Clarke. In her pageboy bob and tangerine gabardine dress, she looked too young to be a thirty-four-year-old actress with two children and two failed marriages.

In the legal parlance of the time, Janie charged "extreme mental cruelty," a hollow, empty phrase. She told the judge of Ronnie's endless political discussions with his friends and colleagues. "Most of their discussions were far above me," she said. Ronnie had insisted that she attend meetings with him and sit in on interminable discussions, though her ideas "were never considered important."

"Finally there was nothing in common between us, nothing to sustain our marriage."

Ronnie was not there that day to hear Janie's harsh words, and his attorney, William Berger, had nothing to say. The agreement had already been worked out between the two attorneys. Community property worth $75,000 was to be divided almost equally. Janie was to have custody of the two children. Ronnie was to pay $500 a month in child support. If, through illness or accident, Janie couldn't work, he was to pay an extra $500 a month.

Shortly after the divorce hearings, Gregory Peck came up to Janie at a party. "I'm really sorry to hear about you and Ronnie," he said earnestly. "What happened?"

"I just couldn't stand to watch that damn *King's Row* one more time."

To someone like Gregory Peck, Janie would toss off a callous remark like a thoroughbred shaking its mane. But she didn't want to talk or think about Ronnie anymore. Well before the divorce became final on July 18, 1949, Janie had moved out of their house into a new residence in Holmby Hills.

When Ronnie needed a bachelor apartment, he called their old Hollywood landlord. The man offered him the same apartment (a block from the Mocambo nightclub) where he and Janie had lived when they were first married. Many a divorced man would have cringed at the idea of living in the very rooms where he had first brought his bride, but Ronnie took the apartment right away, as if there he might discover the secret of what had gone wrong.

In 1948, during the trauma of his divorce, Ronnie costarred in *The Girl from Jones Beach*. The film was as substantial as marshmallows and Coke. Ronnie played a magazine illustrator who, like the then popular Vargas, made his living drawing beautiful women. His costar was Virginia Mayo, who looked like one of Vargas's gorgeous blond pinups. There were a dozen other beautiful young actresses and models in the film. Ronnie credited the film with going "a long way toward solving my social problem."

"He didn't seem depressed or anything," said Virginia Mayo. "We did a day's shooting at the beach. We romped around, leapfrogging, all kinds of fun things. He was awfully attractive. If I hadn't been married, I probably would have gone out with him."

In the spring, one of his first dinners was with Doris Day. He spent the evening talking about Janie. His name was also linked with Ruth Roman, Shirley Ballard, Kay Stewart and Ann Sothern, the vivacious blond comedienne.

Ronnie took Sothern to Ciro's, where they sat laughing and talking. He even gave her a gold saint's medal that she cherished for years. But she knew that Ronnie's heart was not up for grabs.

"The press always exaggerated things," Sothern said. "I was a big star, and publicity was a way of life. The photographers would come in and take pictures. We even knew their names. We were accustomed to that.

"Ronnie has infinite charm and he was marvelous-looking. He always acted as if he was sort of embarrassed to be an actor. He had a wonderful body because he rode horses all the time. He was a charming, sweet man.

"But he's an Aquarius and I'm an Aquarius. You can't pin an Aquarius down. We hate to get tied down."

Ronnie's greatest performance in 1948 was pretending that he was a carefree bachelor. He didn't like being alone. Night after night he went out. As he later admitted in his autobiography, he was spending $750 a month in nightclubs and restaurants. He was so unaware of the realities of his own life that he didn't even realize he was spending so much until his accountant told him so.

Years later when he'd had a few drinks, Ronnie would enjoy a few rounds of manly reminiscing about his conquests. In the 1950s Ronnie told Joe Santley, a public-relations man, that one morning he found himself in the Garden of Allah, the famous bungalow court that in lore and legend was the scene of half the sex in Hollywood. "I woke up one morning and I couldn't remember the name of the gal I was in bed with," Ronnie said. "I said, 'Hey, I gotta get a grip here.'"

Ronnie couldn't get away from Janie. He ran into her at the studio's makeup department. When he had lunch at Warners, her portrait as Belinda smiled down from the wall. She seemed to be everywhere.

Ronnie went alone to the premiere of *Johnny Belinda*. So did Janie, wearing a dress Ronnie had given her especially for the occasion. It was the same ice-blue color as her wedding dress. He told reporters, "I'm not saying this simply because Jane is my wife but because I believe it with my whole soul: her performance in this picture is one of the greatest things I've ever seen." Ronnie was not alone in his judgment. Janie was nominated again for an Academy Award. This time she won.

Janie wasn't dating anybody seriously either, though her name was linked to Lew Ayres, her costar in *Johnny Belinda*. Janie and Ronnie often dined together to talk about the children. Ronnie was occasionally a guest at dinner parties at her new house.

Ronnie spent a great deal of time away from the social life of Hollywood at his little ranch in the San Fernando Valley. Janie and he had named it "Yearling Row" in honor of *The Yearling* and *King's Row*. He liked to ride and jump horses or just putter around. On weekends he sometimes took Dick Carroll, a young Warner public-relations man, up with him. They dug postholes and worked together. Ronnie liked to be around people like young Carroll, who never ventured into his own private psyche.

At the studio Ronnie knew almost everybody's name. Wherever he went at Warners, it was "Hi, Ronnie," "How ya doin', Ronnie." He was a popular man, but he talked too much. It was as if he could not be quiet. His subordinates had no choice but to appear at least moderately interested. But with his peers, it was another matter. They grew tired of his endless monologues. One day a good friend took him to lunch. "Ronnie, you've got to stop this talking all the time," the friend said earnestly. "You're a great guy, but you're boring people to death."

While Janie's career seemed to go from triumph to triumph, Ronnie's was petering out in one humiliation after another. All he wanted was a big Western, but Warners kept using him like a utility outfielder, throwing him in at the last minute. The studio had funds frozen in England. So Warners sent him and Patricia Neal, his costar in *John Loves Mary,* to London for four months in November 1948 to play in *The Hasty Heart* with Richard Todd, a newcomer. Ronnie had only the second lead, making him, as he said sarcastically at the time, "Hollywood's most expensive supporting player."

There is no way to upstage a dog, a kid or a dying actor. *The Hasty Heart* belonged to thirty-year-old Todd, a Scottish actor who played a soldier dying in a Burmese hospital. Ronnie was his good, compassionate friend, a role he had played too many times before.

The London weather was as bitter as Ronnie's mood. Rationing had yet to end, and he couldn't even eat and drink his way into a good mood. He had steaks shipped over from the 21 Club in New York. The Savoy Hotel where he was staying kept them in their freezer. Good meat was so rare that the hotel workers sampled his stock. And after he had eaten a half-dozen or so of the steaks, the waiter regretfully announced that the others had spoiled.

Pat Neal and Ronnie lived in adjoining suites in the hotel and often ate together in one of their rooms. They spent much time together. The young actress had just broken up with a very married Gary Cooper, an affair that was the talk of Hollywood. She could commiserate with Ronnie. "I went out with him because I wasn't looking for anyone and he wasn't looking for anyone," she said. "It was so sad because he had two little children and he did not want a divorce but Jane Wyman did. When we would see other people, I don't think he knew it, but I would cue him to tell a funny story. And then I would cue him again. He could tell good stories."

During the four months in London, Ronnie took a special liking to Jack Warner, Jr., and his new bride, Barbara. Jack, Jr., was his father's representative on the film, and Ronnie spent time at the Warners' flat behind the Dorchester Hotel. "He was in a depressed state," Warner remembered. "We discussed his personal situation. He was like the elder statesman giving advice. He talked about having to work things out."

One thing Ronnie enjoyed talking about was his *next* role. For months he had been consumed with the idea of starring in a Western. It was as if only in such a role could he regain his own manhood. He was obsessed with playing a Western hero. Out on the frontier lived good men and bad men. The one law was the six-shooter, and the good men had to be faster on the draw than the bad men, but the good men always won.

He had gotten Warners to purchase a Western story for him: *Ghost Mountain*. The studio promised that he could star. When he got back to Hollywood, he would have his chance. It would be a world away from the drizzle and fog of London and the gray austerity of the socialist government.

The day his ship docked in New York, in March 1949, Ronnie read an article in *Variety* saying that *Ghost Mountain* had been scheduled for production starring Errol Flynn. Ronnie was infuriated. He felt that Warners was rewarding his years of good work by diminishing his career, shackling him with one inadequate role after another. He was tired of betrayals, not only personal and political but now professional. He threatened to do whatever he could on his next picture to create problems for the studio.

When Lew Wasserman, Ronnie's agent at MCA, heard his client's rantings, he worked out a more practical solution. Wasserman renegotiated the last three years of Ronnie's contract so that he would do only one picture a year at half his annual salary.

Warners was only too glad to unload their aging contract player. The studio was in trouble. Between 1947 and 1951, the studio's net profits had declined from $22,094,979 to $9,427,344. Warners was getting rid of public-relations staff, secretaries, even long-term contract players like Ronnie.

Ronnie had better luck in agents than he had in films. A week later Wasserman negotiated another contract: five years, five pictures at Universal. Ronnie knew perfectly well that Universal wasn't the top studio in town. But it was work. He liked the way the new studio immediately put him in a film, *Fugitive from Terror,* a thriller with Ida Lupino. For Ronnie, it was a fresh start.

On June 19, four days before he was to start filming, Ronnie was one of a number of stars taking part in a charity softball game. It was a show more than a game, and as usual Ronnie was playing the hero. "One of the gags was very realistic," wrote Al Wolf, a local columnist. "A hero whacked the ball pretty good, streaked for first and dove in, only to be blocked by a huge meanie. Down they went in a cloud of dust—but only the villain arose. The hero lay there writhing until a stretcher team ran afield and lugged him off. The incident drew a hearty laugh from the stands."

Ronnie, the hero, had broken his right thigh in half a dozen places. He spent eight weeks in casts and splints at Santa Monica's St. John's Hospital, months more recuperating on crutches. Universal gave another actor Ronnie's part. And on July 18, 1949, as he lay in the hospital, the divorce he didn't want became final.

For the next months Janie was in London starring in Alfred Hitchcock's *Stage Fright.* Ronnie recuperated with the two children in Janie's new house. Originally, Janie had wanted to take the children with her to England, but Ronnie had talked her out of it by telling her that London would be too tough on Maureen and Michael. Often when Maureen got home from school, a letter from her mother was waiting. "Dear Maureenie," Janie wrote in a typical letter. "I wish you and all your school chums could have the opportunity to come here. My love to you both, darlings. I wear the locket with your pictures all the time so that I can feel you very close to me."

The children loved both their parents a great deal. One day when a journalist came to take Ronnie to a beach party, Maureen and Michael called out, "Take good care of daddy."

Ronnie always looked at the best of things, and he had convinced himself that even a broken leg had its good side: He felt that he was getting a more philosophical outlook on life. He hobbled around on crutches wearing a steel brace from his ankle to his hip. He did what he could with his days. He prayed that his leg would heal well and strong.

He tried to smile, but his smile often looked like a grimace. He was a thirty-eight-year-old divorced man who was a transient even in Janie's house with his own children. He wasn't working and he could see now that for years his career had been declining. He was a lonely man, and, worse yet, a lonely man who didn't realize that, as he later wrote, "real loneliness is not missing anyone at all."

Actor Ronald Reagan and his fiancée, actress Nancy Davis, at the premiere of the movie version of *A Streetcar Named Desire*, 1952. *(UPI)*

──10──
"IT'S ABOUT TIME"

One day in the fall of 1949, Mervyn LeRoy, the director or producer of a score of films including *Little Caesar* and *The Wizard of Oz,* called Ronnie. LeRoy was no longer a top director, but he still had a credible reputation. Ronnie hoped that he had a part to offer. However, as was usually the case these days, LeRoy wanted to talk to him as president of SAG.

LeRoy had a favor to ask. In his current M-G-M picture, *East Side, West Side,* LeRoy had a new contract player, Nancy Davis. This Nancy Davis was finding her name on lists of Communist-front organizations and on leftist petitions. She was receiving Communist propaganda in the mail as well. She was scared it might hurt her fledgling career.

To be exposed as a Communist was enough to end a career. Ronnie had no quarrel with that. During his period as chairman of the Motion Picture Industry Council (MPIC) and SAG president, Ronnie was actively involved in rooting out Communists. At the same time, he wanted to make sure that only real Communists had their careers ruined. Ronnie was capable of *clearing* people, taking the testimony of repentant Communists and leftist sympathizers and shepherding their reentry into what he considered real Americanism.

Ronnie went down to SAG headquarters and discovered that there was another Nancy Davis. He called LeRoy and told him that if Miss Davis got into trouble, he and SAG would defend her as innocent. That finished the matter as far as Ronnie was concerned, but LeRoy called back. Miss Davis wanted to meet Ronnie personally.

Ronnie was still on crutches and if he had sought an excuse, he had a ready one. But he knew that a woman under contract at M-G-M had to be a knockout. Nonetheless, he had been hurt enough by women, and he was eternally wary.

He telephoned. "I've got a very early call in the morning," he said, lying through his teeth. "If you don't mind a short dinner date, I'd be very happy to talk to you about your problem."

"It's awfully short notice, but I think I can manage it," Nancy said. "I've got an early call too." She was lying as well, but she, too, was defining her own turf. She had used the Communist business in part as an excuse to meet Ronnie. She had asked the director to call back and set up a face-to-face meeting. But though she was willing to admit that she didn't have a date that evening, she wasn't about to throw herself at him.

A little later, Ronnie showed up at Nancy's two-story apartment in Westwood, a suburb west of Hollywood, near the UCLA campus. He stood before the door a moment, leaning on two canes. As he knocked, he expected to see this new M-G-M starlet come rolling out of the apartment like one of Detroit's latest wonders, flashy and polished. Instead, he was greeted by a rather demure brunette whose most striking features were her big hazel eyes. She was pretty but did not possess the flamboyant allure of Ruth Roman or Ann Sothern or other actresses he was dating.

Ronnie took her to LaRue's for dinner. Then they drove to Ciro's, where he had been dropping a good part of the $750 he was spending each month in nightclubs and restaurants. Ronnie was full of jokes and stories. Nancy listened and laughed, her feminine chortle applauding his every tale. Sophie Tucker was opening that night. Nancy and Ronnie sat through both shows, after which Sophie joined them at their table. It was 3:10 in the morning before Ronnie left Nancy at her apartment door.

"I don't know if it was love at first sight," Nancy wrote later in her autobiography, "but it was something close to it. We were taken with one another and wanted to see more of each other. We had dinner the next night and the night after that and the night after that . . .

"Ronnie and I went together for about a year, but I think I knew from the moment I opened the door on our first date that this was the man for me."

In fact, Nancy went with Ronnie off and on not for a year but for close to two and a half years before they finally married.

When Nancy met Ronnie, she was already twenty-eight years old, though no one in Hollywood knew it. She had never been married. She was beginning to feel her youth slipping by. As for Ronnie, he had been profoundly hurt in his first marriage.

"The truth is, I did everything wrong . . . in short, doing everything which could have lost her if Someone up there hadn't been looking after me," Ronnie wrote in his autobiography. "In spite of my determination to remain footloose, in spite of my belief that the pattern of my life was all set and would continue without change, nature was trying to tell me something very important."

Ronnie continued to date other women and traveled to New York and across the country on SAG business. Nonetheless, he was seeing Nancy often enough for his name to be linked frequently with hers in the gossip columns. As early as February 1950, there was conjecture about marriage. "Ronnie, as anyone who talked to him about it at that time well knows, was scared to death," *Modern Screen* reported later. "He had honestly never thought of marriage—and when he did, it terrified him."

After such gossip, Ronnie decided not to be seen with Nancy within a country mile of photographers or columnists. For the *Hasty Heart* premiere, Ronnie's date would be duly noted. As if to prove that his heart wasn't hasty at all, he took not Nancy but glamorous Ruth Roman, starting a spate of rumors about a "new romance for Ronnie?" Later in 1950, observers thought that he was serious about Penny Edwards, Roy Rogers's new leading lady. That went nowhere either.

Nancy continued to see other men. She frequently dated Robert Stack, one of the most socially prominent actors in Hollywood. In March 1950, she was pictured in *Movie Stars Parade* with him at the premiere of his movie *Battleground*. She was identified as Ronnie's onetime girlfriend.

Ronnie was still drawn toward Janie. He gave her a miniature poodle to keep her company. He sent her flowers at the studio when she began shooting *Three Guys Named Mike*. In February 1950, he went out to Janie's house for her thirty-sixth birthday. In honor of the occasion, Michael and Maureen had been allowed to stay up. Maureen had already been sent off to boarding school, the Chadwick School in Palos Verdes, and soon five-year-old Michael would be following her.

Janie told writer Adela Rogers St. John that nine-year-old Maureen danced with Charles Feldman, the producer of Janie's new picture, *The Glass Menagerie,* and with another of her favorites, Kirk Douglas. Then she went to sit on her daddy's knee, and fell half asleep. When Janie walked over to her daughter, Maureen perked up. "Oh, mother, isn't it a problem? In spite of it being such a beautiful party, you go and get sleepy." Ronnie put Maureen and Michael to bed.

On Saturdays Ronnie often took Maureen and Michael out to the San Fernando Valley ranch. He had trained his two children to cool down the horses after he had given them a brisk workout. Maureen and Mike rode two of the gentler horses he had purchased for them around the exercise ring. This wasn't quite the weekend that Hollywood bachelors were supposed to have, but Ronnie liked being up here by himself or with his kids.

On the evening early in 1950 when Ronnie was honored by the Friars

Club, Janie arrived with a group of friends and sat in the back. When Ronnie was praised and praised again, her eyes filled with tears. A few days later when Janie received the *Photoplay* Gold Medal award for her role in *Johnny Belinda,* Ronnie was sitting in the auditorium applauding as loudly as anyone. Hopes of reconciliation still peppered columns whenever they were seen together.

"Are they haunted by their perfect Love?" asked Louella Parsons about Ronnie and Janie in the February 1951 *Modern Screen,* over a year after Ronnie and Nancy had started dating, and when their relationship was finally becoming a steady one. "Not long ago, I went to a dinner party at their home and Maureen came in to cut her birthday cake. Her mother and father stood by her side, polite to each other and respectful—so different from those gay kids who went barnstorming with me. I turned away so they couldn't see the tears in my eyes.

"Since then, when I see Janie, she seems self-sufficient, independent, and oh, so gay. But I know that not long ago she said to someone, 'What's the matter with me? I can't seem to pick up the pieces of my life again. Will I ever find happiness ahead?' And, one of the lovely girls Ronnie seemed interested in for awhile told me he recently said to her, 'Sure, I like you. I like you fine. But I think I've forgotten how to fall in love.'

"I wonder—do those embers of the once perfect love they shared still burn deep with haunting memories that won't let them forget?"

Nancy hadn't sat around waiting for Ronnie's next phone call. Being an M-G-M starlet was a full-time job. Other women bridled at the constraints, upset at the way the studio entered into personal and private lives. But growing up with Dr. Loyal, Nancy was used to a life of rigorous discipline. She complied with the publicity setups.

When Nancy moved into her new split-level, five-room apartment, the publicity department gathered together a couple of other young M-G-M contract players and pretended that they were helping their dear friend Nancy Davis move. Pete and Marshall Thompson and Pete's wife, Barbara, showed up at Nancy's apartment and a photographer took pictures that ran for four pages in the May 1950 issue of *Movie Life.* For all the people out in the movie heartland knew, the foursome were the best of friends. But as Marshall Thompson said later, "I didn't know Nancy. It was all a publicity stunt."

For a supposed date with Peter Lawford, a rising M-G-M actor, she dressed in jeans, a plaid shirt, and rode a horse ("Peter Lawford turns dude for a day, takes city-slicker Nancy Davis on a cowboy caper"). She modeled suits, raincoats and jewelry for ads and promotions. She cooperated for fan-magazine profiles ("Nancy lives alone in a small apartment in Beverly

Hills, helped only by a maid who comes in each afternoon to clean and sometimes remain to prepare dinner"). She gave interviews for articles about the life-style of Hollywood's new crop of starlets ("Nancy doesn't worry about wolves. 'You have to open the door to most wolves, anyhow,' she says"). She told the fan magazines how to remain beautiful while traveling, and her beauty regimen was featured in another four-page spread ("Insurance for all-day freshness comes immediately post-bathing. A trusty underarm anti-perspirant, of course . . . Dusting powder with a deodorizing ingredient is puffed on next"). She modeled at fashion shows, including an occasion in the spring of 1951 when she appeared with Elizabeth Taylor, Ann Miller and Carmen Miranda, whom she had imitated a decade before at Smith.

In almost all her publicity shots, Nancy appeared doggedly unglamorous. When *Movieland* featured her alone in a story, "A Star is Born," Nancy popped into her jeans and was photographed cleaning house. She was supposedly working out anxiety the day of the premiere of her first major picture, *The Next Voice You Hear.* In contrast to the stunning pictures of Janie Wyman that often appeared in the same magazines, Nancy looked positively dowdy.

Nancy tried. Often a woman in M-G-M's publicity department escorted Nancy to Amelia Gray's store to borrow dresses for photo spreads. Amelia's was the first store in Beverly Hills to sell many French designers. Nancy loved traveling to the slow-paced business village graced with palm trees. Trying on clothes at Amelia's, she was like a child dressing up in her mother's finery. Amelia offered her customers coffee and seemed as interested in gossiping as selling dresses. The clothes Nancy borrowed and bought were the clothes not of a young actress but of a rich, thirtyish society matron.

Ronnie went with Nancy to the premiere of *The Next Voice You Hear,* in which she costarred with James Whitmore. Ronnie had not seen Nancy in her earlier films, *East Side, West Side* and *Shadow on the Wall.* Afterward, as they sat in the theater, Ronnie told Nancy that, "she could go home and unpack—she'd be around for quite a while."

The film was Dore Schary's special project. It would play at New York's Radio City Music Hall, and Schary thought that the film would touch America's sentimental heart. *The Next Voice You Hear* was based on the idea of God's voice speaking over the radio for a week. Unfortunately, God had very little new to say. This unexpected visitation did no more to change the world's habits than a Sunday sermon. The film did even less to halt M-G-M's declining fortunes.

Nancy played Whitmore's pregnant wife, Mrs. Joe Smith. She wore a wire form underneath her maternity clothes and walked with the heavy stride of a woman about to give birth. Nancy was adept at making the best of bad lines, and she gave a competent performance as the good Fifties wife—homebody, cook and mother. Her husband was the genial, joshing, mocking, boyish breadwinner, seemingly a tower of manly strength, but on a deeper level it was Mrs. Smith, not Mr. Smith, who was the moral strength of the family. She was the one concerned about problems with her son and his paper route. In a subtle, sometimes devious way, she directed the family, even helping her husband to remember the words of grace. She was the one who held things together. In the *New York Times,* Bosley Crowther said that Nancy was "delightful" as Joe Smith's "gentle, plain and understanding wife."

After *The Next Voice You Hear,* Nancy found herself typecast as a pregnant wife in a series of bad films. These movies, like many of the time, reinforced a role of the American woman that was much more complicated than it appeared. Just as Ronnie had done throughout his film career, Nancy was playing an American archetype, a role that fit her as perfectly as the white gloves she wore to ladies' teas.

Her role in *The Next Voice You Hear* won her more recognition and speculation of success than any of her other eight movie roles at M-G-M. As the "dark-eyed and dramatic" star of the film, Nancy was one of ten candidates named for stardom in *Photoplay*'s "Choose your Stars" contest. In November 1950, readers chose Nancy fifth, behind future stars Mercedes McCambridge and Piper Laurie, ahead of Barbara Bates and Judy Holliday. This role would also win her a Christopher Award alongside Ronnie for "creative work of spiritual significance."

There was no such recognition for her roles in *Shadow in the Sky,* again with James Whitmore; *Night into Morning* with Ray Milland, one of the few where she wasn't a wife; *It's a Big Country,* in which she played with Fredric March in one of the film's seven episodes; and *Talk About a Stranger,* her 1952 film with George Murphy. *Talk About a Stranger,* her last film at M-G-M before she ended her contract, was so dismal that even Nancy refused to see it.

Ronnie praised Nancy's acting. He was not unaware, though, that he was dating a woman whose movie image was a kind of pleasant frumpiness. He even suggested to Nancy that "she send her movie wardrobe to the cleaners and lose the ticket." Nancy herself felt that people "cast sly glances in my direction—almost as if they expected me to look pregnant off the screen too!"

Off screen, Nancy was no housecoat-wearing wife and mother, but she didn't have the youthful glamour so prized in America during the Fifties. Unlike other starlets, she was not a chattering, flirting thing. She was quieter and a good listener. She was the kind of young woman whom older men liked. When her dates arrived at her apartment door, they often showed up carrying the heavy baggage of their pasts. Robert Walker was the other actor with whom Nancy's name was often linked. He was a sad divorcé with two sons. Nancy had the dubious distinction of dating both Walker and Ronnie, who along with John Agar were named in July 1950 by *Modern Screen* as Hollywood's three loneliest male stars.

Nancy was a pretty adornment, like a Boehm figurine. She was often invited to parties where some of her less well-bred peers would not have been comfortable. On Sunday evenings she frequently went to the home of Dore Schary, the head of M-G-M. In Hollywood, Schary was considered an intellectual; Schary thought it a mark of his seriousness that M-G-M was promoting a Nancy Davis who had more to offer over dinner than boobs and bromides.

Nancy had other friends. Leonard Spigelgass, the screenwriter, was one of those who visited her apartment. He found her "charming." Spigelgass had a wicked wit. Sitting in her small living room, he skewered one Hollywood notable after another as if he were making brochettes. Egged on by Nancy's titters of laughter, he continued for hours. There were others, too, who saw a gay, carefree Nancy who liked nothing better than an evening of gossip, the more pungent and personal the better.

With Ronnie, though, Nancy was more serious. In mid-1951, thirty-year-old Nancy felt the tide of time pulling her away from the prospect of the husband and home that she had always wanted. She had given up her romance with Benny Thau soon after she met Ronnie.

Ronnie was no longer the kind of man she had dreamed of when she'd sat in the movie theaters of Northampton during her college years swooning over the silver images of men like Errol Flynn, Jimmy Stewart and Ronnie. Although he looked younger, Ronnie was a forty-year-old actor whose last big picture had been filmed a decade ago. He was a divorced man whose ex-wife's image seemed to appear wherever Nancy looked, from the covers of fan magazines to the marquees. He was a man with two children whom he saw on Saturdays.

He had begun to grouse publicly about his career. "I'd love to be a louse," he wrote in the November 1950 *Silver Screen*. "You know the kind of fellow who leers at the dolls and gets leered back at? The guy who treats women rough and makes them love it. . . . You know why I'd love to be a louse? Because the public loves him. He makes money for his employers. He's talked about and swooned over. He grimaces forth from the pages of *Silver Screen* and people bring mouse-traps to *his* doorstep. And because the louse business is the sure, the open road to Fame in Films."

In his political life, Ronnie was still far from the rigid, right-wing views of Dr. Loyal. He was very much a liberal. In fact, in 1950 the campaign staff for Congresswoman Helen Gahagan Douglas rejected out of hand the idea of asking for Ronnie's help in Douglas's Senate race against a young, Red-baiting Richard Nixon. "He [Reagan] had a reputation as a far-out liberal, and we felt it would only imprint more deeply the idea of Helen as a liberal," said Lionel Van Derlin, who later was elected to Congress himself.

But a bitter quality had crept into his beliefs. As he considered the divorce a betrayal of his personal values, so he considered the Communists the betrayers of his political values. Although he didn't vengefully seek out Communists and fellow travelers to destroy them, he did spray them with an ugly, intemperate rhetoric that spread far beyond its intended targets, helping to fuel the fires of the McCarthy period. In an article in the January 1951 issue of *Fortnight,* he wrote that "several members of Congress are known Communists." Ronnie went on to write that during recent years, "even the most conservative newspapers went on blaring headlines about the 'dirty Reds'—not realizing they employed drama and book critics who (in the same editions) were praising the creative efforts of their little 'Red Brothers' while panning the work of all non-Communists."

Many of his contemporaries would look back on the whole business of trying to "clear" Communists as either morally ambivalent or a truly sordid business. In 1980, two weeks before he died, seventy-five-year-old Dore Schary, a liberal, admitted to journalists Ellen Farley and William K. Knoedelseder, Jr., that he regretted his role.

Another of Ronnie's colleagues in "clearing" people felt the same way. "I worked with Ronnie on the Motion Picture Industry Council," said Leonard Spigelgass. "It was the most wrongheaded thing I did in my whole life. We did it because we thought we could help people who were accused of being Communists. We gave them the opportunity to come to us and tell us that they weren't. Wrong! Wrong! Wrong! We were falling into the trap."

As Ronnie saw it, repudiating the party and standing up to condemn communism and naming names were heroic acts. Sterling Hayden was one of the first Communist party members to come to Ronnie and the MPIC for help. He went on to recant before the House Un-American Activities Committee. When asked what had happened to the Hollywood Communists, he said, "We ran into a one-man battalion named Ronnie Reagan." Having cleansed himself, Hayden went back to work as an actor. Years later Ronnie was still calling Hayden a hero for testifying, though the actor wrote in his 1963 autobiography, *Wanderer,* that "not often does a man find himself eulogized for having behaved in a manner that he himself despises."

It was a tortured time for a man to act well, and Ronnie had tried to act honorably. What set Ronnie apart from men like Spigelgass and Schary was that he never questioned the results of his acts. He refused to admit that there had ever been any blacklists, those arbitrary, privately circulated lists of names that destroyed the lives and careers of scores of innocent people. The only innocent people he saw hurt were those who had stood against the Communists and leftists. He simply would not or could not even try to understand the complicated political reality of his age.

Ronnie's life wasn't only politics. With his broken leg healed, he was finally working more steadily. In 1950 he filmed the comedy *Louisa* for Universal, in which he was well cast as a harassed husband alongside Ruth Hussey and Spring Byington. His next Warner film, *Storm Warning,* was an ambitious, crusading movie about the Ku Klux Klan, costarring Ginger Rogers and Doris Day. For the rest of his days, Ronnie would be ridiculed for his next Universal film, the 1951 trifle *Bedtime for Bonzo,* in which he costarred with a chimp. But his two Universal films and his last Warner film showed that Ronnie was a professional, a characterization he found not unflattering.

His outstanding distinction as an actor remained what it had been in 1937 in his first film, *Love Is on the Air.* He was extraordinarily likable. In 1951, readers of *Modern Screen,* the fan magazine that had most promoted Ronnie and Janie as the ideal couple, voted him their fifth most popular star, after John Wayne, Alan Ladd, Clark Gable, and Farley Granger.

Finally in 1951, after forty pictures and fourteen years in the business, Ronnie got his chance in a Western. *The Last Outpost* was based loosely on the true story of Confederate soldiers trying to capture gold being shipped west.

Western wranglers and actors were pretty much a breed apart from other movie people—a rough, manly, hard-drinking, hard-living lot who traveled from one Western to another like cowboys moving from ranch to ranch. With men like these, Ronnie had to prove himself. When the producers shipped Ronnie's horse, Tarbaby, to Arizona, some of the wranglers thought that the thoroughbred would fade in the 100-degree heat. But the horse did fine. So did Ronnie. "I found him one of the best horsebackers I ever worked with," said Bill Williams, a veteran of scores of Westerns.

These Universal films were produced by William H. Pine and William C. Thomas, specialists in ramming through adventure films on tight budgets, using a big name or two to draw the crowds. Rhonda Fleming, Ronnie's costar, was a stunning redhead. Until now she had been starred in main features, but the industry was in flux, and without a major studio behind her, she found herself trapped in a series of "B" films.

"Ronnie was in his element having his own horse," Fleming remembered. "I'm kind of a country girl too, and he was delightful to work with. He was very private. On the set he was very social, but he didn't socialize. He was very dedicated, very serious. The only time he would take time to discuss current issues was when we were changing sets."

Before his divorce and his fight against communism, Ronnie would have fit right in, but now he was a breed unto himself. On location in Tucson, Ronnie played the loner. "He was still very much on that kick of Americans who were out for the Russians," said Williams. "A lot of time was spent on the phone. He never came down to the coffee shop to be with the boys. He'd always have his meals in his room."

Early in 1952, Ronnie costarred in a second Warner feature with Virginia Mayo: *She's Working Her Way Through College.* The coeds at the local college where the film was being shot made eyes at Ronnie, but Warners made no pretense that this film was anything but a vehicle for their rising young star, Virginia Mayo. "This was a big picture written with me in mind," Mayo said. "He would never upstage. He was always a gentleman, Mr. Ideal, Mr. Perfect."

Since his divorce, Ronnie had been dining twice a week or more at Chasen's. The comfortable restaurant with its plush banquettes was a favorite Hollywood hangout that Ed Chasen, a former actor, had begun modestly when Ronnie was starting in Hollywood. Ronnie usually arrived early and ate his dinner sipping a glass of wine while he did his SAG paper work. Among the chatting guests, the half-inebriated drinkers at the bar, Ronnie appeared even more solemn.

For years Nancy's mother and her friends had discussed the "Nancy problem": When would she finally meet somebody and get married? Edith *knew* that Nancy's happiness lay in marriage. For fifteen years Edith's friends Colleen Moore and Lillian Gish had observed the constant stream of boyfriends. During the war, Lillian Gish, star of the silent film classic *Birth of a Nation,* foresaw that Nancy would never marry her fiancé, Jim White. "He's nothing like Dr. Loyal," she told Colleen Moore.

On one of his train trips to the East Coast, Ronnie met Edith and family friends in Chicago. From the beginning, Edith and Ronnie hit it off. When Gish took one look at Ronnie, she knew that Nancy had found her man. "It will take," she said, pointing out the similarities between Ronnie and Loyal. Colleen noticed it, too. As she saw it, both Dr. Davis and Ronnie were small-town Illinois men with great integrity and honesty, men who spoke out on the controversial issues of the day. She thought they even looked a little alike.

For a woman who sought a courtly Spenserian romance, Ronnie might seem a strange choice indeed. He was a man too scarred by past romantic failures to fall easily into an impassioned union typical of a youthful first love. But Ronnie was the first man Nancy had ever met who measured up to Dr. Loyal. She loved Ronnie. She wanted him, a man whom she could admire uncompromisingly, the way she admired Dr. Loyal.

Ronnie's heart was frozen. To him, spring was not the harbinger of summer but only of another winter. Nancy put up with all of Ronnie's ambivalence. She listened to his endless political talk as Janie had not. She even went with him to the premiere of Janie's film *The Blue Veil.*

Ronnie needed Nancy as much as she needed him. She believed in him as no one had before. Other actresses expected him to listen as much as he talked, but Nancy loved his every word. She thought his most banal political remark rang with profound meaning. She looked at him with pure adoration.

He was drawn to her out of trust in her belief in him, her willingness to weld herself to him, to support him with all her energy and love. It was a rare trait in Hollywood actresses, and the kind of love his mother had given his father. It was the Fifties dream of what a wife should be.

Eventually Ronnie introduced Nancy to Maureen and Michael and took her out to his new 350-acre ranch at Malibu Lake. He had bought it in the summer of 1951, and it symbolized his determination to make a new and bigger life. Nancy had learned to ride as a teenager and had ridden regularly at Smith. But, suddenly, she was a helpless little thing. "I remember the first time he got me up on a horse he told me to take charge," she wrote in her autobiography. "I was sitting so high up, I didn't think I could reach the ground."

"Nancy came through the horse stage with flying colors," reported *Modern Screen,* "she began to ride, badly at first, but later regularly and excellently. The kids admired this and Nancy scored one."

Nancy was more willing than most Hollywood actresses, obsessed with the limelight and night life, to recede into the privacy and anonymity of Ronnie's ranch. She did everything he wanted her to do on his new spread. Her idea of housecleaning was calling the maid, but she pitched in, cleaning up after the horses and hauling manure. She had never learned to cook, but she rustled up scrambled eggs once in a while. She was a good sport, hammering away, hauling water, helping with the sundry chores of the ranch as if she had been born on a 3,000-acre spread in Montana.

One evening Nancy invited her old New York friend Ron Fletcher to her apartment to meet Ronnie. "Ronnie talked about the problems of SAG," Fletcher remembered. "I was so into show biz that I was pretty bored. Nancy didn't talk very much. I think if he had wanted to talk about

The bride and groom with their best man (William Holden) and their matron of honor (his wife, Brenda Marshall), cutting the cake for the press. *(UPI)*

rubber cement, that would have been fine. Sometimes when you have a couple together he's so concerned with *his* success and she's so concerned about *hers*. She was allowing him to be first, but without any feeling of sacrifice.

"They were a stunning couple and very caring of one another. You could feel the trust there. They were totally involved with one another.

"I had seen her as a playmate and friend and buddy. Afterward, I asked her if she wanted to go out and have dinner. She said she didn't think it would be a good idea, like a good old-fashioned girl, because it wouldn't look right. I was kind of stunned by it."

For the first time in his life in a relationship with a woman, Ronnie was the undisputed lord and master. He loved it. Finally, after close to two years, he began to realize just how good Nancy made him feel. He wanted to be around her all the time. Now when he drove his green Cadillac convertible up to Chasen's for dinner at 7:45, he almost always had Nancy with him. They sat at a front table and had a leisurely meal. No photographers were allowed in the dark, paneled restaurant, but the gossip columnists didn't miss the meaning of Ronnie's regular dinner guest. ("The only logical follow-up . . . is a wedding cake some night and the corks popping out of champagne bottles.")

Ronnie was still outraged over their handling of his divorce and what he considered invasions of privacy. The last thing he wanted was a spate of articles about him and Nancy in the fan magazines.

The couple often spent quiet evenings with the Bill Holdens at their Toluca Lake home and with the Glenn Fords. New Year's Eve a friend dropped in and found Nancy in slacks, Ronnie in jeans, eating popcorn and watching TV. Soon after that, they went together to the annual Hollywood press agents' Panhandle dinner. A reporter at the same table noted that "Ronnie kept up a steady stream of conversation on everything from Hollywood public relations to what a pretty dress his date wore, and Nancy hung on every word he said."

What Nancy and Ronnie had, as Ronnie wrote later in his autobiography, was "a wonderful world of warmth and deep contentment." He had not fallen dramatically in love but had slowly, gently been led there. If anything, he took Nancy a little bit for granted.

One day he was sitting in a meeting of the Motion Picture Industry Council, but he wasn't listening to the discussion. He picked up a pad of paper, wrote a note and handed it to Bill Holden, who was sitting next to him. Holden read the scribbled message: "To hell with this, how would you like to be best man when I marry Nancy?"

"It's about time!" Holden exclaimed. The two men bolted up from the table and walked out.

There was not time even for an engagement ring. On March 4, 1952, Nancy and Ronnie were wed at the Little Brown Church in the Valley. Bill Holden and his wife, Ardis (Brenda Marshall), served as best man and matron of honor. If the new Mr. and Mrs. Reagan needed an example of the facades of Hollywood, they had one standing beside them. The Holdens weren't even talking to one another. Before the ceremony, they sat on opposite sides of the church.

Nancy had waited so long for this day. She was almost thirty-one years old. She had been dating Ronnie for two long years filled with as much uncertainty as romance. From the first date she had wanted him. No one but Nancy knew how hard she had worked and how patiently she had planned, how carefully she had wooed him, how hard she had tried with his kids, and the horses, and the ranch, and the politics.

"Let me be the first to kiss Mrs. Reagan," Holden said, standing before her.

"You're jumping the gun," Nancy said in a daze, not realizing that the ceremony was over.

"I am not," Holden said, leaning forward to kiss her.

The Holdens had arranged to have a photographer and a wedding cake at their home. Then Nancy and Ronnie drove away to spend their wedding night at the Riverside Inn. To the manager, Ronnie was still a star, and there was a bouquet of roses in their room. The next morning as they set out for Arizona, they left the roses with an elderly lady in a room across the hall.

11

STARTING OVER

Two weeks after their honeymoon, Ronnie took Nancy to the Academy Awards ceremony. Those who had known Ronnie before were amazed at how different he seemed. Gone were the youthful gaiety and frivolity that were such a part of Janie and Ronnie's early years together. In its place was a quiet, earnest and very loving relationship. The new Mr. and Mrs. Reagan didn't look like a Hollywood couple at all. One observer wrote that "the smiling dignified young couple looked like the more promising young civic-minded citizens of your most exclusive country club set."

The marriage changed both Nancy's and Ronnie's lives as much as a marriage can change two people. Nancy immediately cast off her career and contract at M-G-M as if they had been shackles. "Her thank-you to me was to say that she left Hollywood because all she was given were roles of people with aprons on—which hardly was true," Dore Schary reflected years later. "But that happens. People say things when they don't want to say something else."

At M-G-M, no one knew better than Benny Thau why Nancy's career had floundered and why she had jumped so completely into this new role. "She was an actress who wanted to make good in every way," Thau said. "But there were two hundred stars at M-G-M that she was competing with, and she was no Katharine Hepburn."

Nancy devoted all her energies to being Mrs. Ronald Reagan, housewife. With the "chameleonlike quality" that Ron Fletcher had noticed, she became what she thought the wife of Ronald Reagan should be. "Suddenly she became rather proper in a sense, almost suiting herself to his way of going," Fletcher remembered. "There was a letting go of a whimsical part

Lew Ayres and his concerned wife, Nancy Davis, in *Donovan's Brain. (EBC)*

of her personality. She became like a Chinese wife walking five paces behind."

While the Reagans looked for a house, they lived in Nancy's Westwood apartment, frequently stopping at Ronnie's place in Hollywood to get fresh clothes. The house they finally found was the perfect symbol of their atypical Hollywood marriage. The four-bedroom, ranch-style house stood on Amalfi Drive in Pacific Palisades, where houses cost an average of $24,000 in 1952 dollars, well beyond the aspirations of most Americans. Yet by Hollywood standards it was a modest home, not in one of the prestigious neighborhoods like Beverly Hills or Bel Air.

The area had been nothing but a few cattle ranches and lemon groves on bluffs overlooking the ocean when in the 1920s the Methodists had built a camp meeting grounds. Naming the area Pacific Palisades, the church began to develop what became a real town. By the time Ronnie and Nancy moved there in 1952, Pacific Palisades had grown beyond its Methodist beginnings. It was still a hybrid, open in its architecture and aspirations, and yet retaining many of the qualities of a very closed, upper-middle-class midwestern town, a Republican town that believed in the flag and in keeping things the way they are. As a local history of the town expressed it: "We sense the threat from natural elements of fire, earthquake and landslides as the steep seacliffs and canyons seek their angle of repose—and the threat of man, as well, ruining our Paradise."

"A lot of our friends felt we were foolish to move so far from the heart of Hollywood," Nancy wrote later. It was not a swanky place. In the early Fifties, less than a dozen stores lined Sunset and Antioch—only a market, a liquor store, a stationery store, and a dance studio run by the sister of Buddy Ebsen, the actor, whom Nancy had met years ago in summer stock. But the Palisades prided itself on its small-town atmosphere; clean ocean air and panoramic view of the Pacific.

The Reagans weren't the first Hollywood couple to migrate to the community; Gregory Peck, Joseph Cotten and Lawrence Welk all had homes within a mile of where the Reagans settled. But with all the new homes going up, the neighborhood had the feel of a suburban tract for the upper middle class. The Reagans' neighbors were mainly doctors, dentists, businessmen, upwardly mobile Americans who knew a good deal when they saw one, and bought in early.

Newly married couples almost always want some time by themselves before taking on the burden of family. But Nancy was pregnant. Her baby showers were like the house they had bought: substantial, simple and decidedly middle-class. Nanette Fabray remembered that the gifts were practical; no useless Hollywood silver trinkets, but blankets, bottle warmers and clothes.

Nancy gave birth to seven-pound Patricia Ann ("Patti") by cesarean section on October 22, 1952, seven and a half months after her wedding day. During the Fifties, America's favorite newlywed game was to count to nine, and there was speculation that Patti was not the only thing that was premature. Nancy seemed sensitive to the obvious implication; in her 1980 autobiography, she did not list Patti's birth date, though she did list her secondborn's.

Ronnie was faced with serious new difficulties. For most of his adult life, he had been a contract player at Warner Brothers, protected and nurtured like a hothouse rose. But now he had no one to watch out for him. He was an aging actor who had largely disappeared from the speculation and gossip of Hollywood. He had a new house with a big mortgage, a new wife, a new child and child-support payments from his previous marriage. His financial plight was well enough known that whenever he went through Chicago, Edith talked a local young PR man into taking Ronnie to lunch and putting it on the company bill.

Like so many other stars, Ronnie was being cast out of the studio gates to fend for himself. With exquisitely bad timing, he was looking for good roles during a period of great uncertainty in the industry. There were no stars on the street corners peddling apples or begging quarters, but the halcyon days of Hollywood were ending, Ronnie's movie career fading with them.

Pine and Thomas offered him a starring role opposite Rhonda Fleming in *Tropic Zone*. When he read the script about corruption in Central America, he could see that the movie was likely to be as rotten as its subject. But he accepted anyway.

Ronnie had never been one to insist upon all the perquisites of stardom, but he was used to being treated with a certain deference. Pine and Thomas weren't going to waste money on all the little niceties that the studios usually gave their stars. The only thing the producers squandered money on was bananas. Ronnie didn't complain. Between scenes he usually sat on the set telling stories.

Lewis R. Foster, the director, often berated the performers. Rhonda Fleming frequently started crying, while Ronnie attempted to mediate. "Ronnie would handle the director with kid gloves, with a little light humor," Fleming remembered. "At the time I thought it wasn't the strongest way to do it."

Toward the end of shooting, Foster told the crew that they would have to finish up that day, working until midnight. Fleming was not a temperamental star, but the director had pushed her and pushed her, and she had been up since four that morning.

"I'm exhausted," she said.

"Well, we've just got to finish tonight."

"I just can't."

Fleming was about to walk off the set, an act that would have seriously damaged her professional reputation, when Ronnie came forward and almost magically worked things out. He arranged things so his costar could rest in her dressing room, have a nap and eat some dinner before continuing. "He was the peacemaker," Fleming said. "I could only take so much. Ronnie prevented me from being called temperamental."

Ronnie realized that he had already dissipated much of his name in a series of bad movies like *Tropic Zone*. He had seen what such films did to a star. It was a sad business, and Ronnie wanted no more of it. He decided to wait to work until he was given a decent script.

After filming *Law and Order,* a Western as swaybacked as the horses, Ronnie dropped out of his contract, losing $150,000 worth of work. He sat at home turning down other unpalatable parts, looking at a financial situation that day by day grew more gloomy. During the war he had deferred paying federal income taxes and, with his 95-percent tax bracket, he had found himself in hock to Uncle Sam. He had had to put a second mortgage on one of his two properties. During his first year and a half of marriage, he was unable to fully furnish their living room. He needed money as much as he had ever needed it, but he continued to turn down parts that he considered unworthy.

Years after, Nancy would protect Ronnie's pride by suggesting that the early years of their marriage were idyllic. In actuality, Nancy had all the more difficult burdens of marriage thrown upon her immediately: a new baby, a husband whose career was faltering. Almost anyone can have a good marriage when things are going well. The real test is when they are not, when a man sits home waiting for a phone call that never comes, when a man realizes that he's showing his years. It was a hard time for Ronnie, and it would have been far harder without Nancy. Even then she was his supporter, his protector, his biggest fan.

Nancy acted as if she would have given almost anything to have been Ronnie's first and only wife. She appeared to be racked with insecurities, made worse by Jane Wyman's image. Here was Janie, one of the great stars of her time, a formidable, funny, difficult woman, lauded, applauded, gossiped about and criticized. And here was Nancy, a forgotten starlet, now a suburban housewife whose conversation centered on shopping and babies. Ronnie learned never to discuss Janie in Nancy's presence. But with Michael and Maureen spending Saturdays with their father, Janie seemed always present. Soon after the marriage there were reports of a dispute involving Nancy, "the Reagan kiddies" and Janie, "a fiercely devoted mama!"

How many would subsequently remember Ronald Reagan's movie career: *Law and Order*, Universal, 1954? *(MS)*

Five months after Patti's birth, Nancy costarred with Ronnie in a Ford TV Theater presentation of *First Born*. Ronnie played a serious, decent doctor as devoted to his practice as Ronnie had been to SAG. At the beginning of the half-hour drama, the doctor is married to a beautiful, artistic blonde played by Paula Corday. Upset over her husband's workaholic ways, the doctor's wife drives alone to a party and is killed in an automobile accident.

Nancy played the doctor's second wife, a decent, uninspiring woman who finds it difficult winning acceptance from the doctor's son. "I know [he loves me]," she told the son. "But not like that. I'm not beautiful. And I'll grow old. But he'll always remember her as lovely and childlike. Nothing's as important . . . as your first love and your first born."

For the first two years, Nancy had no close friends in Pacific Palisades. Then in 1954 Robert Taylor and his new German wife, Ursula, moved into a house on San Remo Drive within walking distance of the Reagans. Bob and Ronnie had known each other since their early Warner days, when Ronnie was touted as "the new Robert Taylor." Now Ronnie and Bob could joke about it, for Taylor's suave, almost too-perfect looks were nothing like Ronnie's.

Ursula and Nancy became close friends. The two women had much in common. Ursula was a former actress and had arrived in the States under contract to RKO. She had two children from a previous marriage and had given up her career to build a new family. When pudgy little Patti threw her periodic tantrums, Ursula was there to reassure Nancy from experience that her daughter would one day get over such antics. Nancy finally had a real female friend, and a relationship without jealousies and insecurities. This was not a showy friendship to be paraded through the fancy restaurants of Beverly Hills, but two mothers sitting around the pool discussing their children. The two families spent many birthdays together at the Reagan ranch. When the Davises came for Christmas each year, Bob Taylor and Edith would go off in a corner and Nancy's mother would tell the handsome actor her latest dirty jokes.

Once in a while the two young mothers would get away, for a luncheon, a fashion show, or sometimes even a trip with their husbands to Tijuana, Mexico, for a bullfight. Leaving their car at the border, the two couples would take a taxi, careening with abandon down the streets of the city. One time Nancy wanted to tell the driver to slow down, but she could not bring herself to do it. Then she suddenly relaxed. "Look," she smiled, pointing to the baby shoes dangling from the rearview mirror. "He must be all right. He must know what he's doing. He has a baby."

Ursula saw a Nancy Reagan who had found happiness in the sanctuary of marriage. She didn't need anything but her husband and family. "We spent quiet evenings together," Ursula remembered. "We weren't club people, party people. The affection between Ronnie and Nancy was the same even then, Nancy the perfect wife, always there one hundred percent for him."

Pacific Palisades was not what Ursula called "a neighborly place" and the Reagans made no other close friends. They took almost no part in local civic activities, and Ronnie didn't bother transferring his American Legion membership from Hollywood. During most of the Fifties, the Reagans' social circle remained tight-knit, narrow and family-oriented. Among their other close friends were A. C. Lyles and his wife, Martha. The two couples had double-dated during their courtship. A. C. was a producer, a man of genial, warm temperament, and the two burgeoning families hit it off.

The Reagans also regularly saw Robert and Goldie Arthur. Robert Arthur had produced *Louisa,* the 1950 comedy in which Ronnie played a middle-aged architect. *Louisa* was the kind of light, very American comedy that left audiences feeling good not only about their evening's entertainment but about people in general. The Arthurs had met Nancy at a World Series game in New York right after the war. They thought that the match between Ronnie and Nancy was as good a job of casting as Hollywood had ever produced. Like the Taylors and the Lyleses, the Arthurs were "just folks," successful, unpretentious people with strong, traditional values. The Arthurs didn't have any children and the two couples usually dined together weekly at Chasen's. On New Year's Day, they went to the Rose Bowl game together.

"It was just great warmth," said Robert Arthur. "We'd all get together. The Davises would come in from Phoenix or Chicago, Moon would come up with his wife—all part of a tradition. You can see that Ronnie's values aren't politically motivated or brought out of left field. They're just things he's grown up with."

Ronnie's agent kept him going by plugging him into one thing or another. Ronnie went so far as to agree to appear as a headliner in Las Vegas. He could not sing, tell dirty jokes, dance or do card tricks, but he was amiable enough to emcee the act. He received good reviews and more Las Vegas offers, but he knew that he did not belong, and after two weeks he and Nancy returned to Los Angeles.

In February 1954, just before his Las Vegas debut, Ronnie complained to Bob Thomas, a Los Angeles journalist, about the end of the studio star system. It seemed that almost everyone was being sent packing, even Clark Gable and Greer Garson. "The studios are driving us into other mediums," Ronnie said. "Few actors are supported by the studios alone.

The Reagans' first close friends and neighbors in the Pacific Palisades: Robert Taylor and his wife, Ursula Thiess, 1954. *(UPI)*

The others have to spread themselves into radio, TV, legit theater, nightclubs and wherever their services are in demand."

Later that year, Taft Schreiber of MCA, the giant entertainment corporation, told Ronnie about a possible role introducing a new weekly television anthology series, "The GE Theater." Schreiber liked Ronnie personally and wanted him to succeed. Schreiber owed his position as head of MCA's new Revue Productions to a SAG decision in which Ronnie played an instrumental role.

It had long been one of the few fundamental rules in Hollywood that if you were an agent, you did not produce films. An agent was supposed to get the most money for his client; if he was producing the film, he had a conflict of interest. Yet in Hollywood now everyone was sticking their fingers in other aspects of the industry. And on a movie-by-movie basis, SAG was willing to waive this stipulation.

What Ronnie had done shortly before leaving the SAG presidency was unprecedented. On July 3, 1952, after a series of meetings, Ronnie sent a letter to MCA granting the agency the blanket right to produce films.

Within a few years, MCA was a dominant force in show business. In television, the forty or so shows that Revue Productions produced each week far surpassed the output of other programming suppliers. (In 1959, Ronnie returned for another term as SAG president.)

When Schreiber wanted to give Ronnie a proper test for the new "GE Theater," he simply gave him the lead in an episode of another MCA-produced television series, "Medallion Theater." After the live program was finished, Henry Denker, the coproducer, remembered that "the cameras were kept running while two MCA guys got Reagan up against a gray background. They filmed an opening, middle break and closing as if he were host on a series."

Ronnie fit the role of host like a light bulb fit a socket. He exuded a healthy, optimistic quality that GE wanted to project, an optimism doubtless aided by his new salary: $125,000 a year. That wasn't all, either, since according to Arthur Park, his personal agent at MCA, Ronnie also received "a very fancy sum" from Revue Productions.

Week after week, "The GE Theater" was one of the best drama anthology series on television. Almost from its premiere, "The GE Theater" was among the twenty most popular programs on television. Ronnie starred occasionally on the half-hour program, including Thanksgiving 1960 when he played opposite Nancy in *A Turkey for the President*. In his role as host, Ronnie introduced stars such as Joan Crawford, Alan Ladd and Fred Astaire in their dramatic debuts on television. Introducing the program was hardly arduous work. Sometimes Ronnie would come down from his ranch and knock off half a dozen introductions in an afternoon.

In 1956, with the success of the program, Ronnie built a new house high on a bluff just a few minutes from their old ranch-style home on Amalfi. With this new house cradled on the secluded plateau, the Reagans graduated to the Riviera, the more exclusive part of the Palisades. The Riviera is a high ridge protected from outsiders by the wilds of Rustic, Sullivan and Mandeville canyons. When the Reagans moved into this ultramodern residence designed by architect Bill Stephensen, San Onofre Drive was still an oiled-down dirt road on which only a few homes had been built. Even when ten more houses were added and the street was paved thanks to Ronnie's petitioning, the Reagans' house remained isolated. Beyond stone gates bedecked with white azaleas, surrounded by trees, up a hedge-lined driveway, the house could not be seen from the road.

As the voice of General Electric, it would not have done for the Reagans to have anything but an all-electric home—indeed, the most completely electric home in the nation. That was GE's gift to Ronnie. Each department vowed to put in its newest gadgets and improvements. "It'll have everything electric but a chair," Ronnie joked at the time.

It was a wonder to behold, with the 3,000-pound switchbox on the back wall, big enough to power a town. But guests at the five-bedroom, 4,764-square-foot, stone-fronted house looked in vain for a simple switch to perform the mundane business of turning the lights on and off.

Ronnie and Nancy had often climbed the hill to watch construction. They carved their initials into the wet cement of the swimming pool and in the three-car garage. Hidden from the prying view of the world below, they stood on the sun deck and looked out on the Pacific Ocean.

For Nancy, everything was new. But this was Ronnie's second "dream house." The house he had shared with Janie—with its hunting prints and rustic, manly, comfortable furnishings—had been *their* house, in decor and spirit. But this sprawling white California residence on San Onofre Drive was really the house that Nancy built. Ronnie liked to trim the hedges with his fancy new equipment and putter around the swimming pool, but the house was Nancy's.

Nancy's old friend, Leonard Spigelgass, describes Nancy's style as "conservative Chicago—everything must be the best and match." And so it did. Nancy liked bright colors and pastels, soft corals and pale greens, and the decor was feminine and flowery. Two matching yellow couches framed an ebony cocktail table and faced a fireplace and eighteen-foot floor-to-ceiling windows looking out onto the pool and patio. The Reagans had few books or original works of art, and the house, always so neat, and surrounded by bright bougainvillaeas, looked like a picture from *House and Garden*.

Nancy immediately set out to make the street itself meet her standards.

She and Ronnie unsuccessfully petitioned for streetlights. She later managed to get "no parking" and "Caution: Children at Play" signs installed to make driving up the steep road safer. Her neighbor, Maribe Nowell, found a certain irony in that. "She was the fastest and scariest driver of them all," she said.

On Saturdays, Ronnie usually drove to Beverly Glen in Bel Air to pick up Michael or Maureen for the day. Janie's house was in an area more appropriate for a star, just around the corner from Debbie Reynolds's place. Janie's house had been burglarized more than once, and the plate underneath the rug on the stairs was so sensitive that Michael was forever setting it off.

Michael was a small, feisty lad who often got into trouble in school. He loved to see his dad pulling up in his wood-paneled Ford station wagon. One weekend at the ranch, Ronnie showed his son a palomino horse called Rebel that he said he was keeping for a friend. In the meantime, he said, he wanted to teach Mike to ride the horse. On Mike's birthday, the boy walked out to the stable and there stood Rebel wearing a big birthday ribbon. "I went absolutely crazy," Mike said later, remembering one of the happiest moments of his childhood.

Michael was devilish. One day when Ronnie yelled for his two kids to come and get into the station wagon for the trip home, Mike and Maureen were already waiting for him. Ronnie was not a suspicious father, but when he noticed something moving underneath a blanket, he figured Mike was up to his tricks. As Mike pulled the blanket off his favorite goat, he begged Ronnie to let him take the animal home with him. Ronnie agreed, but when he deposited the two kids and the goat on Janie's doorstep, he accelerated away like a drag racer. As soon as Janie opened the door, the goat dashed into the living room and promptly defecated on the off-white rug.

The goat spent the night tethered on the front lawn. By early morning, the animal had chewed enough flowers and shrubs that the front of the house looked like a set for *Tobacco Road*. After one look at the lawn, Janie called Ronnie and gave him five minutes of withering Wyman, a performance that got Ronnie back to the house to pick up the goat almost as fast as he had left.

Another time, Ronnie drove Michael and his close friend, Doug Prestine, to the ranch, stopping at the Malibu Lumber Company. The two boys were looking forward to a weekend of romping around the ranch, playing in the barn and riding horses. But when they saw the cans of white paint, the three brushes and three pairs of gloves, they knew that Ronnie had other ideas.

Ronnie wasn't quite a Tom Sawyer, making the boys trade their prize possessions for a chance to paint the fence. But Michael and Doug enjoyed the work. As the day wore on, Ronnie and the two boys grew giddier and giddier. Finally, someone threw a dab of paint, and before long all three weekend painters were as white as snowmen. Nancy came out of the house, took a few pictures for posterity and sat with them, trying to get the paint off.

There were many good times, but there was little of the mundane, day-to-day business of fathering for Ronnie. As for Nancy's role as a surrogate mother, in her early years she had been brought up largely by relatives. She knew what it meant to be an orphan by fiat. She might have reached out to the two children to understand them and love them. She wasn't mean or hostile to Michael and Maureen, but it appeared that she didn't want Ronnie weighed down with the complex burden of his first marriage; she wanted him fresh as his laughter. This new marriage and new family were so distant from Ronnie's first marriage that years later Michael said that he often felt jealous of a "First Family" of which he didn't consider himself and Maureen a part.

Hollywood children were often sent to boarding schools at an early age, and Maureen and Michael were both shipped off. Janie loved her children, but she was constantly working. She had married again, to Freddie Karger, a bandleader. Michael spent two years with Ronnie and Nancy during high school, but almost all that time he was either away at an Arizona boarding school or off in summer camp.

"I didn't get to know my mother and father personally until I was twenty-five," said Michael. "Mom was working double time. I was more or less raised by Carrie, who was mom's cook. I would go to her with my problems and my inner feelings.

"Many of the kids I went to school with had money," Michael said, remembering his years in boarding school. "They had the bicycles, the toys. Their families took care of them. Mom said that 'you build men, not boys.' And dad didn't believe in giving kids a lot of things. You meet other kids and they go home every night. I was jealous because these kids could spend time with their parents."

Maureen felt the divorce like an enormous, unpalatable dose of adulthood. A divorce "makes you grow up pretty fast," she said. "I guess it's unusual to be at a very young age and realize you have to take care of yourself and make your own decisions—but then, if we had lived at home, it would have been the same because my mother's favorite line was 'If I get hit by a Mack truck tomorrow, you're going to have to take care of yourself.'"

Patti was Nancy's real daughter. She was raised with an omnipresent, smothering concern that in its way was as great a burden for her as the lack of it had been for Maureen and Michael.

When it came time for Patti to go to school, she could have gone to the first-rate public schools in Pacific Palisades as did most of the children on San Onofre Drive. But Nancy wanted her daughter to have the same kind of private education that she had had. In 1958 Patti went to the John Thomas Dye School* in Bel Air. Cathryn Dye, the school's matriarch, had come from Iowa in the 1920s. In 1929 she and her Indiana-bred husband, John, had founded the strongly conservative, family-oriented school. To be admitted, children and their parents had to pass the rigorous scrutiny of the formidable woman the students called "Auntie Cathryn." Auntie Cathryn didn't care how much money parents had, how fancy their connections; if they didn't seem concerned, socially conservative folks, their child was not admitted. Auntie Cathryn thought that the glittery Hollywood world was synonymous with sex and salaciousness, and she took it as a mark of honor that there were so few movie offspring at Dye. But Nancy and Ronnie didn't seem like Hollywood at all, and little Patti was admitted.

Nancy drove in a car pool that took a group of the children back and forth from school. At Dye, Patti wore an old-fashioned navy-and-white checked pinafore with a white, puffed-sleeved blouse. She attended classes in the huge main building that looked like a great Iowa barn complete with its own weather vane atop the bell tower. Patti was a quiet little thing, shuttled between her home and this genteel school that was far from the realities of the world below in Los Angeles.

In part the Reagans sent Patti and later Ron, Jr., to Dye because the school espoused what they considered their values. They were the values of a small midwestern town at its best—honest and caring, but parochial and narrow. "There were no black students, of course, and I was one of only three or four Jews," said Francine Applebaum Warner, who was a year ahead of Patti. "If there was a question about race, we got a lecture on skin pigmentation and that was that. There were two blacks who worked there—the cook and the janitor—and we would have been severely disciplined if we had treated them with any less respect than we showed the Dyes."

The principle of good citizenship was instilled daily at the school, a citizenship that basically meant good manners. Each Monday, Auntie Cathryn presided over a good-citizenship assembly. Awards were given not

* The school was then called the Brentwood Town and Country School. The following year it was renamed the John Thomas Dye School in honor of the Dyes' son, killed in World War II.

so much for specific deeds as for quiet demeanor and consideration for others. "By being good, you were contributing to the community by not making it hard on other people," said Warner. Every morning on the plateau overlooking the fashionable neighborhood of Bel Air, students raised the American flag and recited the Pledge of Allegiance and the Salutation to the Dawn, a Hindu thanks for the day and its opportunities.

For the traditional May Day celebration, Patti wore a white gown and danced with the other young girls and boys. Ronnie and Nancy were always there with other parents looking on proudly. She was on the Mothers Club Board and attended monthly meetings to plan for the special events. One year Nancy was in charge of the maypole, seeing that it was properly fixed with ribbons and set into the earth.

Whenever Ronnie appeared at the school, whether to see a play, or to sing with the white-clad children in the candlelight Christmas caroling, or to man the hot-dog booth at the yearly fair, no one treated him like a well-known movie actor. He was just another dad, a role that he appeared to relish.

Patti went through her years at Dye making little impression on most people. She had outgrown her plump stage and had become tall, slender and gawky. She was so tall that she stood a head above her classmates and didn't look quite right in her school dress. "I don't remember her except as being shy," one of her classmates recalled. "She had very little self-esteem, but maybe that was the way kids were."

Whatever ambitions Nancy had had for herself, she now transferred to her husband and children. Her final film, *Hellcats of the Navy,* a 1957 movie in which she costarred with Ronnie, was a dreary bit of business, nothing to make Nancy wish for a renewed career. She was a housewife and mother. She reveled in that role. But she was not the typical suburban wife. She could not cook, and while most women also had to clean their houses, mop and polish, do dishes, and wash clothes, Nancy was freed of most of this by her housekeeper, Anne Owens.

Nancy would do the grocery shopping at Brentwood Market, a maze of specialty shops that catered to a well-to-do clientele. Occasionally she would pop into Colvy's in Pacific Palisades to buy Ronnie a pair of C-long pajamas in pima cotton, but neither of the Reagans were seen in town much. On his way to the ranch, Ronnie might drop off a toaster or iron to get it repaired at a little electric shop, but that was about it. Nancy and Ronnie were leading as private lives as they could, and there were few who sought to intrude upon them.

In later years Ronnie would talk so much of the Bel Air Presbyterian

Nancy and Ronnie, together on the screen, in *Hellcats of the Navy*, 1957—her last movie role. *(MS)*

Church and its pastor, Rev. Moomaw, that it was assumed the Reagans were members. But they were not, and only attended infrequently.

Ever since Patti's birth, the Reagans had wanted another child. During those first years of marriage, Nancy had several miscarriages. She and Ronnie badly wanted a boy. Ronnie wanted a boy because he was such a boy himself. He wanted a son who could go romping through the ranch, a son to teach to ride, a son who would play catch with his dad in the yard. Nancy wanted a son too, because Ronnie wanted one so badly, and because by giving birth to his natural son, she would give him something Jane never had.

When she became pregnant once again, Nancy took the advice of the physician who had delivered Patti. She spent three months in bed. On May 20, 1958, again by cesarean section, she gave birth to Ronald Prescott Reagan.

Ursula Taylor went to the hospital with Ronnie and Edith, who had come to help her daughter. Ursula and her husband, Bob, were named Ron's godparents. A year later, Nancy spent hours waiting for Ursula to give birth to her daughter, Tessa, of whom Ronnie was named godfather.

As Ron, Jr.,* and Patti grew up, Nancy became very demanding. Her closest neighbor, Maribe Nowell, who lived just across the street, remembered what a perfectionist Nancy was. "Ronnie's nursemaid used to bring him down here to play with my grandchildren's toys," Mrs. Nowell said. "He always liked the dirty old ones and he'd carry them home with him. They'd always be returned cleaner a few days later. The nurse told me that Nancy demanded absolute perfection from the children. She felt that she was in competition with Jane Wyman and her children and wanted them to be just as good or better so Ronnie couldn't compare them—not that he would."

"I have a distinct memory that Mrs. Reagan wasn't interested in the emotional aspects of the children, the giving, the nurturing," said a childhood friend of Patti's. "She was only interested in the outside appearance, having these nice, bright kids. Mrs. Reagan very much doted . . . on her son, and everything Patti did was wrong: the way she talked, the way she dressed. Even when we were sitting at the swimming pool, Mrs. Reagan would criticize. Mrs. Reagan used to listen to us talking."

Ursula Taylor saw Nancy differently, as "a natural mother." She remembered how, when the two couples went out to dinner, leaving Patti at home with her English nannie, the child would press her nose up against

---

*Ronald Prescott is technically not a Junior since his middle name is different. But for clarity in this book, he will be called Ron, Jr.

Christmas, 1960. From their Pacific Palisades home, Ronnie, Nancy, Patricia Ann (eight) and Ronald Prescott Reagan (two and a half) host a moving dramatization of *The Other Wise Man* for *The General Electric Theater,* CBS TV. *(LGC)*

the window. Seeing this, Nancy would run back several times and say "I love you." "That child was smothered with love," said Mrs. Taylor.

Nancy's closest friend at this time admits that "Nancy was very protective with her children, especially with little Ronnie. She had wanted a male child so badly that she was overly protective of him during those first years."

Nancy was a woman who dressed perfectly even when she sat out by the swimming pool, and she wanted Ron, Jr., and Patti to be just as perfect. She had many of the very fears to which the television and magazine ads played. Like so many women of her generation, she had a horror of getting caught with a dirty living room, or with scuffed linoleum, or with holes in her children's shoes.

Dr. Loyal had taught her the regimens and safety of discipline. Nancy acted as if she sought to control her children's lives. She also had the fears of a southern Californian, the nagging foreboding that one day all this might end. To prosperous southern Californians, life seemed only a quarter-step away from paradise. Yet they feared that at any moment it might be taken away, by natural disasters, thieves, changing life-styles and other unseen forces. The Reagans had friends whose careers had gone from incredible fame to nothing in a matter of a few years. They had friends with homes in the Hollywood hills, villas propped on the side of great brown hills like squatters' shacks. One earthquake and it would all be gone. Pacific Palisades was full of classic California homes, open in spirit and form, yet with their own security systems and security patrols to guard against theft.

During the dry season, there was the fear of brush fires. In 1961, a devastating fire swept down from the hills into Bel Air, destroying over 600 homes on a ridge that included Dye School. Nanette Fabray was the carpool driver that morning, and she had scarcely gotten home when she received a call to return to the school. Nancy drove to the school as well to pick up Patti and three-year-old Ron, Jr., who had just entered Dye's nursery school. From fifteen miles away, the smoke could be seen filling the sky, like the aftermath of a bombing raid. For the last few miles up the hill, the police had set up flares to guide the cars through the swirling, enveloping smoke. Children piled into the cars helter-skelter, and both Nanette and Nancy drove off without their own children. "Nancy and I had the same situation," Fabray said. "She was as distraught as I was. It was very frightening. But we had to stay with the children we had with us. It was awful, a terrible fire."

All the children were safe; but minutes after the last car departed, the fire reached the school's barnlike main building and burned it to the ground, taking with it all the records, an extensive library and the antiques that the Dyes had laboriously collected.

Although Fabray had known Nancy only through the studios, they saw more of each other as mothers at Dye. Fabray's son, Jamie, was in the same class as Ron, Jr. She would drive her son to the Reagan ranch for little Ron's birthday parties. "They'd have clowns for the children or a little rodeo that the kids would put on themselves," Fabray said. "There would be around ten to fifteen children, mostly from Dye. Ron and my son were the two largest boys in the class. They were very shy and very quiet. They were observers who would stand back and watch. Nancy was always very sweet and gentle with Ron. She was so proud of him."

On "The GE Theater," Ronnie introduced the stories and starred in an occasional half-hour drama. His other work consisted of lecturing around the country as GE's "corporate ambassador." For a total of about three months a year, he went from plant to plant, press conference to press conference, luncheon to luncheon. He loved to talk, and it was almost like running for office. He didn't just roll out the same tired speech wherever he went. He listened to his audiences and then tinkered with his words, stitching in a new anecdote there, ripping out a tired joke, enriching the whole tapestry of story and emotion. As he rode trains across America, usually accompanied by a PR aide, he clipped newspaper stories, tore out articles from the *Saturday Evening Post* and jotted down facts he had heard.

When he had started out on the GE trail, his speech was a politically benign mixture of patriotism linked to a general defense of Hollywood. But as the years went by, the speech developed into a vigorous, impassioned defense of American capitalism, and an attack on big government.

As Ronnie evolved into a right-wing populist, there were those who thought that Nancy instigated it. "He did meet Nancy, his wife, around that time," said Dore Schary, not the only person to note that coincidence. Others saw the figure of Loyal Davis behind it, pointing out that the Reagans had even spent their honeymoon in Arizona with Loyal and Edith.

Ronnie's brother, Neil, was ready to take some of the credit. He had registered as a Republican six months after Roosevelt took office. Neil was as conservative as Ronnie had been liberal, and over the years they had had fierce, endless arguments. Neil was a success in his own right, a top executive at the McCann Erickson advertising agency. What irritated Neil was now that Ronnie had seen the light, he acted as if he were the one who had discovered conservatism. "From early on I started to campaign on him, things like his supporting Helen Gahagan Douglas. I made snide remarks about that. When I'd give one of my speeches to him, he'd say, 'Ah, you're just saying that.' When he had become a conservative too, I'd remind him. And he'd say, 'I never said that.' "

Others have gone so far as to credit (or blame) *Time* magazine publisher Henry Luce and his formidable wife, Clare Boothe Luce. "I would be flattered to think that I had an impact on his thinking," said Mrs. Luce, who as a playwright/congresswoman/diplomat has intrigued many of the more interesting men of her time. "I think his ideas were formed through his experience with the guild, seeing that there were subversives in these do-good organizations. He was a healthy, normal guy who liked to saw wood. Then he started to socialize with the better class in L.A. People haven't liked to admit that the rich are often smarter and better."

In the late Fifties, Ronnie was increasingly in a different social milieu. He had a conservative wife. He was living in a conservative neighborhood. Now traveling in high corporate circles, he had come to see the freebooting American entrepreneur as America's great hero. The fact that GE executives had been convicted of price-fixing, an onerous crime against free enterprise, was an irony that did not trouble him.

During his liberal years, Ronnie had looked at one side of the political canvas and seen that workers were often abused and cheated; that people needed the protection and succor of government; that unions protected workers against the arbitrary will of large corporations. Now he was looking elsewhere and he saw other truths: that government bureaucrats often stifled the energy and creativity of business; that big government was a danger to the individual liberties of Americans; that people often wanted to be left alone to solve problems their own ways. He was incapable of integrating these varied, contradictory truths into his own thinking. Truth to him was almost always an emotional reality, and he took these new truths and ran with them as he had run with his older, more liberal truths.

In the late 1950s, Ronnie started pushing highly ideological, generally right-wing programs onto "The GE Theater," much the way he had accused Communists and their sympathizers of pushing pro-Communist material into movies. In 1961, for instance, he wanted to do a program featuring three young Russians, one of them an ex–Red Army officer, talking about their experiences in Russia. It was assuredly a worthy idea, but hardly the typical dramatic fare of a popular television series.

At the studio Ronnie often disagreed with Stanley Rubin, who in the early 1960s was senior producer. The two men had met at Fort Roach, and Rubin was still very much a liberal. With his new contract, Ronnie had a right to produce several shows a year. The programs he wanted to do were, in Rubin's words, "almost exclusively political, highly anti-Communist. One was about a teacher who was a spy. His suggestions either came from the *Reader's Digest* or the *Saturday Evening Post* and I began to suspect these were the only reading he ever did."

Rubin was not the only person to comment on Ronnie's choice of reading material. A few weeks after "The GE Theater" presented Irving Stone's drama of Lincoln's youthful romance, *Love Is Eternal,* the historical novelist invited Ronnie to a large dinner party. When the Stones' houseguest learned that Ronnie was coming to the party, she asked to be seated next to him. Afterward, in the living room, the novelist asked the houseguest about her dinner companion.

"As soon as we sat down, Reagan said he had read a *Saturday Evening Post* story that morning," Stone remembered the woman saying. "He told the whole story from beginning to end, without missing a comma. He spent the entire hour and a half telling that entire story."

On the set, Ronnie was well liked. He would bring in eggs from the ranch for the crew and sit around telling Errol Flynn stories for hours. But Ronnie could be a terrible bore, particularly when he started talking politics. At the TV studios, Rubin and Ronnie were having many heated political discussions. Even in the most fervid debate, Ronnie was his old amiable self. But the constant arguments were getting on the producer's nerves. "I came home one night," Rubin said, "and I said to my wife, 'I'm not going to fight with him anymore. I'm not going to have any political arguments. He sits there and invents his own statistics. It's spoiling the fun we're having on the show.' "

Ronnie's political ideas were beginning to spoil the fun for GE as well. He had started attacking the Tennessee Valley Authority, proud symbol of New Deal activism and a General Electric client, gathering $50 million in government contracts. Some of the GE executives weren't about to stand by while their employee attacked TVA. Ronnie learned that he was in grave danger of being fired. After hearing that Ralph Cordiner, the chairman of the board, had defended him and said he wasn't about to dictate what anyone at GE said, Ronnie called the chairman.

"I understand you have a problem and it concerns me," Ronnie said, speaking to the executive for the first time.

"I'm sorry you found out about that," Cordiner said, reassuring Ronnie that he could go on speaking his mind.

"Mr. Cordiner, what would you say if I said I could make my speech just as effectively without mentioning TVA?" Ronnie asked.

"Well, it would make my job easier."

Ronnie neatly exorcised TVA from his speech, substituting another example of what he considered government waste.

Despite Cordiner's assurances that he could say whatever he pleased, Ronnie's decision to stop attacking TVA probably saved his job for another season or two. With John F. Kennedy as the new president, and millions of dollars in government contracts in the offing, Ronnie was marching to a different drummer. "An executive for GE came to me," Rubin recalled. "He said, 'What if next year we had not only Ronnie as host but three or four hosts?'

"I said, 'What about Ronnie?'

"He said, 'Well, he could be one of the four or maybe not at all. Truthfully, some of the highest executives at GE are embarrassed by the overly conservative tone of his speeches.'

"I kept that story from Ronnie. I went and discussed it with my boss, Taft Schreiber at MCA. He rarely interfered, but he got into the act and it was squashed."

Schreiber's move only temporarily quelled the disquiet. All across America, Ronnie had become a much desired speaker, not to talk about toasters and television sets but to talk about "Encroaching Government Control" and "Our Eroding Freedoms," speeches that seemed aimed at the Democratic administration. Electric ovens and hair dryers are bought as much by liberals as conservatives, and the more popular a right-wing activist Ronnie became, the less desirable he was as GE's corporate ambassador. In 1962, pleading bad ratings, GE canceled the program.

Nancy was always supportive of Ronnie. She was by no means a woman of pure social calculation, but she pursued successful people. In a society of such fluidity as Los Angeles, she knew that a person was known primarily by externals. One could not afford a bad friend, a bad neighborhood, a bad school.

At the Dye School, Auntie Cathryn was the director of the children's education and in part the arbiter of their parents' social success. Among the women who took turns car-pooling the children to school was Mary Jane Wick, wife of Charles Z. Wick, a Los Angeles producer and businessman. Mary Jane, a blond former model, was spending most of her time raising five children and caring for her husband. Her oldest son, nicknamed C.Z., was in Patti's class. Charlie was a character that Sinclair Lewis might have invented, a diminutive, brash Hollywood hustler whose greatest production was *Snow White and the Three Stooges,* and who made a timely jump into a burgeoning new industry: nursing homes.

The Reagan children and the Wick children hit it off as well as their parents, and the two families developed a friendship. Ronnie enjoyed Charlie, but Ronnie was not a man of great or easy intimacies and the friendship between the wives was far more serious.

The two women became involved with the Colleagues, one of Los Angeles's most prestigious charities. The Colleagues was formed in 1950 to raise funds for the Barton House, a halfway home for troubled women. In the early Sixties when Nancy became an active member, the Colleagues were planning to build an infant-care center for battered children. Every May they put on the clothing sale of clothing sales. "We called it our glamour-clothes sale," said Virginia Milner, an L.A. society lady whose twenty-year friendship with Nancy developed in the Colleagues. "There were so many movie people around who would wear clothes once for a ceremony or show and give them to us."

For many years the sale was held in a private home in Bel Air that gained nationwide familiarity pictured as the home of television's Beverly Hillbillies. The most popular room was the so-called blue room, which housed the most coveted and expensive dresses. This room was Mary Jane Wick's special project. The ladies not only gave clothes, they sometimes bought them. Sorting through the clothes, pricing them, taking her turn as a saleslady, Nancy was relentlessly charming.

Getting into the Colleagues was as difficult as being chosen for the most exclusive sorority in college. Money wasn't enough. A new member had to be attractive and stylish. She had to be "with it," not a far-out liberal, mind you, but aware of social and cultural nuances. The Colleagues provided Nancy not only with a way to add an occasional inexpensive addition to her wardrobe but with a new kind of friend. During the monthly luncheon meeting for the members, Nancy planted her social pitons higher yet toward the peaks of L.A. society. Through the sixty Colleagues, she either met or became a social friend of some of the women who would later become known in the press as "the Group," the most publicized clique in Los Angeles. Marion Jorgensen was the head cashier and treasurer. Betsy Bloomingdale always donated a wide selection of items to the sale.

The ladies of the Colleagues were serious indeed about their projects. They roamed the precincts of Los Angeles in Mercedes and Rolls-Royces, picking up boxes of clothes, and gowns on hangers. Nancy was driving only a station wagon at the time, but she was one of them. For the most part these ladies did not have full-time careers; but for Nancy and many of her compatriots, charity work and social life were practically a career by themselves, bringing honor, camaraderie and access to greater wealth and celebrity. The ladies were relentless gossips. They knew who was having an affair or a face-lift, whose children were on the verge of being disowned, whose daughter weighed 200 pounds, which husband had his finger bitten off by an enraged mistress. But these were *their* stories; to the outside world, they presented a solid front.

Nancy had other new friends through Ronnie's contacts. Ronnie had first met Holmes Tuttle, one of L.A.'s biggest car dealers, in 1946 when he had bought a Ford. Now that Ronnie and Nancy were a couple traveling in Los Angeles's non-Hollywood social circles, the Tuttles began seeing the Reagans. One year the Tuttles invited Ronnie and Nancy to go with them to the Autumn Cotillion, one of the many charity balls. That evening, Tuttle introduced Ronnie to Earle and Marion Jorgensen, whom Nancy got to know much better in the Colleagues. Ronnie was his inevitably affable self, and he was impressed by the tough-talking, conservative tycoon. The son of a sailing captain, Jorgensen had started working as an office boy when he was thirteen. After World War I, he had taken $200 and a rented desk and built the giant Jorgensen Steel Company.

Nancy seemed to be picking up rich new friends wherever she went. The Reagans had met Alfred and Betsy Bloomingdale at a party. Bloomingdale had developed Diners Club, one of the major credit cards, and he was a multimillionaire. Betsy was a vivacious, striking woman, perfectly coiffed and groomed. Nancy admired her style and the clothes she wore to the Colleagues luncheons, but she had her first long talks with Betsy when she and Ronnie took Patti to the Douglas Camp, which the Bloomingdale's daughter also attended.

Ronnie was a man who needed to believe in heroes, and he came to see these new friends as the genuine heroes of his age. To Ronnie there was something real, something tangible, about these men that he did not find among Hollywood people.

Nancy was no longer the homebody sitting around with Ursula Taylor at the pool talking about children. She didn't see Ursula as frequently. She felt right with her new friends and she enjoyed driving into Beverly Hills for shopping and luncheon. In the exclusive stores, she was known as a sharp shopper, buying much less frequently than her friends. Her problem was that she did not have enough money to keep up as she wanted to keep up.

—12—
"A TIME FOR CHOOSING"

"**N**ot a day goes by when someone doesn't come to the house and ask Ronnie to run for senator or governor or even President of the United States," Nancy wrote a college friend in 1962 in a letter the woman remembered years later. "It boggles the mind but maybe it'll get me out of the carpool."

For years people had been asking Ronnie to run for office, first for the U.S. House of Representatives as a Democrat, then for the Senate as a Republican. He was proud that his contemporaries thought so much of him, but he didn't think of himself as a candidate. He saw himself "as a Paul Revere sounding the alarm."

Ronnie went from town to town, speech to speech, decrying the encroachment of government on individual liberties. He joked that government "was like a baby—an alimentary canal with a big appetite at one end and no sense of responsibility at the other." But he was dead serious. He joined the American Medical Association's fight against President Kennedy's Medicaid program. He produced Ronald Reagan Record Kits to warn listeners of what he considered to be the spreading virus of socialized medicine. He continued his battle against communism by speaking for Dr. Fred Schwarz's Christian anti-Communist campaign. He was a member of Project Prayer, a Hollywood movement against the Supreme Court's decision ending prayer in the schools.

Ronnie was perfectly happy in his chosen role as an impassioned salesman for conservative candidates. He had gone back to work again, too, thanks to his brother. After the cancellation of "The GE Theater," Neil had come to him with an offer. One of Neil's advertising accounts at McCann Erickson, U.S. Borax, needed a host to introduce their syndicated television program, "Death Valley Days," and to peddle their soap, 20 Mule Team Borax. "I wanted to sign him for a contract," Neil said. "He didn't want any part of it. I rather suppose he didn't want to work." In the end, though, Ronnie did sign, for about the same salary he had been receiving from "GE Theater."

That same year, 1964, Ronnie's candidate for president, Mr. Conservative himself, Barry Goldwater, won the Republican presidential nomination. Visiting Nancy's parents at their winter home in Phoenix, Ronnie had often talked to the Arizona senator. Ronnie admired Goldwater's straightforward, uncompromising brand of conservatism. And he went to work for the nominee as California cochairman of Citizens for Goldwater-Miller.

Ronnie was an avid booster. For six weeks he traveled the state, making several speeches a day. He was a hit, but President Lyndon Johnson and the Democrats had an easy time portraying Goldwater as an extremist and war hawk who as president would bring great peril to the Republic. As the election neared, it was clear that Goldwater was going down to one of the worst defeats in modern political history.

In late October, Goldwater was unable to speak at the big $1,000-a-plate fund raiser at the Ambassador Hotel in Los Angeles. Ronnie's friend and a big Republican fund raiser, Holmes Tuttle, asked Ronnie to pinch-hit.

Asking Ronnie to talk about "the cause" was like getting Billy Graham to discuss sin. He had been preparing his speech for more than a decade as he toured the country for General Electric. He had tried out each bit and piece scores of times. He had tested the response to each of his anecdotes, each of his stories of outrage, each of his shocking facts a score of times.

Some of the rich Republicans in the audience had already heard the speech a number of times, but to them it was like listening to Kate Smith sing "God Bless America." They never grew tired of hearing it. To Ronnie it was just another speech, another audience to charm, but it was a call to arms to the dispirited Goldwaterites, a warning against the Soviet threat, and to many a signal to rally around a new conservative champion.

"We are at war with the most dangerous enemy that has ever faced mankind in his long climb from the swamp to the stars, and it has been said if we lose that war, in so doing lose this way of freedom of ours, history will record with the greatest astonishment that those who had the most to lose did the least to prevent its happening," Ronnie said in his melodious, beseeching voice, a voice both earnest and passionate.

"They say we offer simple answers to complex problems. Well, perhaps there is a simple answer . . . not an easy one . . . but a simple one. If you and I have the courage to tell our elected officials that we want our national policy based on what we know in our hearts is morally right, we cannot buy our security, our freedom from the threat of the bomb, by committing an immorality so great as saying to a billion human beings now in slavery behind the Iron Curtain, 'Give up your dreams of freedom, because to save our own skin, we are willing to make a deal with your slave-masters.'"

Tuttle sat next to Henry Salvatori, a multimillionaire entrepreneur involved with the right-wing Anti-Communist Voters League and Project Alert, and the finance chairman of the Goldwater campaign. They were two of the most powerful, most committed conservatives in the state. They were looking for a candidate to take on Governor Edmund G. ("Pat") Brown in the 1966 gubernatorial campaign.

"Henry, that's a terrific speech," Tuttle said in his abrupt, stop-and-start voice. "Let's run him for governor."

"Oh, for Christ's sake," Salvatori sputtered, "you can't run an actor for governor."

Although Salvatori doesn't specifically remember that comment, he says that it is something he might have said. Many of the most powerful California conservatives considered Ronnie little more than an after-dinner entertainer and cheerleader. Nonetheless, his potential as a fund raiser was evident. Televised statewide, the speech brought in so much money that the state committee agreed to pay for a national telecast.

On October 27, 1964, "A Time for Choosing" played on national television. The speech was not, in a sense, a Goldwater campaign speech. In the entire speech, Ronnie only mentioned the presidential nominee five times. It was a speech for Ronnie and for his ideals, a speech that inspired Goldwater conservatives as had nothing else in the campaign. Here was idealism about the American experience, anger at the corruption within the burgeoning bureaucracy of government, and faith that to restore itself all America had to do was return to simpler, older ways.

"You and I have a rendezvous with destiny," Ronnie concluded. "We will preserve for our children this, the last best hope of man on earth, or we will sentence them to take the last step into a thousand years of darkness."

Conservatives knew that even if Goldwater went down in defeat, they had a new champion who might yet lead them to the White House. In Owosso, Michigan, a group immediately formed a Reagan for President committee.

While all across the country Ronnie's speech was being praised and discussed, he was in Gallup, New Mexico, stripped to the waist, tied to a stake, being threatened by an Indian brandishing his captive's own saber. For Ronnie, giving a speech for national television and playing a part as a cavalry officer captured by the Indians in "Death Valley Days" were all in a day's work. As the crew prepared for a close-up, the propman's hand slipped, and Ronnie received a slight cut on the shoulder.

"Where were you when I was standing there bleeding to death?" Ronnie asked Joe Santley, the show's PR man.

"I was downtown having a couple of bloody marys," Santley said, knowing that Ronnie was joking.

Santley tromped back downtown to the newspaper and wrote up a story about Ronnie, the wound and the famous speech, mildly exaggerating the extent of Ronnie's scratches. By the time the story hit the wires, it read as if Ronnie had bled like a stuck pig. "I forgot to tell Nancy," Santley said. "She heard it on the radio. By the time it got through to her, it was as if he had been run clean through."

In a few days it was Goldwater who was run clean through in the most stunning defeat in contemporary times. He won only 27 million votes as against 43 million for President Johnson.

As a young man, Ronnie had been open and trusting. But his experiences with Communists in Hollywood and the Goldwater campaign had made him a person who saw the world in terms of *them* and *us*. "We don't intend to turn the Republican party over to the traitors in the battle just ended," he told the Los Angeles County Young Republicans the week after the election debacle in which Goldwater won only six states. "We will have no more of those candidates who are pledged to the same socialist goals of our opposition and who seek our support," Ronnie said. As he saw it, Goldwater had been the victim of the "worst campaign of vilification and the worst betrayal of those who should have given us their trust."

In Reagan, the disjointed, defeated Republican Right had a new hero. Tuttle, Salvatori, A.C. ("Cy") Rubel, chairman of the board of Union Oil Company, and other millionaire businessmen pressed Reagan to run for the Republican nomination in 1966. They thought he could defeat Governor Brown, the liberal who personified big spending and big promises.

"When some of the boys got together to talk about Ronnie for governor, they asked me to come up to the house for a meeting," remembered Neil Reagan. "They said he's really got his feet dragging. They were pitching him from one side to the other. I said I thought he could be elected."

As Ronnie recalled, Tuttle finally turned to him and said, "Would you agree not to give us a flat no? Just kick it around in your mind."

To men like Tuttle, Salvatori and Rubel, the business of America was, indeed, business. Politicians and candidates, even Ronnie, were an inferior breed. "Reagan doesn't have great depth," Salvatori admits, "but I don't know any politician who does. He's not the most intelligent man who ever was, but I've never met a politician with great depth. I don't know of any politician who would be smart enough to run my business, but Reagan just might."

In the spring of 1965, forty-one rich businessmen formed "The Friends of Ronald Reagan." For $50,000 a year, they purchased the considerable savvy of the Spencer-Roberts public-relations firm, which had managed Nelson Rockefeller's close 1964 presidential primary campaign as well as a host of Republican candidates who had successfully sought congressional seats. Stuart Spencer and William Roberts gave Ronnie a crash course on issues and political stage presence. Ronnie agreed to stump for a six-month trial run starting in June 1965. He wouldn't have to announce formally until January 1966 when he would know if he had enough support to win the primary.

Though he had given himself a way out if his "friends" didn't arouse sufficient support, Ronnie was not as reluctant as he appeared. When he traveled to the East Coast to address the National Association of Broadcasters, he had the race on his mind. Returning on the *Twentieth Century Limited,* the classy New York–to–Chicago express train, he sat in the club car talking to Joe Santley.

"We'd really like to know if you're running or not," Santley said. If he was going for it, "Death Valley Days" would need a new host.

"They're doing a feasibility study," Ronnie said, giving his standard reply. "If it's positive, I'll run."

The more Santley heard Ronnie talking, the more sure he was that Ronnie would run. Ronnie would need to film twenty-six "Death Valley Days" introductions before beginning his run. The four shows in which he acted would have to be aired before he announced his candidacy in January, when opponents would demand equal time.

"You know the first thing I'm going do, if I'm governor?" Ronnie asked.

"No?"

"The first thing I'm going to do, by God, is get rid of that Clark Kerr at the University."

No one seemed to like the president of California's public university system—not the right wing, who saw the universities as playpens of anarchy, profanity and promiscuity; not the radicals in Berkeley, who considered Kerr the big daddy of the multiversity that they believed was turning people into human IBM cards; and not even some of the more moderate state politicians, who thought that Kerr was politically inept.

Ronnie's rhetoric was too raw for electoral politics. He denounced the graduated income tax as having been "spawned by Marx as the prime essential of the socialistic state." His advisers began snipping his most fiery rhetoric out of what everyone now called "the speech," the addres. electrified conservative America. He was cut off from many of his contacts.

He had associated with the right-wing John Birch society. In 1 had spoken at a fund-raising dinner for John Rousselot, a Birch member who then was running unsuccessfully for the House. Rousselot was now the society's national public-relations director. Ronnie announced at a private meeting of the California Republican Assembly that Rousselot had offered to endorse him for governor or attack him, whichever would do more good.

Ronnie may have been trying to show how shrewd and astute he had become. But he didn't sound so astute when in August 1965 his words appeared in the newspapers. The taint of the John Birch support continued to plague him throughout his "trial run." And the campaign staff had orders that never was Ronnie to be photographed with any member of the society.

Because of Ronnie's extremist affiliations and his actor's past, Governor Brown considered him merely the latest California right-wing nut. Brown spent his energies blackening the reputation of Ronnie's opponent, the former mayor of San Francisco, George Christopher, a moderate Republican.

When Ronnie announced his candidacy in January 1966, he had known for several months that he was going to run. He sat before 150 reporters in the Pacific Ballroom of the Statler-Hilton Hotel in downtown Los Angeles. He was flanked by two six-foot photos of himself and his signature reproduced in glittery silver on a twenty-foot-long banner. Backstage, Joe Santley thought that Nancy looked "a nervous wreck, on the verge of tears, flying off the wall, so glad to see a familiar face in this crowd of strangers, of media people."

From that day on, the Reagans would have a new kind of public life, where opponents would try to magnify every slip into a pratfall, every blemish into political acne. In Hollywood, both Ronnie and Nancy had been contract players, watched over by PR directors, lackeys and makeup artists, and they knew how to use people and use them well. But now more than ever, the fortunes of their aides were tied to their well-being and to the image that the Reagans portrayed.

Nancy thought that running for office would be similar to being a movie star. She was shocked to see how little it was like her cushioned existence at M-G-M. "Politics is a completely different life," she said later. "In the picture business you're protected somewhat—by the studio, by your producer, and so on. In politics you aren't protected in any way. You don't belong for a night to a theater audience; you belong to everyone all the time. There's a wider, deeper penetration; people write and tell you *everything* that's on their mind. And we can't go anywhere without people coming up to us and asking questions. On movie tours and junkets, studio staffs would surround us and create a little privacy. But you can't do this in politics."

Ronnie handily won the Republican nomination in June 1966 over George Christopher with 64 percent of the vote. For a few days' rest, the Reagans headed over to Malibu, the exclusive beachfront town north of Pacific Palisades, to the home of a wealthy supporter.

"I'd like you to run into Hollywood and get something for me," Nancy asked a personal aide.

"What would you like, Mrs. Reagan?" the man asked, thinking that it must be an important mission to go all the way back into the city.

"I'd like a copy of *The Making of the President* by Teddy White."

For all Nancy's natural reticence toward campaigning and her dislike of the sweaty hurly-burly of politics, she saw no limits to where Ronnie might go. Even before the fall campaign, she had hired Melvina Pumphrey, a public-relations executive and an old friend from M-G-M's publicity department, to be her part-time press secretary. She was immediately accused of hiring Pumphrey to give her a "Jacqueline Kennedy gloss," a charge that was quickly disavowed.

When the campaign needed it, Nancy appeared at ladies' groups, teas and fund raisers, answering general questions, parrying personal queries. But she much preferred to campaign with Ronnie. She had heard "the speech" hundreds of times, but she stared up at him as if he were giving an hour-long dissertation on the wonders of his wife. It hurt her that some reporters suggested that there was something false or calculated about "the stare."

She was, said Paul Beck, then a reporter for the *Los Angeles Times* and later Ronnie's press secretary, "a tigress protecting her favorite cub." Nancy always protected Ronnie's health. Early on in the campaign, the staff learned that if they pushed Ronnie too hard, woke him up too early or tried to maneuver around him, there was no wrath like Nancy's. Whatever the staff thought of her personally, they never doubted the sincerity or depth of her love for Ronnie.

In private, Ronnie often called Nancy "mommy." Ronnie had called his mother "Nelle" and Nancy was the first woman he had ever called "mommy." Nancy called him "daddy," the first man whom she could easily or regularly call by that name.

In her campaign performances, Nancy acted as if she had the perfect family. That was part of the ritual of politics. Even without that, Nancy would have sought to project a harmonious veneer, but now that image was even more crucial.

Some of the staff members felt that Nancy was all for putting a decided distance between the campaign and Maureen and Michael. In Maureen's case, there was a certain irony in that, since she was the real politician in the family, a conservative who as early as 1962 had written Ronnie about running for office.

Maureen was by now a statuesque blonde with an almost haunting resemblance to her mother and conservative beliefs to match her father's. Ronnie's eldest daughter had grown up more a child of boarding schools than of either parent. She appeared full of enormous self-doubt. Although she did not see her father very much, Maureen adored Ronnie and seemed haunted by a fear of losing her father completely to Nancy. "She is very much in love with him," Maureen said later. "She would like to be the only person that ever was. I can understand that. Reality interferes, but it's perfectly understandable."

Her lonely life had marked Maureen. "To this day I am very sad at goodbyes," she said. "When someone goes to the market, I get sick to my stomach."

When she was seventeen, Maureen had entered Marymount Junior College in Arlington, Virginia. After a few months she dropped out. "I was tired of being institutionalized," she said. In Washington, Maureen took a $60-a-week job as a secretary at Walker and Dunlop, a local real-estate firm, and rented a dreary little room on Sixteenth Street, a marginal area. She didn't tell Ronnie any of this. "I didn't call him when I left school," Maureen said. "I just left. He said, 'I wish you hadn't done that.' I said, 'I know.' He said, 'Well, whatever you do, be good at it. People are paying you money.'"

One day Maureen met a policeman, John Filippone, directing traffic. Filippone was the son of an Italian shoemaker. He was twelve years older than Maureen, but she and the thirty-two-year-old policeman eventually married. To Filippone, Maureen was "screwed up." After a year, she paid for the divorce.

Maureen returned to Los Angeles. While trying to enter show business, she fell in love with a Marine Corps officer; but after less than three years, that marriage was about to end. "I didn't like being married," Maureen said years later. "I don't like being a nonperson. I've been someone's daughter all my life, and I'm not going to spend the rest of my life being someone's wife. I'm a person!"

With Maureen's immense interest in politics and general flair as a speaker, she might have been a worthy asset to the campaign. But she was considered more a liability.

As for Michael, he was a boisterous, beer-drinking, let-me-buy-you-a-round kind of guy, hardly Nancy's cup of tea, or someone to be propped next to Ronnie during the campaign. Ronnie had paid Michael's tuition for six months at Arizona State University, but when he left Arizona to attend Los Angeles Valley College, neither of his parents helped him. To earn money, he worked on a trucking dock. But like his sister, he had dropped out of college and seemed to be floundering.

At eight years old with his front teeth missing, Ron, Jr., was too young to understand what was happening, but his older sister, Patti, was beginning to sense what politics might mean to her private life. Moreover, she was ready to publicly affirm her nascent liberalism. According to Norman Cagle, one of her teachers, she wore a Pat Brown T-shirt to Dye School one day.

The following year, 1965, as Ronnie's campaign drew nearer, thirteen-year-old Patti was sent away to the Orme School in Arizona. The 250-acre campus sat in the midst of a 40,000-acre working cattle ranch on the edge of the Rocky Mountain plateau seventy-five miles north of Phoenix. It was rugged cowboy country and the 180 students got up in the morning and did chores like any ranch hand, milking cows, slopping hogs, gathering eggs. Horsemanship and desert survival were two interests pursued at the school.

Patti was one of fifty students on the equestrian team. All 40,000 acres were open to their riding, and students like Patti were taught western rodeo skills as well as traditional show riding. Twice a year Patti helped round up the cattle. In the spring, the students inoculated, branded and castrated the new calf crop. In the fall, they separated them for sale to the market. But even out on the range, the rules were stringent. And back at the school, beds were checked every night and rooms inspected every morning.

Many wealthy Americans like Nancy and Ronnie were willing to slap down hard cash to see that their children were not contaminated by the permissiveness and excesses of the Sixties. The Orme School was just the place to send a teen-ager who needed good old-fashioned discipline. And for the adolescents themselves, it was not a bad deal, not a bad way to grow up.

Nancy was not content to leave that to the school, though, and she was forever calling, wanting to know all about Patti. "She was very concerned," said Charles Orme, Jr., the headmaster and son of the founder. "The Reagans were conservative and getting more so. We are a conservative school, but she didn't feel [we were] conservative enough to counteract the typical rebellion of the time nor Patti's exposure as a young child to the glitter and tinsel of Hollywood. But the era and Patti's exposure [to the less rigid Hollywood life] caused problems. There was tension with her parents."

Patti was tall and lean. She had radiant good looks. But at times her face became set in a troubled grimace, and she slumped along as if she did not want people to look at her. "Patti was self-conscious about her parents being in politics and didn't want to talk about it at all," Orme said. "She had the normal resistance to parental authority. It was stronger with her because she so resisted her father's going into politics. That was part of the tension between them, but not the sole cause."

Patti considered her parents so far removed from her world, that probably no matter what Ronnie did, she would have struggled with her parents. For Thanksgiving 1965, the Reagans made their first trip to visit the school. Ronnie and Nancy had sent Patti to Orme to get her away from what they considered the vulgar, immoral dangerous world of the Sixties. But what they saw in their daughter was a walking, breathing incarnation of everything they publicly deplored and privately feared.

What greeted them was not *their* Patti but a Julie Christie clone: thick hair parted to one side and hanging down her face; black eye makeup; white lipstick; a miniskirt so short that she would have risked arrest a few years back.

Ronnie and Nancy gasped. "As long as you're getting upset about *everything*," Patti said, "how about *this?*" With that, Patti flung her hair back and displayed a pierced ear.

Ronnie was not about to show any anger or bewilderment. "Just do us a favor, okay?" he said with a soothing touch of humor. "Before you have your appendix taken out, will you let us know."

Nancy wanted Patti to grow up and become her genteel, well-brought-up daughter. She didn't understand what Patti had to protest. She wanted to shield her from the violent realities that lay beyond the pale of Pacific Palisades.

In August 1965, a great riot had broken out in Watts in L.A., the black ghetto that had become a bloody symbol for militant civil-rights groups. Thirty-four people had died before it was put down. Nancy thought that these people had had opportunities and freedom, and yet they had savaged their own neighborhood.

She knew very little about the minorities that were making Los Angeles one of the most diverse cities in the world. Los Angeles had more citizens of Mexican descent than any metropolis but Mexico City, more Japanese than anywhere outside Japan except São Paulo, the largest community of Koreans outside Korea, as well as the largest black population in the West.

One day when she was being driven home, her car got stuck in a line of vehicles. She was running late, and by the time the limousine managed to work its way to the front of the thirty or so vehicles, she was fuming. Finally she saw the cause of the trouble: two black men pushing an old car.

"That figures," Nancy said, remembered one passenger, as her chauffeured car accelerated past the stalled vehicle.

Pat Brown had been a popular governor. But he was trying for a third term and he was tired. He tried to attack Ronnie as a dangerous right-wing radical, but he had little luck against Ronnie, who managed to seem both well meaning and comforting.

When Ronnie had begun campaigning in the summer of 1965, he had known as much about California's problems as he did about nuclear fission, but he read position papers and he was quick on his feet. On television, there was already no better, no more persuasive a candidate than Ronald Reagan. In person, giving "the speech," he was effective as well. The reporters, many of them liberals, liked Ronnie. They had heard "the speech" so many times that they could have given it themselves, but Ronnie broke up the tedium by telling stories on the campaign bus about Errol Flynn or Jack Warner, tales miles away from the campaign.

Still, Ronnie's lack of knowledge became embarrassingly apparent.

"Reagan had just entered politics and he was inexperienced," said Henry Salvatori. "Once, he didn't know a goddamn canal and where it went. Another time, he was standing in the Eagle River and didn't know where the hell he was. It's a hell of a big state."

It infuriated Ronnie that he hadn't been better briefed about the Eagle River. He maintained his composure in public, but that evening at a motel he let go. Taking a pack of Smith Brothers Cough Drops, he threw them at the window so hard that he chipped the glass.

Pat Brown knew all about the Eagle River, but the voters didn't seem to care. In August 1966, a Gallup poll indicated that Ronnie had a comfortable eleven-point lead over Brown. In desperation, Robert Coate, the Democratic party chairman, issued a twenty-nine-page report entitled "Ronald Reagan, Extremist Collaborator, an Exposé." But even moderate Republicans and Democrats didn't buy the idea that Ronnie was a dangerous extremist. As the election neared, every indication was that Ronnie would not only win but win in a landslide.

Even with all his campaigning, Ronnie had time for little things. One day Kathy Davis, his secretary, showed him a letter from a man who said that his nephew was a newsboy hawking papers on the corner, and that every time he sold a paper he said, "Vote for Reagan." Two weeks later, Ronnie told his driver, "Let's see if we can find that kid." And though the candidate was running late, the chauffeur drove through the streets of L.A. until they found the boy. Ronnie spent twenty minutes with him in the back of the limousine.

To Ronnie, America was indeed the blessed land; but even in his own country politics were now often full of blood and rancor. Three years before, Kennedy had been assassinated, and there was a violent tempo to the politics of his day. During the campaign, Ronnie's headquarters were broken into and documents were stolen, an incident that was immediately and thoroughly hushed up. He had received threats of bodily harm, and he didn't think of the radicals at Berkeley and elsewhere as playacting kids. They were young men and women, many of them no older than Patti, but to Ronnie the leaders were dangerous revolutionaries capable of almost anything. He was not a fearful man, but Nancy and Ronnie both sensed that, in entering public life, he was taking the highest kind of risk.

But that was nothing they thought about on election night. They were on their way to an election-eve party when the radio announcer said that Ronnie had won. "It can't be over," Nancy declared. "We're not at the party yet." In the end, Ronnie won by an enormous margin, 993,739 votes in all.

Citizen politician Ronald Reagan, fifty-six years old, is sworn in as governor of California while his wife looks on, 1967. *(UPI)*

═13═

THE GOVERNOR AND
HIS LADY

W hen Ronnie had driven into Los Angeles on a warm spring evening late in May 1937, Americans east of the Mississippi thought of California as a distant island. To the rest of the world, the state still meant movies and sun and exotic romance. But California's 19-million population made it the biggest state in the Union. The gross state production was larger than the GNP of all but five countries.

California felt like the future. All one had to do was look at the state to see what would soon happen in the rest of the country. The "generation gap" had begun in California. Ronnie and his contemporaries felt that their prosperous, middle-class society represented California. But while Ronnie was looking forward to his inauguration, bizarrely dressed young "hippies" were taking up quarters in a slum area of San Francisco called Haight-Ashbury. In a few months, thousands of young Americans would converge there for what was supposed to be "the summer of love." In Berkeley, the free-speech movement had signaled the beginning of what would become one of the most sustained periods of mass protest in American history. There were not only promises of love and peace but militant parades and anti–Vietnam War demonstrations.

The discontented middle-class and working-class voters who provided Ronnie's election margin didn't understand this any better than Ronnie. And they didn't want to understand it. They wanted a return to *their* idea of the future, an America that fought its wars in Vietnam, not in the home, and offered prosperity to morally upright people. During the campaign, they had applauded and cheered when Ronnie promised to "clean up the mess at Berkeley," where there had taken place "sexual orgies so vile I cannot describe them to you."

When it came time to celebrate his election to office, Ronnie did it among his kind of people—not in some kind of aw-shucks people's inauguration, but at the biggest, most expensive ($100,000) inaugural bash California had ever seen. Ronnie was sworn in at one minute after midnight in January 1967 in the Capitol rotunda. Standing next to the governor-elect were a few good friends, including Senator George Murphy, the former actor and Nancy's costar in her most forgettable film, *Talk About a Stranger*. Murphy had broken the political trail for Ronnie. He had been the first professional actor in modern political history to be elected to a major office. Ronnie was indebted to the old song-and-dance man who had played his father in *This Is the Army*. "Well, Murphy, here we are on the Late, Late Show again," Ronnie said.

For the full outdoor inauguration, the *Proceedings Manual* was so detailed that it reminded one reporter of a "1930s M-G-M movie script." Because of death threats, a helicopter buzzed overhead while the Sacramento State College band played "America, the Beautiful." On the Capitol roof stood at least four rifle-carrying police officers.

Not since her debut had Nancy had such an opportunity to show her style and glamour as at the great Inaugural Ball. She wore an extraordinary white, one-shouldered gown by James Galanos, the young Los Angeles designer. The gown was beaded with diamond-like glass daisies. Her dark brown hair was set in a bouffant and she wore emerald-and-diamond earrings. She looked a good ten years younger than her forty-five years.

As for fifty-five-year-old Ronnie, he didn't look a day over forty himself. He had the bounce in his step of a rookie who has just pitched the winning game in the World Series. He hadn't served a day in office and the national media already considered him a presidential contender. Around him, aides, advisers and friends played their own game of musical chairs, trying to be near him, to be indispensable, to be touched by his mantle of celebrity and power.

Even Ronnie's brother suffered. Ronnie was his brother, and Neil had worked harder than most in the campaign, yet he and his wife, Bess, hadn't been invited to some of the parties. Neil didn't blame his brother, but he was angry. During one dinner party given by a Reagan aide, Neil sat at the hotel bar having a drink.

"What's up?" one of Ronnie's aides asked as he breezed by. "Aren't you going to the party?"

"We weren't invited. And Bess is upstairs crying."

After considerable coaxing, Neil's wife finally came down, and the governor's brother and sister-in-law entered the party.

Although Nancy liked the idea of being First Lady of California, she would gladly have moved Sacramento south somewhere between Beverly

Hills and Bel Air. She knew practically nobody from California's Central Valley, the flat, fertile area between Redding and Bakersfield. Most of the money in the area came from politics, agriculture and oil, three commodities that people of Nancy's background often associated with dirt.

Her immediate problem was the Governor's Mansion downtown at Sixteenth and "H" where she, Ronnie and Ron, Jr., were supposed to live. If she had been the wife of the richest merchant in central California in 1877, she would have been ecstatic about moving into the magnificent Victorian structure. Back then, the four-story house with its added two-story cupola, studded with wrought iron and Italianate windows, was worth a buggy trip just to see. But this was 1966, a full decade before most people began to appreciate Victoriana, and Nancy was appalled at the idea of living in the drafty firetrap.

When Bernice Brown had shown Nancy through the rundown mansion in mid-November, the First Lady–to–be wasn't critical. "It's lovely, just lovely," she'd swooned as Mrs. Brown led her through the upstairs bedrooms. "I'm sure we'll enjoy living here."

But when it was just Nancy, Ronnie and two aides touring their new home, Nancy was appalled. "That fireplace isn't right!" she said, finding things to criticize in almost every room. She couldn't stand the neighborhood, either. Back to back with the Governor's Mansion was an American Legion hall, and next door two gas stations and a motel. Nancy considered it no place to raise a child.

As Ronnie walked through the house beside Nancy, he said practically nothing. Ronnie didn't care much about his surroundings; he could have been happy in a trailer or bunkhouse. Moreover, as his political aides were advising him, if the house was good enough for Pat Brown and Earl Warren, then it was good enough for a new governor elected to cut down on government spending.

The Reagans moved into the house, but to Nancy it was little better than camping out. With its old yellow wallpaper, crystal chandelier and faded red carpet, all the living room needed was a spittoon to complete the image of a parlor left over from 1890. Ronnie would sit downstairs in his pajamas and bathrobe, a blanket around his shoulders, making the best of it. But the day she and Ron, Jr., had to scramble out when a fire alarm went off, Nancy insisted that they move out to a rented house—politics be damned. They did so by April.

For the most part the wealthy men who had backed Ronnie's campaign weren't looking to have legislation passed to benefit their specific industries or businesses. "When Reagan won, he had no obligations," said Salvatori. "It never came up with us. That's something."

All Salvatori and his friends wanted was for Ronnie to cut away the brush and brambles of government so that business could go grow tall in the California sun. They weren't looking to be named to a Sacramento job, either. After the transition and appointments were completed, they tended to lose interest in the day-to-day business of government.

In addition to Salvatori, the kitchen cabinet included Tuttle; William French Smith, Ronnie's lawyer; Taft Schreiber, who had gotten Ronnie his "GE Theater" position; Leonard Firestone, president of the tire company; Jaquelin Hume and Arch Monson, Jr., San Francisco businessmen; Edward Mills, vice-president of Holmes Tuttle Enterprises; and Leland M. Kaiser, a retired banker. They attended monthly advisory meetings and talked to Ronnie by phone, but they had businesses to run, money to make.

As governor, Ronnie was not about to become a nuts-and-bolts administrator, worrying about the squeaky valves of government. He had his staff to do that. His campaign manager, Philip Battaglia, had become executive assistant, Ronnie's top aide. Battaglia was a successful lawyer. A bright young thirty-one-going-on-fifty-year-old, he was an archetype that was becoming familiar in Washington, as clean and sleek as a Siamese cat.

With Ronnie's blessing, Lyn Nofziger had named himself "director of communications." A former reporter for the conservative Copley chain, Nofziger had a subtle, deep understanding of the media, and an ego as big as a redwood tree. He was already in trouble with Nancy. Not only did Nofziger wear clothes that he could have picked out at the Salvation Army, but Nancy felt that he had cued Ronnie during the campaign as if the candidate were Howdy Doody. Nancy got along much better with the twenty-nine-year-old cabinet secretary, William P. Clark, a courtly, rather self-effacing attorney. He had managed the Reagan campaign in Ventura county.

Ronnie trusted these men to bring the big decisions to him and to take care of mundane daily details. During his years in Hollywood, he'd gotten used to people doing things for him, making him look good, and as governor he set out the same way. When it came time for the major decisions, he liked neat little memos with the alternatives laid out clearly and cleanly. And that's what he got.

Governor Brown had left a startling welcoming present: a previously undisclosed 1967 budget deficit of an estimated $200 million. Thus the conservative new governor would not be able to cut taxes. He would have to raise them. In his first three months in office, Ronnie announced three controversial and unsuccessful budget-balancing proposals. He was all for socking the state universities with tuition charges, making students pay at least part of their education bills. He also proposed an across-the-board 10-percent cut in department programs and the elimination of 4,000 state jobs.

Almost every night at five or six o'clock, a limousine drove Ronnie

The seventy-year-old Victorian mansion in Sacramento, home of California governors since the turn of the century, which Nancy found unsuitable for her family. The Reagans moved out of this mansion and into a rented house only four months after taking office. *(Wide World)*

home to his new twelve-room, two-story Tudor-style house on Forty-fifth Street, rented for $1,250 a month. If Ronnie arrived a little late, Nancy often stood waiting to welcome him with a kiss. If they didn't have a political meeting or dinner somewhere, Ronnie was into pajamas and robe, ready for dinner—macaroni and cheese if he was lucky—and such favorites as "Bonanza" or "Mission Impossible" on television.

Nancy did not care a whit about policy. Her power did not lie there. She cared about Ronnie and how he appeared, and berated anyone who made him look bad. Early on in the administration, Ronnie was talking to a reporter in his office when a phone call was put through. The state's new finance director, Gordon Paul Smith, had just made a statement in Los Angeles directly contradicting a statement that Ronnie had made in Sacramento.

"It's my wife," Ronnie said, picking up the phone.

"Yes, dear," he said. "Yes, dear. . . . No, dear. I don't think he was being insubordinate. It's just when I say something in Sacramento and he says something in Los Angeles, we'll have to get together."

To Nancy, "that first year in Sacramento was a miserable one." Nancy hated the fogs of Sacramento and the state politicians. But she kept busy. The governor's offices on the ground floor of the state capitol had not been redecorated since 1951. She set out to make them more representative of the state and a more comfortable environment for her husband.

She had the halls leading to Ronnie's sanctuary recarpeted in bright red and lined the walls with prints depicting historic moments of California and the West. She hung new red-and-white draperies in Ronnie's office, reupholstered his couches and presented him with an antique desk for his birthday. She set photos of the family in the office and placed an apothecary jar filled with hard candies on his desk.

To mitigate the furor over the move out of the Governor's Mansion, Nancy wooed Republican women by giving them tours of the mansion and its deficiencies. She attended countless lunches and brunches and teas. She refused to give speeches, saying, "That would be presumptuous on my part." She did engage in question-and-answer sessions. She refused weekend obligations unless they were family outings where Ron, Jr., could go along.

It had been hard pulling him out of Dye. She had enrolled him as a third-grader in Brookfield School, a small, private elementary school that stressed the creative arts as well as the basics. But he was picked on as the governor's son.

Patti was becoming a problem as well. It was a difficult time for Nancy. Patti was developing into one of these Sixties children, unruly and difficult.

Nancy also missed her friends in Los Angeles. They did what they could to make her happy. At their luncheons in Beverly Hills, Nancy had a reputation of almost never picking up the check. They didn't mind. Betsy, Betty, Mary Jane and the other ladies knew that she didn't have as much money as they. Now that she was California's First Lady, they didn't mind helping her decorate the governor's home, either. The rented house needed some new furniture, and the ladies donated whatever they could, $25,000 worth in all. Of course, it was all tax-deductible and afterward would go to the state, but it was for Nancy. Betsy and Alfred gave a mahogany dining table that could seat twenty-four and was worth $3,500. Marion and Earle donated two Queen Anne–style chairs and twelve side chairs worth $3,000. Virginia Milner gave furnishings valued at $17,365, including what became Nancy's favorite, a French Regency fruitwood secretary. Two years later, when the owner of the house wanted to sell, seventeen of Nancy's and Ronnie's friends bought the house for $150,000 and rented it to them for the same $1,250 they paid before. It was a neat bit of financial dealing that the post-Watergate age would not have looked upon kindly.

Nancy loved her house in Pacific Palisades and she was happy that Anne was still housekeeper. But she worried that on Anne's day off the dog might not get fed properly. According to a staff member, one aide made weekly trips to Los Angeles to feed the dog and spend the night in the house.

"Thank heavens we can escape to Beverly Hills on the weekends," Nancy was quoted as having told a journalist in Stephen Birmingham's *California Rich*. She felt that she simply had to fly south because "no one in Sacramento can do hair." She was reported to have gone shopping once at I. Magnin's in Sacramento, but once was enough. "Here everything is scaled down for these Valley farm women," she said.

Two and a half months after Ronnie took office, a reporter at a press conference asked the governor just what his legislative program might be. "I could take some coaching from the sidelines," he said, "if anyone can recall my legislative program."

In his first year in office, Ronnie was able to accomplish at least one of his goals. He had wanted to get rid of University of California president Clark Kerr. He had done so without leaving any fingerprints. A few weeks after the election, with impeccably bad timing, Kerr asked for a vote of confidence from the state board of education. With Ronnie threatening a proposed $30-million budget cut, that was the end of Clark Kerr.

Faced with a mammoth deficit and a state law that mandated a balanced budget, Ronnie's team put together a record-high $5-billion budget and tax increases totaling a billion dollars a year. Another conservative governor might have blustered and ranted and lost half his constituency, but Ronnie was a marvel on television and in press conferences.

In the governor's office, several members of his staff had that look of earnest intensity that comes from dreaming of the White House. They weren't the only ones contemplating Ronnie's chances in the 1968 campaign against President Lyndon Johnson. The prospect had already been featured in articles in all types of publications, from *Newsweek* ("Eastern Republican leaders now scoff at the suggestion that Reagan might be nominated—just as they scoffed at Goldwater's chances four years ago") to *Cosmopolitan* ("What girls should know about California's golden-boy [at 56] Governor and Presidential Hopeful") to Evans and Novak in the *Saturday Evening Post* ("In his campaign for governor last fall he time and again pledged that he would light a 'prairie fire' visible across the country. Reagan intimates are convinced that that fire is now blazing and might just possibly light his way to the presidential nomination next year").

Ronnie joined in as if he found himself in the middle of a parade, the marchers carrying his banner, the bands blaring his song. Although he played down his potential candidacy, he made speeches out of state and spent a lot of time with national reporters and editors. Many of the eastern journalists thought of Ronnie as a California rube, and the mere fact that he could talk coherently was news to them. Whether a man who had so little knowledge of national and foreign affairs should be president was a question rarely asked. In fact, his press conferences almost always went well. Afterward, reporters would look at their notes and wonder what had sounded so convincing.

On September 12, 1967, Ronnie was in San Diego at the Coronado Hotel, away from the paper work and details of Sacramento. He was in his pajamas and a robe when into his suite walked an extraordinary group: eleven of his top aides and associates.

Nofziger had been the one to bring the group together. He had learned that two of Ronnie's other aides were part of a homosexual clique within his administration. For Nofziger, it was one of those happy occasions when virtue and ambition are fully allied. If the two alleged homosexuals left, Nofziger believed that he would have served Ronnie well, while getting rid of his greatest competition within the administration. The director of communications had discussed the situation with Clark and other staff members and had the charges investigated.

"My God, has government failed?" Ronnie said. It had never occurred to him that he might have homosexuals on his staff. He considered homosexuality an illness, and his aides' activities a betrayal of themselves and "the cause." He was shocked as he was told about an orgy in a cabin at Lake Tahoe.

The more Ronnie heard, the worse it got. There were further allegations about other young men and political figures. Some of the men were married. All in all, it was an unsavory stew, particularly at a time when homosexuals either lived in the closet or suffered rebuke, shame or ostracism.

The next day, a high-ranking aide who was suspect was asked to resign. Soon afterward a second aide resigned, and several others discreetly left the administration. Some members of the staff felt that what had been done was an abomination; they considered it a betrayal of the basic principles of fair play for which Ronnie was supposed to stand. Ronnie was told as much, but, as he always did in emotionally difficult and complex situations, he distanced himself from the realities and went on.

It didn't seem to occur to Ronnie that there was something bizarre about an administration where eleven of its top people came barging into a hotel room 513 miles from the capital to tell the chief executive a shocking story about which he knew nothing. He felt personally betrayed, but he went on as before, delegating away authority and duties. He made Clark his top aide, and assumed that the whole scandal would go away like a temporary rash.

In late September the story surfaced, as a blind item about a "top GOP presidential prospect" and "a potentially sordid scandal" in *Newsweek*. Believing that the tale was bound to come out more fully, Nofziger went to three California reporters and three national reporters and told them what had happened. Nonetheless, on October 31 the story appeared first in one of the places where the administration would least have wanted it: the national column of the liberal journalist Drew Pearson.

To minimize the damage, Ronnie could have gotten up and simply named the men involved, but he was not about to do that. Pearson had said that the administration had knowingly harbored the homosexuals for six months. Puffing himself full of moral indignation, Ronnie called Pearson a "liar." Later he vowed that if Pearson came to California, if he didn't want to be arrested he had better "not spit on the sidewalk."

In trying to cover up what he considered a sordid private matter, Ronnie lied to reporters by denying that Notziger had leaked the story. Nofziger had handled the leaking of the stories in a clumsy manner, and Nancy blamed him for the extent of the scandal. He was not soon forgiven. He was never again Ronnie's confidant, which he so much wanted to be. For six months Nancy would not even talk to Nofziger. Then she saw to it that he was fired.

With the scandal behind them, several of Ronnie's aides and advisers were all for getting Ronnie into the presidential race. Although later Ronnie would say that he knew he wasn't ready to be president, he allowed a

$450,000 fund to be set up to pay for all the hoopla and professional enthusiasm of a real race.

As the wife of a potential presidential candidate, Nancy was receiving all kinds of attention. She was happy being the governor's wife, but she dreaded the prospect of Ronnie becoming president. Not that she thought he couldn't do the job—her Ronnie could do anything.

In March 1967, at a press conference in Washington's Madison Hotel, a reporter asked how Nancy would like to live in Washington. "I've never thought about it," she said, and then broke out in deep, inexplicable laughter. A year later she sat in a curtained room in that same hotel while outside smoke rose up in the gray sky. A half-dozen blocks away, the city burned during rioting after the assassination of Martin Luther King, Jr. More than ever, she didn't want Ronnie to run.

That same spring, Joan Didion, then a columnist for the *Saturday Evening Post,* paid a visit to Nancy in her Sacramento home. Nancy believed that civility was one of the highest virtues. She was comfortable with reporters who considered civility more important than mere journalism. Didion seemed civil enough, and Nancy showed her the house and tried to introduce her to a reluctant Ron, Jr.

Late in May, Nancy was flying to Chicago on a three-day trip when she started reading the latest issue of the *Saturday Evening Post.* "Pretty Nancy Reagan, the wife of the governor of California, was standing in the dining room of her rented house on 45th Street in Sacramento, listening to a television newsman explain what he wanted to do. She was listening attentively. Nancy is a very attentive listener."

Nancy laughed. But as she read on, she was puzzled and hurt. Didion described Nancy as "playing out some middle-class American woman's daydream, circa 1948. The set for this daydream is perfectly dressed, every detail correct. . . . Everyone on the set smiles, the social secretary, the state guard, the cook, the gardeners."

Nancy shook her head and set the magazine down. "I thought we were getting along well," she said. Later she turned to her companion, a social reporter who would never write that way. "It may sound corny, but I like people and I assume that unless there's something to indicate otherwise, they like me. It's just plain courtesy to be nice to people when you meet them. Do you think she might have liked it better if I snarled?"

Nancy never snarled. When she got mad, she got into a warm bath and soaked while having imaginary dialogues with the malefactors, be they journalists or politicans. She considered that so much in life was ugly these days, and she did whatever she could to avoid ugliness. She couldn't understand people who would go see sensationalistic films "just out of curiosity." She couldn't understand people buying vulgar books, or wearing see-through blouses. She was upset at the new movies because she knew that they influenced peoples' actions. She thought it was time for Hollywood to start censoring itself, and bring back more wholesome fare.

Nancy believed that Ronnie would be the kind of president the country needed, but she didn't want it, not for him, and not for her. As it happened, another Californian, Richard Nixon, had the nomination sewed up by the end of the primaries. Nonetheless, Ronnie's most fervent supporters and most ambitious advisers pushed him to enter the race. At the convention, while Nancy was off attending to other duties, Ronnie, the favorite son, listened to the counsel of William Knowland, a former senator, who wanted him to keep the convention open by running. Ronnie told the California delegation that he was a candidate.

Nancy learned of Ronnie's decision on the radio while she was waiting to give an interview. She was totally surprised. For the first time in their married life, Ronnie had made a major decision without consulting her—and it was a bad decision. If Ronnie had had such timing as an actor, he would have been eternally unemployed. Nixon rolled to nomination on the first ballot.

While Nixon and his supporters celebrated, Ronnie and Nancy borrowed a yacht and spent the weekend cruising the Florida Keys. And Ronnie never again made a major political decision without Nancy's advice.

When the Reagans were in private, at home or riding in the state limousine, they might argue or discuss their unhappiness with Patti or Maureen or Michael. Ronnie's oldest daughter had taken a public-relations job with PSA, the California airlines, a high-flying position indeed for a high-school graduate with little experience in the field. For years she had had little to do with the family, but now she was a frequent presence in Sacramento. To some members of Ronnie's staff, she was a minor irritant, a high-strung young woman who had a constant need for attention.

Maureen saw things differently. "As governor he was a littler easier to find [than before] because he was in office," Maureen said. "But there was a little intimidation to it. Boy, this better be important if I'm going to call him. He didn't think that way. But I did. We had a long talk about that when it was all over. He said, 'But you're very busy too.' And I said, 'But it's not the same.'"

Michael was off racing boats, ranking fifth in the inboard national circuit in 1967. "I did that to try to get an identity of my own," Michael said. "It's very hard when you're trying to do something and you go out and win and everybody thinks you're just your parents' child." Nonetheless, Michael needed business sponsorship for his sport, and he, too, was a potential political liability, to be kept at a distance.

Ronnie's ex-wife, Janie, had become a potential time bomb as well. Her career seemed to be at an end, and there were allegations that she had serious problems. According to a personal aide, during his first year in office Ronnie was helping Janie. But Michael, her son, says that Ronnie did not help.

In public, the Reagans played a family that could have been scripted for "Ozzie and Harriet," but in private there were many undercurrents. The day Ronnie was to receive a national award as Father of the Year, one member of his staff received a mildly hysterical, highly secret phone call from Nancy. Patti was home from school. She had left a note and run away. It was important to find her, to find her fast, and to keep the whole business quiet. Patti returned later that day and the staff member heard that Patti had run away after being caught smoking.

For a young woman who identified with the causes and ideals of the Sixties, it was no easy matter having Ronald Reagan for a father. Patti believed in the very forces that her parents thought meant anarchy and doom. In teach-ins, classes and a score of popular books, students were learning of a hidden America where democracy was manipulated by corporations and the Pentagon, and governments were subverted overseas by the CIA and American business interests. Students took to the streets, protesting the Bank of America, the draft and the bombing of North Vietnam. In California there was a cultural war going on between educated young Americans and their parents' generation, the two sides confronting each other with distrust, misunderstanding and belligerence.

As Patti and several of the governor's younger aides realized, Ronnie was as ignorant of college students as if they came from a different galaxy. One day he had been down at the University of Santa Cruz. As he was leaving an administration building through a gauntlet of students, one lovely blond woman screamed profanities at him and followed him to his car. As the limousine pulled out, Ronnie turned to his aide. "Her eyes were full of hate," he said with bewilderment, taken aback by the young woman. "I really don't know her."

Ronnie thought that "alienation" was no more than a new form of malingering. He couldn't understand why students didn't just study, and push all the freaks and kooks and spongers off campus. It made him sick that students didn't take advantage of the world that lay before them. The Sixties made no sense to him, a unique age when wisdom was supposed to reside in the unwise, and youth alone was considered a mark of virtue.

The great symbol of Ronnie's war with the youthful minions of protest was People's Park in Berkeley. Until the spring of 1969, People's Park had been a 270-by-450-foot vacant lot owned by the university near the Berkeley campus. Hippies, street people, townspeople and activists sodded the

Michael Reagan, age twenty-two, racing his speedboat at Lake Havasu City, Arizona, 1967. "It's very hard when you're trying to do something and you go out and win and everybody thinks you're just your parents' child." *(UPI)*

Christmas, 1967: Governor Reagan, Nancy, Ronald, Jr. (nine) and Patti (fifteen) after putting the finishing touches on the tree. *(UPI)*

field, planted flowers and added slides and sandboxes, turning it into a community park. As delightful as the park may have been, the land still belonged to the university, and the university decided to put up a fence around the property.

Like most confrontations between two rights, the battle over People's Park was an ugly one. Ronnie had already declared a "state of extreme emergency" during student strikes in February, and on May 15, 250 police moved in, pushed the 70 hippies and street people aside, and set up an 8-foot-high fence. The word spread, and soon several thousand people began to arrive. Someone turned on a fire hydrant, someone threw a brick, a policeman fired a shotgun, another tossed a canister of tear gas. By the time the melee was over, one young man standing on a roof nearby had been shot dead with buckshot, another young man had been blinded by a shotgun blast, a police officer had been stabbed, and 63 other people had suffered injuries serious enough to be treated at a hospital.

Ronnie had not been directly involved in the People's Park decisions and he might have tried to bring some peace, or at least to calm things down. But in his way, he was just as headstrong and militant as many of the street people. He saw in People's Park the harbinger of revolution, saw the flowered garb and long hair as the disguises of new Lenins and Stalins.

Patti suffered through all this in her last two years in high school. She was already five-foot-eight, a good four inches taller than her mother, and she dressed with the calculated casualness of her generation.

"I was pretty rebellious," Patti remembered. "I think my feelings stemmed from opposition to the Vietnam War. He was very patient with me. But one of the laws of the Sixties was that you didn't listen to the other side—you just plowed ahead. . . . It was difficult. The press portrayed him as an ogre. They were very inflammatory times, and he responded to the radicalization of the time by being very strong about things as well. So it was difficult. It was hurtful. There was so much conflict, so many inflammatory things."

Ronnie could get up and authoritatively tell a convention of newspaper editors that "for the first time, the radicals have got a majority of students behind them in the antiwar movement." But he couldn't understand the one person of that generation whom he knew and loved: his own daughter. And Nancy couldn't understand her either.

Whenever Patti was home from Orme School, she reportedly told her troubles not to her mother but to Carolyn Deaver, the wife of Mike Deaver, her father's assistant cabinet secretary. Recently married and still in her twenties, Carolyn was a sympathetic ear.

Nancy intended to make sure that Ron, Jr., didn't turn out the way Patti was developing. She coddled him as if he were still a baby, so much so that one of Ronnie's aides wondered how the boy would turn out. After the fourth grade, she had moved him from Brookfield School to Sacred Heart, a Catholic school in downtown Sacramento. That had only lasted a year. Ron, Jr., was now enrolled in Sacramento Country Day, an exclusive private school in the residential area of Sierra Oaks. She wanted him to go to school in a car pool like all the other children, but soon a threat was made on his life and he had to be driven to school in an unmarked police car.

In her autobiography, Nancy wrote about watching Ron, Jr., play touch football and hearing the other boys say, " 'There's Reagan—let's get him.' He never mentioned it to me, but I practically had to be held back from going after those boys."

"Sometimes if the other team found out who Ron was, they'd go after him," said Frank Pignata, assistant principal of Country Day and young Ron's algebra tutor and softball coach. "But his teammates looked after him because he played hard for them. I remember one time I was filling in for the coach and Mrs. Reagan made a point to come tell me that it had happened before. So I talked to the referee and we nipped it before it got bad. . . .

"She was very protective," Pignata said. "It did embarrass Ron a little. After all, he was at the age that he felt like he's growing up and doesn't want to be protected."

Ron, Jr., was turning out to be a bit of a mischief-maker. On occasion, Nancy saw this firsthand. She happened to attend an assembly at the school when a park service official lectured, using animal skins to illustrate his talk. Like most boys, Ron, Jr., didn't want to be seated next to his mother; he was as far away as he could get, up in the front row. With a twinkle in his eye, he reached out, picked up one of the skins and started mimicking the speaker. The ranger turned around, catching the young prankster in the act. Then everyone in the audience laughed—the speaker, the teachers, the students—everyone but Nancy.

Despite his hectic schedule, Ronnie tried to keep up with his son's activities. He came to watch young Ron's tag-football games. Once he was early and offered to help warm up the team. "He pulled off his coat and started passing the football to the kids," remembered Pignata. "They all thought he was great." Another time, when Ron's class was touring the state capitol, Ronnie invited the students to his office and to a surprise lunch at the Reagans' home.

Nancy tried to be home when Ron, Jr., returned from school. She paraded him into the living room for a quick turn before an approving journalist or took him to social events. "I was aware that I was treated differently," Ron, Jr., remembered. "Not so much by my friends, but by adults. They'd always go out of their way to be nice to me and that kind of bullshit. They'd say, 'How's my boy?' It was kind of good in a way because it taught me early on how to see through the bullshit."

On Christmas Eve in Pacific Palisades, the family gathered in the living room to trim the tree for the benefit of the press. As much as Ron, Jr., and Patti enjoyed the festivities, they hated being photographed for publicity. "Nancy would hand them an ornament and they'd hang it," said Zan Thompson, then a Reagan administration press aide and now a *Los Angeles Times* columnist. "It was very hard on them. They didn't like it at all."

One Christmas Ron, Jr., tired of the photographers pushing him into place. "Oh, bug off," he said, while Nancy stood by aghast.

When Nancy wasn't with family, she was busy with official duties and social life. There were fund-raising events everywhere, from San Mateo to Washington; charity events all over the state; trips with Ronnie to Hawaii and Tulsa and the Oroville Dam in northern California. There were the minor indignities such as the time she christened a midget sub, the *Roughneck,* battering away at the hull with a magnum of champagne. The bottle finally broke on the fifth try. And there were the teas, and the dinners, and luncheons galore, and other involvements. She took a special interest in the Foster Grandparents, a two-year-old program started by Sargent Shriver that matched elderly people with handicapped and retarded children.

She took trips to hospitals. "A doctor's daughter, I'd always been in the habit of visiting hospitals," she wrote later. So much of Nancy's life had been spent avoiding what was ugly, sickly or poor, and yet she walked the corridors of veterans hospitals cheering the infirm and the wounded. One day in 1967, at Pacific State Hospital in Pomona, a hydrocephalic child named George took her hand and held it most of the day. When it was time for her to leave, both Nancy and the child cried. Then she was gone, off to visit another hospital another day, to cry over another child and to move on.

Nancy was often driven into San Francisco for lunches and events in this most formal of western cities. The social elite of the city looked upon Los Angeles the way carriage makers looked at the first automobiles: as rude and vulgar experiments that would soon pass from the scene. But Nancy and Ronnie were welcomed, gracious adornments at the Opera Ball, the most prestigious event of the social calendar. By the estimation of Robin Orr, society editor for the *Oakland Tribune,* the Reagans attended more social functions in the city than the Browns had, though the former governor hailed from the Bay area.

Nancy had achieved a sleek, lean look, nothing like the plump college girl, the actress condemned to play mothers or a matronly housewife. "Physically she looks thinner, some of the soft roundness of the pre-political days is gone," wrote *Women's Wear Daily* in 1969, chronicling Nancy's emergence as an arbiter of style. "Always well groomed and well dressed, she looks even better these days. That wide, generous smile is more captivating than ever. Even a non-Reagan fan like Herb Caen [the columnist] admitted after the San Francisco Opera opening this year that 'Mrs. Reagan has a smile that can unhorse a dragoon at 20 paces.' Emotionally, she seems more at ease in her new role. More sure of what she's doing. More involved. And although she still prefers her Beverly Hills pals and her Pacific Palisades home . . . she seems happier in the Sacramento based role these days."

Most of Nancy's friends were still in Los Angeles. That's where she went to have her hair done, to buy her clothes, to lunch and gossip at the Bistro Garden Restaurant in Beverly Hills. When Nancy had come west, Beverly Hills had a village atmosphere. In 1969, however, Gucci, a sophisticated, celebrated Italian-owned store, opened for business on Rodeo Drive. Gucci had first become prominent in the United States when First Lady Jackie Kennedy bought from their modest showroom in New York. Gucci was a hit in New York, but many felt the store was just too expensive, too eastern for laid-back casual L.A., and that Dr. Aldo Gucci would soon go back east, carrying his leather slippers and handbags with him.

To help get things started, Gucci hired Carlo Celoni, a handsome young salesman with a personality as extravagant as any of his merchandise. Celoni knew that to be successful in L.A., the store couldn't simply sell fine, doe-soft leather shoes and delicate evening bags. In slipping on the shoes or carrying one of the bags, the users had to be putting on a magical amulet that would mark them as successful, stylish and rich. The way to accomplish that was to get movie stars and social leaders to wear his goods. "I made myself liked by these people," Celoni said years later, and so he did. There was no one better to have wearing his clothes than the governor's stylish wife, and Celoni called Nancy and invited her to visit the store.

Nancy simply adored the way Carlo swooned over her, brought her lunch, or pulled out some new item that no one else had seen. She liked the idea of designer names, certifying her good taste. With her support and that of other socialites and stars, Gucci became a phenomenon, helping to draw all sorts of exclusive international stores to Rodeo Drive.

Nancy didn't just stop at Gucci. She would go down the street to Amelia Gray's, where she had been a customer since coming to Los Angeles. At I. Magnin's, she had her own *vendeuse,* Miss Donahue, a self-effacing woman whose dress was as subdued as that of a French widow. Miss Donahue always had something special for Nancy, a dress in the new collection that she knew would be just right for Nancy's slender frame.

Nancy loved to shop and then have lunch with her friends. She could have spent the whole afternoon sitting in their banquette at the Bistro Garden, giggling, telling stories with Betsy or Betty or Mary Jane.

Nancy was hailed statewide, even nationwide, as a stylish woman. She was courted by designers, philanthropists and society ladies she admired. She had been named to 1968's list of best-dressed women, had a rose named after her and was featured in an hour-long color documentary for national television. But personal losses would soon interrupt.

In the spring of 1969, Robert Taylor was dying. Taylor smoked too much. For months Nancy heard Bob's hacking cough and worried about him. When Bob learned that he had lung cancer and was to be hospitalized, Nancy flew down to be with him and with Ursula. Nancy was good and she was strong. When on June 9 she was told that Bob still had a few more days to live, she decided to fly back to Sacramento. After leaving the room, she turned back and kissed Bob on the cheek.

As soon as her plane reached Sacramento, Nancy was told that Bob had died. She returned to Los Angeles on the next flight. "She took over for me," Ursula remembered. "I was in shock. She made all the phone calls, all the arrangements, picked out my wardrobe—everything. Nancy could never separate herself from Ronnie for more than a day if she could help it, and she stayed with me several days and took care of me."

Patti, too, had come to see Bob in the hospital, and sat by his bedside. The whole Reagan family was there at the funeral. Ronnie spoke, his voice breaking, eyes flushed with tears, bringing Bob alive in vivid tales.

A week later, Ursula's twenty-three-year-old-son, Michel, died. "It was an overdose, what seems to have been an overdose," Ursula said. "He just went to sleep and didn't struggle at all. There were so many letters, but Patti's was so sensitive, after all those tragedies. Of all the letters I received, hers was the most beautiful."

——14——
"A GOOD BREATH OF CLEAN AIR"

On Labor Day 1970, a bus carrying Ronnie, his aides and a group of reporters cruised along the highway toward the Orange County fairgrounds. Ronnie was campaigning for reelection and Orange County was Reagan country, as solid an enclave for Ronnie as south Boston was for the Kennedys.

To the liberal media, the name "Orange County" was an epithet, synonymous with rednecks and reaction. Here outside Los Angeles lived aspiring middle-class Americans who didn't want to be taxed to pay for welfare and do-good programs. The orange groves that had been here when Ronnie arrived in California had been plowed under, and mile after mile of tract housing had gone up, interspersed with shopping centers, gas stations, fast-food outlets.

A reporter from the *New York Times* looked out and saw "little stucco bungalows with aging Fords in the driveways, women in Bermuda shorts . . . and freeways carpeting the sun-charred landscape with wall-to-wall concrete." Ronnie looked out the same window and saw not an unchic people ripe for satire but the greatest darn miracle America had ever seen. In the postwar world, common, everyday people by the millions had scrimped and saved and bought their own homes, and gotten a real stake in America. These monotonous subdivisions were proof of their financial success, proof that anyone in America could scramble up into the middle class. Sure, the orange groves had been pretty, but as far as Ronnie was concerned, they could bring the fruit in from Florida, and build more houses and set down another freeway.

Nearing the fairgrounds, one of the labor leaders apologized for the small turnout. Working people didn't come out to these Labor Day celebrations the way they used to.

"You youngsters probably don't remember," Ronnie said to the labor leaders, whose youthful days in the movement were long gone, "but when I was young, golf was a sissy, rich man's game. So was boating and skiing and horseback riding. Today, they're weekend sports for the working man. He doesn't have to go to Labor Day picnics."

Ronnie's first term had been in part on-the-job training, learning how to work with the legislature, and how and where to compromise. Now he was running against Jesse Unruh, the rotund Speaker of the Assembly. Unruh looked like a classic American pol, a minor character in *All the King's Men*. A brusque, savvy politician, he loved the dealmaking, sweet-talking business of politics. He was a talented, dedicated legislator, but he was no match for Ronnie's television or personal appearances as the conservative's prosaic Walt Whitman, singing his song of the people, a hard-working, God-fearing, blameless people.

"We have been picked at, sworn at, rioted against and downgraded until we have a built-in guilt complex, and this has been compounded by the accusations of our sons and daughters who pride themselves in 'telling it like it is,' " he told the state chamber of commerce. "Well, I have news for them—in a thousand social-science courses they have been informed 'the way it is *not*'. . . . As for our generation, I will make no apology. No people in all history paid a higher price for freedom. And no people have done so much to advance the dignity of man. . . . We are called materialistic. Maybe so. . . . But our materialism has made our children the biggest, tallest, most handsome and intelligent generation of Americans yet. They will live longer with fewer illnesses, learn more, see more of the world and have more successes in realizing their personal dreams and ambitions than any other people in any other period of our history—because of our 'materialism.' "

Ronnie was a man without guilt in a nation that was losing its sense of righteousness. Other Americans whose children had run away from them and their dreams, flinging accusations, sat bewildered, wondering what they had done wrong. Not Ronnie. He believed in the same small-town, middle-class values of hard work, patriotism and reverence that he always had, values that to him didn't seem rigid and narrow. Other Americans chased after the rainbow of affluence, loading up on boats, campers, snow-mobiles, color TVs, and wall-to-wall carpeting, borrowing unprecedented amounts, all the while worrying about their future. Not Ronnie. He wasn't concerned with out-of-control consumer spending; he believed that people deserved these things because they had worked for them, and should work more, buy more, enjoy more. Other Americans watched the maimed, the bloodied and the dead of Vietnam on the television news and sensed the moral ambiguity of the war. Not Ronnie. The war remained for him a grand and noble cause.

The very issues on which he chose to base his campaign distanced him from some of the nastier realities of California: Taxes, the size of government, the state's financing of higher education, law and order, the environment, and building the state's economy. As Steven Roberts of the *New York Times* wrote, Ronnie didn't mention "poverty, slums, disease, discrimination, job training or justice."

Ronnie sensed one great truth about the nation that he loved so much: that the future of America depended on people having an optimistic sense of themselves and of their nation. The economy depended upon people expressing their faith by buying and borrowing. Beyond that, democracy depended on people having faith in themselves and their government, acting positively in the myriad decisions of their daily lives, dealing fairly with other people, paying taxes, carrying out minor civic duties, adding strong threads to the fabric of society.

"It seems like so often today that the world we know is coming unglued," he told the annual Labor Day picnic of Local 324 of the Retail Clerks International Assocation, AFL-CIO at the Orange County Fairgrounds. In the last election, Ronnie had done well among working-class Democratic voters. These men and women stocked the shelves of Safeway and Alpha Beta with the bounty of American agribusiness—frozen pot pies; oranges from Florida; a wealth of bread, ice cream, soda pop; whole rows of cereals. They wanted their share of the dream for themselves and for their children and they looked up at Ronnie and listened attentively.

"I've got a new way to stop smog," he said. "Stop burning down the schools." These clerks hadn't been able to take advantage of California's tuition-free system of higher education; it rankled many of them to see college kids rampaging in the streets. "The young people want three political parties, one in power, one out of power and one marching on Sacramento. . . .

"Welfare is the taxpayer's greatest domestic expense, and it is increasing in cost faster than our revenues can keep pace," he said. "I am also convinced there is a sizable percentage of people who have taken advantage of loopholes . . . to augment their incomes at your expense."

When Ronnie spoke, it all sounded so plausible. Kick the slackers off welfare. Boot the "brats," "freaks" and "cowardly fascists" out of school. Cut down taxes. Leave people alone and things would be all right. They would even be great.

Ronnie was a superb campaigner. He outspent Unruh two to one. He won with 52.9 percent of the votes, polling half a million more votes than his opponent.

If there are no second acts in American lives, as F. Scott Fitzgerald believed, then life is often a series of one-act plays, each one having little to do with the previous one. Change a job, change a spouse, move on. In his official biography as governor, Ronnie didn't mention that he had been married to Janie and had two children by that marriage. As for Nancy, her one-page biography began: "Nancy Davis Reagan was born in Chicago, the only daughter of Dr. and Mrs. Loyal Davis."

The past, however, had a way of intruding, like a ghost at Macbeth's banquet. Back east in New Jersey, Nancy's father, Ken Robbins, was nearing the end of his days. His wife, Patsie, had died. He was selling his house and settling accounts. "My doctor last week told me I should join the Retired Persons Club and get to see people," Ken wrote his niece, Kathleen Young, on May 20, 1970. "I'm so terribly lonesome here it's awful. Six months ago, last Friday, my sweetheart Patsie left me."

More than a year later, when things got worse, Young decided to contact her cousin Nancy. Young remembered: "Ken was in the hospital and Patsie had died and I didn't know what to do. I couldn't afford to go back there and help out. I tried to get hold of Nancy. I called up the Republican party. I said, 'Hey, I'm her cousin. I don't want anything.' They said to call the governor's office. I did and talked to a secretary and told her about Ken and asked for Nancy and they said they'd get back to me, but they never did."

On February 2, 1972, Ken Robbins died.

Nancy tried to forget not only much of her early years but a good deal of what she had experienced as a young woman. In the theater and film industry in New York and Los Angeles, she had lived a life far less rigid than that lived by most of her contemporaries. But now Nancy had morals as uncompromising as if she had been raised in a convent. Although Ronnie had signed a bill legalizing abortions, Nancy believed that abortions were a crime and that women did have a choice. "It starts with a movement of the head, either yes or no. This cheap, easy thing they say—that I can do whatever I want sexually and not take responsibility—I don't agree with that at all."

She had no truck with women's liberation.

"Ridiculous," she called it. "They're going to end up being unhappy women." She couldn't understand the use of this new term "Ms." or the fact that married women had started keeping their maiden names. "The happiest day of my life was when Miss Davis became Mrs. Reagan." She couldn't stand the idea of pantsuits in public "where a woman should look like a woman."

Two decades earlier, when she had filled out her studio biography, Nancy had described her phobias as "superficiality, vulgarity . . . untidiness of mind and person—and cigars." Like many women of her generation who had grown up believing that outward niceties were reliable barometers of character, she made matters of style and taste into moral issues. She could say, as she did in her weekly question-answer column of the *Sacramento Union* on June 4, 1972, that "I think we forget that every age has its fads. . . . I admit I'm getting tired of jeans and long hair." But when she looked at her daughter's straight long hair and jeans, she was not so philosophical. To her, Patti's dress meant that she was living a life that rejected social rules and propriety, exchanging it for nothing more than anarchy.

Nancy hated obscenities. "I've heard people use certain trigger words they know will raise emotions and I've gotten sick to my stomach," she wrote. "From a woman's standpoint, it frightens me when I see students shouting obscenities," she told one interviewer. "I think of Hitler's Youth movement."

To Nancy, the youthful protesters were a bizarre and terrible race symbolizing the instability and disrespect that she hated and feared. After Ronnie left the governorship, she happened to be going to a fund-raising event in the San Francisco area. Her driver and companion that day was Dennis Hunt, a handsome young public-relations executive, and a fervent admirer of the Reagans. Hunt didn't know the Bay Area very well, and as he drove the Granada through Berkeley, he listened intently to Nancy while looking for street signs.

"You know during the Manson killings they threatened to send one of the victim's heads to the governor," Nancy said as the car moved quickly through the university community.

"I'm afraid I'm lost, Mrs. Reagan," Hunt said. "It's the long way but we'll get there."

Nancy looked out on Berkeley, a city her husband considered full of political infamy and moral squalor. She reached back and locked all the doors. "You never know," she said. "You never know when one might recognize me."

In Sacramento, Nancy gave her teas and interviews, the daily knitting of political wifedom. As often as the Reagans could, they left Sacramento Thursday evening for their home in Pacific Palisades, not returning until Monday.

Nancy's group of friends was becoming one of the most exclusive sets in Los Angeles. Martha Lyles and Mary Jane Wick were old family friends. Jean Smith, the wife of Ronnie's attorney, William French Smith, was one of the most recent arrivals, Nancy's good friend since the early years of Ronnie's governorship. William Wilson was one of Ronnie's advisers, and Nancy was close to Betty, his petite, well-dressed wife. In the next years, the Reagans enjoyed flying down to Mexico to spend a weekend at the Wilsons' ranch and hacienda where Betty would serve her guests elegant food in a relaxed, peaceful atmosphere.

Two of Nancy's friends were former movie actresses whom Ronnie had met years before. Ronnie had known Jane Bryan since he had played beside her in the 1938 movie *Girls on Probation* as well as two other movies. That was well before she had married Justin Dart, whose first wife had been a drugstore heiress. He, too, had become one of Ronnie's advisers and financial backers. Bonita ("Bunny") Granville was another old acting colleague of Ronnie's; she had appeared with him in Warners' *Angels Wash Their Faces* in 1939. Her father had been a star of the Ziegfeld Follies, and Bunny had come to Hollywood at age seven. She had been nominated for an Academy Award when she was twelve for her performance in Lillian Hellman's *These Three*. Before she had retired to raise a family, Bunny had appeared in fifty-five films. Now she was Nancy's friend, married to Jack Wrather, Jr., a big man in oil, entertainment and real estate, and another of Ronnie's advisers, with whom she coproduced the television series "Lassie." The two couples, along with the Wilsons, became frequent dinner partners at Chasen's.

Virginia Tuttle went way back with Ronnie. They had met in 1946 when Ronnie bought a Ford from her husband, Holmes. Virginia had worked for Ronnie's election as governor in the campaign office her husband and Henry Salvatori opened on Wilshire Boulevard across from I. Magnin's. Virginia and Holmes had hosted the gubernatorial victory celebration in their Hancock Park home. The Tuttles had introduced the Reagans to Marion and Earle Jorgensen at the Autumn Cotillion. Earle, the steel magnate, became an important adviser to Ronnie, serving with Alfred Bloomingdale on the committee that helped him select his first-term cabinet. Marion was a stylish lady, beautifully coiffed and typically clad in Galanos gowns and Maximillian furs.

Betsy Bloomingdale and Nancy had first become friends taking their children to camp. During Ronnie's second term, Nancy became close enough to Betsy that Ronnie's press secretary, Paul Beck, considered her "Nancy's best friend." Despite her three children, Betsy had a figure and manner that were positively girlish. Along with Betty and Marion, Betsy was a perfect size eight. Her passions were parties and clothes. She did her part selling clothes in the Colleagues, but much preferred chattering away at the Bistro with Nancy. "She's like a totally wired writer who is totally

The best of friends: Nancy with Betsy Bloomingdale and Jerome "Jerry" Zipkin. *(Guy Delort, Women's Wear Daily)*

fascinating, a dynamic character," said one of Betsy's admirers. Another acquaintance describes her as "the too-tall girl in class: precise, pristine, a cinnamon stick, the kind of woman who appeals to gays."

Sitting together, Nancy and Betsy were like two teen-age "best friends," believing that the friendship gave each one added status. Betsy's husband, Alfred, whom she had married in 1946, had made millions of dollars developing Diners Club, a credit card used by businessmen and others. The success of the card was spawned by the expense-account world of postwar America, and the Bloomingdales were sitting pretty.

One of Betsy's friends was Jerome ("Jerry") Zipkin, the son of Annette Goldstein and David Zipkin. Jerry's father had made a fortune in New York real estate. Jerry had attended Princeton, but did not graduate with his class in 1936, and went out into the depression with nothing but money to buffer him against cruel fortune. He traveled to California and Europe, beginning a lifetime of taking seriously what others considered frivolous.

To some, Jerry seemed to be nothing but an upturned nose. Yet Jerry had taste, and charm, and was the most civilized and gracious of friends. Somerset Maugham, the aging, world-weary novelist, was one of those who enjoyed Jerry's company. Maugham's biographer, Ted Morgan, thinks the British author may have patterned Elliot Templeton, a snobbish character in *The Razor's Edge,* on his American friend.

In 1949, Jerry visited Maugham in his Riviera home. Afterward, the novelist wrote his lover, Alan Searle, about Jerry's "completely mad" spending spree. "We had the greatest difficulty in preventing him from buying up the entire contents of every shop he went into," he wrote. "As it was, he went back laden with antiques, shirts, and pullovers, most of which he could have got in New York at half the price. But as he owns not apartment houses on Park Avenue but rows of apartments, I don't suppose it mattered."

When Betsy introduced Nancy to Jerry and his circle, Nancy was simply enthralled. For wealthy ladies who could not fill the void of their free time, he was there, sexually benign, constantly entertaining. He was a lover of the exquisite moment. He chased these moments as if they were rare butterflies, netting them, pinning them in his memory, and then chasing again. And yet wherever he was, no matter how glorious the party, how witty the dinner conversation, he exuded a certain malaise, as if it all weren't quite right.

"Jerry is like a character in a Balzac novel who is always in the know," says one close Reagan friend. "He isn't someone that you climb on. He takes care of people by being totally fun, good company. Betsy and

Jerry are both totally engaging. Nancy has little tolerance for people who aren't interesting."

Watching Nancy, Betsy and Jerry, some of the society ladies thought that Nancy's two friends were remaking her, giving her a style and *savoir faire* that she had lacked before. But Nancy was already making the best-dressed lists. Her friends only helped refine and enrich what was already there. Jerry watched over Nancy, telling her what to wear and whom to see and what to do. Nancy loved Ronnie profoundly, but she couldn't titter with him over lunch at the Bistro Garden, discussing Bill Blass's new show or savaging some grotesque matron in the corner with a *bon mot*. For Nancy, it was a world of conversational pastels and sweet nuance far from the gray precincts of politics.

Through Betsy and Jerry, Nancy was collecting an entourage of fashionable, effervescent people. Her other friends couldn't understand how she could spend so much time with them. "There is this crazy fagotage around her," said Leonard Spigelgass. "They're so embarrassing. I like Nancy very much but I find her friends absurd, just absurd. Imagine spending any time with Betsy Bloomingdale."

There were dangers in this life for Ronnie and his political career. It was one thing for a conservative columnist like William F. Buckley to be an intellectual snob, indeed to make snobbishness seem almost endearing. It was quite another for the wife of the governor of California to be a social snob. Members of Ronnie's staff worried that Nancy's associations would offend voters.

Some of Nancy's new friends had life-styles that would have given the boys back in Dixon's barbershop a lot to chew over. According to her sworn testimony, in 1971 seventeen-year-old Vicki Morgan began having an affair with fifty-three-year-old Alfred Bloomingdale. A social pillar in his own community, Bloomingdale allegedly enjoyed spanking and beating his young mistress. "Nancy told her [Betsy] about me 11 years ago when she saw me and Alfred together," Morgan told the *Los Angeles Herald Examiner* in 1982. "Alfred and I were out to lunch together and Nancy saw us." Nancy denied knowing about the affair; but if she did not, she was an anomaly among Betsy's set in Beverly Hills.

In 1975, Ms. Morgan married and it appeared to Betsy that Alfred had returned to the convivial bliss of wedlock. In later years, however, he continued a relationship that one day would shame Betsy, and embarrass Nancy and Ronnie as well.

During Ronnie's second term as governor, he thoroughly enjoyed his work. He was very much the paternal governor, acting with a confidence that he had lacked before. In later years he would try to turn his gubernatorial record into a series of epic achievements. Here was Ronnie standing alone in the high noon of big government, shooting it out with the dark forces of collectivism and sloth, turning back the welfare hordes, cutting down the government bureaucrats in their tracks, attacking the dark forces of crime and anarchy.

Ronnie did have a right to brag about some of his performance. So did the Democratic-controlled state legislature with whom the governor worked to achieve many of the reforms. The California Welfare Reform Act of 1971 was an honest rendering of Ronnie's ideals into a working piece of legislation. Actively consulting with Bob Moretti, the new assembly speaker, Ronnie's staff put together a bill that on one hand sharply reduced the numbers of fraudulent welfare recipients while raising the benefits for the truly needy by 43 percent.

Some of Ronnie's purist philosophies had to give way to pragmatism. Ronnie had vowed to cut down state government. But people were still pouring into California, and what he was able to do was to slow the growth of the number of state workers, from 158,400 when he entered office to 192,400 when he left. Despite his campaign promises, he sponsored the greatest tax increases in the state's history. The state budget more than doubled, from $4.6 billion when he took office to $10.2 billion when he left. At the same time, California property owners pocketed $4 billion in property-tax relief. As for Ronnie's pledge to be tough on criminals—despite the forty bills he signed to do just that, the number of homicides doubled, and armed robberies grew at even a greater rate.

Ronnie had unsheathed his sword and hacked away at the tentacles of government, but, like the brush in the hills above his house, it just kept growing and growing. He thought that if he started knocking the ne'er-do-wells off welfare and making welfare recipients get out and work, the lists would shrink dramatically. But unwed and abandoned mothers, the sick and the illiterate clogged the lists, and, Ronnie or no Ronnie, they stayed there, the pathetic underbelly of America.

Nancy couldn't have been prouder of Ronnie, and she was infuriated by the criticism he was receiving. In 1971, Ronnie's 1970 California income-tax return was leaked to the press. It disclosed that the governor had paid no state taxes. Citing business losses, Ronnie had to admit that he had not paid taxes in 1970 or in one other year. For all he groaned about the burden of taxes, like most rich people, he didn't pay anything like what the working stiff figured a rich man paid. In a few years, Americans would yawn cynically when they read yet another story about a politician, a corporation, an individual who had paid no taxes. But in 1971, most Ameri-

Alfred Bloomingdale, founder of Diners Club, with his wife, Betsy, and interior decorator Ted Graber. *(WWD)*

cans didn't realize yet that accountants had become the *artistes* of business, constructing tax shelters and business "losses" so that people like Ronnie and his friends wouldn't have to fill Uncle Sam's coffers with *their* money. It was all legal—Ronnie had the lawyers and accountants to prove it—but it rankled some people no end.

Nancy was so "deeply hurt" by "dirty" politics that she hoped Ronnie would never run for office again. Nevertheless, "I still basically believe that men who are not politicians should get into politics," she told Sacramento's KCRA Television in 1971. "I do believe that. I think the whole thing needs a good breath of fresh air."

Nancy continued to do what she could to protect her two children from public life. In 1970, Patti had gone off to Northwestern University in Illinois, where she was interested in writing, but she only lasted a year before returning to the West. She went on to USC and studied drama, but left after her junior year. Patti was a child of the Sixties who once had wanted nothing more than to dance off to Haight-Ashbury and live as a hippie. The idealism and energy of the decade had dissipated and the streets of the Haight were a tough, hard place, but in Los Angeles the rock musicians remained one of the last symbols of the Sixties.

Patti took up with Bernie Leadon, a guitarist and sometime banjo player for the Eagles, one of the more popular groups of the early 1970s. Patti could empathize with Leadon. The musician had found it hard handling sudden fame and fortune and had twice dropped out of the group. A native southern Californian who dressed in T-shirts and jeans, Leadon preferred anonymity, a sentiment that appealed to Patti. The Eagles had become a symbol of the restless generation that bought its records by the millions. "The whole way of life they had come to represent undoubtedly accounts for part of their appeal," wrote *New Times* in August 1975. "The restlessness, the self-pity, the curiously romantic misogyny . . . all contribute to the portrait of Hollywood angst that the band has conjured up. But what completes the picture is the especially poignant air of ennui, of confusion, of painful insight."

Nancy was horrified that her daughter not only liked this music but was living with one of its leading proponents. It would have done no good to tell Nancy that shaggy Bernie and his friends weren't freaked-out rebels but merchant princes, cultural entrepreneurs, making more money from the music than Ronnie ever made from films. It was as if she had lost her daughter to a world that directly challenged all the principles and decorum in which she believed, a world where drugs were almost a constant presence, a world full of dangers not only for Patti and her reputation but for her father's reputation and honor as well. Nancy had seen what drugs had done to Ursula Taylor's son. And Patti was in a world where drugs were almost omnipresent.

Ronnie was perfectly willing to discuss political issues with Patti, but he didn't like hearing about what she was doing. "When they were having their disagreements with Patti, I remember my father saying, 'What ever happened to just not saying anything?'" Maureen recalled. "He said, 'I can remember as a kid doing things that I knew my mother wasn't going to like. And I used to pray that she wouldn't find out. Now we live in an age when everybody can't wait to tell everybody else. Why don't they just not tell me? I'd be a lot happier really.'"

The Reagans continued to project an image of the classic American family. In fact, they did have the classic American family. But it was the new model. In the early 1970s, families were being torn apart by children rejecting their parents' mode of life, and parents delivering ultimatums out of their battered pride.

The decade and all its disintegration were even more perplexing for people with the strict doctrines of the Reagans. They believed in the family, in the country, in discipline, in work, in community spirit. They didn't believe in questioning those values. They were a given, the basis for dealing with day-to-day life.

More than ever, Nancy wanted to protect Ron, Jr. When it was time for him to enter high school, she actively explored which private boarding school would be best for him. She wanted a strict, conservative school with high academic standards. She visited the Webb School in Claremont, California, thirty miles east of Los Angeles, and found what she sought.

Situated outside town in the foothills of the San Gabriel Mountains, the campus appeared far from the din and temptations of the outside world. The 165 boys wore coats and ties for dinner, couldn't have long hair and had to have the lights off at 10:30 P.M. They were severely disciplined with a demerit system, and immediately expelled if caught drinking or off campus at night without a pass. Webb was just the kind of place Nancy thought Ron, Jr., needed. Once she had made up her mind, she brought him out for an inspection.

When Ron, Jr., entered the secluded school in the fall of 1972, he was quiet and subdued. Nancy had requested that Cham Rand, the son of a family friend, be placed in Ron's dormitory to serve as a model to her son. Cham was a mother's idea of the perfect young man: studious, polite, unquestioning, neat.

Ron soon found another group of friends, none of whom personified Nancy's definition of the all-American boy. "It was obvious that he had been very sheltered," said Marty Briner, a freshman who became one of Ron's best friends at Webb. Early that freshman year, several of his new friends decided that something had to be done about the bell that regulated their day from 7:00 A.M., when it sounded the last chance for breakfast, to 10:30 P.M. when it sounded lights out. One night they climbed up the bell tower and wrapped towels around the clappers. The next morning, there was no clanging.

These were inquisitive young men. They didn't accept the strict conditions of the school simply because of ancient rules. They questioned the curriculum as well, and the society for which Webb was grooming them. "We were all pretty philosophical," said Marty Briner. "We saw the prep-school educational environment as a cog of the social machine. We had reservations about our only chance for individuality in that society being reserved to drinking beers on Sunday. It wasn't interesting enough for us."

Ron, Jr., did join the B football team, but he wasn't a gung-ho player like his father. He would just as soon have been off writing poetry. "He didn't write for the paper, because they would have wanted him to write about what happened on the football field," said Bill Ripley, his adviser, "and he would have rather written about the sunrise."

Ron, Jr., was an avid reader. Unlike his father, who as a young man had accepted the world around him as good and preordained, young Ron was challenging and questioning everything. He and his friends roomed in the same one-story dorm their sophomore year. They lounged in the smoking room, endlessly discussing the world in trenchant, searching conversations. "Each of us felt that if you disagreed with something, you asked. If you didn't like the answer given, then you had to resolve it yourself with your own values and ideas," said Doug McCowan, another member of the group.

These discussions often led to confrontations with the administration. "Ron was very bright and talkative," remembered Roy Bergesen, dean of students and now director of admissions. "He was fun to argue with because he was so quick. He was like a barroom lawyer coming up with every possible reason for not having to do something."

The group had not completely given up on their pranks. In their junior year, they rolled the head coach's VW beetle into the dining room, set it on blocks, painted a face on the windshield and crowned it with a baseball cap. They weren't beyond slipping off campus at night to a party with female students from St. Lucy's. They weren't beyond toking a little marijuana, either. To cover up the telltale scent, the boys burned incense until the dorm smelled like a Hindu temple. When the incense was outlawed, they used oil instead, burning it to the gods of discretion.

The counterculture tenor of the group and its constant questioning began to rankle the school. "We were a thorn in their sides," said Briner. The administration admonished the boys for their "negativism." So they nicknamed themselves "the negos."

By his junior year, Ron, Jr., was an articulate, determined young man, and he became the negos' spokesman. "Ron was very quick," said Chris Avant, a member of the group. "He was so articulate. Most of us would get mad and be unable to voice our anger coherently. We couldn't present our grievances or debate them like Ron did."

Nancy began to sense the change in her son. "She had the feeling that she had sent Ron to the school pure and that we corrupted him," said Avant. "But really he was just growing up."

Whenever Ron, Jr., went over to Briner's house during vacations, Nancy worried. "She would call my mother and ask, 'Where are they going, who are they with?'" Briner said. "She was so overly and unnecessarily protective of him. My first inclination was to like and trust Ron's father. And my first reaction with Mrs. Reagan was to fear and disdain her. Even when she was being friendly, you had the feeling that she was holding something back or condemning you."

Nancy began to call the school, checking up on Ron and his education. "His mother was much more the active parent," said Bergesen. "She is a very strong woman. She would call about anything that she felt wasn't right. She would worry about anything. She was very concerned about drugs even then and was very alert to drugs on the campus. She didn't miss much. She's pretty sharp that way. If she felt a teacher or a class or his dorm wasn't right, she'd call and say so."

Ron, Jr., was not without his own shrewdness in dealing with Nancy, at times withdrawing from the burden of her concern, at times standing up to her.

One day Nancy called Bergesen. As the dean of students remembered it, Nancy said: "My son's coming home for the weekend, and to avoid a fight with his father, could you get him to cut his hair?"

"I can't make him, Mrs. Reagan," Bergesen said. Students could grow their hair down to the collar but not below, a compromise with the styles of the Seventies. "His hair conforms to the rules."

"But he sees his father so infrequently, I'd really like it to be a pleasant visit."

The dean of students considered the Reagans "a typical upper-middle-class family where there's a domineering mother," and he sympathized with young Ron. As he promised he would, though, Bergesen went to see his young charge and forwarded Nancy's request.

"You can't make me," said Ron, Jr., who had grown into a tall, lean young man with a mime's face that displayed his every emotion. "You can't make me. I know the rules."

"Your mother would like to avoid an argument."

"Absolutely not. I won't do it."

Bergeson left privately impressed that Ron was not afraid to confront his mother. "It was far better for Ron to be in boarding school," Bergesen said years later. "No one could have survived at his home. She was not used to being countermanded."

Ron, Jr., continued to lobby for reform so adamantly that the school administration became even more impatient. They separated Briner and Ron by moving Ron to another dorm. "Ron became more blatant in his defiance than I was about to be," said McCowan. "It was almost as if he wanted to get kicked out. That would be the ultimate rebellion."

At the end of his father's second term as governor, after trouble with Webb's administration, Ron, Jr., returned to Pacific Palisades to live and go to the Harvard School. When he left Webb for the last time in December 1974 in the middle of his junior year, it was a relief to all three parties: Ron, Jr., who was finally released from the stringent school rules; the administration, rid of its most articulate dissenter; and Nancy, who was relieved to have her son out of the clutches of the group she saw as his corrupters.

Nancy appeared glad to have direct control over her son again. When Briner called to talk to his friend, Nancy would answer and say that Ron, Jr., wasn't there. Briner returned some of Ron's records to Nancy at the house one day, a note secreted inside one of the album covers. "It was hard to keep in contact," Briner said, "and we drifted apart quickly."

With its flower-strewn walkways and red-tiled roofs, Harvard looked more like a Mexican monastery than a highly reputed prep school. Despite having started out as a military academy, the manners, demeanor and ideas of the students weren't neatly cropped. Ron, Jr., let his hair grow long and felt himself a part of his time and generation.

He took up with an old Dye School acquaintance, Neil Leonard, the son of Nancy's friend Betty. Leonard introduced him to his friends, John Ungerleider, Dan McCabe and Charlie Stack. These young men were a tight clique like Ron's Webb friends had been. They, too, were bound together by an inquisitive nature that the majority of Harvard students lacked. But Ron's new friends took the talk of reforms out of the smoking room. Ungerleider was the campus newspaper editor and had his own office at the school.

"There was a very dynamic intellectual atmosphere with that group," said one teacher. They often gathered at the office talking politics for hours while planning the next newspaper issue. Ron, Jr., fit in immediately and began drawing political cartoons that savaged conservatives.

Ron was not an outstanding student, but his instinctive humor and creative writing impressed several teachers. The arts were becoming his special sphere and another bond with his friends. "The group wasn't totally political," said McCabe. "We were more interested in the arts. That's how he fit in. Ron would be quiet during the political talks. We were sensitive to the situation for Ron and were reasonably careful about not making him take a stand on his father. He had a lot more input into the artistic discussions. We talked about film and listened to music. Jazz was the big thing."

Nancy was holding her son up to daily scrutiny, like a wineglass smudged with fingerprints. She began to worry about his involvement with this group as well. "The whole ambience of the group worried her," said one teacher. "She was an establishment conservative and as she saw it these boys weren't headed for business school." She had called Webb to check up on Ron, Jr., but now her calls to Harvard were becoming even more persistent. He warned his teachers about his mother's impending calls to their homes. She often telephoned during the dinner hour, letting an instructor's meal grow cold while she talked on and on.

Other staff members saw something poignant, almost pathetic, about Nancy's concerns and lack of understanding. She and Ronnie acted as if they wanted their son to fit one precast mold. Nancy loved Ron, Jr., profoundly; but no matter how often she talked to the teachers, she didn't seem to learn anything, to assimilate, to grasp the realities of her son, his creativity and promise. The teachers found it bizarre to receive one of her phone calls and then hang up and realize that this was the Mrs. Reagan whose husband was preaching about the family as America's salvation.

Ron, Jr., had a hard time getting away from Nancy. Mrs. Nowell, the next-door neighbor, occasionally heard young Ron's shrill screams: "Leave me alone! All I want is to be left alone!"

Nancy soon had something totally new to worry about. A new teacher, John West, the first black instructor at Harvard, persuaded the administration to let him teach a dance class as an alternative to the prescribed PE courses. A lot of young men would have preferred taking a knitting class to dancing around like a sugarplum fairy in *The Nutcracker,* but Ron's group was all for it. It helped that West was married. He had no dance studio, no mirror or *barre,* but he gave his four students a feel for the form and beauty of dance. They were young men who, as West saw it, needed discipline, and he worked them until they sweated and ached as much as if they had gone out for football.

West saw that Ron, Jr., was a sixteen-year-old with a dancer's body, beautifully contoured, supple and fluid. As Ron struggled to dance with grace and form, he lost himself in the movements, feeling a wondrous control. Until he started dancing, he had never even seen a live ballet performance. "What's it like to be a dancer?" he asked West one day, and the teacher knew that Ron was serious about dance.

"It was funny to get into that and to see that Ron could really do it," said McCabe. "Going into the arts for Ron was a refuge. In other areas his father would have been more of an issue. Dance ended up being a solution to his interests and his problems. It was something that he is good at and something that could be totally his own."

"I've always been sort of athletic but never a jock," Ron, Jr., said later. "I never liked the idea of beating up on anyone in football. But I enjoyed athletics, at the same time enjoying writing and drawing, creative things. I guess dance was a fusion of those two impulses."

As long as Nancy and Ronnie thought that their son was taking dance as a lark, they didn't mind. But as Ron, Jr., began talking more and more about dance, they became worried. "I wasn't the favorite teacher in their household," West said. "Ron always wanted to step out of himself and try something new, but his parents wouldn't let him. The boys always used to ask him, 'What are your parents going to say about this?' Ron respected his father always. He'd be more vocal about his mother. They'd have a falling out and he'd pack up and go stay with his sister for a while. Ron needed space. All he wanted was to be accepted as himself."

Despite their disagreements over dance, Ron was becoming closer to his father. "The bonds were there before, but tenuous," said West. "Ron's a very warm young man, and the boys told me that Reagan was very likable as well. They used to spend time at Ron's house. They liked his father and used to talk politics and argue with him. He was very tolerant and encouraged the boys to dispute with him. Even though they never agreed with him, they respected him."

"Reagan was such a villain in California's political history," said McCabe. "There was such animosity toward him then. It was part of the culture. He was the guy they loved to hate on California campuses."

"It upset me—it always does when someone you care for is misrepresented," said Ron, Jr. "He was portrayed as some kind of ogre for a long time. And he's such a gentle guy and such a real person. I always wanted to take those people and shake them."

Wherever Ron, Jr., went, he was cast as the governor's son. People whispered as young Ron entered a party. One time Ron and Ungerleider were attending a party at McCabe's house. The group had nicknamed Ungerleider "Bob Dylan."

"This is Bob Dylan and Ron Reagan," McCabe said, introducing his two friends to a young woman.

"Bob Dylan I believe," the woman said, looking at them. "But Ron Reagan, never."

As much as Ron loved his father, he did not want his identity eternally tied to Ronald Reagan's. He wanted to be free. In the 1976 yearbook, Ron, Jr., didn't put the usual pictures and synopsis of his school career on his senior page. Instead, he had reprinted a fanciful Maxfield Parrish print of a nude youth swinging in front of a castle. Over the painting was a poem credited to San Juan de la Cruz:

The conditions of a solitary bird are five:
The first that it flies to the highest point;
the second, that it does not suffer for company, not even of its own kind;
the third, that it aims its beak to the skies;
the fourth, that it does not have a definite color;
the fifth, that it sings very softly.

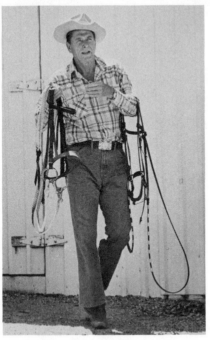

At the country house, Rancho del Cielo, in California's Santa Ynez Mountains, Ronnie prunes a stubborn tree and prepares to saddle up. *(Roger Sandler; UPI)*

═15═

FROM RANCHO
TO RODEO

D uring the last months of Ronnie's second term as governor, he drove up into the Santa Ynez Mountains, northwest of Los Angeles, with William A. Wilson, a gentleman rancher, investor, adviser and friend. For six miles the Refugio Canyon Road twists tortuously up along sheer cliffs, traveling through raw, mesquite-covered land. Suddenly, at an elevation of about 2,200 feet, the road levels out onto a plateau that rests like a natural throne above the world, looking out toward the ocean thirty-five miles away.

Wilson was the kind of tough, blunt-spoken businessman Ronnie admired. Wilson owned property nearby, and the two men rode on horseback over the land. Ronnie was a westerner to whom unrestricted space was the beginning of freedom. As he rode across the untamed, unfurrowed land, he felt right with himself. He needed space, and as he prepared to leave the confines of office, he decided he needed it even more. Wilson showed Ronnie the 688-acre ranch that was for sale. The going price was $527,000 with a $90,000 down payment, a steep commitment with Ronnie's uncertain financial future. He already had the expenses of a 778-acre ranch south of Los Angeles in Riverside County that he had purchased in 1968 for $347,000. He had intended to turn the spread into a working ranch, but he couldn't get the water or power that he needed. To have the kind of ranch he wanted, Ronnie knew that he had to buy his new "Rancho del Cielo" (Ranch in the Sky). And in November 1974, he purchased it.

At Rancho del Cielo, Ronnie felt far above the complexity and compromises of the world below. But his ranch itself was a product of that new America where businessmen didn't make products but deals, and a shelter wasn't a place in which to live but an investment to avoid taxes. In California, the value of agricultural property had increased so dramatically that farmers and ranchers were being taxed out of their lands. Many of them were being forced to sell out to developers, builders ready to put tract houses, gas stations and shopping centers where once there were grain fields and pastures. To forestall this, the state had recently passed a law designating "agricultural preserves" where taxes were kept extremely low. It was a law to be taken advantage of; by grazing twenty-two head of cattle, Ronnie's ranch was considered an "agricultural preserve." In 1979, instead of being socked with over $40,000 in probable property taxes, Ronnie had to pay only $862.

Up here Ronnie didn't think about such things. Wearing old jeans, a cowboy hat and leather gloves, he often chopped wood. The ax blade rose and fell in rhythmic pattern, a woodsman's ballet, as next to Ronnie rose neat cords of wood that would warm the Mexican adobe house against winter's chill. Helping him he had William ("Barney") Barnett, a former California State Police officer who had been his driver and bodyguard during his years as governor. Barney was a far different sort from the rich men with whom Ronnie socialized. He didn't want to talk politics and wasn't looking for any reward. He would have fit right into Dixon. Many felt that Barney was the one man with whom Ronnie felt most comfortable. As they worked together, there was no telling who was a possible presidential candidate and who was his chauffeur.

On weekends, the two men drove up from Pacific Palisades, with some sandwiches in a bag for lunch. As they worked side by side, they talked about their renovation of the eighty-seven-year-old, two-bedroom house. They took down some of the walls and put in a new kitchen. They built a good-size family room where before there had been an ugly screened porch on the small 1,500-square-foot house. They tore off the old corrugated roof. Ronnie wanted to put on a roof of old-fashioned tile, but that would have been too heavy for the walls. So they settled for reddish-brown fiber-glass tile.

Nancy came up, too, but Rancho del Cielo was Ronnie's in the same way that the house in Pacific Palisades was Nancy's. In her jeans and cowboy clothes, she looked more like the heroine of a Hopalong Cassidy movie than a rancher's wife. She pitched in, but she also spent a lot of time on the telephone. For Ronnie, that was just as well. Once he was up here, he didn't want to hear the confounded phone ringing.

Ronnie was a man of immense public charm, but he was also a man who enjoyed being alone. Unlike many actors, he didn't need an entourage around him. Those who tried to get close to him discovered it was like grasping at an image on a screen. He held his intimacies, his vulnerabilities close to himself like a gambler his high cards. "I think that if he were not married, if there were no Nancy, he would be perfectly content by himself," said Lyn Nofziger. "Emotionally, I've just never seen him really need people. That's why he likes people. When you're with him alone or with a group, you never feel alone or shy or shunned. Nevertheless, he's perfectly capable of doing without you."

In his eight years in office, Ronnie had made contacts but not friends. He cared about his old friends in Dixon and in the film industry, but as charming as he might be, he treated his professional associates with professional distance. The staff looked out for him, but he did not look out for his staff. Early on in the administration, one personal aide had quit in a moment of personal pique, simply packing up and heading home. During the first gubernatorial campaign, the man had spent as much time with the governor as anyone else, seeing to his every need. For days the man sat by the phone, but neither Ronnie nor anyone else ever contacted him to find out what had happened.

"He's not the kind of guy who when someone leaves is going to worry about how you're going to pay the mortgage," said one former aide. "Maybe he doesn't think about the mortgage deliberately."

Leaving office in December 1974, Ronnie had an enviable setup from which to preach his gospel and to further his undeclared campaign for president. Two of his former aides, Michael K. Deaver and Peter D. Hannaford, had set up a public-relations firm whose main function was to service Ronald Wilson Reagan. For sixty-four-year-old Ronnie, it was not a bad life. Barney Barnett picked Ronnie up several times a week and chauffeured him to the Deaver & Hannaford offices at 10960 Wilshire Boulevard in Westwood. There Ronnie would look over a dozen three-minute radio commentaries to be heard on 200 stations across America. Those he hadn't written himself on a yellow legal pad, Hannaford had prepared. Then he might chat a while or go through the mail. "He always had time to talk to everyone, the secretaries, everyone," said Mary Nimmo, then an executive at Deaver & Hannaford.

Often Ronnie was off speaking, receiving up to $10,000 a speech. In one month alone during 1975, his schedule took him to London; Malibu; Des Moines, Iowa; Jackson, Mississippi; Paramus, New Jersey; Oakland County, Michigan; and Boca Raton, Florida. It didn't leave him much time for the ranch, but the money wasn't bad. In that year he made an estimated $800,000.

What set Ronnie apart from most politicians was that he enjoyed daily living so much. When he went up to the ranch, it was as if he had lived all his life herding cattle. Even in Los Angeles or on his speaking tours, he exuded a pleasure and never-ending amazement at life that was rare enough to see in a young man, much less in the sixty-five-year-old former governor of California.

Ronnie was a modern-day Horatio Alger protagonist. Those nineteenth-century heroes did not rise merely on their own initiative. As John G. Cawelti writes in *Apostles of the Self-Made Man*, "From the beginning of his career, the Alger boy demonstrates an astounding propensity for chance encounters with benevolent and useful friends, and his success is largely due to their patronage and assistance." From the day in Dixon when young Ronnie had chatted with rich businessmen as a lifeguard, he had ingratiated himself with men of wealth. Holmes Tuttle. Justin Dart. Bill Wilson. Jack Wrather. Henry Salvatori. Alfred Bloomingdale. Walter Annenberg. Earle Jorgensen. These were the conservative kingmakers backing Ronnie, advising him on investments, putting money into his campaign, promoting him among the hierarchy of the Republican party. For the most part, their wives were Nancy's friends, and as Ronnie rose toward the White House, the wives rose, too; the whole social and political circle moved upward together.

Ronnie's friends were not part of the Protestant business establishment. Alfred Bloomingdale and Walter Annenberg were Jewish, as was Charlie Wick, another friend and adviser. Salvatori and Wilson were Catholic. During the Thirties, Annenberg's father, Moses, had reputedly the highest earned income in the country. His son, a media magnate, couldn't pretend to have pulled himself up by the bootstraps, but most of Ronnie's other advisers considered themselves "self-made men." Bloomingdale was the grandson of the founder of Bloomingdale's department store. Dart had married Ruth Walgreen, a drugstore heiress. Wrather came from oil money and made his own fortune in entertainment and real estate. As for Salvatori and Jorgensen, they had struggled up, the sons of immigrants on Manhattan's Lower East Side.

Even if these men weren't all "self-made," they were plungers, business gamblers whose expansionary, optimistic visions had matched the world of post–World War II California. Jorgensen had developed a major steel company, and Salvatori had founded Western Geophysical, an oil company. But Ronnie's friends had not built railroads, great ships or vast oil empires like the generation of Rockefeller and Carnegie before them. Nor were they daring innovators operating on the frontiers of technology and change, developing computers or microchips. As their legacy, these men had such things as Tupperware, *TV Guide,* "Lassie," "The Lone Ranger," *Snow White and the Three Stooges,* Duracell batteries, drugstores, Diners Club, Ford and Lincoln auto dealerships.

Ronnie's friends had supported him to reestablish the kind of freewheeling, hands-off environment that had nurtured their achievements. They were getting old and they wanted to assure their legacy. Nothing would top their achievements like helping to put Ronnie in the White House and getting America back on track.

When Ronnie left Sacramento, he had expected his rich friends to help him the way they always had—put him on corporate boards, send all sorts of deals his way. But he was able to make big money with his radio commentaries and speeches, and his friends did not help him to the extent that they might have. "I am told that it changed forever his relationship with them," said Jim Lake, who joined Reagan during his last year as governor because he was told that Reagan was planning to run for president. (The new campaign law that limited personal contributions to a presidential candidate to a thousand dollars also diminished the importance of Ronnie's wealthiest friends.)

The dream of the presidency was still there. After Nixon's two terms in office, Ronnie's advisers expected Ronnie to win the nomination. As early as May 1974, when Nixon was still president, Ronnie met with a group of advisers to discuss his presidential prospects. It was the usual mix of wealthy businessmen, including Dart and Tuttle; retainers and former aides like Deaver, Hannaford, Ed Meese and Nofziger; and a few outsiders, including Lake and Washington attorney John Sears.

Sears was a political technician and strategist who had orchestrated Nixon's search for delegates in 1967 and 1968. Among the top campaign aides, Sears was an anomaly. Deaver, Hannaford and Nofziger owed their own prominence almost completely to Ronnie. To a large extent, Meese and Clark owed their careers to Reagan, too. Sears was a principal in his own right, an ambitious, complex man. Sears lived not for politics but for campaigns. Like a jockey who without a horse is just a tiny man, Sears without a candidate was only another dark-suited Washington attorney.

"Well, what do you think?" asked Meese, in his usual courtly, soft-spoken manner.

"Nixon's got to stay in office," someone said, an opinion that was quickly seconded. To some of Ronnie's advisers, Nixon's greatest crime was not Watergate but the possibility that he might ruin the scenario for getting *their* man to the White House. The group agreed that if Nixon stayed as president, Ronnie should run in 1976. And thus it was important to keep Nixon in the Oval Office.

"Forget keeping Nixon in office," Sears said dramatically. "I think the race can be won. I think it should be done; the party needs it, the country needs it; but I disagree that Nixon has to stay as president. In fact, Nixon will be gone in six months."

The comment jolted Ronnie to full attention. Even when those in his own party had begun to desert Nixon, Ronnie could not understand the seriousness of Watergate. He was sure that Richard Nixon's crimes had been grossly exaggerated.

Sears continued: "Jerry Ford can't cut the mustard, he's not perceived as a leader; he can't lead the Congress or the country. He will be vulnerable and we can beat him. He will not be seen as a true incumbent; you have as much support around the country as he has. We can challenge him successfully in New Hampshire."

Sears gained little support that day. But with Nixon's resignation in August, Sears seemed more and more the prophet. Now ensconced in the Oval Office was an accidental president, Gerald Ford, a squatter who had no intention of vacating the premises to make room for Ronnie. And sitting right behind him was Nelson Rockefeller, the scourge of the Republican Right, who had been chosen for vice-president over Ronnie.

Ronnie kept chopping wood, giving speeches and biding his time. Nancy was still his closest adviser. She was as fiercely protective of his honor as of his health, and she thought long and hard before agreeing that Ronnie should go for the ultimate prize in American politics. More than ever, she was not a woman to have against you. As Jules Witcover wrote, she was "painted in some quarters as a kind of West Coast Dragon Lady." She was never a lady to forget or forgive. She went along with letting Nofziger join the campaign, even though she had not liked his work in Sacramento, but she was soon siding with Sears in reducing Nofziger's role to running only the California primary campaign.

Sears and Nofziger both wanted Ronnie to get hopping and make his run. But he waited and waited to make his commitment. "He's the kind of man who pulls stuff and sees what the reaction is going to be," said Paul Beck, his former press secretary. "He pulls them to see if people are ready." It didn't matter whether it was asking Jane Wyman or Nancy to marry him, or announcing for the presidency, he always made sure of his reception before risking the issue.

It was said that Ronnie was an idealist, not a man of raw ambition. The fact was that he was contemplating taking on the seated president, a man of his own party, a bland yet decent politician at a time when decency and blandness were high virtues. If Ronnie had been ten years younger, perhaps he would have seen Ford differently, but Ronnie was sixty-five and the 1976 election was bound to be his last shot at the presidency.

If Ford had been smarter or more wily, he would have tried to flatter Ronnie out of running by asking his advice or offering him a high cabinet position. When Ford first became President, Ronnie had expected to be considered for vice-president. He was passed over for Nelson Rockefeller, a man despised by conservatives. Moreover, he wasn't even told of the decision by Ford. Then Ford had offered him what Ronnie considered a meaningless cabinet post, tossing the position of secretary of transportation in his direction.

Now Ford was desperately trying to keep Ronnie from challenging him. In April 1975, the Reagans went to visit the Fords, who were vacationing in Palm Springs. Ford had invited Ronnie with hopes of dissuading him from running. But his efforts were too late. According to Mrs. Ford, when the Reagans left that evening, the Fords knew without even speaking to each other that Ronnie was going to run. Neither Ronnie nor Ford was a hater. Though they took full measure of each other, there was not the vindictive loathing of which the Kennedys or Johnson were capable. Much more intense was the reaction between Nancy and Betty Ford. "She is a cold fish," Mrs. Ford told an aide afterward. "Nancy could not have been colder. Then the flashbulbs went off and she smiled and kissed me—suddenly an old friend. I couldn't get over that. Off camera—ice. On camera—warmth."

Often people who are very similar take a visceral dislike to one another; in the other person they see a mirror image of what they might have been. Although Nancy considered Jackie Kennedy her model, Betty Ford was the contemporary First Lady with whom she had the most similarities. They were of the same generation, Betty three years older than Nancy. They were women who had always been admired for their good looks. They had attended well-known New England schools—Nancy going to Smith, Betty to the Bennington School of Dance. They had both gone to New York and pursued artistic careers while modeling and dating their share of Princeton and Harvard men. Betty's first marriage, to a Michigan businessman, ended after five years, when she was twenty-nine. In her twenties, Nancy had had several serious relationships that ended short of marriage. Both women had married their husbands when they were thirty years old. Both had four children, though two of Nancy's were from Ronnie's first marriage. Emerging from the anonymity of being suburban wives and mothers, they both enjoyed the national limelight and yet were frightened by it.

What separated Nancy and Betty so dramatically was how they dealt with the world around them. If the Reagans were playing "Ozzie and Harriet," then the Ford family was a *cinéma vérité* documentary. The day Morley Safer asked Betty on "60 Minutes" what she would do if her daughter told her she was having an affair, the First Lady told him: "Well, I wouldn't be surprised. I think she's a perfectly normal human being, like all young girls. If she wanted to continue it, I would certainly counsel and advise her on the subject. And I'd want to know pretty much about the young man." The First Lady believed that premarital sex might lower the divorce rate, that the Supreme Court was right in legalizing abortion, and that her kids probably had smoked marijuana.

Privately, Nancy was appalled at Betty's performance. Publicly, she expressed her counterbeliefs without specifically rebuking Betty. She presented a portrait of decorum and decency. On September 19, 1975, she told the Women's Republican Club in Grosse Pointe, Michigan, that she couldn't abide this so-called new morality that included premarital sex. Moreover, she objected to young people being able to get abortions so easily.

The irony of it all was this: Nancy, conservative protector of hearth and home, had a daughter, Patti, living with a rock star. Patti was reputed to have toked the weed more than once. Betty, brave voice of the new feminist, had an eighteen-year-old daughter who had experimented with neither drugs nor sex and felt that her mother's remark had given her dates the mistaken idea that they had *carte blanche* on her maidenhood.

Susan Ford worked actively in the campaign, while Patti wanted nothing to do with it. "I didn't deal with him running for president that well," Patti remembered. "I guess I wasn't [glad]. I guess I'm fairly apolitical. I kind of deliberately stayed out of the limelight. . . . It was rather selfish."

On November 20, 1975, Ronnie formally declared his candidacy at the National Press Club in Washington, and headed off on a five-state tour. In Miami, he and Nancy were standing on a platform during a speaking engagement when a voice called out, "Hi, Dutch, glad to see you."

"Hi, I'll be down to see you afterward," Ronnie said, recognizing the fellow as an old midwestern friend.

Later, Ronnie and Nancy plunged into the crowd, turning off course to try to link up with Ronnie's old buddy. Suddenly, the Secret Service agents surged forward to envelop a young man. The gun he was carrying was only a toy, but it looked real. Nancy now had a whole new level of worry.

Ronnie was a great campaigner; and if the reporters tired of hearing variations on "the speech," the audiences found freshness in his words. But campaigning for the presidency was not just show biz, a perennial road show moving from city to city. Words mattered, whether spoken casually to a reporter or read from a speech that someone else had written.

Two months before his formal announcement on September 26, 1975, Ronnie had made a fatal mistake while speaking to the Executive Club of Chicago. The speech had been written by Jeffrey Bell, a conservative intellectual. It was a variation of Ronnie's old theme that the federal government and its taxes were strangling the country. Ronnie proposed transferring duties performed by the federal government to the states, thereby cutting federal outlays by a whopping $90 billion. With that savings Ronnie promised to balance the federal budget, begin paying off the national debt and cut income taxes by an average 23 percent. It wasn't pie in the sky, but pie on earth, cut 225 million ways and distributed in every home in America.

The broad outlines of the speech were not that different from things Ronnie had said scores of times before, and he read the speech with his usual fervor. But what was striking was the $90 billion figure. Ronnie had blithely used dubious statistics before, but this time he had outdone himself.

The Ford people, under the leadership of Stuart Spencer, who had helped Ronnie win the governorship, saw that $90 billion could be made to symbolize what they considered Ronnie's kookiness, his wrongheaded, naïve attempt to dismantle government. They waited until the right moment, then dissected the speech and turned the $90 billion into a gooney bird that they tied tightly around Ronnie's neck. Squirm as he would, Ronnie could not get loose.

He moved onward, into the snows of New Hampshire. He was staking his campaign on blowing Ford out early, in a few humiliating defeats. Primaries are a grueling boot camp for would-be presidents, but Ronnie moved through these cold white streets and into homes and stores with great energy. He appeared to be leading.

His campaign manager, Sears, was trying to run the most subtle of campaigns. As Sears said later, "The perception of Reagan was quite far to the right, close to George Wallace." Ronnie had to move toward the center while not alienating the true believers. He also had to avoid slinging mud at Ford. "Republicans are very sensitive about unity and you couldn't savage Ford," Sears said.

It was a fancy *pas de deux*. "Reagan was a very easy guy to work with," Sears said. "He would understand what you were trying to do. . . . He's an excellent up-front man in politics, but the whole rest of him needed work."

What Ronnie did not do was control his own organization. He preferred to play the star of a play produced and directed by others. As the New Hampshire primary day drew near, the Reagan polls showed the candidate roughly 5 percent ahead, both Sears and Lake, the New England coordinator, said later. According to pollster Richard B. Wirthlin, Sears kept to himself information and polls that showed the race far closer. As the February 24 primary approached, Wirthlin knew that it was going to be close indeed, and that the New Hampshire campaign needed its ultimate weapon: Ronald Reagan crisscrossing the state. But his top campaign staff believed that the most important thing on the day before the election was to make sure that loyal workers were ready to get voters to the polls. To prepare for that task, the candidate's presence and the attention that went with it were counterproductive. Following that strategy, Sears scheduled Ronnie to be out campaigning in Illinois for the two days before the primary.

On the evening before the primary, Ronnie flew back to New Hampshire. As the plane droned northward, Wirthlin told the candidate for the first time about his polls and how close the election would be. "I hope someone down there lights a candle for me," Ronnie said as the plane slid down into the darkened city of Manchester.

When the returns started coming in, Ronnie was leading. He let himself be photographed smiling and holding a newspaper with a headline showing him winning. But as the votes kept coming in, Ronnie's lead diminished. By 1 A.M., Ford had taken the lead. In the end, Ford won, 54,824 to 53,507, a difference of only 1,317 votes out of the 108,331 votes cast.

It was tough enough to lose, doubly tough to lose by so little, and to be pecked to pieces by second thoughts as to whether he should have stayed in New Hampshire to campaign instead of flying to Illinois. In such a close election, any single factor could be blamed, from Reagan's scheduling, to the $90-billion statement, to premature boasts about a Reagan victory. The campaign staff blamed the factor with which they were least involved. But presidential campaigns do not allow the luxury of perspective, and Ronnie forged ahead.

When Ronnie's campaign was being planned, Florida was supposed to be his second big victory, but this time he knew what the polls said—and it wasn't good. In Florida he tried to switch the media interest from his $90-billion gaffe to Ford's foreign policy, specifically the Panama Canal treaty that proposed returning jurisdiction over the fifty-one-mile canal to Panama. Ronnie was adamantly opposed to it, and so were a great many conservative Floridians. Ronnie pulled up in the polls, but not far enough. He lost to Ford, 53 to 47 percent.

Then came Ronnie's birth state, Illinois, where the Republican organization was locked up for Jerry Ford. If it could always be the way it was in Dixon, though, he would have been voted president by acclamation. In the years since he'd left, Ronnie had come back to Dixon for three big public occasions: Louella Parsons Day in 1941, Injun Summer Days in 1950, and the Dixon High School Honors Banquet in 1963, plus other, unpublicized visits. Each time he came here, he took away a renewed faith in his ideas about people and their lives, just as a visit to his ranch renewed his spiritual sustenance.

This time Ronnie had a special private visit to make to see Winston ("Wink") McReynolds, with whom he and Neil had played high-school football. Wink was one of the few blacks whom Ronnie had known well enough to call a friend. Ronnie's idea that blacks could obtain full civil rights without much government regulation came largely from his unfeigned friendship with Wink and a few black Eureka football players. Ronnie never could see why people couldn't get along with blacks the way the Reagan brothers did with Wink. Ronnie's mother had helped Wink out when they were all boys, and Ronnie figured that's the way people should behave. Wink had done well in his life. He had served on the county board and helped put together a housing development for the elderly. But now Wink was in a nursing home with a brain tumor.

"My husband and I had a call about ten o'clock at night the week before Dutch's visit," said Carrie Redebaugh, a nurse who had known the Reagan boys since school days. "They wondered if it was okay for Dutch to visit Wink in the nursing home. But they said if you tell anyone, he won't come."

On the appointed day, Ronnie spoke at Dixon High School. Then the cavalcade of limousines, Secret Service, and press pulled up in front of the Orchard Glen Nursing Home. It was to be a visit among friends, and Ronnie would allow no press coverage. It didn't matter that publicizing the visit would have mitigated his image as racially insensitive. The journalists were kept outside, and one local reporter was bodily taken out of Wink's room.

Ronnie and Nancy entered the room together. Wink was blind. Ronnie stood over the bed and squeezed his hand. No photographer was there to take pictures. No journalist stood recording the scene.

Two weeks later, Wink died.

On March 16, Ronnie lost the Illinois primary, garnering 40 percent of the vote against 60 percent for Ford. Even those in the campaign thought they heard the drum rolls of doom. Although Ronnie was loath to admit it, if he lost the North Carolina primary on March 23, his glorious crusade would look like a divisive last hurrah.

It is a show-business adage that when things get tough, a performer should go with what he does best. Ronnie had given one version or another of "the speech" for two decades, and he knew if he got on television with it, he would be boffo. John Sears was the kind of sophisticated man who wouldn't cry at *Love Story*. He didn't think people would sit in their living rooms listening to Ronnie for a half-hour. He felt that success in the South would only be had by centering the campaign on patriotic issues, defense and foreign policy, rather than the economic questions they had stressed in the Northeast. But others in the campaign recognized Ronnie's oratorical powers. They revised a film made during the Florida primary. When this version of "the speech" played on fifteen North Carolina television stations, Carolinians sat listening to a vocalization of their beliefs and world that played like a John Wayne movie.

On March 23, primary day in North Carolina, Ronnie flew north to Wisconsin to make a speech at Ducks Unlimited, a hunters' club. Then, instead of campaigning anymore in Wisconsin as was planned, he flew directly to Los Angeles to make a speech on national television asking for contributions. For weeks he had been saying that he should go on television to make his plea. Now, with the campaign a good $2 million in debt and finances drying up, it made sense, even to Sears.

When the first returns from North Carolina started coming in, Ronnie could hardly believe the good news. On the plane to Los Angeles, the pilot announced authoritatively that Ronnie had won 52 to 46 percent. Now he was ready to celebrate. As aides strutted up and down the aisle singing "Nothing could be finer than to give Ford a shiner in the primary," Ron, Jr., and his dad played catch with a football.

Ron, Jr., had received permission from the Harvard School to spend his last term campaigning for his dad. It sounded like a great idea, helping with the baggage and other mundane tasks. But staff members noticed Nancy picking at her son, making demands, and they understood when he left the campaign. "His mother and father seemed hardly to notice that he was gone," said one campaign aide.

Nancy was upset about her son's aspirations to become a dancer, but she knew that at least he would be going off to Yale in the fall. "When he first said he was going to Yale, he said he was going because they wanted him to," said John West, his dance teacher at the Harvard School. "But he said that he knew he wouldn't finish. He threatened to flunk himself out because they wouldn't respect his wishes."

Buoyed by his upset victory in North Carolina, Ronnie spoke on NBC on March 31. Ronnie could have sold light bulbs to the Amish. He raised an extraordinary million and a half dollars that kept him in the race. Even with that money, however, the campaign funds were low, and he arrived in Texas not by chartered plane but on a commercial flight. Ronnie did better as an underdog than riding high. Helped by Wallace supporters who distrusted the federal government, he swept the May 1 Texas primary, 96 delegates in all. Three days later he took Indiana, Alabama and Georgia, for the first time moving ahead in the delegate count. On May 11, he took Nebraska while Ford won in West Virginia.

As Ronnie moved on to challenge the president in his own state of Michigan, he indulged in the favorite reverie of front-runners, talking about a running mate. But the voters went for the home-state boy, 65 to 34 percent, and in the last primaries the president caught up and surpassed Ronnie by 100 delegate votes. Neither man had the votes that would be needed for the nomination at the Kansas City convention; and in the two months left, the two candidates wooed the uncommitted delegates.

Ronnie tried during the eight weeks before the convention, but he was no match for the pomp, power and prestige of the presidency, and the promises Ford could make. At the Kansas City convention, Sears masterminded one last gambit. To capture the votes of moderates, Sears had Ronnie declare on July 26 that Richard Schweiker, the middle-of-the road senator from Pennsylvania, would be his running mate. Ronnie knew next to nothing about Schweiker until Sears mentioned him, a condition that Ronnie shared with most Americans. To many of the true Reaganites, it was an unseemly idea, a repudiation of what Ronnie stood for. It succeeded only in creating a momentary spectacle.

Even Nancy became a momentary public spectacle. On the second night of the convention, shortly before Nancy took her seat in the amphitheater, Betty Ford and her entourage had entered. Seated in her box was her daughter, Susan, wearing a blue denim shirt with FORD spelled out like the sponsor's name on a bowling shirt. Tony Orlando was there as well, a singer who is to pop music what a 7-Eleven Taco is to Mexican food. When Nancy entered, the loyal Reaganites welcomed her with thunderous bursts of applause, drawing attention away from Mrs. Ford. Then the band struck up "Tie a Yellow Ribbon Round the Old Oak Tree." Susan said, "That's your song, Tony. Come on, you and mom get up and dance."

All America watched while Betty and Tony danced. Susan, no longer a media novice, spun like the Goodyear blimp, flashing her FORD. It was the battle of the wives—the demure, dignified Nancy bowing graciously to applause while the First Lady boogalooed.

For the Reagans, though, the great endearing story of the convention was the underlying faith among Ronnie's supporters. Around him was a coterie of the rich and the privileged, the lords and ladies of the Reagan court. But most of the Reagan workers were simple, unadorned, God-fearing folk who had sacrificed time and money to work for Ronnie. Idealistic and naïve they might have been, but they had believed that Ronnie could change America. And they still believed it.

"Don't get cynical," he told them the morning after it was all over, Nancy standing beside him crying. "Don't get cynical, because, look at yourselves and what you were willing to do and recognize that there are millions and millions of Americans out there that want what you want, they want it to be that way, they want it to be a shining city on the hill."

Ronnie may have lost the nomination, but Betsy, Jean, Jane, Bunny, Virginia, Marion, Martha and Mary Jane already considered Nancy the First Lady. Her group of friends had become one of the most exclusive circles in Los Angeles. No one had entered "the Group" for over a decade.

"When we were younger, these were people we'd never heard of," said one prominent socialite. "Anytime in life when you have a clique, it's always insecurity. It's like when you're in college and you're a Theta, and they want to keep the prettiest girl or the smartest girl out of the clique. And I think the group around Nancy is very insecure. A lot of these women felt the need to get something in their lives. When Nancy was the governor's wife, they saw it as an opportunity. It's a group that doesn't mind playing handmaiden to a person. They need each other desperately.

"They want to be at a dinner party at eight P.M., have a glass of white wine, and leave at ten-thirty, get up the next morning and go to dinner again wearing another new dress. They're living in an illusionary world. They don't want to say anything about anything."

Often Nancy drove into Beverly Hills for lunch with her friends, leaving her car with an attendant on Rodeo Drive. When she had first walked this street thirty years ago, there had been a pleasant meld of local stores that could have been in Greenwich, Connecticut, or Bethesda, Maryland. Since the arrival of Gucci, a whole swath of expensive international stores had arrived, making the street one of the most celebrated shopping thoroughfares in the world. Between 1976 and early 1978 alone, eight of the original seventeen stores on the block with Gucci had been replaced by more prestigious boutiques. Lothar's. Yves St. Tropez. Jewels by Edwar. Jax. Matthews. Right Bank Clothing Co. Gunn Trigère. Bilari. Polo. Jerry Magnin. Knight, Inc. Ted Lapidus. Celine. Omega. Wally Findlay Galleries. Hermes. Gucci. That one block alone contained a treasure of gowns and silver and furs and silks and diamonds.

Chic and sophisticated in their jewels and designer attire, the ladies wore Adolfo suits or Yves Saint Laurent dresses and carried Gucci bags. At night they often wore custom-made Galanos, Oscar de la Renta, Bill Blass, and Dior gowns and carried Judith Leiber purses.

The ladies and their husbands had both their admirers and detractors. "The men are largely self-made, high achievers," said Midge Clark, a Los Angeles socialite active in charity work. "They are all married to beautiful women who are high achievers in their own right. They've had careers. They are dynamic fund raisers and charity organizers."

"These ladies are so isolated from experience," said another participant in L.A. social life. "In their houses they have few books and tons of doodads. Pictures are part of decorating. They have the cultural tradition of teen-agers in small towns, always going to the same places."

These were ladies who for the most part had decided to live as blondes. They were mothers and grandmothers, but with the help of face-lifts, facials, beauty spas, exercises and the camouflage of cosmetics, they all looked remarkably young. Over the years they had come to look more and more like each other. Seated next to their older husbands at Chasen's, the ladies were glamorous, supportive and charming, another accouterment of wealth, like a Mercedes or a home in the Hollywood Hills.

The Reagans and their friends weren't aging and declining like so many of their contemporaries. How could anyone wonder whether Ronnie would be too old to run for president in 1980? The men were vibrant, virile. They were at the top of their professions. They had struggled up, and they still enjoyed a good scrap. The women were demure sweethearts soothing their men after a day's toil. They tried to be the entrancing Helen, inspiring their husbands to work even harder to gather wealth to complement and display their beauty. They believed that the greatest homage to their practiced allure was an admiring husband.

The ladies kept up with each other. They walled off the young and the irreverent, and in their dinners and galas they were stunning in their youthfulness, daring, yet ever tasteful. They oohed and aahed over each other's gowns. They sang each other's praises. And reigning over them all were Ronnie and Nancy. Ronnie was as young and vital as the America they all believed in, and Nancy was the loveliest lady of all.

Rich ladies who aspired one day to sit at the table of the Group, nibbling salad and tippling a glass of California Chablis, frequented the same shops, paying full price for their dresses and gowns. But in the stores on Rodeo Drive, *the ladies* were known as liking to hold on to the money in their Gucci purses. Some of them insisted on special discounts, or had other ways of paying less than full measure.

Despite her husband's millions, Betsy Bloomingdale saw no reason why she should have to pay duties on gowns that she brought into the United States from Paris. The customs inspectors had a nose for these rich ladies and their ways, and on April 14, 1975, Betsy was caught trying to smuggle in two Christian Dior dresses worth $3,880 at Los Angeles International Airport. Betsy knew that her face would still be gracing the pages of *Women's Wear Daily,* displaying one designer dress or another. But it was embarrassing, especially when the gowns were auctioned off and she was fined $5,000.

Nancy wasn't beyond accepting her own alms for the rich, either. Her friends were always giving her gifts. Her birthday was a day of tribute. The stores along Rodeo Drive sought her patronage, even though she treated some of the salespeople like liveried lackeys.

"Nancy's a taker, not a giver," said Dorothy Tupper, who now manages Amelia Gray's. "She would call and say, 'Oh, Dorothy, bring me lunch.' One time she said, 'Would you like part of my sandwich, darling?'

"I said, 'Oh, that would be wonderful, Nancy, a quarter would do. That way I won't have to buy lunch.'

"Then I came back. She said, 'Oh, I'm sorry, darling, I ate the whole sandwich.' I could have poured the carton of milk over her head.

"All that Amelia has done for her! A coat came in worth twenty-five hundred. Amelia gave it to her. And now Amelia's an invalid in bed. When Nancy comes in she says, 'Oh, no, poor Amelia.' But will she go out and visit her? She's a taker."

For Nancy and her friends, life was not simply a matter of endless parties. They made sure that they did their share of charity work, one of the requirements of being socially prominent. Betty, Jean, Marion and Bunny were active in the Amazing Blue Ribbon 400, an exclusive society that supported the Los Angeles Music Center. Betty and Marion were copresidents of the 400, and Bunny its executive vice-president. As coproducer of "Lassie," Bunny had crossed the country lecturing on the importance of wholesomeness in TV programs. She and Nancy had discussed the deterioration of morality many times.

But no matter how busy they might be, the ladies were perfectly turned out in feminine suits, bobbed hair and often circle earrings. They were never seen on the streets in jeans. They always looked stylish. Theirs was a hybrid look, far more conservative than most younger California women, and yet more relaxed than their eastern counterparts. To maintain their looks, no one had any idea how many hours they spent on pedicures, manicures, face-lifts, hair tinting, hairstylings, brush-outs and facials. They were always preparing for the next season.

Miss Donahue, Nancy's favorite saleslady at I. Magnin's in Beverly Hills, said of the group, "They're professional ladies," referring to the profession of being a lady. "Mrs. Reagan has come in for years. I've helped most of them for years. They're lovely people. They're all very sweet."

"They come in on a regular basis, weekly or biweekly," said Doris Fields, the store's manager. "They do so because they have such enormous social calendars. They all have salespeople, *vendeuses,* to call them and tell them if we have something. We know everyone, what size they are. The salesperson will say, 'Don't you think Mrs. So-and-so will like this?' Nine times out of ten it's a sale. We have shows in August and they preorder their clothes. They're the special ladies of the city."

⟫16⟫

"GOODNESS, GOD, HOME AND COUNTRY"

Nancy had become a woman of authority and social prominence, openly ambitious for herself and her husband. Three weeks after Ford's defeat by Jimmy Carter in the 1976 presidential election, Nancy dominated a luncheon meeting during which Ronnie and his top aides and backers discussed his future. Nancy was full of rancor at Jerry Ford. Ronnie had campaigned for Ford against Carter, but Nancy asked how many in the room had voted for Ford. Only three people admitted to voting the Republican ticket. By the time the meeting was over, it was clear that Ronnie would go for it once again in 1980.

Left to himself, Ronnie might have ridden into the sunset to chop wood and breed horses up at Rancho del Cielo. But Ronnie was not just a person anymore. He was a cause, a symbol. He had a whole retinue of people whose fortunes were tied to him.

By the spring of 1978, it was clear to his supporters that Ronnie's time had finally arrived. After the experimentation of the Sixties, the country was turning to the right with such force that, to stay in office, "liberal" politicians were repudiating the very term. President Jimmy Carter was preaching to the country on everything from energy conservation to morality, and the country was tiring of Carter's church. The people appeared ready for Ronnie's optimism and his promise to turn America back to the good old days of small government and unfettered opportunity.

Ronnie's most dramatic problem was no longer his conservatism but his age. If elected, he would be seventy-three years old at the end of his first term, by far the oldest president in American history. It rankled him when reporters suggested he dyed his hair or chopped wood only for the cameras. Few men in their mid-sixties were as vigorous as he.

For Ronnie, the beauty of his undeclared race was that he could go on as before, knocking off a speech or two a week opposing the Panama Canal treaty, giving interviews and radio commentaries opposing President Carter's energy and tax policies, spending time at the ranch or with old friends, while his minions were preparing the way.

Lyn Nofziger was the head of Citizens for the Republic, a front organization for Ronnie's 1980 campaign. Using a million dollars left over from the failed 1976 campaign, Nofziger mailed hundreds of thousands of newsletters and press releases to Ronnie's conservative constituency, attacking everything from the Panama Canal treaty to the villainy of Castro and the Kremlin. He had a receptive audience of people who would support Ronnie's run for the Republican nomination.

John Sears had returned for the race as well. Unlike most of Ronnie's other aides, Sears was not interested in any sort of personal relationship with his candidate. He had worked for Nixon, and he realized that neither man had real friends. The difference was that in Nixon's case, everyone realized that fact. "I worked for Nixon and nobody was close to him." Sears said. "But that was fairly open and known. Reagan's isolation is different. It's more a product of Reagan, the actor. The star is the star. For the people who work with him, he's the star. There's a built-in separation. I'm a great believer that you become what you are. If he became a star, it's because he was capable of becoming it in many ways. He could achieve the discipline of it."

As Ronnie's campaign director, Sears sought to use that star quality. He saw himself not as a starmaker but as a president maker. To win in 1980, he had to be in control. But Ronnie was unwilling to give Sears that complete control, and instead spread the power around more broadly. Jim Lake and Charles Black, two Sears protégés, joined the team, too. Then there were Mike Deaver and Peter Hannaford, whose public-relations company had in its beginnings depended largely on Ronnie. Richard Wirthlin, the pollster, was regularly consulted as well. In the California headquarters, Ed Meese, the courtly former assistant district attorney and top adviser during Ronnie's second term as governor, was chosen to keep Ronnie informed on issues and to serve as chief of staff.

Nofziger and Sears were ambitious, driven men of Shakespearean complexity, and their own competition would be the first battle of the campaign. Each man thought that politics was life. To Nofziger it was ideology. To Sears it was strategy and technique. They discussed politics endlessly, thinking they were talking about the world when they were only talking shop. Each had suffered his own humiliations in the service of Ronnie's advancement. Nofziger had been fired during the Sacramento years and pushed aside again during the 1976 campaign, but he did not blame Ronnie personally. Sears had struggled with and conquered a drinking problem in 1976. He became everyone's favorite scapegoat for the loss to Ford. Both men had egos that served them as life preservers, expanding automatically at any sign of disaster and carrying them back into yet another campaign.

Despite all his years of service, Nofziger knew that Ronnie could forget him like a cherished but worn-out pair of riding boots. He intensely disliked Sears, who was not a *real* conservative and, to Nofziger's mind, had lost the 1976 campaign. Nofziger cared about Ronnie, but Sears was like an editor who thinks that publishing would be great if only authors could be eliminated. He sometimes considered candidates the curse of politics.

Sears's first target was Nofziger. In October 1979, with Nancy's help, Sears made his case against Nofziger and, using Deaver as his messenger, made it well. Sears accused Nofziger of doing such a dreadful job of fund raising that he would have to go. When Deaver came to Nofziger to tell him that he was being dismissed, the bedraggled former press secretary predicted that Deaver would be Sears's next victim, and that Sears would not be content until he had eliminated all the old Californians.

Deaver was responsible for three benefit concerts, including one in Boston with Frank Sinatra and Dean Martin, which almost lost money. "A campaign is like an orchestra," Sears said later. "Everyone has to sit in a chair. And everyone has to play the same music. From my point of view, Deaver was having trouble sitting in a chair and playing."

"There were a lot of undercurrents," Nancy said later, "and it was very difficult for Ron. He doesn't understand undercurrents. He can't function when there is tension and people aren't getting along. Everyone tried to work it out. But we were Band-Aiding it for a long time, and it just wasn't working."

Nancy understood undercurrents better than any of the Reagan people. She was as alert as a deer in the hunting season, scenting any danger to Ronnie. She listened for muffled innuendo and complaints. Practically the only member of Ronnie's staff in Sacramento with whom Nancy had developed a mutual trust and liking was Michael Deaver. Deaver was a born public-relations man. He was self-effacing and cautious, and he had risen in good measure because of his relationship with Nancy.

Nancy liked Deaver for his loyalty. She respected Sears for his ability. She couldn't understand why the two men couldn't work together more amicably. Lake tried to get them to work together, but they were constantly at loggerheads. At the time of Ronnie's formal announcement on November 13, 1979, tension between them was so bad that Deaver wasn't even talking to Sears and stayed away from the New York gathering.

The endless bickering and infighting threatened to undermine the entire campaign. At Nancy's instigation, a meeting was held on November 26 at the Reagans' Pacific Palisades home to resolve the whole business. Deaver and Sears went at each other like a cat and dog in a burlap bag. Sears said it straight out: If Deaver didn't go, he would leave, taking Lake and Black with him. Despite all his legendary talents of conciliation, Ronnie couldn't get the two men to agree to work together.

"Yes, honey, you're going to have to make a choice," Nancy said pointedly.

"No, governor, you don't have to make that choice," Deaver said. "I'll resign." He stood up abruptly and walked out the door.

Ronnie pleaded with him, trying to get him to return. But Deaver walked on.

"The biggest man here just left the room," Ronnie said when he returned. "He was willing to accommodate and compromise and you bastards wouldn't."

The fact was, however, that Deaver was gone and Sears was still sitting in the living room. As he did in his own family, Ronnie stood above the squabble. He liked Deaver. Indeed, four years before, when Ronnie had been choking on a peanut, Deaver had saved his life. But Ronnie let Deaver walk out that day to go home and hear that most modern of silences: a phone that never rings.

Partially in preparation for the race, Nancy decided to write her autobiography. She wasn't a writer, so she hired Bill Libby, a free-lance journalist, to write the book, using her taped recollections. Once or twice a week early in 1979, Libby drove up from Orange County to tape interviews and to have Nancy look over what he had just written. He was a prolific writer, author of close to fifty books, many of them coauthored. His task was not to ferret out the truth but to put down what Nancy wanted said, in a voice that was a reasonable approximation of her own.

To help him write the book, Nancy asked Libby to read a book about morals. She saw her life as a moral lesson, and she wanted Libby to write an edifying text almost appropriate to the nineteenth century in its reticence. "Human beings need moral standards to guide them," she says in *Nancy.* "Self-restraint marks the difference between adult and childish behavior."

She saw this book as *hers,* and although she mentioned her love for Ronnie, she put little of her husband and children in the book. She went over the pages that Libby had written, culling away personal anecdotes, stripping the book of vitality. She didn't want to hurt Ronnie or her friends. She didn't want to talk about the men she had dated, give her age, or give any details about her own family. When Morrow saw the manuscript, they decided that they would not publish what they considered a boring, bloodless book. An editor from Morrow went to see Nancy to get her to add some life and detail. Reluctantly, she threw in some more anecdotes, but she refused even to mention Jane Wyman's name or to say very much about Michael or Maureen.

Nancy made her childhood in Bethesda appear a time of relative emotional deprivation, not mentioning that she had gone to an expensive private school. She said that she had not seen her father since her early teens, when she had seen him years afterward. She said that she had dated Ronnie for only a year before marrying him, when it had been more than twice that. She said nothing of the difficulties of being a mother in the Sixties.

"The main warmth she [Nancy] has is for Ronnie," said Bill Libby after his experience writing *Nancy*. "It is a strong relationship in which they need each other. They are both very sincere when they meet and part again. . . . Nancy wields influence over Ronnie. She wants that limelight more than she admits. The reason, I think, is that she feels so strongly about her way of life and wants to impose it on others. Goodness, God, home and country are what Nancy believes in. She lives in a narrow world. She is not intellectual. She's a tough, clever woman who knows what she wants. She has street smarts, has a certain grace, and whatever her temper is, she can control it. She really loves her husband and thinks he will give us the moral leadership the country needs."

For years Ronnie had lived in a rarefied social world isolated from the pursuits and problems of most Americans. While George Bush, whose résumé was longer than his speeches, campaigned from dawn to dark in Iowa, Ronnie dropped into the state for papal-like visits—a speech, a blessing of the flock, and out again. While John Connally, Senator Robert Dole, Senator Howard Baker and Congressman John Anderson struggled for recognition, Ronnie stayed apart from the fray.

If Ronnie thought that he was to be anointed president, he was rudely awakened in January's Iowa caucus. He won only 30 percent of the votes, against 33 percent for Bush. In Hollywood, the hero never won until the last reel anyway, and Ronnie was much better playing the struggling candidate in the New Hampshire primary than the rich front-runner. Riding in campaign buses, standing in the New England cold, answering questions from the local press, he moved on day after day. At sixty-six he was more resilient than reporters half his age who dragged along covering him.

A good crowd invigorated Ronnie, no matter how exhausted he might be. What tired him was the perpetual bickering among his aides. After Deaver's resignation, Sears had gotten rid of Martin Anderson, a conservative economist and a Californian, sending him back to the groves of academe. Meese was the only old Californian left.

Late in January, when Ronnie got back to the hotel in Andover, Massachusetts, after campaigning all day, his stomach knotted up with tension. If it hadn't been for that, the infighting might have gone on until the convention. But Nancy simply wouldn't tolerate Ronnie's feeling so anxious about the dissonance around him.

"Nancy's biggest help to Reagan was to lead him in the direction of his natural instincts," said Frank Donatelli, a regional campaign director. "You have to listen to advice, but you must follow your instincts to make a decision. And she was very good at leading him back to his natural instincts."

In early February, Sears came to talk to Nancy. "She was the one person close to him," Sears said later. "That's why I went to her."

Nancy had a way of making men feel as if she understood them. From his triumph over Deaver, Sears had every reason to trust her. The campaign director told her that through the thin wall of a motel room in New Jersey he had overheard Meese talking on the telephone to Dave Fischer, a Reagan aide. Meese had said that after the New Hampshire primary, Sears and his two associates Lake and Black would be summarily fired. Sears had heard such rumors before, but he felt that he no longer could ignore a situation that fractionalized and demoralized the campaign staff. Moreover, he felt that Meese was largely incompetent in the campaign.

"The original setup never worked," said Donatelli. "Sears was never campaign manager. That was the problem. No one was. They'd all get together at Reagan's house and they'd try to reach an agreement but couldn't. Sears never had any authority. Nor did anyone else."

Nancy soothed Sears's ego and the two talked about bringing in a new campaign administrator. Nancy had the opening that she needed to resolve the brutal squabbling once and for all. She flew to California to talk to Ronnie's former aide, William Clark, now a California Supreme Court justice, to ask him if he would become the new chief of staff. When that didn't work out, the Reagans talked with William J. Casey, the former chairman of the Securities and Exchange Commission. Casey agreed.

Sears had gone to Nancy seeking to unburden himself of Meese, and now he found himself and his authority challenged even further. In the evening in the motel room in Andover, Sears went to the Reagans' suite with Black and Lake.

Sears proceeded to outline his charges against Meese. He accused Meese of undermining the campaign by leaking stories. They were serious accusations against a man Ronnie admired and respected.

"You did in Mike Deaver," Ronnie yelled. "But, by God, you're not going to get Ed Meese."

"Governor," Sears said, almost demurely, "this is your campaign. You have to do what you need to do. But I can't stay under these conditions."

"Goddamn it!" Ronnie stormed. As he got up to confront Sears, Lake thought that "if Reagan hadn't been restrained, he might have hit Sears." Nancy took Ronnie's arm and held him.

"I will not get rid of Ed Meese! You guys have forced me to the wall! If you leave now, it's over!"

As the three campaign aides left, they knew that it was already all over. They knew that it was now just a matter of time before they would be eliminated. They thought about leaving the campaign, believing that if they did so, Ronnie would lose the primary and then the nomination. But they didn't want to be the spoilers. Moreover, they still believed that Ronnie was the best candidate. They decided to stick it out.

The drama of the New Hampshire primary could not quite match the drama playing inside the Reagan campaign staff, but it came close. It was total theater. Theater when six candidates debated in Manchester on February 20, sponsored by the League of Women Voters; theater again three days later when a dual debate scheduled for Nashua turned into a dramatic free-for-all.

Ronnie had done well in Manchester, but his debate with Bush, the front-runner, on February 23 was even more important. In debates, Ronnie wasn't great on the specifics of issues; he would slide past questions like a halfback greased with Vaseline. It usually didn't matter, but Bush looked to be a formidable opponent. His career as a public servant was unmatched by any candidate, everything from member of Congress, to director of the CIA, to ambassador to China, not to mention a successful career in business. He had also been a far better baseball player in college than Ronnie had been a football player. But he often sounded like a hyperkinetic preppie whose idea of fast food was a tailgate picnic before the big game at the Yale Bowl.

There may have been something a mite unfair about a two-man debate since there were still five other candidates in the running. But this was politics, not participatory democracy, and both candidates thought the debate to their benefit. Nonetheless, realizing that the Reagan camp was paying for the debate, John Sears got a wickedly good idea. Why not call the other candidates and have them show up in Nashua and ask to participate?

Ronnie didn't learn what Sears had done until noon the day of the debate when Lake brought him a press release. On his way to the Nashua High School gymnasium that cold February evening, he had no idea what was about to happen. He met the four other opponents who had decided to come—Anderson, Baker, Crane and Dole—in a classroom in the school and tentatively agreed not to debate Bush unless the others could join in. Meanwhile, Sears informed Bush and his campaign manager, James Baker, about the new arrangements. Bush had not gone to Yale for nothing. He insisted that the rules were the rules. Ronnie was a quick study, and he was always good at puffing himself up with righteous indignation. As Bush sat stiffly on stage, Ronnie led Anderson, Baker, Dole and Crane toward the podium.

"What am I supposed to do?" Ronnie asked Lake as he walked up the aisle, his face a harsh grimace. "What exactly am I supposed to do?"

"We're going to go up there," said Lake. "You're going to make this statement that these guys should be allowed to speak. If they leave, you've got to stay and debate."

As Lake sat watching Ronnie's furious face, the press secretary became worried. The audience had turned on Bush already because of his unyielding stance, and Ronnie could win this thing hands down as long as he didn't blow up and walk off with the other candidates. That was the one way he could lose. Lake penned a note on a borrowed yellow pad: "Give 'em hell, Governor. The whole place is with you."

A Secret Service agent took the note up to Ronnie. He looked at it a moment, scowling even more deeply, looked up, winked at Lake and went on scowling some more. Lake relaxed. He knew Ronnie understood that he had the audience.

The crowd grew raucous and shouted to let the other candidates speak. J. Herman Pouliot, publisher of the *Nashua Telegraph,* sponsor of the debate, tried to quiet the audience.

"Turn Mr. Reagan's microphone off," yelled Jon Breen, editor of the *Nashua Telegraph,* seeking to take control of the gathering.

"I paid for this microphone, Mr. Green," Ronnie said, calling the man by the wrong name, the only mistake he made that evening. He spoke with that combination of idealism, anger and naïve faith that Jimmy Stewart had perfected in *Mr. Smith Goes to Washington.* As it was, the sound system was safely in the hands of a company the Reagan campaign had hired, and they weren't about to shut Ronnie off.

If Ronnie had had such delicious parts in Hollywood, he might never have entered politics. He was a sensation, and the debate that finally took place between the two candidates was like the "B" movie after the main feature. But he won that, too.

It was Sears's triumph as well, the last that he would have. The afternoon of the primary, February 26, Ronnie called Sears, Black and Lake into his third-floor suite at the Holiday Inn in Manchester. Ronnie was sitting next to William Casey. Nancy was on the other side of the room, as if she were no part of this.

"We've been having some problems and we want to get them solved," Ronnie said. For the last few days Ronnie had almost certainly known what was going to happen today, all the time treating the threesome with friendliness and warmth. Yet even now he couldn't say directly what had to be said. He handed Sears a typed statement announcing the resignations of the three men and the appointment of Casey as campaign director. Sears read silently and passed the sheet of paper to Black and Lake.

"Well, John?" Nancy said from the other side of the room. "Well?"

"I'm not surprised," Sears shrugged.

"Nancy had a lot to do with Sears's firing," said Donatelli. "She helped bring Casey aboard and was very influential in the timing of the firing. When Deaver was forced out, a lot thought that Sears wouldn't survive much longer. I think Reagan and Nancy decided between them that the next time Sears demanded that Meese be fired then would be the time to fire Sears."

In the New Hampshire primary, Ronnie walloped Bush by 27 per-centage points. Soon afterward, Deaver rejoined the campaign after his months in purgatory. Anderson, the conservative intellectual, returned to mastermind the issues team. And Nofziger was back, too, as press secretary.

In the service of his ambition, Ronnie and Nancy had temporarily pushed aside three of their oldest, most loyal aides and advisers. If Sears had not overplayed himself, Deaver, Nofziger and Anderson might never have been closely associated with the Reagans again. And yet, to his aides and to much of the press, Ronnie remained a benign, benevolent figure above the sordid fray. To use an analogy from the drug world, he was a dealer who never held.

The Reagan children saw their father much the same way. Michael was now the father of a two-year-old boy, Cameron. He had hoped that Ronnie would be a real grandfather to the child, but Ronnie had little time for his grandchild. Michael had been invited up to Rancho del Cielo only twice, and, if anything, he felt even more the orphan. At one point early in the campaign, he had had a rare moment alone with Ronnie. As he confid-ed to a reporter later, he had told his father that he hoped that one good thing would come out of the race: the family would grow closer together. But Nancy entered the room. According to Michael, after Ronnie left, she told him pointblank that would never happen.

Michael believed in Ronnie and his ideas, and he was a good cam-paigner. At times he felt that he really wasn't wanted though; that the campaign staff considered him and his sister almost embarrassments. "I suppose it makes dad look old, having older children," he said. And yet when the staff wanted him for an appearance, they didn't care about his personal life. They knew that Michael would drop anything to help his

On the campaign trail for the presidency: 1980. *(RS)*

father. The one thing he looked forward to all year was skiing for a couple weeks in Aspen during January. But he was told that he was needed in Iowa, and so he went skiing for only four days.

As for Maureen, she was sometimes campaigning by car in Iowa when her father was flying overhead. She rarely saw him or talked to him as week after week she kept campaigning. When she couldn't get through to him, she didn't blame Ronnie. She blamed Nancy.

Ron, Jr., was dancing in New York, and he hadn't even voted in the New York primary. He was making it on his own, and though he wanted his father to succeed, he was concentrating on his new career. He planned to have as little to do with the campaign as possible.

Patti wasn't about to campaign, either. In the spring of 1980, floods in the Topanga Canyon drove Patti out of her rented home. She returned to stay in the family house until she found a new apartment. It was hard to say which was more incongruous in Pacific Palisades: Patti, her little Toyota, or her antinuke bumper stickers. Her career wasn't going well, but the twenty-eight-year-old actress didn't want to capitalize on her father's fame. Nor did she want to be known eternally as Ronnie's daughter. She found it difficult to talk to outsiders and reporters.

"Your father and your mother's personal views about how people should live their lives differ from most members of our generation," a young woman reporter said to Patti one day. "And some of the choices you've made. How have you resolved that, if you have, with them?"

"How do you mean?" Patti asked, her voice sounding much like Jane Fonda's.

"I mean about people living together. Your parents very much believe in marriage and that's it."

"I don't want to get into personal comments or private life," Patti said quietly.

The reporter was determined. "But I mean that's very much a part of the message he delivers in public. He talks about morality, sex, and marriage and . . . fidelity and divorce and the deterioration of the family."

Patti thought a moment. "Well, I believe in fidelity," she said, laughing exuberantly. "I'll go for that one."

While her two children went on with their lives, Nancy was actively campaigning. She preferred to be with Ronnie, but often she had to be his surrogate. At times she even had to give full-fledged speeches. Early in the campaign, when Ronnie's plane was snowbound in New Hampshire, Nancy subbed for him before 200 well-heeled supporters in Chicago. She looked out on the crowd and said that she wished Ronnie could be there to "see all these beautiful white faces . . . " She stopped for a moment. That didn't sound quite right. " . . . Beautiful black and white faces."

In Florida the week after Ronnie's stunning triumph in New Hampshire, Nancy was by his side. Ronnie was still dropping incredible, unverifiable facts that sounded as if they were taken from a "Ripley's Believe It or Not" column on the comic page. The previous evening in a debate in South Carolina, Ronnie had claimed that marijuana was the most dangerous drug in America. One of the reporters was so graceless as to read Ronnie's quote back to him. What he had said, Ronnie corrected the reporter, was that scientists considered marijuana *one* of the most dangerous drugs. Then he came up with a new fact: Scientists had discovered that "a marijuana cigarette probably is several times the cancer hazard for lung and throat cancer than a tobacco cigarette is."

The reporter, doubtless thinking that he knew few pack-a-day marijuana smokers, said that one didn't have to smoke that much marijuana to get high.

Listening to this arcane discussion, Nancy smelled trouble for Ronnie. With Ronnie's deafness, Nancy couldn't whisper. "You wouldn't know," she said firmly.

"I wouldn't know," Ronnie said.

Neither Ronnie's nor Nancy's occasional *faux pas* mattered much, and Ronnie moved from success to success. One by one they dropped out— Baker, Dole, Crane, Connally and finally Bush, with Anderson leaving the party to run as an independent.

The Reagan campaign people knew that when Ronnie departed from the script and started ad-libbing, they were often in trouble. In late June, when the nomination was cinched, two busloads of journalists were ferried up the mountainside to Rancho del Cielo. Today was to be a "photo session" and the reporters were threatened with being left behind if they asked any news questions.

For a day, Rancho del Cielo was turned into a movie studio. Ronnie stood in cowboy hat, jeans and cotton plaid shirt saddling his horse and telling cowboy stories. The only other sound was the clicking and whirring of the cameras. When Ronnie put his arm around Nancy, some of the 100 journalists could have sworn they were looking at Roy Rogers and Dale Evans, and they broke into Roy's theme song, "Happy Trails to You." Nancy and Ronnie held hands long enough for everyone to get a good shot. Then they got on their horses and rode slowly off into the mountains. When they reached the top of the hill, they spun around and faced the cameras. This was to be the ending, the final shot, and the early takes hadn't been that good. This time they wanted to get it right.

"What are they waiting for?" one cameraman grouched, holding his heavy equipment.

"A cue," another cameraman said.

"Action!" yelled Marty Kasindorf, Los Angeles bureau chief of *Newsweek*.

Nancy and Ronnie came riding in like a scene from "Death Valley Days."

The campaign staff could orchestrate a day like that one at Rancho del Cielo, but they couldn't control the articles that were written about Nancy. For the most part, women journalists writing profiles of Nancy were feminists, strong supporters of the Equal Rights Amendment. In Nancy, all the traits that they disliked in their mothers' generation had come to fruition in one human being. Assigning them to write about Nancy was like asking Barry Goldwater to review the *Communist Manifesto*.

Sally Quinn of the *Washington Post* didn't even like the way Nancy sat ("She never seems to get an itch, her lips never stick to her teeth, she hardly blinks. Don't her legs ever go to sleep?"). Lyn Rosellini of the *Washington Star* let nameless sources carp at Nancy ("'She's always mad at somebody,' said a former longtime Reagan staffer who has experienced her wrath"). Julie Baumgold of *New York* magazine named Nancy "Ronald Reagan's Total Woman" ("She does not provoke; she flatters and always suppresses the little touch of the bitch inside").

Nancy was appalled by the stories. The national press corps picked on everything. She couldn't understand the criticism. When she read some of the reports, she wanted to go and hide. *Everything* was fair game. Her legs. Her clothes. Her every gesture. Even her love for Ronnie.

On Monday afternoon, July 14, Ronnie and Nancy arrived at the Detroit Plaza Hotel, headquarters for the Republican convention. Standing before the crowd, the Reagans looked like fashion models displaying the latest summer wear for the gentry of Grosse Pointe, Greenwich, Potomac, or Pacific Palisades. Ronnie was decked out in dark pants and a white jacket, while Nancy wore a beige Adolfo suit. "Nancy and I were just flying by and thought we'd drop in and see what's going on," Ronnie said. "I had a dream the other night. I dreamed that Jimmy Carter came to me and asked why I wanted his job. I told him I didn't want his job. I want to be president."

Maureen, Michael, Patti and Ron, Jr., had all arrived in Detroit, too. This was their father's week of triumph. But for each one of them, there was a curious distance from the spectacle that was unfolding.

In recent years Maureen had put on a lot of weight. She was a big woman with a booming voice and an ego that more than matched her height. She was divorced again, and at thirty-nine she vowed that it would be a long time indeed until she married again. Her television career had petered out and she was now involved in a business promoting the exporting of American goods. She had taken off a great deal of time to work in the campaign.

"Maureen was very active," said Donatelli. "She was good to put with groups of women, especially younger women. She's an excellent campaigner, well informed. She understands politics. She had a reputation for being brash, but she was an asset really."

Another campaign staffer remembered how Maureen could energize a crowd while her father was speaking. "She'd jump up and applaud at the appropriate times and really get the crowd going. She's a real character. He'd wink at her each time she did it." By her efforts, Maureen thought she could gain a new closeness with her father. But that had not happened, and though she still hungered for her father's love, she understood why it was not forthcoming.

"Nancy and dad have an incredibly unique relationship," she said. "They are not only of course each other's best friend, they are married, they are in love. All of the good things in the world that we wish that we were. But I would assume that because of the closeness that they have, that it would be a bit of a barrier to the children they've had together as much as to us. Because they don't need anybody else but themselves.

"I think I said that to him one day. I said, 'You have to understand it's terrific and I'm all for it. But for those of us on the outside, would you wave at us once in a while so we'll know that you know that we're here.'

"It was difficult for him to understand. He thought I was trying to tell him he was doing something wrong. I wasn't. I was trying to say I understood, but know that we're trying. But he kept saying, 'What am I doing wrong?'"

Although Michael had campaigned long and well for his dad, he didn't expect that alone to bring him closer to Ronnie. He thought that Cameron, Ronnie's only grandson, would be the epoxy that would bond them together. At the convention, the child was hauled in and out for family pictures like a stage prop. He appeared not even to recognize his grandfather. "He only sees me on television," Ronnie joked.

Patti was willing to come to Detroit, but that was about all she was willing to do. "I'm not a terribly political person and I have my own work and my own aspirations that I'm working toward," she said, explaining why she wouldn't campaign for Ronnie. "I think it's fine if somebody wants to do that, but I don't."

She wanted to become "rich and famous" but things weren't going too well. "I'm trying to get some work," she said. "Things are a little slow." At twenty-eight, she was the age her mother had been when she arrived in Hollywood, and she felt that time was passing by. If she was going to be a star, it had to happen soon. The week before the convention, she had talked to Mike Wallace for "60 Minutes." Wallace was an old friend of Nancy's and he led Patti amiably through the interview. At the end of the segment, Patti picked up her guitar and sang a song she had written, "No Place Left to Hide."

In 1976 Ron, Jr., had taken off a semester from high school to campaign with his dad. But now, if anything, he was even less willing than Patti to become involved in politics. "It takes a lot of energy to go out and campaign and I can't do that and dance at the same time," he said during the campaign. At twenty-two, he felt the pull of advancing age far more than his sixty-nine-year-old father. He hadn't started dancing until he was a senior in high school. He had dropped out of Yale after one semester and returned to Los Angeles to study at the Stanley Holden School of Dance. To earn money, he had worked at the school's dancewear shop and in the men's department of I. Magnin's. He took several classes a day and learned quickly. Now he was an apprentice with the Joffrey Ballet, rehearsing eight hours a day, and he had his chance. He had done it on his own. Through concerted discipline and hard work, he had achieved in a few years what had taken many others twice as long. Though he was willing to put in an appearance in Detroit, that was the limit of his efforts.

The Republican convention in Detroit's Joe Louis Arena was Ronnie and Nancy's convention, then, the fruition of a quest that had begun when Ronnie had first run for governor fourteen years ago. Detroit was a Democratic city, a beer-drinking, car-making, rawboned industrial city, but this week it was Ronnie's city. It was a far cry from Kansas City four years before, when Ronnie's aides had wheeled and dealed, fending off the inevitable defeat. This week all Ronnie had to do was prepare his acceptance speech and choose a running mate.

In June, Ronnie had visited Ford in Palm Springs to urge his former opponent to support his run against Carter. Only a couple of months before, Ford had contemplated a last-minute run for the nomination simply to stop Ronnie. But now Ronnie charmed Ford and he agreed to support Ronnie's candidacy. Ronnie asked Ford to be his running mate. The former president turned him down, but the idea stuck in Ronnie's head. It seemed an even better idea when the party's leadership presented him with George Bush as an alternative, a man he actively disliked.

After Ford's fiery speech on Monday, July 14, Ronnie again approached him. Ford was interested, but he was a proud man and, as he told Walter Cronkite on CBS, he would settle only for what amounted to a copresidency. It was great television. But sitting in his suite watching this strange spectacle, Ronnie was appalled. He quickly offered the nomination to Bush.

As for Nancy, there was no Betty Ford to upstage her this time. She was the queen of the Republicans, and as the party leaders spoke, their wives sat with Nancy.

The events of the convention had been beautifully structured for television, many of the speakers moving on and off as quickly as guests on the "Johnny Carson Show." Everything had led to Ronnie's acceptance speech on Thursday, July 17, the climax of the week. Scheduled for prime-time television on the night that most Americans watched the convention, he would have the greatest audience he had ever had.

Before his arrival, the delegates and viewers were shown a film about Ronnie's life. There were Dixon and Eureka; Jack and Nelle; Neil, too; Hollywood and the Screen Actors Guild; the years in Sacramento; and Nancy. It was not much different from an old Frank Capra movie or "This Is Your Life," a warmhearted tribute to what a person could do and become in America. "He believes in the boundless opportunities of the American idea," the announcer said, and Ronnie's life seemed a personification of that idea.

When Ronnie and Nancy appeared on the podium, the delegates erupted in emotions that were beyond mere politics. They clapped until their hands were numb, screamed until their throats were raw, and stomped in frenzy.

Ronnie stood before them in a blue suit, the waves of applause washing over him. When it came time for the family to join him, Ron, Jr., and Patti stood to their mother's left; Maureen, Michael and Colleen to Ronnie's right, instinctively dividing themselves by marriage.

In his forty-five-minute speech, Ronnie said things he had said so many times before. He talked about inflation, tax cuts, putting people back to work, cutting down the size of the federal government, the decline of American strength.

"Family." "Neighborhood." "Work." "Peace." "Freedom." He said the words as if the very force of his voice could etch them in marble. He took his audience back to the beginning of the American experiment, when the Pilgrims had signed a compact and a people had "pledged their lives, their fortunes, and their sacred honor to found this nation." He carried them through American history, their history, to Abraham Lincoln, and Franklin Roosevelt, and on to the future with the words of the past. He quoted Thomas Paine that "we have it in our power to begin the world once again."

Like any great performer, Ronnie sensed the spirit and pulse of the audience as if it were but one person. If the audience was with him to the end, he intended to ask for a silent prayer. In this cavernous arena, it would be a daring gesture. As he looked out at the throng that had already interrupted him seventy times with applause, he knew that it would work.

"I'll confess that I've been a little afraid to suggest what I'm going to suggest, what I'm going to say," he began, his voice quivering. "I'm more afraid not to.

"Can we begin our crusade joined together in a moment of silent prayer?"

All across the great arena, people stood and bowed their heads. Ronnie raised his head, and spoke his final words: "God bless America."

Labor Day weekend, Ronnie opened his presidential campaign at a rally in Liberty Park, New Jersey. Standing in a slightly rumpled white shirt, his sleeves rolled up, with New York Harbor and the Statue of Liberty behind him, he spoke of the glories of the working man. If the entire campaign went like this day, not only would Ronnie win, but voters would buy a ticket to vote for him.

But a campaign is not set pieces, and Ronnie was already making a series of blunders that were diminishing his substantial lead in the polls. In August, speaking before the Veterans of Foreign Wars, he had added a line in his speech, calling the war in Vietnam a "noble cause," a description that opened unhealed wounds. He considered America's support for Taiwan another noble cause, and proposed an "official relationship" with Taiwan, a suggestion that he was willing to risk jettisoning America's hard-won diplomatic ties with mainland China. In Dallas he told a group of reporters for religious publications that he thought the biblical account of the world's creation could be taught in the schools alongside modern evolutionary theory. In early September, he wrongly called Tuscumbia, Alabama, where President Carter opened his campaign, "the city that gave birth to and is the parent body of the Ku Klux Klan."

Like most people, Ronnie frequently gave his opinion on matters he only half understood, regurgitating half-remembered facts as gospel. That was fine before. But now every word, every gesture, would be analyzed, picked apart and, if possible, thrown back at him.

Nancy understood what was happening, and she decided that Stuart Spencer must be brought full-time into the campaign. Spencer and his partner, Bill Roberts, had helped mastermind Ronnie's original gubernatorial campaign. Irreverent and at times almost studiously vulgar, Roberts was hardly a gentleman that Nancy liked to lunch with at the Garden. Moreover, in 1976 he had worked against Ronnie, helping to win the Republican nomination for President Ford. But Nancy knew they needed Spencer.

Spencer understood the court and courtiers around the Reagans well enough not to expect to be welcomed with flowers. The first thing he wanted to know was whether Nancy wanted him. And when he was told yes, he arrived on *Leadership '80,* the campaign plane, to shepherd Ronnie through the campaign.

In early September, on the first swing through the South, Ronnie sat in the plane looking over the speech he was to give at the next stop, New Orleans. He had enough time to add a few zingers of his own. He looked up and realized that Spencer was looking at him.

"Okay, Stu, okay," Ronnie laughed. "I'll stick to the script."

From then on, there were far fewer gaffes and ad libs. Ronnie and his campaign took on a new confidence.

It didn't hurt having Jimmy Carter as an opponent. Carter had proved to be as difficult to like as Ronnie was to dislike. On June 25, the president's own pollster, Patrick Caddell, had told Carter in a confidential campaign memorandum that "the American people do not want Jimmy Carter as their President . . . indeed a large segment could be said to loathe the President." Loathed or not, Carter was already sitting in the White House. Thus the pollster believed that Carter's reelection was "not only possible, but likely."

Carter's opponent would first have to pass what Caddell called the "acceptability threshold." "I am fairly convinced that a moment exists for every non-incumbent challenger in which a majority of the public decides that the person, even if he is not their choice, is qualified and able to be President," Caddell wrote. "The passage from prospective candidate to possible President of the United States is invisible and perilous. . . . From that failure there is no recovery, no matter what the campaign's course."

Thanks to Spencer and others, Ronnie had already made that invisible, perilous journey. On the Reagan plane itself, Spencer tried to create a convivial we're-all-in-this-together atmosphere that would spill over into the news stories. Ronnie chatted to reporters, and Nancy did her part, too. Each time *Leadership '80* took off, she rolled an orange down the aisle to the applause of the journalists. She passed out chocolates to the reporters, too. She walked up the aisle, her words as sweet as the chocolates she offered.

Several of the journalists thought that Mrs. Reagan was waiting to make sure they had popped the chocolates into their mouths before moving on. Still other journalists believed that there was a direct relationship between eating the chocolates and getting interviews with Ronnie. It was an interesting theory. But a reporter who would turn down a chocolate was often the surly sort who wrote words devoid of sweetness. They wouldn't have gotten interviews anyway. As it was, when Nancy found herself being criticized in the media for merely being polite and genteel, she was doubly devastated.

Nancy would have campaigned with Ronnie every day, listening to his speeches hundreds of times, but she had to be his surrogate, traveling to places where there was no time for Ronnie to go. Wherever Nancy campaigned, she made sure that she called Ronnie once or twice a day.

Whether she was with her husband or not, her chief aide was Peter McCoy, who seemed born to the job of handling Nancy. He was a Californian, a movie brat whose father, Horace McCoy, had written the Thirties novel of protest *They Shoot Horses, Don't They?* When his father died, leaving the family what for Hollywood was considered poor, fourteen-year-old McCoy began an upward struggle that started by selling popcorn and tickets in a movie theater and progressed to dealing with literary properties as an agent at William Morris. He finally became head of the Los Angeles office of Sotheby Parke Bernet, the antique and art dealer. McCoy married Kathleen Doheny, who arrived with the dowry of an oil fortune.

McCoy hadn't gone to college, and he wasn't the most brilliant man in the world, but he was charming, dapper, witty and, at thirty-nine, made a balding head appear the new style in debonair looks. He looked as if he had been groomed for years to carry Nancy's purse, watch out for her, deal with her every whim.

"These trips were hard on her," McCoy said. "She's very disciplined on the campaign trail, but she was working on six hours' sleep. She was doing her own makeup. There's a time when she looks bad."

Politicians have an almost natural adrenaline that drives them on when they are tired, half sick, or discouraged. For Nancy it was simply drudgery, the polite chatter, the bad food, the pushing, but she insisted on meeting people, on getting out there and working the crowds. She traveled by commercial and private plane, moving on, another city, another rally, another interview.

It was not only fatiguing but sometimes dangerous. "During the campaign we were getting on a private plane to take us to New York from Champagne-Urbana in Illinois," McCoy said. "I went to put the bags on the plane and noticed a little oil leak on one of the engines. I talked to one of the pilots. I said we weren't taking off until they checked it out. It was a valve. They had an aviation school there, and they fixed it."

When the Reagans weren't campaigning, they were staying at a rented estate in Virginia. Although for years they had had an entourage around them, they had always been able to retreat to their ranch or home. But the campaign flowed into the innermost precincts of the house. McCoy saw how the constant rush of people was affecting Nancy. "It was difficult for her with all these strangers coming in and out," McCoy said. "She would talk about it. I tried to limit it so they could have a semblance of a private life."

No one, least of all Ronnie and Nancy, had time to sit around day-dreaming or reflecting on what it would be like as president and First Lady. Jimmy Carter, whose own mother described him once as "a beautiful cat with sharp claws," was a formidable antagonist. The Reagan campaign feared an "October surprise," perhaps the release of the fifty-two Americans held hostage in Iran, and they did everything they could to bolster Ronnie's supporters and to capture groups that weren't his natural electorate.

Ronnie had originally been a supporter of the Equal Rights Amendment, but Nancy felt the amendment was unmitigated feminist silliness, and Ronnie changed his mind. He was a man's man when it came to voters, too, more popular among men than women. To woo female voters, Ronnie announced that, if elected, one of his first appointments to the Supreme Court would be a woman.

The real presidential battle of 1980 was fought in media strategy. Here Ronnie was undisputed champion. The Republicans' convention film about Ronnie was a warm, irresistible piece of propaganda. The Democrats' film was a tedious lecture featuring Carter pondering the world at his desk in the Oval Office. The film was a marvel as an advertisement for office furniture, but an embarrassment as a campaign device.

As effective as the Republican campaign was, Ronnie was the leader of a minority party, espousing forthrightly conservative ideas that a majority of Americans had always opposed, and running against an incumbent president. As the campaign headed into its last weeks, the two men stood roughly even in the polls. The upcoming October 28 debate with Carter took on greater and greater importance. Ronnie's people were worried. He had done well against John Anderson, the independent candidate, in an earlier debate in September. But Carter was something else. Not only was Carter president, but the man had the knowledge and instincts of a champion debater.

In preparation for the debates, the campaign staged several trial debates, with David Stockman, an articulate, ambitious Michigan congressman, playing Carter. Stockman argued Carter's positions better than the president could do himself. Warming to his task, Stockman/Carter savaged Ronnie on nuclear proliferation, making him appear a bomb-happy, thoughtless Neanderthal. Ronnie answered as best he could, but afterward he said, "I was about to say, 'There you go again.' I may save it for the debate."

In the real Cleveland debate, Carter attacked Ronnie's position on everything from Medicare to nuclear proliferation. They were serious questions and Ronnie neatly parried them by accusing the president of misstatement. Time and again a frustrated Carter came back at Ronnie, until, as one of the president's own advisers observed later, "Jimmy looked like he was about to slug him."

Ridicule is a democracy's final rebuke, and when Carter talked about his daughter, Amy, discussing nuclear proliferation with him, he appeared the fool.

Carter went on to attack Ronnie's Medicare record.

"There you go again," Ronnie said, looking with bemused amazement at the president of the United States.

Ronnie had the last word. "Are you better off than you were four years ago?" he asked. That was the basic question in an election, and it was a wonder that no presidential candidate had asked it so starkly before. "Is it easier for you to go out and buy things in the stores than it was four years ago? Is there more or less unemployment in the country than there was four years ago? Is America respected throughout the world as it was? Do you feel that our security is as safe, that we're as strong as we were four years ago?

"If you answer all of those questions yes, why then I think your choice is very obvious as to who you'll vote for. If you don't agree, if you don't think that this course that we've been on for the last four years is what you would like to see us follow for the next four, then I could suggest another course that you have.

"I would like to have a crusade today, and I would like to lead that crusade . . . one to take government off the backs of the great people of this country, and turn you loose again to do those things that I know you can do as well, because you did them and made this country great."

There was no "October surprise," though the weekend before the election it looked as if Carter might be able to have the hostages released. Flying back to Los Angeles on *Leadership '80,* Ronnie and Nancy were full of good cheer. Wirthlin's polls said that Ronnie would win by a large margin.

On Election Day morning, Nancy and Ronnie voted in Pacific Palisades. Ronnie got a haircut and went home. They showered before beginning the long wait, leaving the television on, tuned to NBC.

"I ran out, and I wrapped a towel around me," Nancy said later. "And Ronnie got out of the shower, wrapped a towel around him, in time to hear that they were giving him the election. It was five-fifteen, five-thirty in the afternoon. And there we were, standing in the bedroom with towels wrapped around us, dripping wet, hearing that he'd been elected President of the United States. And I said to him, 'I don't think this is the way it's supposed to be. . . . I somehow saw it completely differently from this.' And with that, the phone rang and it was Jimmy Carter. President Carter conceding the election."*

*Reagan received 43,899,248 votes, or 50.75 percent. Carter received 35,481,435 votes, or 41.02 percent. Anderson received 5,719,439 votes, or 6.61 percent. In the electoral vote Reagan defeated Carter 489 to 49. Reagan carried all but six states.

═17═

A GREAT NEW BEGINNING

S oon after the election, many of Washington's top politicians, philanthropists, attorneys, businessmen and clergymen received an invitation to a sit-down dinner at the F Street Club to meet the president-elect and the new First Lady. They were amazed that the incoming Republican president should make such a friendly gesture. After all, most of these people were nominal Democrats, and some had actively campaigned against Ronnie. They had gotten used to the Carter people, who had been so disdainful of Washington society. The Carterites had arrived in the Capital four years earlier like an occupation army ready to discipline the slothful, morally corrupt political establishment.

But Nancy and Ronnie wanted to be residents, not just detached officeholders. Nancy had consulted with her old friend Nancy Reynolds, who now lived in Washington as a vice-president of Bendix. "We're sort of new to Washington," Nancy said, thinking ahead to January. "Who are the local people? Who are the movers and shakers?"

The Reagans decided to host a party on November 18 to befriend the community. With the help of columnist George Will, Nancy Reynolds put together a list of some of the most prominent people in Washington. The guests included Joseph Hirshhorn, the philanthropist who had donated his art collection to the nation and built a museum to house it; National Symphony Orchestra conductor Mstislav Rostropovich; attorney and Baltimore Orioles owner Edward Bennett Williams; publisher Austin Kiplinger; the governors of Maryland and Virginia; D.C. mayor Marion Barry; chairman of the board of *National Geographic* Melvin Paine; John T. Walker, bishop of Washington's Episcopal diocese.

The evening began rather stiffly, reminding Reynolds of a PTA meet-

Ronald and Nancy Reagan in their new home, the White House, 1980. *(Michael Evans, WH)*

ing. But George Bush played host. He had lived for many years in Washington. The way Bush worked the crowd, introducing city leaders to the new administration, he could have been the vice-president-elect of the D.C. Rotarians, not of the nation. "Hey, Ron, you want to meet Abe Pollin," he said, introducing Ronnie to the sports entrepreneur whose Capital Centre would house the inaugural gala.

The guests sat down to a candlelight dinner of sherry consommé, Veal Piccata, raspberries and California wines. To Washington's old guard, it was an elegant respite and a welcome return to more gracious entertaining. One socialite ordered a scotch and soda saying, "Thank goodness the Carters are gone." After dinner the fifty guests retired to the drawing room of the private club for coffee. Seated before a large fire they listened to Ronnie's tales of Hollywood, and were thoroughly charmed.

The Reagans returned to California knowing they had left behind a new feeling of goodwill. Ronnie's main task in Los Angeles was to choose his cabinet and staff. Meeting in a boardroom of William French Smith's law firm high above Los Angeles, the nineteen members on the "Transition Advisory Committee" helped put together the new administration. Half the advisers were his old millionaire friends: Bill Wilson, Holmes Tuttle, Alfred Bloomingdale, Earle Jorgensen, Jack Wrather, Henry Salvatori and Justin Dart.

"He's too old," one of them said, condemning a candidate.

"What!" said eighty-three-year-old Jorgensen loudly. "He's only a kid!"

The "kid" in question was sixty-five years old.

Seventy-four-year-old Dart didn't care how old a man was, or how young, as long as he was a tough-minded s.o.b. Dart limped on an artificial hip. The doctors had just put in a pacemaker. He was supposed to slow down but he wasn't about to let any doctors tell him what to do. He was going to be the one giving advice. The year before, he had learned of the Soviet invasion of Afghanistan while giving an interview. He'd picked up the phone and called Ronnie. The reporter listened as he told Ronnie that he should call for Carter to send in the marines.

Dart was upset when Ronnie decided to name Donald Regan secretary of the Treasury. The man he should have named, as Dart saw it, was William Simon, who was also part of the Transition Committee and who had held the post before. Dart felt that Simon was not only "brilliant" but "a goddamn near essential." But most of Ronnie's top-level appointments pleased his old friends. Salvatori told Dom Bonafede of the *National Journal* that they agreed on 99 percent of the final decisions. And according to Smith, Ronnie accepted almost all their recommendations.

They chose men who were Reaganites, Republicans and conservatives, in that order. If others might call it a cabinet of millionaires—well, let them. To Ronnie's aging advisers, it was largely a cabinet of men who were younger versions of themselves, men who had made it on their own in the real world, men who had seen their world, and made money, lots of it. Included in the cabinet would be one of their own: Smith, as attorney general. Others they knew and trusted were given prominent posts: Meese, counsel to the president; Deaver, deputy chief of staff; William Casey, director of the CIA; Caspar Weinberger, secretary of defense. The group would have its own office in the Executive Office Building, next door to the White House; they planned to see that the rest of the appointments were just as solid.

Ronnie was happy with his choices. He was less happy with what he saw happening to Nancy. Even before he was sworn in, she was a major figure of controversy. She told a reporter that she kept "a tiny little gun" near her bedside. When the words appeared in print, her new press secretary, Robin Orr, was blamed. Orr, the former society columnist for the *Oakland Tribune,* had been sitting in on the interview, and to her it hadn't sounded so terrible.

Nancy managed to offend the Carters as well. She told Jack Watson, the head of the president's transition staff, that she wanted to begin redecorating the White House and wouldn't it be nice if the Carters moved out of the White House a little early, into Blair House, so that she could get on with the job? On a Saturday morning in mid-December, Nancy made her second tour of the White House. She had asked that the West Wing be cleared of Carter staff, but that request had been turned down. None of this set well with the Carters and they were reported to be hurt and angry over Nancy's behavior.

For this new controversy, Orr again was blamed. After twenty-eight days, the fifty-year-old journalist was told to resign and was shuttled off to San Francisco with a temporary position at the International Communication Agency.

For Nancy, the whole inauguration was a dream, an incredible week that was one memory after another. She and Ronnie hadn't even settled into the White House when, a week after the inauguration, there came yet another grand and noble day, the honoring of the hostages who had survived 333 days of captivity in Iran. Ronnie was supposed to go up to West Point to greet the fifty-two returning hostages. "No way," he said when shown the State Department plan. "This is a time for these people to be with their families." He waited until they arrived in Washington on January 27.

As the sixteen Metro buses carrying the hostages and their families drove from Andrews Air Force Base to the White House, Washington displayed unabashed elation, the likes of which had not been seen since V-E Day. The buses drove through the bedroom communities of suburban Maryland, the bleakest ghettos of Washington, the gentrified regions of Capitol Hill, the edge of the downtown business district. Republicans and Democrats, rich and poor, lawyers and secretaries, blacks and whites, thousands of Americans lined this route—they waved flags and they shouted and they cried and they exulted on this springlike afternoon.

In the hostages Ronnie saw a personification of his belief in the everyday heroism of Americans. As he stood on the South Lawn of the White House greeting the former hostages, he was proud of his nation and its people. Ronnie knew this was not his day, though, and he spoke only briefly. "I'm sure you will want to know that with us here today are families of the eight heroic men who gave their lives in the attempt to effect your rescue," he said, referring to the abortive rescue mission. "Greater glory hath no man than that he lay down his life for another."

Afterward, Ronnie and Nancy met the former hostages and their families in the Blue Room of the White House. Waiting silently in the adjoining Green Room were the families of the dead servicemen. For them it was a day of deep, almost tortured remembrances and emotions. Nancy and Ronnie entered the Green Room. For a moment there was silence. "I just have to hug you," one of the women said, moving up to enfold Ronnie.

Later, the two groups met in a reception in the Blue Room. Among them were L. Bruce Laingen, the soft-spoken diplomat who had been the highest U.S. official held captive in Iran. Also in the room was Colonel Charles Beckwith, the dashing army officer who had led the May 1979 raid.

"Thanks for trying," Laingen said.

"We didn't come far enough," Beckwith said. A military aide standing nearby thought that the two men might cry.

Ronnie enjoyed greeting the hostages, but being president was more than ceremonies, no matter how moving. Every day there were decisions to be made. Ronnie worked a lot fewer hours than his predecessor. He left the details of government to a staff headed by James Baker, Deaver and Meese. Baker had been chosen as chief of staff, by tradition the most powerful position in any administration. The fifty-year-old Texas lawyer and millionaire was an outsider. He had managed both Ford's 1976 campaign and Bush's 1980 effort. At the troika's daily breakfast meeting, Baker sat at the head of the table, but he did not really preside over the 7:30 A.M. gathering. Ronnie's counsel, Meese, had as much to say as did Deaver, the deputy chief of staff.

Ronnie met with the trio each morning, signing off on many decisions that they had already made. In the early months of the administration, the three men to a large degree complemented one another. "At first they kind of mystified Washington," said Joseph Canzeri, then Deaver's top aide. "To understand it, you have to understand them. Meese worked as a prosecutor. He thinks that way. Deaver is a preceptor, an image kind of guy. And Baker's a business type and a pol. The three principals did well together."

Before Ronnie took office, David Gergen, the former communications director for Ford and now a Reagan aide, had written a long document entitled "The First 100 Days," comparing the first days of the seven administrations since Roosevelt. These first weeks, Ronnie outlined the themes and initiatives that would dominate the next four years. There were no breadlines in the street, no foreign troops massing at the border, no threats of internal insurrection. The problems, as Ronnie saw them, were more insidious than that: a government that was growing uncontrollably and uncontrollable, and a Soviet government that he thought now had greater military might than the United States. Furthermore, inflation stood at 13 percent, interest rates at 21½ percent, and productivity growth was down for the second year in a row.

Immediately after being sworn in, he signed an executive order freezing federal hiring. "It's time to recognize that we've come to a turning point," he told the American people on February 5 over television. "We're threatened with an economic calamity of tremendous proportions, and the old business-as-usual treatment can't save us. Together, we must chart a different course."

On February 18, Ronnie called for a $41-billion cut in the Carter budget. With his supply-side economics, Ronnie promised that the cuts would be a wondrous tonic, letting loose untapped energies and capital in the country's populace.

Ronnie didn't simply sit there and jawbone on television. Unlike Carter, he not only tolerated congressmen, he liked them. During the first two months, directed by his staff, he personally made his case to 400 legislators. The legislators liked him for his charisma, his genuine warmth and because he was popular. The voters had given him added power by choosing a Republican majority in the Senate and a far more conservative House.

Some Washington politicians said that Ronnie was an actor playing a role. But there was little difference between the public and the private man. Ronnie recorded a great many of his meetings on videotape or film for the National Archives. In the White House, Joe Holmes, an old Sacramento aide with a neatly trimmed moustache and a roving eye, oversaw two camera crews that filmed or videotaped much of Ronnie's day. Visits with dignitaries, heads of state, friends, journalists; cabinet meetings, discussions—

very often Joe's team was there. Ronnie was as comfortable with the filming as he was wearing shoes. Sometimes a guest appeared nervous or ap-
prehensive, but Ronnie reassured him.

It was Ronnie's joke both on Hollywood and history. A hundred years
from now, when John Wayne, Clark Gable and Cary Grant were only
vaguely remembered, Americans would still be playing Ronald Reagan's
greatest movie: the story of his presidency.

Nancy had her own exquisite moments in the media. There was no
more elegant a scene in Washington than the arrival of a foreign head of
state for a formal dinner at the Reagan White House. It had always been a
special moment, but Nancy and Ronnie carried it off with extraordinary
panache. As they stood waiting on the steps in their formal clothes, on a
platform across the driveway stood scores of cameramen and photographers, the working class of journalism. The only sounds were the clicking
and whirring of their cameras. Ronnie and Nancy stood in the sweet light
of attention, looking like a dream of what the president and First Lady
should be.

Nancy hosted her first formal party a week after the inauguration,
January 27, the same day the hostages arrived in Washington. It was a
formal reception for the diplomats of 141 countries, the first white-tie affair
held in the White House since the Ford administration. Nancy wore her
inaugural gown and greeted her guests with such warmth and hospitality
that they felt they were entering a private home.

The Reagans were a hit in the Capital. Washingtonians depended on
access to power for their livelihood, and many of them mimicked whoever
was in power. Four years before, at the beginning of the Carter administration, Hamilton Jordan, the new White House chief of staff, had attended
the annual black-tie White House correspondents' dinner at the Hilton
Hotel. Afterward, at a private party given by the *Wall Street Journal*, Jordan took up station in the middle of the room. He pulled off his tie and,
sucking on a bottle of beer, began discussing the mammaries of the women
in the suite. Within minutes, other males had begun shucking their ties and
drinking from beer bottles. If Jordan had stripped naked and run down the
corridor singing "Dixie," he might well have been followed by half a dozen
nude lobbyists, reporters and hangers-on singing harmony.

There would be no more drinking beer out of bottles. Indeed, there
would be almost no beer drinking at all. It was fine to be rich again. At
black-tie affairs, short dresses were no longer acceptable, and many ladies
would spend as much as $2,000 for the requisite designer gown. Nancy
Reynolds said that during the first weeks of the new administration she
was invited to five parties that included private orchestras or bands. John

Orcino, of the prominent catering firm of Avignone Frères, had been "wined and cheesed to death" by the Carter people. Now he was serving smoked Nova Scotia salmon, escargots stuffed with mushrooms, and calamari sautéed in garlic butter. The luxury hotels were full of ladies in mink and gentlemen in cashmere topcoats, the limousines purring quietly in the driveways like great sleek cats. At night the Reaganites filled expensive restaurants like the Jockey Club or Jean Louis.

With Nancy as First Lady, a different kind of woman was coming to prominence in Washington. In the late Seventies, the predominant image of the "Washington woman" was an ambitious professional to whom a leather briefcase was what a horse is to a cowboy. But now it was all right, even salutary, to be at home, raising a family and enjoying the bounty provided by one's husband. The exclusive boutiques had never done so well. Designer gowns and dresses sailed off the racks at Saks-Jandel and Neiman-Marcus. "Someone said when Reagan was elected you didn't have to be ashamed of what you have anymore," said one socialite. "At the tea parties the children come in blue velvet and the ladies in three-hundred-dollar suits. You discuss difficulty with maids and you discuss social events."

Nancy was excited about Washington, but for her the first months in the White House were full of mixed blessings. She had professed the intention of doing something serious as First Lady, but during her first weeks in the White House she was preoccupied with settling in. "I'm a nester by nature," she told reporters curious about her lack of activities. "Until I get all the boxes undone and unpacked, I'm not much good to anybody."

As she had done as the governor's wife, she saw her first task as redecorating the family rooms of the White House. She brought in Ted Graber, a sixty-one-year-old California decorator. Ted was another of those perennial California bachelors who hovered around Nancy and the ladies of her group. He was as charming as a maitre d'. He had been Betsy's friend for thirty years, and he had decorated her house as well as touching up Nancy's home in Pacific Palisades. He had written a book called *Decorating for Celebrities* and called his clients "the merchant princes who are today's royalty." He had even flown to Washington with the Reagans on *Air Force One* and out to Camp David with Nancy on the White House helicopter. He was staying at the White House, taking measurements of the nineteen-room private quarters and deciding how to use Nancy's personal pieces, English antiques and Chinese porcelains.

Each new president received $50,000 for redecorating. The Carters hadn't even spent all of theirs, and they had left the private rooms of the White House in what Nancy considered threadbare shape. Nancy knew that $50,000 wasn't even a beginning, that the renovations would cost several times that. Ted Graber normally spent $50,000 per room, and that was without art and antiques. In the White House there was a debate over whether to announce that they were going to accept $200,000 in private donations to redecorate. To many Americans, that might have seemed a reasonable sum, but it was obvious that much more would be spent. They announced it anyway, and the money came pouring in from the Reagans' friends, supporters and from private foundations. Earle and Marion gave $50,000; Alfred and Betsy $20,000; Justin and Jane $10,000; The Annenberg Fund, Inc., $70,000; Holmes and Virginia $10,000; Jack and Bunny $10,000. By March, a total of $735,911.91 had been received from 212 donors. All of the private donations were tax-deductible.

Justin and Holmes and Ronnie's other old friends in the Kitchen Cabinet had set up shop in the old Executive Office Building. It wasn't the White House, but it was next door, connected by a tunnel, in offices shared with Lyn Nofziger, who was running the political operation.

Holmes had helped raise money for Nancy's decorating, and some of the big oil people he'd approached, asking for $10,000 contributions, weren't happy. But Ronnie had just decontrolled oil prices, and they felt obligated. The Kitchen Cabinet was out raising money as well for "The Coalition for a New Beginning," which was supposed to lobby the public to support Ronnie's economic program. The money came rolling in, $800,000 and more. The future of America was at stake, and Holmes and Justin weren't too subtle about the whole business. To one of those approached, they seemed as dangerous to Ronnie as "a loose cannonball rolling around the deck" of a ship.

The Californians had come to Washington and made it *their* city. Alfred and Betsy had taken an eleventh-floor pied-à-terre in the Watergate, the crenellated co-op complex on the Potomac River that was the most expensive and exclusive in the city. A two-bedroom apartment sold for $200,000 and a parking space in the garage $15,000. There were rumors that Alfred was going to be named an ambassador. The Bloomingdales came flying in at the drop of an engraved invitation. Mary Jane and Charlie rented an $1,800-a-month apartment in the same building, Watergate South. Charlie was the new head of the International Communication Agency. Walter and Lee Annenberg took a three-bedroom suite next door at the swanky Watergate Hotel; the suite usually rented for $750 a day. Lee was going to have the first job she had ever had: the new chief of protocol. Justin and Jane Dart stayed in the hotel so that "Punky" and her husband could be just seven blocks from the White House. So did Betty and Bill Wilson, who had been named special envoy to the Vatican.

The hotel management had a *savoir faire* that the millionaires liked. The manager, Gabor Ollah, an urbane Hungarian, had known Greta Garbo, Hedy Lamarr and Ava Gardner from his days as manager of the exclusive Hotel Splendido in Portofino, Italy. He had a charm and European manner the California ladies adored. Usually, Ollah escorted them to their suites, taking their arms, complimenting them in a soft voice.

Jean and Bill Smith stayed not here but at the Jefferson Hotel, nearer the Justice Department, where he was the new attorney general. But Jean was often at the Watergate Beauty Salon or shopping in the Les Champs mall with its exclusive boutiques such as Gucci, Saint Laurent, and Valentino, where a simple day suit could cost over two thousand dollars.

To be near Betsy, Punky and Mary Jane, Jerry Zipkin stayed at the Watergate, too, where the management kept guest histories of VIPs and treated them to their known likes—fresh fruit, roses, champagne, Godiva chocolates, or a Christian Dior bathrobe. Of course, when Jerry was in New York, he was still just a phone call away, and Nancy loved talking to him. *Women's Wear Daily* dubbed Jerry "The Walker," one of those sexually benign gentlemen who squired ladies of wealth, but to Nancy he was "a sort of modern-day Oscar Wilde." In his bedroom in his sprawling apartment on upper Park Avenue were scores and scores of pictures of his friends: Nancy, Betsy, Mary Jane and the others. They were in silver frames and when the light struck them they glimmered like a hundred candles at a shrine.

Now in the White House, Nancy felt she needed sixty-six-year-old Jerry even more. He was honest and had good judgment and she was surrounded by dissembling. He was witty and she was in the midst of the dullness of political servitude and insecurity. He told her how to dress, how to act, whom to see, and he wanted nothing more than her friendship.

Jerry knew all about the biggest event of Nancy's first weeks in the White House: Ronnie's seventieth-birthday party on Friday, February 6. She had discussed it with her friends over New Year's at the Annenbergs' great 250-acre Palm Springs estate, Sunnylands. *Everyone* went there for New Year's, and Nancy talked with Jerry and Betsy and the others about the surprise party. The Annenbergs, the Deutsches, the Jorgensens and the Wilsons were happy to pay for the party, but Nancy had to do the planning and keep it from Ronnie.

Californians dominated the 100 names on the guest list. Alfred and Betsy, Betty and Bill, Jane and Justin, Virginia and Holmes, Jean and Bill, Charlie and Mary Jane were coming. So was Jerry. And. Francis Albert and Barbara were flying in, too. Maureen was the only offspring attending.

Nancy tried to keep it a secret. She got Ronnie into black tie by telling him that a small group was coming for dinner. When he walked into the

Charles and Mary Jane
Wick; William French
and Jean Smith. *(WWD)*

grand hall to see all his friends standing there, he looked properly surprised.

Nancy loved flowers and the dining room was filled with lilies, tulips, jonquils and ficus trees. Entering the room was like walking into spring itself. The ten tables were covered with white organdy and green moiré cloths. For every table there was a vanilla sponge cake rich with raspberry brandy and topped with a white horse; chefs in white coats and hats carried the cakes into the room.

In her toast, Nancy looked around the room and said, "I know there is nothing he wants more than a continuation of your friendship."

It had been so long since anyone had had such a gay, glorious time in the White House. The guests weren't about to simply sit between the courses of lobster, veal and dessert. Following Nancy and Ronnie's lead, they began to dance.

"The most wonderful thing happened," remembered Nancy Reynolds. "Everybody was cutting in and double-cutting. I was absolutely tickled. I haven't been to a dance in thirty years where people cut in. Maureen asked her father to dance. The people danced between courses. It was good for their digestion. I believe the doctors would approve. The waiters loved it. They got to clear the tables. People were laughing. Laughter is in because Ronald Reagan has a funny bone. His friend Frank Sinatra says that nobody has a funny bone like Ron's."

They danced into the night, the ladies in their gowns by Adolfo and Galanos, the gentlemen in tailored black tie. They were old, these friends of Nancy and Ronnie Reagan, but this evening they did not know that or see that. Francis Albert was not a rotund senior citizen with the face of a bulldog and a ghost of a voice; for them he was young Frank Sinatra, bobby-soxers delight. Jane and Bunny and Nancy were movie starlets again, lovely young ladies whom gentleman wanted to hold in their arms.

Wearing a glittery beaded white gown that was one of Ronnie's favorites, Nancy was the belle of the ball, swept from arm to arm, gentleman to gentleman. The orchestra played the romantic old songs like "Nancy with the Laughing Face." At midnight, when White House dinners were usually over, Ronnie and Nancy were still dancing in each other's arms. As much as the guests wanted to stay, they felt that they should leave. They began slipping slowly away, while Ronnie and Nancy whirled around and around, as if the evening would never end.

The celebration didn't stop with the Friday night surprise party. The next evening Mary Jane and Charlie hosted a lavish dinner in Ronnie's honor at the Jean Louis restaurant in the Watergate, where dinner could run $200 a couple. Jean Louis, a thirty-five-year-old French *nouvelle cuisine* chef, had already become a favorite with the Reagan crowd. The

The president's surprise seventieth birthday dinner party at the White House, with the president, the First Lady and Francis Albert Sinatra dancing between the courses, 1981. *(Michael Evans, WH)*

Wicks dined in his small, exclusive restaurant several times a week. Reached through a long corridor lined with wines as old as a 1916 La Tour, and separated from the rest of the hotel, the restaurant had a privacy and intimacy the Californians loved.

When Jean Louis knew they were coming, he would prepare their favorite menu. Tonight he cooked an eight-course meal that included foie gras on toast, scallops and salmon, and ravioli stuffed with wild mushrooms. He served French wines and champagnes. "Everyone sang and wandered around," Jean Louis remembered. "The president sang first, and then everyone joined in. They are simple people. They enjoy each other."

Without Nancy's toughness and social ambition, Ronnie never would have become president. Yet Nancy was still shy and painfully vulnerable. She didn't like most journalists and she dreaded having to deal with them. So much of her life was not what she said it was, and as she told Diane Sawyer of CBS later, she thought that "there's a certain point, yes, that's—that's public, but then beyond that there is—that is part that's—that's mine."

Nancy would have to make an appearance before the White House reporters. Rosalynn Carter had given a tea party to introduce herself and had mingled with the reporters, but Nancy wanted nothing like that. Instead, she agreed to a "background briefing" to introduce her staff and talk about the Foster Grandparents Program, a program funded by ACTION, the federal agency. No pictures would be taken, no questions allowed.

The seventy-five reporters, mainly women, sat waiting for Nancy to make her debut. They were a motley lot: middle-aged ladies who had covered several First Ladies; ambitious professional women who couldn't wait to get out of this female beat; old ladies whose White House press passes were their one social cachet, and who covered for tiny, distant journals; a few self-styled social arbiters who considered real reporters riffraff, and the regular crew who covered the West Wing and this afternoon had nothing else to cover.

On February 9, Nancy arrived in a bubble of Secret Service and staff, wearing a pink-and-rose suit. The reporters knew of her interest in clothes, and that the professional dowdiness of the Carter years was over, and they had dressed to fit the occasion. Out in front of the First Lady was a sea of pearls and suits. Elizabeth Mehren of the *Los Angeles Times* wrote in her notebook that except for one reporter in an "Exxon jump suit," it looked like "Peck and Peck's last stand."

Nancy stood behind the lectern, petite and feminine, nervously slipping her small foot out of her burgundy shoe. She introduced her staff, beginning with chief of staff Peter McCoy, whom she called laughingly the East Wing's "token male." She introduced the rest of her entourage including her new press secretary, Sheila Tate, a former public-relations executive at Hill and Knowlton; and Muffie Brandon, the social secretary, and the wife of Henry Brandon of the *London Sunday Times*. Though these ladies had garbed themselves in frills, satins and bows, they remained big-boned women who could have been Nancy's bodyguards.

Nancy talked a bit about the Foster Grandparents Program.

"You're not going to let your husband cut it out, are you?" asked Helen Thomas, the UPI correspondent and the dean of White House reporters.

"It's not a press conference, Helen," Nancy said. "But no, I'm not. Nor would he want to."

After twelve minutes, Nancy told the reporters that they better "get your Kleenex" out for the film they were about to see about the program. When the film was over and the lights went up, Nancy was gone.

Inside the White House, Ronnie and Nancy tried to change their personal lives as little as possible. There was little privacy in the 132-room mansion. Nancy could hear the patter and chatter of the tourists on the first floor. The sounds drifted up the vaulting stairways to her private quarters.

Nancy and Ronnie were outdoor people. Ronnie, in particular, couldn't stand being cooped up in the White House with its sealed windows and climate control. He loved his ranch and after only a month in the White House he and Nancy flew back to California for a long weekend vacation at Rancho del Cielo. Ronnie wanted to take a break, chop some wood and ride Little Man. But he wasn't about to turn *his* ranch into a western White House, like Nixon's San Clemente estate. He wanted it to stay just as it was. The Secret Service was housed in trailers, and the press was sequestered in Santa Barbara.

Back in Washington, Nancy had begun to take her own part in the social scene. To help her she had Letitia Baldrige, who had been Jacqueline Kennedy's press secretary. "Tish" stayed in the White House the first two weeks, setting up the East Wing. Working in the same office as she had twenty years before, she had a sense that America's attitude toward the White House and the First Lady had changed dramatically since those days. "Mrs. Kennedy was young, and beautiful, and had just given birth," she said. "She had pedigree and style and enjoyed the same kind of popularity as Elizabeth Taylor. In those days we still had a 'we' philosophy. We loved our country and cared about our astronauts' children. Vietnam and Watergate have turned us into cynical revolutionaries. We don't worship anything anymore and it shows in the press. Before, the press was in awe. Today, they look for all the drunkenness and problems they can find."

Baldrige set up a series of luncheons for Nancy. "These were to intro-

duce Mrs. Reagan to real Washingtonians who could tell her about the city
into which she was moving," Baldrige said. These "real" Washingtonians
were aging matrons who as often as not spoke as if their noses had been
trussed with silver filigree. They lived mainly in Georgetown, where
quaintness comes high and eternal war is waged against bars and burger
joints. The "Bright Old Things," as the *Washingtonian* dubbed them, were
almost all in their sixties or older. Unlike Nancy's wealthy California
friends, most of the B.O.T.'s had allowed themselves to age, as is the fashion for part of the eastern establishment. They were like cherished antiques, pleasant to look at but difficult to handle.

The luncheons with Nancy were wonderfully sedate. Nancy was polite
to a fault, sometimes sending flowers beforehand, and of course a personal
note afterward. Most of the B.O.T.'s did not have that much in common
with Nancy. Evangeline Bruce's deceased husband had been ambassador to
France, West Germany and Great Britain. Evangeline, with the sleek look
of a prize polo pony, was more used to a salon where policymakers discussed world events. Lorraine Cooper's husband had been a senator and
ambassador and she was comfortable sitting at the dinner table talking
about current issues. But the ladies liked Nancy, and the luncheons tinkled
with Nancy's high-pitched laughter.

"If more people could see her on a one-to-one basis, they'd love her,"
said Ann Hand, wife of LBJ's chief of protocol, who met Nancy at one of
the luncheons. "She's funny and she laughs so easily. I can see why the
president loves to go home to her. She has a very cozy manner. We were all
perfectly charmed by her."

One of the first ladies to give a luncheon for Nancy was Mrs. Robert
H. Charles, who had a cottage in Newport as well as a tall Victorian house
on "R" Street in Georgetown. "Oatsie" Charles had been brought up, as
she would say, "by loving black hands in the South." She had the hardy
figure of a Wagnerian diva and the shrill voice of a tobacco auctioneer. She
wore her hair in a bun and spoke with a candor, often laced with profanity,
that had spiced up more than one dowdy dinner party. "I find myself at the
age of sixty-two and I don't do a goddamn thing," she said.

Of course, Oatsie knew Jerry, and one day in the late winter she received a call from Zipkin suggesting that she invite Nancy to lunch. Oatsie
dialed the White House and asked for Nancy. The telephone operators
knew enough about Nancy by now to ask if Oatsie was a personal friend.
Oatsie said no, and that was that.

No more than a couple of hours later, the phone rang. "Oh, Oatsie,
I've heard so much about you," Nancy said in her tiny voice. "We have so
many mutual friends."

As Nancy talked on and on, what struck Oatsie was Nancy's "understanding and her reticence and shyness on the phone." She had the feeling, she said later, "I had known Nancy all her life."

"Oatsie, I'd love to come to lunch," Nancy said.

As Oatsie discovered, it was no simple matter having the First Lady to lunch. The Secret Service checked out everything. The day before the luncheon, she received yet another call from the White House, asking if Ted Graber, the decorator, could be added to the guest list of ladies.

"He can come if he doesn't mind playing the pasha," Oatsie said.

The next day "the pasha" arrived with the ladies.

Nancy had an almost childlike way of exploring a new place; and with its library and antiques, the house on "R" Street was something new to her.

"Is Mr. Charles ill?" Nancy asked.

"Yes, he's had a stroke," Oatsie said, almost wistfully. "The cook left the same day."

After the luncheon, Nancy thanked Oatsie profusely and later sent her a touching note. Nancy had tried to instill the same manners in her daughter. But to the women of the Sixties, including many of the younger reporters who savaged Nancy, such manners were a kind of prison, and they sometimes mistook rudeness for truth. Nancy's etiquette was as stylized as that of a Japanese, but her gestures brought touches of joy to society dowagers.

Muffie Brandon called Oatsie. "How would you like to come to the White House for dinner?" the social secretary asked, inviting Oatsie to the first state dinner of the new administration, for Prime Minister Margaret Thatcher of Great Britain on February 27.

"I'm distraught. My hair's a mess," Oatsie replied.

As Oatsie walked through the diplomatic entrance of the White House, past the solo harpist and the reporters and photographers cordoned off behind a velvet rope, she yelled out in her booming voice, "Nancy—I mean, Mrs. Reagan—rang me up last week and very kindly invited me. She thought it would cheer me up since Robert's in the hospital with a stroke for a second time."

Next morning, the quote appeared in the *Washington Post*. And Oatsie remembers receiving a phone call later that day from Barbara Bush, the vice-president's wife. It was rare for someone to say something so nice in print about Nancy.

Oatsie continued to talk to Nancy on the telephone. "She knows I don't give a damn that she's the First Lady," Oatsie said later. "I don't think of her as the First Lady. I think of her as 'Beauty.' I call her 'Beauty.' I said once, 'I wish I had never met you.' I think about the loneliness. You can hear it in the voice. Everything is suspect. Everyone is questioned.

There is nothing you can do privately. She can't say she wants to have tea. She is an anachronism. She is simple. She's extremely sensitive. I think she is utterly stunned by the reception."

The second week in March, Nancy joined Ronnie on his first state trip abroad, to Ottawa for meetings with the Canadian prime minister, Pierre Trudeau. Ronnie didn't pay any attention to demonstrators who feared that his bellicose words about El Salvador would lead to a second Vietnam and that his stance against air-pollution control would increase acid rain over the North American continent. "I thought they were imported to make me feel at home," he joked to the embarrassed Trudeau.

Coming out of the National Arts Centre after a gala, Ronnie noticed a red-coated Canadian Mounted Policeman who looked like Nelson Eddy in *Rose Marie*. Ronnie strode up to the moustached officer standing as motionless as a tobacco-store Indian, and mugged for the cameras. While the photographers snapped away, Nancy laughed as hard as anyone.

The next day, March 11, Ronnie was scheduled to address the House of Commons. Nancy had her own activities. The Canadians knew she had an interest in hospitals and special children. Wearing her Maximillian mink, she visited the Clifford Bowey School for the Mentally Retarded outside Ottawa. She felt uncomfortable when she had to speak extemporaneously or travel into new situations without Ronnie, but she plunged onward, going to one classroom after another. Mentally retarded children often are acutely sensitive to the moods of adults, and Nancy was nervous. "Don't be embarrassed," one of the students told her.

Nancy touched and hugged the children in little cathartic moments. When it was time to leave, one of the retarded children brought Nancy her fur. Across Nancy's face passed a look of horror and disbelief: It wasn't her coat, but a far more modest fur. That mix-up was soon taken care of, and Nancy and her mink headed back into Ottawa. It had already been a long day, but at least Julius, her hairdresser, had flown up to Ottawa to take care of her hair.

Lee Annenberg had flown up to Ottawa, too. Not only was she Nancy's friend, but she was going to be the new chief of protocol, and Nancy knew that nobody had better taste than Lee.

In Washington a few days later, on March 20, Lee was scheduled to be sworn in. *Everyone* was in Washington, staying at the Watergate for the ceremony at the State Department and the luncheon given by Jane Dart at the Watergate Terrace.

"Daaaaahling, how nice to see you," Jerry said, kissing a matron the civilized way, intimate but sanitary, never applying lip to cheek. "I just saw Punky upstairs and I'm on my way to pick up Bets."

Lee was duly sworn in and began duties that included not only plan-

The Reagans with their son after his debut with the Joffrey II Ballet at the Metropolitan Opera House in New York City, 1981. *(UPI)*

ning state and other diplomatic visits but a constant round of parties. Walter, her seventy-three-year-old husband, had gone along with her new job, but his wife's prominence had introduced him to one of the melancholy realities of the modern age: wives who are more important than their husbands. Lee was hardly more successful than Walter, who among other things owned *TV Guide,* had been ambassador to Great Britain and had recently donated a cool $150 million to public television. But in Lee's Washington world, Walter was sometimes the little man who sat in the corner.

As for the aging coterie of the Kitchen Cabinet, they, too, were discovering certain melancholy realities of power, or the lack of it. The administration had received a legal opinion that Ronnie had no business giving out government offices for a private operation, and they had been rudely evicted from their perch in the Old Executive Office Building. Worse yet, because of their alleged arm twisting they had been asked to end their "Coalition for a New Beginning" and return the contributions. "The kitchen cabinet has served its purpose and, unless the President calls on some of us, the cabinet is finished," Dart told Jack Nelson of the *Los Angeles Times.*

Ronnie wasn't about to leave his old friends embittered. There is nothing quite so seductive as being asked for advice, and Ronnie continued to talk to his old friends. But their dream of being the wise old men of the administration, the entrepreneurial role models for the nation, was about over.

In mid-March, Nancy was excited to be going to New York with Ronnie for the weekend. Ronnie did a few political chores, but the Reagans had come to New York to have a good time. Saturday evening, Ronnie, Nancy, Jerry, Betsy and Claudette Colbert, an old Hollywood acquaintance, dined together at Le Cirque. The elegant, terribly *cher* restaurant was a favorite of Nancy's set. Sitting nearby was Bianca Jagger, Mick Jagger's ex-wife. And at another table was Andy Warhol, pale as an albino. Young Ron's new wife, Doria, worked for Warhol's magazine, *Interview,* and Andy came over to say hello.

Ronnie talked to Betsy about Ron, Jr. Tomorrow night for the first time Ronnie and Nancy would see their son perform as a professional dancer. Ronnie, sensitive about implications concerning dancers, told one interviewer that he had checked Ron, Jr., out and he was "all boy," as if homosexuals had a different anatomy. Now that Ron, Jr., was married, that kind of rumor was at least partially squelched, and Ronnie could take pride in his son's debut with the Joffrey II Ballet at the Metropolitan Opera House.

Young Ron's marriage to Doria Palmieri had been a political plus, ending the controversy over their living together, and diminishing gossip about his sexuality. But the match may not have been one Nancy would have made for her son. The couple had met four years earlier at the Stanley Holden School of Dance in Los Angeles. Doria was seven years older, the daughter of an Italian immigrant who designed sets for 20th Century-Fox. She dressed with a dancer's flair and drama, black eye liner circled the dark eyes under the mass of curls. Doria and Ron had married in November after the election at City Hall with a Secret Service man as witness. His parents did not attend the wedding. They now lived in a tiny apartment on the top floor of a Greenwich Village brownstone.

Nancy and Doria had met only a few times. During Christmas at the ranch, Ronnie had spent an hour with his son's bride, walking around his spread, his arm around her shoulder, Secret Service agents trailing a discreet distance behind.

Sunday evening, from their box at the Met, Ronnie and Nancy watched Ron, Jr., perform in an abstract ballet entitled *Unfolding*. The Joffrey II Ballet was the company's farm team and Ron was more used to performing in college auditoriums and theaters in the hinterlands. He was as nervous as any first-time performer, but he did well, lifting his partner with grace, proving to anyone that he was there not because he was the president's son but because he could dance.

Afterward, Nancy and Ronnie went backstage. Ron, Jr., stood there in a blue terry-cloth bathrobe and red sweat pants, appearing slightly bewildered and embarrassed by all the attention. Nancy, stunning in her shimmering gown, hugged her son, theatrical makeup still splashed on his face. Ronnie looked on, as proud as a father whose kid has just scored the winning touchdown for the high-school team.

Ron, Jr., had gotten this far by himself, but now his mother's friends set out to help him. "I received a letter from Justin Dart," said the corporate contributions officer for a major corporation. "The letter said Ron, Jr., is dancing with the Joffrey and Nancy has asked me to get funds. I was infuriated and we turned it down." There were other letters as well, seeking funds.

Most of the Reagan children seemed to be doing well. Patti had moved into her bare new apartment in Santa Monica. And though she could do without the Secret Service agents camped out in the garage, she was getting on with her career. She was represented by a hotshot Hollywood agent, Norman Brokaw of the William Morris Agency, and she had signed a one-year six-figure contract with NBC.

Maureen wasn't hurt by the fact that her father was in the White House. As president of Sell Overseas America, an organization to boost exports, it didn't hurt having a friend in the Oval Office. She was thinking of running for the Senate in California, too. And she was about to take on her third husband, twenty-eight-year-old Dennis Revell, a law clerk.

As for Michael, his father's first two months in the White House had already netted him a slew of troubles. The local district attorney was investigating whether Michael had misused funds given him for investment in gasohol development and whether he had illegally sold stock in his fledgling company. Michael considered it a petty vendetta because his name was Reagan. The whole matter was soon dropped. But Michael was getting fed up with the Secret Service agents around his modest home in Sherman Oaks, their closed-circuit cameras in his yard. His wife couldn't even sunbathe anymore.

━━18━━
"RAWHIDE NOT HURT, REPEAT, NOT HURT"

Washington was very much *their* city. The last Sunday in March dawned sunny and warm, and Nancy and Ronnie decided to walk to church. The cherry blossoms had yet to bloom, but spring was in the air and in the president's youthful step as he and Nancy strode across Pennsylvania Avenue, through Lafayette Park and into the gates of St. John's Episcopal Church. The Reagans were accompanied by a Secret Service detail, and an officer nearby carried the black communications box. The last thing on Ronnie's mind, however, was either security or unleashing a nuclear attack. The Reagans enjoyed sitting in their pew, singing and praying and listening to a special treat, the U.S. Naval Academy choir.

Afterward, Ronnie and Nancy shook hands with the cadets and headed back to the White House through a crowd of well-wishers. Ronnie would have been a smashing success in a country like India or Italy where the president is a largely ceremonial figure. He loved waving happily to the tourists and getting out of the White House to speak to various groups. His predecessor had hated the gooey glad-handing of politics; it was as if Ronnie, not Jimmy Carter, had been the one reared on southern politics.

Ronnie was looking ahead to the following week. He knew that in a political life as in a movie there are one or two symbolic moments whose impact resonates, giving meaning and purpose to all that follows. As the Reagan presidency went into its tenth week, one of those moments was upon Ronald Reagan. Within a few days the Senate would vote on the administration's bill to cut more than $41 billion from the proposed Carter budget. If the bill passed, it would symbolize that government was beginning to shrink for the first time since Franklin Delano Roosevelt took office

---

The inner circle at the Oval Office: President Reagan confers with, clockwise from him: William P. Clark, James A. Baker, David Gergen, Michael K. Deaver and Edwin Meese. 1981. *(RS)*

in 1933, giving a new energy and impetus to the entire administration. If it failed, then he might find the ideals of his presidency fading into the sunset like the last reel of a "B" movie.

The media were gauging Ronald Reagan's first 100 days against FDR's dramatic initiatives, and Monday the thirtieth of March was the seventy-year-old president's seventieth day in office. As he had already realized, there was more routine than drama in his exalted office. This morning, as usual, he met with the troika of top aides, and then heard his daily briefing on the world situation. After that, at 10:00 A.M., he talked to 140 subcabinet-level appointees. They were the people who, as he saw it, were out in the trenches fighting intransigent bureaucrats. He gave one of his patented go-out-and-get-'em speeches, ending with a quotation from Tom Paine—"We have it in our power to begin the world over again." The dark-suited men and women applauded wildly.

At noon, Ronnie took the interminably slow elevator to the private quarters on the second floor. Finishing off a lunch of avocado and chicken salad, red beets and an apple tart, he went to his bedroom for a nap before his 2:00 P.M. speech to the AFL-CIO.

Nancy would normally have lunched with her husband and gone with him to the Hilton Hotel to hear his speech, but today she had what for her was a very busy schedule. In the morning she and Barbara Bush, the vice-president's wife, attended a midmorning reception at the Phillips Gallery, only four blocks from the Hilton. Nancy had grown to hate some of her public duties, but today's activities would be a respite from her more onerous tasks. She wouldn't have to talk to the reporters, whom she disliked so, the old ones who dressed so poorly, the younger ones brash and unpleasant.

Today's event was a gathering of Washington women active in the arts—not painters and poets but philanthropic ladies. And a stylish gathering it was—silk dresses and linen suits and, except for the reporters huddled behind the ropes, nary a rustle of polyester. Laughlin Phillips, the gallery director and heir to a Pittsburgh steel fortune, was one of a few men in the musuem. When he showed Mrs. Reagan around the gallery of French impressionists, she took his arm. "Don't leave me," she said. Watching this from a distance, Phillips's wife, Jennifer, found Nancy "touching . . . like a little girl."

Soon afterward, Nancy and Barbara Bush were driven to Georgetown, the lovely neighborhood that during the Kennedy administration had seemed the center of the universe. Nancy loved the old streets and visiting houses like the one she was entering today, the Italianate Victorian house of Michael Ainslie at 3021 "Q" Street. Ainslie, the president of the National Trust for Historic Preservation, was entertaining Nancy, Barbara and some of the cabinet members' wives for lunch.

At 2:15 Ronnie stood before 3,500 leaders of the Building and Construction Trades Department of the AFL-CIO, the largest group to whom he had spoken since becoming president. He was dressed smartly in a blue suit and white monogrammed shirt, a white handkerchief sticking from his breast pocket. These men spread out before him in the ballroom of the Hilton Hotel on Connecticut Avenue weren't the easiest group to face. Their unions hadn't supported him in the election. Moreover, almost 660,000 construction workers were out of work. His reception was not overwhelming, but four times the union men interrupted his speech for applause, and he could believe that the Democrats' lockgrasp on the unions might end.

At 2:24 Ronnie walked briskly up the long VIP corridor, his shoes sinking into the deep-pile red-and-blue carpeting, toward the gray double doors leading onto "T" Street. When he came out into the gray, rain-speckled day, he raised his right hand toward the office workers peering from the buildings on "T" Street, then his left hand toward the reporters and onlookers standing about ten feet to his left.

"Mr. President," shouted Michael Putzel, the Associated Press reporter, who wanted to ask a question about Poland.

If Churchill's characteristic gesture was his V sign, and Napoleon's a hand stuck in his coat, then Ronnie's was a smiling, half-turned head responding to some reporter's question. No matter how his staff fretted, he always had to say something. Mike Deaver motioned for Jim Brady, the burly press secretary, to move forward to help field the questions.

Shots rang out—not the sharp volley of a movie sound track but pops like a string of two-inch firecrackers going off. The president froze. His face appeared to one bystander, Mickey Crowe, like "a person who has seen death reflected in his eyes . . . saying: 'I'm in a moment of helplessness.'"

As the first shot rang out, fifty-year-old Jerry Parr, head of the Secret Service detail, put his left hand on the president's left shoulder and pushed him down into the back seat of the presidential limousine, the president's head striking the Cadillac's doorway.

"Take off," Parr said as he lay on top of the president, straddling the hump in the floor of the vehicle's spacious back seat. "Just take off."

"You son of a bitch, you broke my ribs," Ronnie told Parr as the limousine sped away from a scene of blood and dismay. Ronnie felt a shattering pain, as if he had been struck by a hammer. Still, he knew he had been lucky—he hadn't been shot. Parr, a seventeen-year Secret Service vet-

The exact moment of the shooting. *(W-W)*

eran, examined the president anyway, running his hands along his chest and back and under his arms. Parr decided that the driver, agent Drew Unrue, had better take them to the most secure place in Washington: the White House.

"Rawhide not hurt, repeat, not hurt," Parr said into the Secret Service radio, using the president's code name.

As the limousine sped through the tunnel under DuPont Circle, a half-dozen blocks from the Hilton, Ronnie started coughing up blood. Parr knew what the bright red color meant; it was oxygenated blood, coming from the lung, suggesting that the president's lung might have been punctured.

"Rawhide is heading for George Washington," Parr told the Secret Service command post at the White House as the presidential limousine and the follow-up car traveled the mile and a quarter to the hospital, buffered by motorcycle police. "We're just going to check you out at GW," Parr said.

In the driveway of the emergency entrance, Parr jumped out. Then Ronnie got out. The ashen face and frightened eyes said that he was a man who should be carried into the hospital, but the agent could tell that Ronnie wanted to walk in by himself. It was as if Ronnie thought that by an act of sheer willpower he could exorcise the pain that grew within him. He walked through the three sets of automatic double doors, three agents close beside him.

"I feel like I can't breathe," he said. His knees buckled. As he sank to the ground, twenty-eight-year-old Kathy Paul, a stout, plainspoken nurse, grabbed his arm. Two agents and a paramedic helped carry Ronnie through the emergency room forty feet to the trauma bay.

"I feel so bad," he said as he lay on one of the two beds used by critically ill or wounded patients.

As in most city hospitals, the emergency room at GW treated the running sores of an often brutal urban society, everything from gunshot wounds to poisonings, psychoses to wife beating. The staff in the ER had seen hundreds of cases like the president's and Kathy Paul and Wendy Koenig, another emergency room nurse, unceremoniously tore away the monogrammed RR shirt, buttons popping, and cut off the blue suit, littering the area with cloth.

Scarcely ten minutes had passed since the shooting, but the emergency room was already packed with people—Secret Service agents, D.C. police, doctors, technicians. Outside, sirens blared. Inside, radios barked urgent messages. The din of conversation was steadily rising, until to be heard a few feet away a person had to shout.

Standing bent over the president, Wendy Koenig tried to hear his

An exhausted and worried First Lady arrives at George Washington University Hospital to be with her husband after the assassination attempt. *(UPI)*

heart through her stethoscope. But the noise was so loud. . . .

"I can't hear anything!" she yelled. "I can't get a systolic pressure."

The nurse tried again. Only 50 to 60 systolic, half what it should have been. Less than ten minutes ago, the president had felt himself in command of his life and his country. Now he lay here in what doctors call "trauma," in a fog of pain, poked at and prodded by white-coated men and women less than half his age. He could feel all his energy and strength seeping away.

At the head of the bed stood Parr. At the foot stood Dr. Daniel Ruge, the White House physician, who had hurried to the hospital. Ruge had once been in partnership with Nancy's stepfather, and he had known Ronnie for twenty years. He was a proud man, though professionally self-effacing. He believed that "when anybody goes into a hospital, the best people to take care are the people accustomed to doing it, and the role of the president's physician is not to create any obstacles."

At her Georgetown luncheon, Nancy decided that she wanted to leave early. She had no special reason, and it was totally unlike her, but she said goodbye and was driven back to the White House. She had scarcely reached the private quarters on the third floor when a Secret Service agent told her, "There's been a shooting at the hotel. Your husband was not shot. Your husband wasn't hurt, but he's at the hospital."

For twenty years Nancy had lived for him and through him. She had always been there when he needed her. But now she was not there, now when he needed her more than ever. As the limousine sped toward GW, she sat quietly, her eyes glistening with tears.

"He's all right, he's all right," she yelled as she ran from the car through the double doors. All her life she had striven for order and discipline. As she hurried into the emergency room, she was entering into everything she had worked so hard to avoid ever seeing or feeling. It was not only the noise and close-packed bodies, the scurrying doctors, the burly D.C. policeman, the Secret Service agents, their faces damp with tension, the sharp smells of medicine and nervous, sweating bodies. It was that Ronnie was somewhere back there among this surging chaos, out of her reach and care.

There stood Mike Deaver, whom she trusted most of all Ronnie's aides. "He's taken a bullet, but he's all right," she was told.

"But I want to see him."

"Well, you can't just now," Deaver said.

"But if it isn't serious, why can't I see him?"

"Well, in a few minutes."

With that, Nancy was shuttled into the tiny ten-by-twelve-foot call room. She was like a fragile *objet d'art* that did not belong in what she called later "that awful little room." She sat on the fold-up bed that doctors slept on during the night shift, next to piled-up boxes. A half-dozen or so Secret Service agents crammed into the windowless lime-green room. Nancy hardly noticed. To Herman Goodyear, the emergency room secretary, Nancy looked "like she was made out of plastic, she was so white and tense."

Everywhere she looked, all she saw was confusion. Police ran down the corridor shouting, "Get those people out of the way!" There was a din of voices, noises, scurrying. Outside at his desk, Goodyear saw officers raise their guns to herd onlookers out of the emergency room.

I have to hold on and not get in the way, Nancy thought to herself. *I have to hold on and not get in the way. . . . I have to hold on and not get in the way. . . .*

With each minute, the president was less in control of himself and the world around him. He knew now that he had been shot. The doctors had found a small blackish hole with blood trickling from it under his left armpit. They had covered his mouth and nose with a lightweight oxygen mask. They had put in a urinary catheter so that he didn't control his bladder any longer. Through the IV in his arm, blood was pumping into his body. A doctor gave him a shot of Xylocaine, a local anesthetic, in the side. Then they made an incision and put a tube into his body to drain the blood that was filling his left pleural cavity.

A nurse pushed her way through the Secret Service agents, who stood in a solid block like a Roman phalanx. "Can't someone see Mrs. Reagan?" she asked.

In the emergency room, Senator Paul Laxalt was insisting that someone talk to the First Lady. Nancy was beginning to understand the scope of what had happened still less than a half-hour ago. Jim Brady had been shot in the head, and Timothy McCarthy, a Secret Service agent, had been downed as well. They were also being treated in the hospital. Officer Thomas Delahanty of the D.C. police had been shot, too, and taken to another hospital. But all she wanted to know was what was happening to her Ronnie.

Dr. Neofytos Tsangaris, the acting chairman of surgery, agreed to talk to Nancy. The Greek-American physician was an amiable bear of a man with a calm voice and he did his best to reassure the First Lady. Tsangaris found her "very controlled." She insisted on seeing her husband.

"If you'll just give us a few minutes, I'll set things up and come back." Tsangaris couldn't let her see the president the way he was now. He hurried back to the trauma bay and saw to it that the president's mauled body was covered up, the discarded clothes picked up, the spots of blood wiped away, and curtains drawn separating Ronnie from Jim Brady, where doctors continued their frantic efforts on his head wound. At first Tsangaris had found the noise level in the emergency room "almost unbelievable" and had had to shout over the Secret Service agents, but by the time he returned to see Mrs. Reagan again, it was far quieter.

In the meantime, Dr. Sol Edelstein, the director of the emergency room, went in to talk to Mrs. Reagan. Like most of the doctors, he was young enough to be her son, but he held the knowledge that would determine the fate of her husband.

"The bullet looks like it's outside the heart," said the young doctor, who had just seen the X-ray.

As she heard the doctor's technical discussion, Nancy became so frightened that she could hardly speak.

Dr. Tsangaris returned and tried to prepare her a little more explicitly for what she was about to see. "There's a tube in his chest and he's short of breath," the doctor said as Nancy was guided through the maze of Secret Service agents and police. She looked as if at any moment she might begin shivering with fear, shattering her tight-lipped composure.

"But she was strong," remembered Dr. Paul Colombani, GW's senior resident, who was working on Brady. "The whole scene was like a horror show. There were discarded bandages, tubes, ripped-away clothes and blood. It was a real mess and very intense for a lay person. But she walked right in, went right up to him and took his hand. She was a powerful strength for him."

Nancy saw Ronnie lying on the narrow bed, an oxygen mask clamped on his face. Then, as she leaned over to kiss his forehead, she saw blood on his lips.

"Honey, I forgot to duck," he said, the words muffled by the mask.

It was a phrase that would have broken many wives up, but Nancy remained composed. As she held Ronnie's hand, it was as if *she* were the one transfusing him with lifeblood, not the bottles that hung above him.

After Nancy returned to the tiny room—where she talked with Ed Meese, James Baker and Lyn Nofziger—the medical team worked on the president more actively again. Two doctors attempted to put a large IV into his jugular vein, but Ronnie could not lie still long enough when they probed for the vessel, and they gave up.

If they had to operate, it would be Dr. Benjamin Aaron, the head of Cardiothoracic Surgery at George Washington, who would hold the scalpel. When the forty-eight-year-old former navy surgeon had first entered the emergency room, he'd thought of Kennedy's death and wondered if history might be repeating itself. Aaron was a born-again Christian, active in church work, but he had no time for either reflection or prayer; he thought only of the man who lay on the bed.

Aaron saw that large amounts of blood were still flowing from Ronnie's chest into the tube. He had already lost over a quarter of his original blood. If this continued and the blood flow increased, he might go into shock before they got him to the operating room.

"Mr President, there's a lot of blood coming from your chest tube," Dr. Aaron said calmly. "And we know the bullet's in your chest. And we don't know what's been injured. But because the blood continues to come, we think it would be safest to take you to the operating room. We don't feel you're in any immediate danger, but we think that would be the safest thing to do rather than to just watch you bleed for the next—we don't know how long."

Ronnie nodded his assent.

Before operating, though, Aaron went to get Nancy's accord as well. Talking to her, Aaron felt that "she really didn't know how badly injured he was." He felt that it was his job "to assure her that he [the president] was survivable." Next to Nancy stood Mike Deaver, who now, as in the White House, was spending much of his time watching out for the First Lady.

"If we don't operate, we might get into some problems," the surgeon said. "The operation's the surest, the safest path at the time."

Legally, before operating the hospital needed Nancy's written consent. But the hospital settled for her verbal agreement. As her husband's bed was slowly wheeled toward the operating room, she took his hand, his arm pierced by the IV, and held it tightly. Dr. Aaron noticed that she appeared "teary-eyed." The narrow bed, with its thicket of bottles, plastic bags, IV lines, blood bags on narrow poles, rolled slowly down the hall surrounded by close to thirty doctors, nurses and aides in long white coats and surgical greens. To let this strange, unwieldy procession move down the halls, the Secret Service agents pressed hard against the wall. "He looks real gray," one of the nurses said as the president's bed moved past the nurses' station. "I wonder if he'll make it."

Right behind Ronnie, a second bed moved toward the operating rooms carrying Jim Brady. Nancy turned and saw "a terrible sight," the press secretary's head looking like one gigantic wound. At the entrance to the operating-room area, Nancy left Ronnie and watched the procession moving on to OR2, the largest operating room.

During major surgery, doctors and nurses are fitted tightly into the operating room. Now the medical staff had to put up with the Secret Service men who took up positions between the operating table and the doors. The agents had never worn surgical clothes before and they were a ragamuffin group, with masks askew and pants on crooked, standing awkwardly, anxious and alert.

Ronnie raised his head slightly as if to take one last look before the operation. "I hope you people are all Republicans," he said, surveying the crowded scene.

"Today, we're all Republicans, Mr. President," said Dr. Joseph Giordano, a liberal Democrat.

"How are you going to put me to sleep?" Ronnie asked. "I can hardly breathe now."

As Dr. George Morales prepared to administer Valium, plus a synthetic narcotic and Pentothal, he reassured the president. With an injection of Pentothal, Ronnie went quickly to sleep, and the operation began.

The FBI had mistakenly told the medical team that Ronnie had been shot by a large-bore .38-caliber bullet instead of a smaller .22. Thus, before entering the operating room, the surgical team had to take an X-ray to search Ronnie's abdominal cavity for fragments of the large bullet. Not until later did they learn of the FBI's mistake, which, by delaying the operation, could have cost Ronnie his life.

In OR2, Drs. Joseph Giordano, David Gens and Wesley Price first tested for blood in the abdomen. Through a small incision, they inserted a catheter into the abdomen, pumped in a liter of saline solution, then drained it, observing the color of the liquid. After a half-hour they were as certain as they could be that the abdomen was fine.

"Does anyone know what's going on out there?" asked Dr. Gens as he sewed up the abdominal incision.

For a moment there was silence, as if the only universe were the green operating room.

Gens tried again. "A lot of people were shot. Is there a conspiracy?"

Gens was finished with his primary job, but no one had any time for such talk.

Now Dr. Aaron would have the most difficult assignment, an exploratory operation near Ronnie's heart. "There was so much to take into consideration," Aaron remembered later. "At any time it's hard to be casual about that kind of procedure. I had to stay ahead of things, knowing that everything would be reviewed and reviewed. I had a strong feeling of security that this mission was suited to come out well as long as I didn't really screw up."

Dr. Aaron made an incision in the left side of Ronnie's chest and began to explore the cavity. Almost immediately he found a large blood clot in the chest cavity and blood flowing from a hole in the lung. He saw the hole the bullet had made, the size of a dime. He followed the bullet's track. The projectile had been heading down until it hit the top of a rib and was deflected upward. It had to be here somewhere. He touched Ronnie's lung, kneading the spongy substance, trying to come up with the bullet. Even as he did so, he thought to himself that Ronnie's lungs were as youthful-looking as the rest of him. Then it struck him. What if the bullet had gotten into the pulmonary vein and now was moving into the arterial tree? What if that had happened?

"How important is it that I get the bullet out?" Aaron asked Dr. Ruge, almost as if he were talking to himself.

"What's important is that the president survive."

Aaron continued his search. In an operating room, there is a language of tension that outsiders cannot begin to fathom. The surgical team looked calm enough, but they feared now that they were up against a problem of dreadful seriousness. Dr. Manfred Lichtmann, who had been the anesthesiologist scores of times with Aaron, knew how anxious the surgeon felt.

"You enjoying yourself, Ben?" Lichtmann said, trying to break the tension.

"I'm just having a marvelous time down here. It couldn't be better."

Aaron continued to probe. He looked at a new chest X-ray that showed he should look higher for the bullet. He pushed a catheter into the track and traced the bullet's path. He pushed his fingers along the route, trying to find the projectile.

"I think I've got it," he said finally, barely containing his excitement. "Just one second and we'll have it."

At 7:30 in the evening, Ronnie began to wake up. He lay surrounded by screens in one of the six bays in the large, open recovery room. He had two chest tubes for drainage. To help him breathe, a tube ran into his mouth down to his windpipe. He was hooked onto an EKG monitor and a respirator. He had all kinds of lines and tubes connected to his body, everything from blood-pressure and pulse monitors to IVs. In his increasing consciousness, he felt that he wasn't breathing, that he couldn't breathe. It was a terrible, terrifying feeling. As he tried to breathe out, air was pushing down his throat. He attempted to raise his head and point to the tube. If he could have, he would have yanked it out of his throat.

"You've got to trust me," said Kathy Edmonston, a nurse hovering over him. "You've got to let me breathe for you." Even as she said it, she thought that this was the president of the United States whom she was asking to trust *her.*

Ronnie still felt as if at any moment he might suffocate. But he stopped raising his head and lay there.

Suddenly, the back door to the recovery room opened. Nancy walked determinedly toward Ronnie across the linoleum floor as the hospital staff cleared a path. She had not seen him since before the operation, when she had walked to the operating-room area holding his hand. She had spent hours waiting anxiously. As she saw him lying there, she started to cry. "I love you," she said, and grabbed his arm. They looked at one another for a long time without saying anything. The doctors and the nurses were mesmerized. How many times had they seen such scenes? But this was more profound. To Dr. Sam Spagnolo, who stood not four feet from the bed, it was "a genuine and absolutely pure display of love, amazing, incredibly touching, overpowering."

After a few minutes, the president wrote a note on a clipboard. "I can't breathe."

Nancy turned on the doctors as if she were the sole protectress of her man. "He can't breathe," she said to Dr. Edelstein, looking him straight in the eyes.

"You shouldn't worry, Mrs. Reagan," the doctor said. "You see the machine is doing the breathing for him. He's having difficulty because he isn't used to it yet."

"He can't breathe," she said again, as if no amount of arcane explanation would suffice.

Ron, Jr., was now in the room, too. The moment he'd heard his father had been shot, he had chartered a private plane to fly from Lincoln, Nebraska, where he was performing with the Joffrey II Ballet. For years the relationship with his father had been as much pain as love, but he knew how he felt about Ronnie. He leaned down and whispered in Ronnie's ear: "Dad, it's all right. What they're telling you is all right. It's like scuba diving, dad. You remember when I went scuba diving and when I put the mask over me, I felt as if I couldn't breathe." Ron, Jr., relaxed his father enough so that the machine could do its work.

When it was time to leave the recovery room, Nancy did not want to go. "I have to be at his side," she kept saying to Dr. Edelstein. "I have to be at his side."

Finally, Dr. Ruge had to tell the First Lady politely but firmly that she had to leave. As she walked out of the recovery room, she turned and saw Ronnie gesturing to her that he couldn't breathe. She stood alone in the doorway looking toward his bed. Then she turned and left. In the corridor on her way out of the hospital, she encountered the parents of Tim McCarthy, the wounded Secret Service agent who had thrust his body between the president and the assailant.

"Your son saved my husband's life," Mrs. Reagan said.

Mr. McCarthy sobbed.

Then, on the ground floor of the hospital, Nancy met Dorothy Brady, the press secretary's mother. During the hours of the operation, Nancy had sat and talked to Brady's wife, Sarah, when the television was reporting that he was already dead and that McCarthy and Delahanty were doing nicely.

"Hi, Nancy," Mrs. Brady said, totally composed. "We are just praying for both of them."

Although Ronnie had scarcely woken up, he had no respite from the regimens of medicine. To clear the congestion from his lungs, the doctors attempted a bronchoscopy, working a fiber-optic tube down his throat. It was a procedure that, as Dr. Colombani said later, gives the "feeling that you're choking to death." When that was unsuccessful, the two nurses squirted saline solution down the windpipe, making Ronnie cough up mucus.

"Was anyone else hurt?" he scribbled on the clipboard.

Denise Sullivan, the head recovery-room nurse, thought quickly. "Yes, there were two other people who were shot," she said, not realizing that Delahanty lay in another hospital. "But don't worry about it. They're okay."

"Did they get the guy who did it?" Ronnie wrote.

"They got him. They got him."

The doctors had begun to wean Ronnie from the morphine, and at around midnight he began to become fully conscious. Once again he began bucking the breathing machine. Marisa Mize looked down at him. As a recovery-room nurse, she had learned that here the rich were no different from the poor, the famous no different from the unknown. Although the doctors were commenting on how well Ronnie was doing, she could tell by his eyes that the patient lying there was "scared shitless."

"You're scared out of your wits," she said in her matter-of-fact voice.

Ronnie nodded.

"You're not alone."

During a moment's rest, Ronnie wrote a message on the clipboard: "All in all, I'd rather be in Philadelphia."

"Oh, no you don't. They played like shit," Mize said, thinking Ronnie was talking about the NCAA basketball championships and not a line from an old W. C. Fields movie.

Ronnie could not stand to be tied down, and here he was now tied down to machines and tubes. During the operation, his ribs had been spread for a thoracotomy, an incision that Dr. Gens considered "the most painful to recover from; most patients complain about a lingering pain for months." Eight hours ago his life had seemed in perfect order. Now he lay not knowing what was happening not only to his own life but to the other victims and to his country.

Ronnie was still afraid, and he was alert enough to the world to overhear Dr. Aaron talking about the dangerous condition of a heart patient upon whom he had just operated.

"Is that happening to me?" he scribbled, as if he feared he wasn't being told everything.

"No," said Mize, who was sitting next to him holding his hand. When she got up to leave for a minute, the president grabbed her hand and looked at her with eyes that said he needed her.

At 3:00 A.M. the medical team took Ronnie off the respirator and put him on oxygen.

"I sure believe in capital punishment," Ronnie said. "What's this guy's beef? He must have gotten off three or four rounds."

No one followed up on his remark. Earlier, David Fischer, a young White House aide, had asked the doctors not to tell the president about the condition of Brady and the other two men. When Ronnie didn't pursue the question, Dr. Edelstein assumed that Ronnie didn't realize that anyone else had been shot.

For an hour Ronnie entertained the doctors and nurses with his jokes and stories. The doctors and nurses hovered around his bed. Marisa Mize, for one, thought that Ronnie was one of those patients who should be told to be quiet; but, after all, he was the president of the United States. Others stood there watching Ronnie so happy to be alive, expressing his profound love and confidence in life.

"How long will I be here?" he asked, the words muffled by the oxygen mask.

"About ten days," a nurse said.

"I recover quickly."

"Good. Keep up the tradition."

"You mean this is going to happen again?"

Everyone laughed.

Ronnie could have talked all night long, but he needed sleep. At 4:30 A.M. a recovery-room nurse, Joanne Bell, put a gauze pad over his eyes so that he would have an easier time sleeping. Even before she had left his bedside, he pulled the pad off and was chatting away. "Mr. President," she said as she stood over him, holding the pad, "in the most polite way I can tell you, when I put this over your eyes, that means I want you to shut up."

With that, Ronnie went to sleep.

In the next few days, Drs. Colombani and Gens, the chief surgical residents, would spend more time with Ronnie than anyone. Now they were themselves getting some sleep in the kidney-dialysis unit. They knew that it had been a far closer call than practically anyone realized.

"If five minutes had been lost, he would have died," Gens said later.

"His blood pressure was so low that his blood wasn't being pumped properly. He probably would have had a stroke or a heart attack. It doesn't happen often that a patient like that coughs up blood. Thank God he did, because if they had continued to the White House, he probably would have died."

"There's no question that if he had lost fifteen minutes going to the White House, he probably would have died or had a stroke," Colombani said. "He had lost a lot of blood into his chest and he had a gray death look about him when he came in. Most people his age can't tolerate that stress."

Before dawn, Ronnie was awakened. "I want to give you a bath, Mr. President," a nurse said, looking at her drowsy patient. "Don't you get up early, Mr. President?"

"I take this job from nine to five," Ronnie said.

At 6:15 in the morning, after less than two hours' sleep Ronnie was wheeled up to the fourth-floor intensive-care unit. A half-hour later, Baker, Deaver and Meese walked into the small room to find a nurse helping Ronnie brush his teeth.

"I should have known I wasn't going to avoid a staff meeting," he said as he sat propped up, tubes in his nose. The outside world had already begun to intrude. He had a bill to sign, and for the first time he began to learn the magnitude of what had happened at the Hilton Hotel.

It fell to sixty-three-year-old Dr. Ruge, the only man of Ronnie's generation around him, to tell Ronnie.

"Oh, damn, oh, damn," Ronnie said when he learned about Brady. "Did it go into the brain?"

Dr. Ruge said that Brady might end up partially paralyzed.

"We've got to pray," Ronnie said.

Ronnie learned that his assailant was twenty-five-year-old John W. Hinckley, Jr., from Evergreen, Colorado. He wasn't nearly as interested in hearing about the man who tried to kill him as in learning about the three other victims. As Ronnie saw it, he was like the sheriff in a western town who, when he put on his badge, knew that people might be shooting at him. But he considered the three others, and especially Brady, innocent victims of bullets that were meant for *him*. "He was very upset that other people were hurt just because of their involvement with him," Colombani said.

Nancy, Patti and Ron made their first visit to the hospital in the morning. Maureen and Michael did not arrive until Nancy had departed. The evening before, Patti, Michael and Michael's wife, Colleen, had flown from Los Angeles in an air-force cargo plane, fighting the damp cold with blankets.

"The last time I saw you like this was when you broke your leg playing baseball," Michael said as he entered the room.

"Yeah, that's right," Ronnie said. "That kid comes from a well-to-do family, and I was wearing a new suit. The least they can do is give me a new suit."

Later in the day, Nancy returned to the hospital. Because she was the stepdaughter of a doctor, she knew enough to ask probing questions. She insisted on learning everything about Ronnie's operation and condition.

"Usually we keep answers to family members very simple, but she wanted more details," said Colombani. "She was pretty savvy and knew how to put us on the spot."

Dr. Edelstein considered her "pretty persistent, a very tough lady."

"She wanted a progress report every afternoon," Gens remembered. "It was tough. She wanted to know everything and would let nothing slip unexplained. She'd ask why incessantly. She couldn't stand it when we'd use centigrade to tell her about the fever. She'd want it in Fahrenheit. I'd always try to be very well prepared for her questions. She wanted exact answers, but it's hard to try to explain in a few minutes what has taken us years to understand. Sometimes it was like being under attack, because she'd double-check anything I'd say. But she was so worried about him. It showed in her face. After all of it, when I'd walk past the room she used to sit in, I had this funny feeling that she was still there waiting to grill me."

One of Nancy's first concerns was the very room in which Ronnie was lying. For security reasons, the drapes had been nailed shut. With the unseasonably warm weather and the large numbers of visitors, the room was insufferably hot. The central air conditioning wasn't on yet, and all the hospital could do was rush to get the special rooms on the third floor ready for the president as soon as possible. The "presidential suite" was eight bedrooms, an office and a treatment room on one corridor that could be partitioned off and protected. Workers painted the president's room beige and put in new drapes. Meanwhile, GW and White House people scurried around getting furniture: a desk from a hospital administrator, a sofa from the White House, Oriental rugs and paintings from the University Alumni House, a silver tea service from the White House mess.

By the afternoon, Ronnie's room was so hot that it reminded Dr. Edelstein of a "steam bath of hot, congested air." Nancy insisted that Ronnie be moved, and moved soon.

"Maybe if the four o'clock X-ray looks good, we can move him then," said Gens, while Ruge, the White House physician, looked on.

"I'll expect a call at four o'clock," Nancy said.

"Oh, well, you can call her," Ruge said after Nancy had left. Dealing with Nancy was not the easiest part of Ruge's job.

At precisely four o'clock, Gens called the White House. Ronnie couldn't be moved yet—the smell of the fresh paint in his new room was still oppressive. But Gens wasn't about to tell Nancy that. "I'm sorry, Mrs. Reagan, but the move has been delayed," he said.

"Oh," she said, and Gens felt a cold breeze coming through the phone line. "I thought we were going to move him after that X-ray."

"Well, Mrs. Reagan, we should be able to move the president between six and nine."

"It will be six," Nancy said.

In little more than six hours, the presidential quarters were ready and secure, all entrances to the hospital closed off except the main one. Ronnie's room had a sofa and two easy chairs. For security reasons, the windows faced on an inner courtyard rather than out to the sun, and with its heavy drapes the room was a dark place to begin convalescing. For Nancy there was a sitting room with a couch, an end table and a rug. Another room was ready for Dr. Ruge. There were two rooms for the Secret Service, plus a closet off Ronnie's room in which an agent sat watching him through a cracked-open door. Outside Ronnie's door sat another agent, whose briefcase contained a machine gun. Near the elevator on the third floor stood portable partitions and a desk manned by Secret Service agents.

Nancy was upset that so many doctors had access to the president's room. "*They* have made a request," Dr. Gens told Dr. Tsangaris after learning of Nancy's concern. From then on, the numbers of doctors with access was severely limited.

As for Ronnie, he was putting up with enough to make a Quaker swear. Another bronchoscopy had to be performed. Typically, when this procedure is done, the patient is given Valium intravenously. But because of trouble in the Mideast, the triumvirate asked that the President not be given any sedatives. "He didn't bat an eye," said Gens. "Most wouldn't have been able to tolerate it."

From then on, Ronnie refused pain-killers, wanting to be clearheaded for his 7:00 A.M. briefings and in case he had to make crucial decisions.

No matter how much it hurt, his chest was pounded and probed. He had to cough and wheeze on command. Countless blood samples were taken. He couldn't even empty his bladder in private.

The second evening, the urinary catheter was taken out temporarily because of the risk of infection. At midnight Dr. Colombani woke Ronnie up.

"Mr. Reagan, I'm sorry but you're going to have to get up," the young doctor said. "I'm going to have to walk you around to see if you can pass urine."

Ronnie was irritated. "I never pee at night!" he said emphatically.

"It's not quite the same," the doctor said. "If we don't do it, the bladder will get bigger and bigger."

After the explanation, Ronnie let Colombani insert the urinary catheter. The next morning, Gens had the job of removing the catheter. When he finished, he threw the tube into the wastebasket. Thinking that the device might be salvaged and sold as a souvenir, one of the Secret Service agents scooped it out to be taken back to the White House for disposal. "It was incredible," Gens said later. "He doesn't even have the privacy for something like that."

Nancy's every moment in the hospital was spent trying to make life easier for Ronnie. She brought flowers and candy to his room. With Deaver, she screened who saw Ronnie, knowing that each visit had a political implication as well as being taxing on him. She made sure that the Mexican president's state visit was delayed until Ronnie would have several weeks to recuperate. No matter how much she longed to be with him, she kept her own visits short and light.

She flared in anger when doctors and others said that Ronnie was young for his age. He was young and vital. Period. She loved pointing out how Lyndon Johnson had taken it easy for a month after his gall bladder operation while 16 hours after the shooting *her* Ronnie was signing bills into law. She hated the chest tubes. "Horrible, horrible," she said, "horrible tubes." She hated the nasal prong they had begun using again to provide oxygen.

Ronnie didn't have much of an appetite, and Nancy *knew* that he wouldn't get well if he didn't eat. She had food prepared by the White House chefs. This rankled the GW VIP dietitian no end, especially when she saw that the White House was sending over such gourmet fare as macaroni and cheese, and meat loaf. When Ronnie still wouldn't eat, Nancy sent to California for a favorite treat, meatball soup. But he hardly touched that either.

The media were clamoring for some evidence of Ronnie's recovery. The triumvirate approached Nancy, suggesting that a photograph be taken. At first she vetoed the idea. "She feels that her primary job is to take care of her husband," said Aaron. "She's concerned about how he comes across. She knows that when he's tired, he looks saggy and it makes him look older. Since that is something of an issue with him, she doesn't want photos that reveal that."

The pressure from the media continued to grow: If there was no photograph, then he must be sicker than the White House was saying. Finally, when a photograph was taken, Nancy made sure the nurse standing next to Ronnie holding the collection chamber for fluid draining from his chest tubes was discreetly cropped out.

In Ronnie's room, the heavy drapes were never opened. Nancy understood the security problems, but she felt that Ronnie should be able to get some sense of night or day, and that fresh air would help him recover.

"It comes with the job," Dr. Gens told her, feeling comfortable enough with the First Lady to make his little joke about the hardships of being president.

Later, he told her, "I'm going home, Mrs. Reagan. I haven't been home since Monday and my wife's a little upset."

"It comes with the job," Nancy said, permitting herself a slight, ironic smile.

"He'd never ask why he had to do something, but she would," Gens reflected. "We'd tell him that he had to do something like walking four or five times a day, and he'd say okay. But she would want to know how far, how frequently, on and on. She would want detailed reasons for his doing things."

On Thursday, Ronnie had started running a fever of 102 to 103 degrees and begun looking pale. This was the meanest irony of all. While the nation was celebrating the president's miraculous recovery, he was suffering what some of the doctors considered a serious, possibly ominous, setback. On Saturday, with the fever still running high, he started spitting up not clotted blood any longer but fresh red blood. Dr. Aaron feared that Ronnie might soon begin bleeding anew.

Nancy had to know everything—everything.

"Why did you change the antibiotics?"

"What's that? What does that mean?"

"Why? Why are you doing that?"

Brought up within the inner sanctum of medicine, she realized that medicine was not an exact science, but she wanted exact answers. She was suspicious that the doctors were giving him new medicine for more than preventive reasons. She feared that she wasn't being told everything. She was frustrated by the doctors' varied readings of the situation.

On the GW medical team, there were two different opinions as to the seriousness of Ronnie's apparent relapse. Dr. Aaron saw the world as a surgeon, and he thought that the fever was a natural aftermath of the operation. Drs. Spagnolo and the internists worried that Ronnie might have developed an abscess in his lung that could require further surgery.

As the debate over Ronnie's condition continued, his fever began to subside. By the middle of the second week, even the most pessimistic of the doctors felt that he was on his way to full recovery. He treated the doctors to his imitation of Jimmy Stewart. When he was doing his laps of walking in the hallway, he called out to Maria Blaz, a nurse, "That's eight!" Actually, he had only made three rounds, but he was himself again—an optimist to his admirers, a hapless exaggerator to his detractors.

While his fever raged, the doctors hadn't let Ronnie shower or take a bath. One evening when he was feeling better, he got up and went into the tiny bathroom for a sponge bath. In the process he spilled water on the floor. When he was finished washing, he got down on his knees and sponged up the water.

"What did you do that for?" George Bush asked on a visit to the hospital, as reported by Lou Cannon.

"I didn't want her [the nurse] to get in trouble."

One morning he lay in bed watching a talk show. There was Knute Rockne himself, Pat O'Brien, talking about his old sidekick, Ronnie.

"Well, Ronald, I hope you're feeling better," O'Brien said, looking out through the camera.

Ronnie chuckled to himself and responded immediately: "I'm okay, Pat. How are you?" He then proceeded to tell tales about O'Brien to the doctors.

Another day, Spagnolo was examining Ronnie's chest. It sounded clearer. "Say ninety-nine," the doctor said, so that he could hear the resonance of the spoken number.

"How about 98.50?" Ronnie joked.

As she saw Ronnie improve and a date was set for him to go home, Nancy also began to relax and joked with the physicians. "She was very warm and very grateful to us," said Aaron. "I'd call her kind of huggy, kissy actually."

Ronnie left the hospital on Saturday, the twelfth of April, holding Nancy's hand, with Patti at his side. He wore a cardigan sweater over a bulletproof vest. His popularity polls were up ten points. As he left George Washington, the top White House staff was concerned with not only how well Ronnie was, but how well he looked. They knew that Soviet and other intelligence agencies would be examining the film of Ronnie's exit, and they wanted to know if he would look better getting into the car or out, and when he was likely to grimace.

All Ronnie's life he had played the hero—in his childhood dreams, in more than fifty films, in speeches and in his political career. But it had not been real, none of it. The only touchdown he'd ever scored was in *Knute Rockne, All American;* his amputated legs in *King's Row* was an illusion created by stagehands; he had fought World War II at home. As for the movie villains and the protesters in Sacramento during his governorship, as soon as the cameras stopped, everyone had gone home.

Ronnie went out of George Washington that day believing that God had saved him for great and noble things. He was a man apart, as only a man can be who has come within half an inch of death.

Nancy was a woman apart as well. All their political lives she had dreaded such an attempt on her husband's life. In her chosen role as his protector, she had acted courageously. But she knew how limited her control over Ronnie's life had become.

⟹ 19 ⟸

"THE SUN'S COMING OUT"

"We have much greatness before us," Ronnie said passionately. "We can restore our economic strength and build great opportunities like none we've ever had before. The space shuttle did more than prove our technological abilities; it raised our expectations once more; it started us dreaming again. The poet Carl Sandburg wrote, 'The Republic is a dream. Nothing happens unless first a dream.'"

As Ronnie spoke to a joint session of Congress on April 28, his presence seemed a dream. Only a month ago he had been near death, and now he was already making his first public address since the shooting. At first his aides had wanted him to broadcast his talk from the Oval Office, but Ronnie wanted to do it in person. As the applause rolled over him, he waved and laughed. To the legislators and television audience, Ronnie appeared as well as before, but listening to the cadence of his words on television, Dr. Gens could tell that he was still short of breath.

Ronnie named the three men who had fallen with him. McCarthy. Delahanty. Brady. Each time he called out a name, the audience responded with cathartic applause. Each time the audience applauded, he looked over to his left where Nancy sat looking up at him with an enraptured gaze.

For years Ronnie had been talking about the everyday heroism of ordinary American people, and now he seemed to personify that ideal. He had come up to the Capitol today, though, not simply on a sentimental sojourn but to sell his economic program, which would cut $41 billion from the projected Carter budget and reduce eighty-three federal programs while raising the defense budget $28 billion. Sell it he did, offering the legislators a chance to join him in truly making history, in changing the modern course of government.

He believed that the economy would right itself when released from the weight of excessive government spending. He promised that interest rates and inflation would go down and that his proposed tax cuts would encourage business expansion and investment. But if Congress was afraid, too much the captive of interest groups, then the members would bear the consequences. "Some eighty years ago, Teddy Roosevelt wrote these instructive words in his first message to Congress," Ronnie said. "'The American people . . . are slow to wrath but, when their wrath is once kindled, it burns like a consuming fire.'"

The House of Representatives was still in Democratic hands, and during the next month the administration set out to round up the necessary votes, particularly among conservative southern Democrats known as "boll weevils."

Ronnie was the best salesman the administration had, through either speeches or talking to individual legislators. In the next weeks, Ronnie spoke to scores of wavering members. Other administration officials lobbied as well and, when it was necessary, offered concessions. An ABC–*Washington Post* poll showed that Americans favored Ronnie's program two to one. Members of Congress were deluged with letters, telegrams and telephone calls. The legislators would be running again in a year and a half, and, like fire lookouts, they were always scanning the horizon for political smoke. Democrats in conservative or marginal districts found it expedient to vote for the Republican program.

On May 7, the budget bill passed the House 253 to 176, with 63 Democrats going along. In order to turn over social programs to the states through block grants, put a "cap" on Medicaid and "zero out" other programs, the administration pushed for a second round of budget cuts, $5 billion in all. Ronnie saw the second budget resolution as an act of belt tightening that would strengthen the economic and moral fiber of the country. Through last-minute lobbying of twenty-nine congressmen by telephone from a suite in the Century Plaza Hotel in Los Angeles, Ronnie helped turn the tide. On June 26, the administration won the crucial vote 217 to 210. He was elated.

Ronnie himself stayed far above the wheeling and dealing over details. But politics is in the details, and, to win, the administration had given away special concessions on oil leases and real-estate tax shelters. The public and media didn't scrutinize the legalistic language of the legislation, but, through write-offs and investment credits, the administration had largely done away with income taxes for many corporations.

"Do you realize the greed that came to the forefront!" David Stockman, the budget director, confided at the time to a Washington journalist. "The hogs were really feeding. The greed level, the level of opportunism, just got out of control."

Ronnie kept a distance from the specifics of foreign affairs as well. "At first his phone calls to heads of states were disasters," said one high-ranking State Department official. "We'd supply him with talking points and he would read them, rather than using them as guidelines. If the foreign leader varied or took another tack, he was lost and floundered."

Unlike Nixon or Carter, who through their interest in foreign affairs sought to be men of the world, Ronnie had little interest in either the broad sweep of foreign affairs or the details. He saw the great international struggle as that between communism and freedom, and cared little for the delicate nuances of diplomacy. Yet he was impressive when he could symbolize America, in greetings to foreign heads of states, and leave the details to others. "Reagan has enormous presence," said a State Department adviser to the National Security Council. "It may be John Wayne in the White House, but he uses his amiability very well. When the foreign minister of Italy was here, Reagan really scored points. Just as the minister got up to leave, Reagan said, 'I just wanted you to know, Mr. Minister, how close our countries are. But I for one have a special thankfulness for Italy because a young Italian cavalry officer invented the Santini saddle which I've used often.' Well, the minister just melted. When you're with Reagan, he makes you feel good."

But despite his personal charm, Ronnie's aides worried that he might seem terribly naïve. In late May when Helmut Schmidt, the West German chancellor, made his first official visit, Ronnie welcomed him on the South Lawn reading prepared remarks. Afterward, during a meeting between the two heads of state in the Oval Office, Schmidt reached into his coat and pulled out a small box. The German leader poured some of the contents, a dark mixture, onto his wrist and loudly snorted it. While dribbles rolled down Schmidt's upper lip, Ronnie tried unsuccessfully to maintain his composure.

After the seventy-minute meeting, Ronnie's State Department aides told him authoritatively that Schmidt had a thyroid problem which required medication. "My God, I thought this guy is snorting cocaine right in my office," Ronnie told an aide. In fact, the German chancellor was indulging in an old North German custom: taking snuff.

When there wasn't an evening social event at the White House, Ronnie usually got into his pajamas and bathrobe as he had for years. Within a couple of months of the shooting, except for an occasional numbness in his side, he was feeling fine. To get back his muscle tone, he was exercising regularly, and to him the assassination attempt seemed like a bad dream.

To Nancy, too, the shooting was like a bad dream, but one that kept recurring. She had always been a worrier, but now at times she was finding it difficult to sleep. She had lost several pounds. Her clothes fit her like a mannequin's, but she was too thin. She had always cried easily. Now, at any mention of the shooting, her eyes would fill with tears.

It was now definitely the Reagans' White House. In its social ambience, its emphasis on style and manners, it was very much *Nancy's* White House.

"There is always a sense of decorum and propriety," said one young White House staffer. "They made a point of establishing a hierarchy. Everyone has his place. The privilege of rank is very important to them. The perk system and inner circles of power is a system like Russian dolls, one inside another. Privilege permeates the whole administration so that when someone has power and privilege, it's really powerful. It's everywhere, that feeling. There's a tight clinch on everything that's said. Even the laughter is controlled."

"Once inside the White House, the Reagan administration lost its feeling of a team effort," said a transition-team member. "During the campaign, Reagan would always come by the offices. He never does in the White House. You became one of the itty-bitty cogs of the wheel. Power became very important. Perks told who's in and who's out."

Most of those within the White House accepted the system and thought it necessary and appropriate. But there were those who were repelled by what they saw. "The whole administration's a fantasy that they have the power to maintain and define as normal," said one staffer after he left. "They all have this terrific personal discipline, but they have no questions. It's an administration without questions. They ignore things that are in the 1980s.

"What's so incredible is Reagan's sense of confidence. But it's like death not knowing itself. It's discipline not in support of anyone's inspiration. Discipline becomes an end in itself."

Nancy did, in fact, believe in discipline, not only for herself but for those around her. She was a difficult woman with whom to work. She almost never praised her staff, and blamed them in part for her problems with the media. She spent hours on the phone, laughing, giggling, exchanging gossip. Her staff was beginning to see that as a problem. If she was going to have a series of special projects as First Lady, it was time to begin. But she turned down most of the ideas her staff suggested. On occasion, Mrs. Reagan's aides staged staff meetings for the media at which Nancy appeared. But according to members of the White House staff there were almost no real staff meetings with Nancy present.

Her press secretary, Sheila Tate, was constantly on the defensive. She answered press queries with abruptness, sometimes surliness. The reporters always asked about Nancy's clothes. "The press started focusing on what she was wearing," said Peter McCoy. "We didn't help by commenting on what she was wearing. We just should have said see for yourself."

"It's a seven-year-old Adolfo," Tate told the reporters, who scribbled down the historic detail. "It's a seven-year-old Galanos," she said. "It's a seven-year-old Blass."

After a few months, one reporter said coyly, "My, Sheila, Nancy must have done an awful lot of shopping seven years ago."

Muffie Brandon, the social secretary, shuttled reporters in and out of social functions as if she thought their unsightly presence might offend the guests. Brandon had no use for some of the ladies of the press. "The president and Mrs. Reagan live in a manner of their generation which is not exactly the manner in which the young reporters in their 20s and early 30s live," Brandon told *Interview*. "Some of the young reporters are unfamiliar with this manner, the politeness, the charm, the attitude towards life."

Brandon felt that she had a unique historic perspective. "I'll tell you, in the corridors of the White House, the difference in the way women are dressed and the way they were dressed in previous administrations," she said. "We don't have to be super chic. But I remember a girl greeting me not too many years ago in clogs at the diplomatic reception door. I never got over it. We do not wear pants. We do not wear clogs. We represent our country."

As chief of protocol, Lee Annenberg did not wear clogs. She was meticulous and fussed over her white-on-white flowers and decorations. At her personal expense, she invited Washington diplomats to dinners at Blair House. A child of Hollywood, the wife of one of the country's richest men and the former ambassador to the Court of St. James's, she was accustomed to being on familiar terms with world leaders.

When Lopez Portillo, the president of Mexico, made a state visit to Washington, he was given a luncheon in the White House. As the Latin president arrived, Lee walked briskly up to him, her blond hair set off against a mint-green dress. "Mr. President, would you like to wash your hands?" she asked brightly. Portillo looked at her for a moment as if he weren't sure he had understood. But Latins have endless ceremonies, and he followed Lee toward a bathroom as if this washing of the hands were an exotic White House ritual.

In the White House, Nancy couldn't do any real shopping, and that was a severe limitation. Unknown to her staff, however, she was accepting dresses and gowns from major designers as well as jewels from Bulgari and Harry Winston. For the inauguration, she had worn a diamond necklace and earring set worth $250,000 designed by Harry Winston Jewelers with

Walter and Lee Annenberg. *(WWD)*

the specific purpose of starting a White House jewelry collection. That was not publicly announced, however, and during her first six months in the White House, Nancy kept the jewels.

Nancy could not venture into the showrooms, but Bill Blass, for one, sent videotapes of his clothes to the White House. During 1981, Blass gave Nancy two daytime dresses, a daytime suit, two evening dresses and two coats. "She was a friend and a client and her clothes were to be used for a public policy," Blass said, explaining why he had given the dresses to Nancy. "That's been going on for centuries. The French government provides clothes for their ambassadors' wives."

Galanos sent Nancy an evening outfit, a coat and two-piece dress ensemble. "It's not a question of our getting more business with her," said Galanos. "I'm in a terribly high business. It does give us extra attention."

Jean Louis sent an evening gown. David Haynes provided two daytime dresses. Betsy Bloomingdale gave Nancy three housecoats that she had designed. Fendi sent an evening jacket.

It was still not clear what Nancy's role as First Lady would be, beyond being the First Wife. She had a staff of seventeen and a half-a-million-dollar budget, and she had to do something. She was interested in the Foster Grandparents program, but there were only two such programs in the Washington area, and she couldn't visit them over and over again. She was interested in drug abuse, but McCoy felt that since the White House had "not appointed people in the drug area, to go out and do things would or might be in conflict with the White House policy. And so there was a slowing down."

Nancy continued to attend a series of luncheons with Georgetown's "Bright Old Things." These were relentlessly genteel events in which the only spicy things were the condiments. Only once was there a hint of a disagreement, and that hadn't set well at all.

At a luncheon hosted by Polly Fritchey, wife of an aging Washington columnist, Nancy began talking about one of her favorite subjects: drug abuse. The youngest lady in the room, the middle-aged mother of grown-up children, listened with increasing dismay. The more she listened to Nancy, the more she thought that the First Lady didn't know anything about the problem.

"We have to get marijuana out of the movies," Nancy said.

"I think the most dangerous drug for the upper middle class is cocaine," said the middle-aged matron, whose own children had experienced problems with drugs. "If you want to have an effective antidrug program, worrying about marijuana in the movies would be counterproductive."

Nancy tittered nervously. "In *9 to 5,* the marijuana scene shouldn't have been made," Nancy said in her tiny voice.

"I agree that such scenes are tasteless and shouldn't be made. But I don't think you should go around emphasizing that."

With that, the discussion changed to a subject as bland as a watercress sandwich.

Nancy attended a whole series of luncheons, but she was far more excited about the social events she herself planned. She had always loved the romance of royalty, and on the first Saturday evening in May, five weeks after the president had been shot, the Reagans hosted a private dinner for Prince Charles in the White House family quarters. This was Nancy's kind of evening, and she invited what Peter McCoy called a "fun group."

Movie stars are the nearest thing to American royalty, and Nancy included Cary Grant; Audrey Hepburn; Shelley Hack, a former "Charlie's Angel"; and Bobby Short, the society pianist. There was a smattering of social types such as Evangeline Bruce; the Paul Mellons; Diana Vreeland, *Vogue*'s longtime editor and eternal doyenne of fashion and style; and the William F. Buckleys. Jerry Zipkin was there, as were Alfred and Betsy, Walter and Lee, First Decorator Graber and First Designer Galanos. Everything had to be just right. She had checked over the menu again and again. Fresh asparagus and crab mousse. Herb sauce and cheese twists. Saddle of lamb with mint sauce. Braised fennel and green beans. And finally "Crown of Sorbet Prince of Wales." That was red raspberry sherbet, white coconut ice cream, and blueberry sherbet in an ice-cream mold. But the chef couldn't get the sugar feathers on top to look just right. She had him do the dessert five times until the feathers looked like feathers.

Nancy was ebullient and looked stunning in her two-piece, floor-length black-and-gold Galanos. She stood next to the future king of England, introducing him to guests. When Chief of Protocol Lee Annenberg had greeted Prince Charles upon his arrival in Washington, she had curtsied, creating no end of controversy. In the *Washington Post*, Miss Manners had pronounced authoritatively that she found it improper "to see an American citizen, much less an American official, bending her knees to foreign royalty." But that judgment wasn't going to stop Diana Vreeland, herself an arbiter of style. When she was presented, Vreeland curtsied with deeply bended knee while Jerry looked on approvingly.

The guests congratulated the prince on his upcoming marriage. Ronnie talked about acting, and Betsy bubbled about the joys of British tea. After dinner, Bobby Short played piano in the Yellow Oval Room. As he left, Jerry pronounced the event "one of the most spectacular evenings I've ever spent."

One of the biggest social events of the year was Nancy's birthday. This would be her sixtieth birthday, though to the world it was her fifty-eighth.

The First Lady dancing with Charles, Prince of Wales, 1981. *(UPI)*

It wouldn't be politically expedient to present Nancy with too many gifts, so nineteen of her friends—including the Annenbergs, Robert Gray and Nancy Reynolds—donated $3,900 to the D.C. Department of Recreation to sandblast and paint a swimming pool for the handicapped. Nancy attended a ceremony at the pool, snipped a ribbon and watched as two children jumped into the water on cue.

For years Marion and Earle, Betty and William had given Nancy a birthday bash, on a private plane, or a ranch, always something special. At one point the plan was for this year's party to be at Dumbarton Oaks, the beautiful Georgetown estate and gardens owned by Harvard University. But that hadn't worked out. Neither had Mount Vernon, another possibility. And so they settled on Woodlawn Plantation in Virginia, on land that once had been part of George Washington's Mount Vernon estate.

Nancy's birthday was not until July 6, but the party was held on the Fourth, while the whole city was in red-white-and-blue bunting. On a rainy Saturday afternoon, the seventy-six guests boarded two buses at the Watergate Hotel to travel through the Virginia suburbs to the antebellum plantation. *Everyone* was wearing red-white-and-blue; on their heads were what the official White House press release called "red, white and blue skimmer hats . . . for the gentlemen . . . gondolier hats for the ladies." On one bus Frank Sinatra walked up and down the aisle giving out soft drinks, collecting $1.35 in tips, including a munificent fifty cents from Alfred Bloomingdale.

The party was supposed to be outdoors under a tent, but because of the rain the celebration was moved inside the nineteenth-century brick mansion. At six o'clock, many of the guests gathered on the balcony to await Nancy and Ronnie's arrival by helicopter.

"The sun's coming out," Charlie Wick reportedly said.

"Wouldn't you know it," said Holmes Tuttle. "The sunshine follows Nancy and Ronnie wherever they go."

As the presidential helicopter zoomed down, the twenty-five or thirty thoroughbred horses at Woodlawn ran across the field. To one guest, "It was right out of a western movie."

In her white Mexican peasant blouse, skirt, and red-white-and-blue belt, Nancy looked fifteen years younger than her sixty years. In his light sports coat, Ronnie might have been a fiftyish movie star visiting from California.

This time Nancy's friends had decided that they would bring her a little bit of California as their tribute, and a patriotic celebration to boot. A West Coast barbecue was served on eight sixty-six-inch-long tables in the two main rooms. The tables were adorned with specially cut and sewn blue tablecloths. On top of the blue cloths were red-and-white checked cloths.

From the center of each table rose a red-white-and-blue helium balloon lifting aloft a small basket carrying tiny American flags and pennants saying "Happy Birthday Nancy."

Nancy was ecstatic, giggling away, hugging her friends. She noticed that Natalie Robinson, an old friend, was wearing blue, yellow, red and green wedged sandals. "Just what I've been looking for," Nancy said. "I love them."

"Happy birthday," said Natalie, taking off the shoes. "Try them on." The shoes not only fit perfectly but matched Nancy's outfit. The rest of the evening she wore the sandals, while Natalie went barefoot.

Nancy sat at the head table in one room, Ronnie in the other. Before dinner, the guests had munched on tostadas and sampled a guacamole dip prepared from Betty Wilson's and Marion Jorgensen's recipe. Twenty-four quarts of chili had been flown in from Chasen's, and Nancy was delighted to be sampling one of her and Ronnie's favorites. They were also served country-fried chicken, barbecued spareribs, corn muffins, herb bread, corn on the cob, beefsteak tomatoes, marinated cucumbers, raw vegetables. For dessert there was homemade strawberry ice cream and a four-tiered white birthday cake with red raspberry filling.

The guests stood while Ronnie toasted his wife, quoting Thomas Jefferson on harmony, happiness and the hearth. Most of them had brought cameras, and they took pictures of each other, of Ronnie and Nancy, the cake, the house. No one was a more prolific photographer than Jerry Zipkin. He had found a new role: the photographic chronicler of Nancy and Ronnie's reign as president and First Lady. He was snapping away when he realized he had no film in his camera.

When it was time to go back to the White House for the fireworks, Nancy and Ronnie flew above the Potomac to Washington while the guests got back on the buses. Before long they were only crawling, stuck with thousands of others heading into town. According to one guest, Marion Jorgensen became so upset at the slow pace that she swore. But for most of the Reagans' friends, nothing could ruin this day. Someone burst into song, and soon everyone was singing patriotic tunes and other old American songs. Bill Clark soloed on "Jimmy Crack Corn and I Don't Care" and "Big Rock Candy Mountain." When the Lincoln Memorial finally came into view, one guest felt that "there wasn't a cynical or jaded thought among us. Just reverence and the thrill of being in Washington on the Fourth of July and watching the fireworks at the White House with our good friends the president and First Lady."

At the White House Nancy and Ronnie had already been led down to the South Lawn for a staged "photo opportunity." For a few minutes, they sat on the lawn amid White House staff families as if they were just folks.

Then they headed to the balcony far above the crowd to watch the fireworks with their friends.

The next morning Nancy was upset. At the party, she had given one of her gifts to a staff man to hold, and the package was lost. The staff man had given the gift to an advance man. The advance man had forgotten the parcel on the bus. And the bus had been cleaned and was on its way to Indiana.

The East Wing and the advance office had only one duty: Retrieve the First Lady's gift. The gift happened to be locked safely in the manager's office at the bus company, but the man was taking a holiday. It wouldn't do to keep Nancy waiting. So the office door was kicked in and the package retrieved.

The birthday had been special, but the event Nancy was looking forward to most was her trip to England for the wedding of Prince Charles and Lady Diana in late July. Ronnie was too busy to go to London, and for the first time in their marriage Nancy would be away from him for an entire week. At first she hesitated to leave him, but Ronnie reassured her: "I know what we went through took a lot out of you. This will be a great vacation. I want you to have a good time."

Nancy wanted to take a special gift to the future king of England and his bride. She chose a Steuben glass bowl that, with its $75,000 retail price, had sat unsold since 1975. But for $8,000 in State Department funds and untold free publicity, Steuben was willing to unload the piece. It wouldn't do to wear the same outfit twice, and Nancy took with her an estimated twenty different dresses and gowns. She brought thousands of dollars' worth of jewelry from Bulgari, including a matched set of necklace, earrings and rings studded with diamonds and rubies. Unknown to Nancy's staff, much of this jewelry didn't belong to her; it had been "borrowed" for an unspecified period from the exclusive jeweler to be part of a White House collection. Nancy also took the diamond necklace from Harry Winston Jewelers.

Traveling with Nancy were her three top aides; a secretary; ten Secret Service agents; a nurse; an official photographer; a State Department liaison officer; thirteen members of the press; Julius, her hairdresser; and Betsy and Alfred Bloomingdale. Betsy was already on board the Boeing 707 jet—code-named "Executive One Foxtrot" by the FAA—when Nancy, wearing a red Adolfo, arrived in her limousine. In her stateroom at the front of the plane, Nancy stored four hatboxes and a makeup case. She was keeping her wedding outfit a secret.

"I've never been to a polo match," Nancy said. "I've never been to Buckingham Palace, well, the whole thing. I've never been to a royal wedding." To Nancy, it was all a fairy tale—Prince Charming and his lady, living in a palace in a kingdom called England. She loved the idea of dressing up, meeting royalty—princes and princesses, kings and queens, a swirl of parties and events, a purely social potpourri as charming and carefree as her long-ago debut in Chicago. To Nancy, romance and ceremony were intertwined. The pomp, decorum and beauty of British royalty and their traditions were so removed from the harsh jockeying of American politics.

After recuperating from her trip at Winfield House, the American ambassador's residence, Nancy was off to the country estate of Jack and Dru Heinz, twenty-two miles west of London, near the Ascot racecourse. It was a clammy London evening and Nancy shivered in a black and white Galanos gown with a halter top. The great black limousine, left from Vice President Bush's recent visit, cruised through rolling countryside. Except for an occasional incongruous red Jaguar, the six vehicles in Nancy's motorcade were dinner jacket black.

Nancy knew all about Jack and Dru. The Heinz fortune came from ketchup, soup and beans, and the expatriate couple gave some of the most scintillating parties in England, inviting at least fifty-seven varieties of royalty, celebrities and socialites. As the limousine pulled up the quarter-mile-long gravel drive in front of the estate, the vehicle looked like the personification of American new money, so big in contrast to the Rolls-Royces, Jaguars and chauffeured Peugeots parked in front of the great house.

At the Heinzes, Nancy was in her element. The reporters weren't even allowed to wait at the front gate of the estate, and she didn't have to worry about what she said. She met her first royalty in London: Princess Alexandra, first cousin to the queen; the duke and duchess of Gloucester; even the Aga Khan. Stars, too, such as Peter Ustinov, and famous television personalities such as David Frost.

Saturday morning Nancy awoke to find that almost every paper in London was attacking her. The papers were upset that she wasn't planning to bow or curtsy to the queen, but that was only the beginning of the criticism. The *Guardian* made fun of her movie career. Even the staid *Times (London)* ridiculed her, commenting that she was squeezing "more engagements into the week before the royal wedding than Alice's white rabbit."

Nancy plunged bravely onward, tooling out to the Chequers estate, Britain's Camp David, for a quiet country lunch with Prime Minister Margaret Thatcher. That evening, back in London, she attended a dinner given by Princess Alexandra. Sunday afternoon, wearing a red Adolfo, Nancy was motored out to the Imperial International Polo Tournament after visiting the Queen Mother.

When Nancy's six-vehicle entourage pulled onto the staid polo grounds, the Secret Service agents jumping out, it could have been the arrival of an American queen. Later Queen Elizabeth II drove through the gates in a green Vauxhall station wagon, with King Constantine, the exiled Greek monarch, at her side. Not to be underdone, the queen's daughter, Princess Anne, arrived driving a blue Range Rover.

Peter McCoy noticed that a car of aides drove in front of the queen, a second car behind, and the contrast between Nancy and the royal family was not as dramatic as it appeared. But the royal family did have a British penchant for understatement that was as foreign to Nancy and her California friends as hot tubs and group therapy.

In the royal box, a modest enclosure set off by a picket fence, Prince Charles rose, greeted the First Lady and introduced her to his fiancé, Lady Diana. Charles had only recently been feted in the White House, and he welcomed Nancy warmly before bidding her to sit down on one of the thin wooden chairs. After trying to explain polo to Nancy while the horses and their riders charged back and forth, Charles left to join his teammates on the England II team for their match against Spain.

Soon after the match began, the queen arrived. This was the great diplomatic/political moment of Nancy's trip. "So nice to see you," Nancy said, shaking the British monarch's hand, curtsying not a millimeter.

Nancy's press secretary observed the greeting as if she were watching a meeting between President George Washington and George III. "She shook hands with the queen and inclined her head slightly, as you would when you meet someone," Tate said. "It was definitely not a curtsy."

Nancy enjoyed the match ("But it seemed to me as if they were all going to kill themselves"). Her schedule was so busy, however, that she couldn't stay long enough to watch Prince Charles and his teammates trounce Spain 10 to 5. She had to get ready for a dinner in her honor hosted by the American ambassador, John Louis. A few hours later, she stood in a red one-shouldered gown by Adolfo at the entrance of the embassy residence in London's Regent Park, greeting friends old and new: Betsy and Alfred; Lee and Walter, who had refurbished the thirty-six-room house at their own expense when Alfred was ambassador; Princess Grace, who had been at M-G-M with Nancy; Barbara Walters; Douglas Fairbanks; Tom Brokaw of NBC; Woolworth heiress Barbara Hutton; David Frost—140 guests in all.

The next evening Nancy attended the queen's ball for 1,500 at Buckingham Palace, to which only royalty and European aristocracy were supposed to be invited. Nancy and Betsy received invitations, however, even though François Mitterrand, the French president, didn't. Tiaras were the fashion. Nancy, *sans* tiara, wore a white beaded off-the-shoulder Galanos and diamonds. She also attended a lunch given by Lord Westmorland, had supper at Buckingham Palace with the royal family, and afterward went to

Hyde Park with the royal family to watch the fireworks. "I think it's wonderful," she told a British television reporter about the monarchy. "I think it's wonderful. I would hate to see it ever disappear."

Then, finally, the day itself, July 30, 1981, the wedding of Prince Charles and Lady Diana at St. Paul's Cathedral. Nancy surveyed the "Beefeaters" in red stockings, carrying pikes, and the Corps of the Gentlemen at Arms, in gold plumed helmets, entering the historic church. She sat among the 2,500 guests wearing a three-piece peach Galanos day suit and a straw hat with a chiffon scarf. She had been married to Ronnie quickly and simply, but she loved the fairy-tale romance of the royal wedding.

Nancy watched intently as Charles and Diana took their vows. "Everybody loves romance," she said later. "Everyone in London was so caught up with the whole thing. It was a wonderful feeling." There were more parties, more celebrations before Nancy boarded her plane. It "was a lovely day, a beautiful day and one I won't forget in a long, long time.

"Lady Diana looked really lovely and I was overjoyed at the graciousness of the whole royal family. Altogether, this was a wonderful week."

──=·20·=──
"I'D NEVER WEAR
A CROWN"

A week after Nancy returned from London, the Reagans left for a twenty-eight-day vacation at the ranch. The White House press office said that the vacation cost the taxpayers $250,000. "I don't think he understands the complexity of going to the ranch," said one aide involved with the arrangements. "I think he'd be happy to get on United Airlines with one aide and fly to the ranch. The ranch input comes from Nancy when she feels he needs a trip. Then we fix the schedule, set things up and only then put it to him, say we can work it out."

Nancy didn't enjoy the ranch nearly as much as Ronnie. Despite the panorama of the mountains and the acres of range and trails, she felt that she had even less privacy here then in the White House. On a neighboring mountain sat the network camera crews with their telephoto lenses. To Nancy, it was as if the camera could poke its snout into her very boudoir; she told a friend she had even put up a curtain in the bathroom.

For Ronnie, the four weeks at Rancho del Cielo were truly a vacation. He read position papers, did what he thought he had to do, but for the most part he relaxed. He spent hours cutting away brush, chopping logs, riding, and just puttering around. "By now it must be the cleanest ranch in the world," said one aide.

"What I'd really like to do is go down in history as the president who made Americans believe in themselves," Ronnie said. He was capable of inspiring Americans as had few contemporary leaders, but the presidency was more than patriotic symbols and noble rhetoric. He had the power to unleash a nuclear war, ordering the deaths of a hundred million Russians or more. His economic policies were beginning to bring down inflation, but the unemployment rate was steadily rising. Housing construction was down, as was the stock market.

What was so extraordinary was Ronnie's apparent psychic distance from the burden of the presidency. He sat in cabinet meetings doodling. Unless held to a rigid agenda, he would start telling Hollywood stories or talk about football in Dixon. Often in one-on-one conversations Ronnie seemed distracted or withdrawn. "He has a habit now," his brother, Neil, said. "You might be talking to him, and it's like he's picking his fingernails, but he's not. And you know then that he's talking to himself."

"If people knew about him living in his own reality, they wouldn't believe it," said one White House aide. "There are only ten to fifteen people who know the extent, and until they leave and begin talking, no one will believe it."

"Maybe the only way to be authentic anymore is not to change, to deny part of the world," said another administration member, who viewed Ronnie more philosophically. "When the rest of the world goes through changes, he stays the same."

That distance from the world he lived in was not always a negative factor. "People need badly to believe in the president," said Sears, who in the 1976 and 1980 campaigns had seen Ronnie separate himself from problems. "In that sense they feel better about the president now than they have in some times. As they see him in public, he doesn't convey the feeling that the job has beat him. That's in part because he can escape the reality of it. He leaves the reality of it with his staff."

Even the staff sometimes needed a break. During the third week in August, Deaver was on Martha's Vineyard hobnobbing with such luminaries as Lillian Hellman, the writer and conservative *bête noire*. Baker was down in Texas taking some time off, too. Meese was tending the store in Washington. On August 20 at 2:04 A.M. in Washington, Meese learned that two navy F-14 fighters had just been attacked over the Mediterranean by two Libyan planes. The F-14s had shot down the Russian-built planes and returned to their carrier.

Meese had helped set up the Sacramento system that only brought crucial matters to Ronnie's attention, and then only after the staff had thrashed out a position. Meese didn't call Ronnie; it was just after 11:00 P.M. in California, and he didn't want to bother the president. Instead, he called Vice President Bush and National Security Council members. Not until over five hours later, at 4:24 A.M. California time, did Meese call and wake Ronnie.

The honeymoon among the bizarre *ménage à trois* of Baker, Deaver and Meese was over. Baker and Deaver were livid. They worried that the country now thought that Ronnie wasn't running his administration, that he was sleeping while American military men and women faced new, uncertain dangers. Nancy was upset, too, because Meese had made Ronnie look bad. And she began looking at the pink-cheeked counselor like a shopper not sure she has made the right purchase.

Soon after Nancy and Ronnie arrived back in Washington on September 3, the White House announced the purchase of a new set of formal china. Each of the 220 nineteen-piece place settings cost $910.49, for a total of $209,508. The new 4,732-piece ivory china set made by Lenox was edged in red and had a raised gold presidential seal. Each place setting included a fish plate, finger bowl, cereal bowl, bouillon cup, cream-soup cup and stand, demitasse cup and berry bowl, as well as a dinner, salad, and bread and butter plate.

Trying to offset criticism, the White House pointed out that it had been fourteen years since the Johnsons purchased the last set, 216 twelve-piece settings for $80,028. Like that set, the Reagan china was paid for by a private donor, a separate gift from the $822,641 raised for redecorating. The imperious tone of the announcements from the East Wing suggested that Nancy was doing the nation an immense favor. The editorial cartoonists sharpened their pens to satirize the three china policies: mainland, Taiwan, and Nancy.

While this minor brouhaha still raged in the media, Nancy's office announced the completion of the redecorating of the second and third floors of the White House. Graber, a Californian, used pink, salmon and yellow in the family quarters to create rooms that exuded the sunny cheerfulness of a smog-free L.A. day as well as Nancy's delicate, feminine taste. Whenever he could, he used pieces that were already in the White House or in storage. He replaced curtains and carpeting and reupholstered antiques. He put most of the Reagans' Pacific Palisades furniture in the West Hall Sitting Room. There he displayed the Chinese blue-and-white vases and urns that Nancy's mother had given her. The two long red flowered sofas sat in front of the great arched window. A pillow needlepointed with "RR" told the visitor explicitly who was in power.

Before state dinners, Ronnie chatted with visiting heads of state in the Yellow Oval Room. Graber and Nancy wanted to make the room more comfortable, more apt to make a foreign leader feel at home. They added new yellow sofas and marble-top tables, and four antique chairs by Sené that had been regilded during the Carter years and were worth an estimated $40,000 to $50,000 each.

The loveliest room of all was Nancy and Ronnie's bedroom. Covering the walls was exquisite hand-painted salmon-colored Chinese paper with birds in swirling patterns. A small table sat between a small salmon-colored sofa and two chairs with needlepoint upholstery. Next to the sofa stood a tiny octagonal table that held Nancy's collection of nine Battersea boxes, one in the middle surrounded by eight others. The legs on the tables and chairs looked as thin as twigs. Above the oversize bed was the painting *Before Moonrise* by Carroll Sargent Tyson. Nancy's adjacent dressing room was covered with flowered peach paper. A painting of Nancy and Patti hung over the chest of drawers. The artist, Paul Clemens, had painted the portrait of Jane Wyman as Ma Baxter in *The Yearling* that had hung over the fireplace during the last years of Ronnie's first marriage. Nancy's second floor office was strié-painted a soothing green and decorated with prints of wild flowers. Nancy also had an exercise room and a dozen double closets for her clothes.

There was no public accounting of the costs, which ran about a million dollars. That didn't include the donated and specially priced goods, or all the equipment and furnishings for the refurbished beauty salon. The White House proudly pointed out that the decorating had been paid for by private contributions and had cost the taxpayers nothing. The contributions were tax-deductible, however, and in that sense the public did foot about half the bill.

There they were, then, these splendid new rooms, Nancy's primary accomplishment during her first nine months in office. She had become the administration's number-one public-relations problem, and at first Mike Deaver wanted to make as little mention of the redecorating as possible. But for Nancy, as for most of the ladies of her set, the only place to show one's newly decorated home was in *Architectural Digest,* the toney publication that decorators and their clients considered quite the *sine qua non.*

Jerry was a friend of Paige Rense, the editor in chief, and Ted Graber thought that the magazine was just the place for *his* White House. Rense insisted on an exclusive, so the pictures wouldn't show up in *Parade* or *People.* Everything was done just right. The photographer she chose was a member of the British nobility, Derry Moore, a viscount and the son of Lord Drogheda. Moore was married to the daughter of Ambassador and Lady Henderson. The White House limousine picked him up at the British Embassy on Massachusetts Avenue to whisk him to the White House.

Eighteen pages of color pictures appeared in the December 1981 issue of *Architectural Digest.* On the cover of the $4.95 magazine was a photo of the undecorated front of the White House, and on newsstand copies a logo slashed in Nancy red: "COLLECTOR'S EDITION: The Private White House apartments of PRESIDENT AND MRS. RONALD REAGAN." In the text Nancy said, "This house belongs to all Americans, and I want it to be something of which they can be proud."

The success of Ronnie's administration domestically depended in good measure on his programs being perceived as fair. He was cutting federal aid to dependent children, food-stamp programs, school breakfast and lunch programs, day-care centers, Medicaid, education grants, job training. He was promising, however, not to remove the social safety net protecting the poor, the sick, and the needy. And, more important, he was promising that once the American people were freed from the shackles of government, the great engines of American capitalism would begin pumping at full speed, and there would be jobs and good times for anyone willing to work.

Ronnie said that it would take time, though, and it rankled the administration when the networks ran stories about the impact of the budget cuts on the poor. Those stories were bad enough, but were doubly devastating when juxtaposed against pictures or stories of Nancy and the Californians.

When Ronnie gave his first news conference after his summer vacation, on October 2, he was prepared for the inevitable question about Nancy's life-style. He was also prepared for the equally inevitable question about the aborted Department of Agriculture classification of ketchup as a vegetable in the nutritional requirements for school lunches.

"Mr. President, the style of your administration is being called 'millionaires on parade,'" a reporter said. "Do you feel that you are being sensitive enough to the symbolism of Republican mink coats, limousines, thousand-dollar-a-plate china at the White House when ghetto kids are being told they can eat ketchup as a vegetable?"

"Well, we changed that," Ronnie said. "Somebody got overambitious in the bureaucracy. . . . I don't think it's a 'millionaire's parade' and I haven't counted any of the mink coats that have been around, but also, you mentioned the china. Let's set the record straight once and for all because Nancy's taken a bum rap on that. There has been no new china for the White House since the Truman administration. Some partial augmentation under Lyndon Johnson, but not a full set of china.

"Now, breakage occurs even in the White House. I know that everyone's supposed to be walking around on feathers and that doesn't happen, but it does. And the truth of the matter is at a state dinner, we can't set the tables with dishes that match. We have to have them mixed so don't look too closely at other tables in there. And this was the result of an anonymous contribution and the company making the china made it at cost. So there was nothing out of the taxpayers."

Later in October, on a five-day visit to New York, Nancy appeared before the $200-a-plate Alfred E. Smith memorial dinner. At such gatherings she usually made a few bland, benign remarks and sat down. On this occasion, however, to try to deflate all the criticism, she had been provided with a series of quips. She made fun of the popular picture postcard that showed her wearing a crown. "I'd never wear a crown," she said. "It messes up your hair." She answered those who criticized the private contributions for redecorating. "I'm very glad I raised as much as I did for the White House. Ronnie thinks I did such a good job, he wants me to help work on the deficit."

On the same trip, Nancy visited Phoenix House, a twenty-four-hour drug treatment center. She spent an hour with young drug abusers, telling them that "if we don't do something, we're going to lose a generation. Brains will turn to mush." Like many other drug rehabilitation centers, Phoenix House faced a 25-percent cut in funds.

Patti was in New York, and Ron, Jr., Doria, Patti and two of the Wick children, Doug and Cindi, helped Patti celebrate her twenty-ninth birthday. Two weeks later, when Patti made her television movie debut in NBC's *For Ladies Only,* Nancy and Ronnie could hardly believe what they were seeing. They had once won awards for the wholesomeness of their film work, and here was their daughter in a movie about a male stripper who made his living gyrating in front of scores of lusting ladies. Patti played his girlfriend, and to Ronnie she "was the only breath of fresh air in a film that was unnecessarily obscene."

Nancy was not happy with Patti, her involvement with antinuke groups, and the nuclear-freeze movement that Ronnie believed was infiltrated by Soviet agents. "For a while [in 1981] Patti and her mother weren't speaking," says one high-level White House staffer. "Nancy may have given up on Patti. Her darling is Ron. As for Maureen, you can't even mention Maureen's name in her presence. Maureen is a nonperson."

When Maureen came to Washington, she did not stay at the White House. She had decided to run for the Senate in California, a race that her father did not want her to make, and in which he promised her no assistance.

Ronnie wanted Washington to become "a shining city on the hill," but the capital remained as it always has been, a city rooted in the realities of power, a political bourse, where a day didn't go by without exchanges, dealmaking and compromises. The White House staff, too, was much as it always is. There were any number of dark-suited high achievers who watched their own futures more carefully than they watched the future of the Republic. There was enough backstabbing that a smart operative never turned his face to the wall.

Ronnie was sickened by the struggles within his staff, and preferred to think of *his* people as a happy band of brothers. If anything, there were fewer leaks to the media than during the Carter and Ford years, but Ronnie considered it a form of betrayal when staff people gave out their versions of meetings and policies. He didn't like to play that game, though it was as valuable to the White House as it was to the journalists. "The biggest surprise [about the presidency] is the extent of the leaks and stories that begin 'Unnamed sources report . . . ' and 'They say. . . . ' It is disturbing to be in a closed meeting on a vital subject and that evening hear references to it on the news. It is frustrating to know the facts, and know that even though 'their' remarks are wrong, you can't answer them because you can't tell what you know."

To Ronnie, *his* people were always the innocents. He had had no idea that since the early days of the administration, David Stockman had been having regular breakfast meetings at the Hay-Adams Hotel with William Greider, then an assistant managing editor of the *Washington Post*. At most of the tables sat other men doing what Stockman and Greider were doing— trading information, contacts and ideas, helping each other move a few steps up the board in the Washington game. As budget director, thirty-four-year-old Stockman was the most publicized member of the administration: little David, the giant-killer, slaying the goliath of government bureaucracy. For the time being, the conversations were not to be quoted or reported; but one day when the battles were over, Greider would write an account of Stockman's derring-do, and both men's time would have been well spent.

By fall, Greider had decided that enough time had passed for him to write his article. His long piece in the *Atlantic* was a richly detailed, vivid account of the process of government. "Supply-side is 'trickle-down' theory," Stockman said. But in order to get the program through Congress, the administration had to sweeten the proposals with benefits for middle- and lower-class Americans. "The original argument was that the top bracket was too high, and that's having the most devastating effect on the economy," Stockman said. "The general argument was that, in order to make this palatable as a political matter, you had to bring down all the brackets." On Ronnie's part, at least, there was nothing cynical about this. He believed that the key to economic recovery was to cut taxes across the board. It was the rich and well-to-do, by definition, who would benefit the most and do the most for society by plowing money into investments and stocks, reinvigorating the entire economy.

Greider presented a portrait of David Stockman grappling with the unpalatable realities of power and economics: a federal government that, like many consumers, had so many fixed costs and payments that it was difficult to reduce; and a political system in which elected officials tried to pass the pain of the cuts onto somebody else, some group other than their supporters.

In January, Stockman had been faced with computer projections indicating that the Reagan tax cut and defense increases would lead to a federal deficit rising to $116 billion in 1984. That wouldn't do. So Stockman simply fed optimistic new data into the computer, predicting declining interests and prices and a stunning increase in productivity. He bargained, cajoled, threatened his way, all the time growing more skeptical about the economic program.

When the *Atlantic* article appeared in November, Deaver and Meese wanted to fire Stockman; but after a private forty-five-minute lunch, Ronnie agreed to keep his budget director. "David Stockman was not doing the sinning, he was sinned against," Ronnie said. "What's happened to the journalistic ethic? Stockman was betrayed by a longtime friend who distorted and misinterpreted things that had been said in complete confidence and the understanding that it was off the record. The author used his own interpretation and, very frankly, I liken it to another assassination attempt—which I hope will be as unsuccessful as the first."

The administration member who paid for his mistake with his position first was Richard Allen, the National Security Council adviser. On January 21, 1981 Allen had led two Japanese journalists from *Shufo no Tomo* to see Nancy for a short interview and photograph. The journalists gave Allen a $1,000 honorarium in cash intended for Nancy and two Seiko watches for himself. Allen stuck the money in a White House safe without making a formal receipt and blithely went on his way. When the money was discovered and an FBI investigation begun, Allen admitted to nothing more than poor judgment. But in November, when the matter became public, Nancy was the first to suggest to Ronnie that Allen resign. Ronnie was already unhappy with Allen's performance, and the NSC head was allowed to go on administrative leave from which he never returned.

"Mr. President," Art Buchwald said, looking up at Ronnie in the center box at the Kennedy Center honors gala, "and readers of the *Atlantic Monthly....* " The audience roared. This was the fourth year the Kennedy Center had given awards to distinguished American artists. With Ronnie and Nancy in the White House, the event had taken on a special élan. Earlier in the day, at the White House reception honoring Count Basie, Cary Grant, Helen Hayes, Jerome Robbins and Rudolf Serkin, Ronnie had spoken passionately about their contributions. "It is our spirit they captured when they danced," he said. "Our hopes played out on stage and screen because of their talent, our imaginations have been set free."

The Reagans went to the ceremony at the Kennedy Center but did not stay for the dinner. The official guest list included Art Buchwald, Mrs. David Bruce, Mrs. Katharine Graham, Audrey Hepburn, Mikhail Baryshnikov, Roger Mudd, William Paley, Senator Charles Percy, Morley Safer, Sissy Spacek, Meryl Streep and scores of other media and political stars. It was as spectacular a group as turned out in Washington. In previous years the most courted, feted and observed people were the leading politicians and movie stars, but this evening the focus of attention, the group that the working journalists hovered around and the knowing Washingtonians strolled by, was at table 110. Here sat Jean, Lee, Marion and Bunny, four of Nancy's closest friends, in their blond upswept hairdos and diamonds, looking like quadruplets. Beside them sat their husbands: William French Smith, Walter Annenberg, Earle Jorgensen and Jack Wrather. Except for Smith, the group had no direct political power, no great careers in films or dance. But they were the first friends, bearers of the style and ambience of the Reagan years.

The Reagans themselves still got out for dinner parties occasionally. At a dinner party at the Georgetown mansion of the *Washington Post*'s chairman Katharine Graham, Ronnie tried regaling the guests with his Hollywood stories. But some of the guests were Washington insiders who wanted to discuss political matters. Others were Hollywood types such as director Alan Pakula, who hadn't come to Washington to hear shoptalk. While Ronnie carried on, some of the guests whispered and joked about him. It was not loud enough for Nancy to hear, but her own romance with the Georgetown set was about over. She and the ladies had very little to say to one another. On a visit to the White House, Ronnie told Jack Lemmon, the actor, how much he missed California, his friends and his life there.

A few glorious months ago, Ronnie had seemed able to change the course of fifty years of economic and political history with the mere force of his rhetoric. That was over now. There were few easy programs left to cut, few decisions that could be resolved with the catechism of supply-side economics. A year into the administration, the inflation rate was falling dramatically, giving a new sense of security to those on fixed incomes. But month by month, unemployment was rising, 8 percent in October, 8.4 percent in November, 8.9 percent in December, with almost nine and a half million Americans out of work.

As early as November, Ronnie had to admit that he had given up his plans to balance the budget by fiscal year 1984. In December, the administration estimated that the deficit would rise to a record $109 billion in 1982, $152 billion in 1983, and $162 billion in 1984. They were incredible figures for a conservative president. They recalled John Anderson's memorable response to the question of how to cut income taxes, raise defense spending and balance the budget. "It's simple," he said during the Iowa debate among Republican presidential hopefuls. "You do it with mirrors."

"A melancholy set in," said one high administration official. "Before,

Reagan had a clean slate and he was popular. Now all that was left was a handful of grungy issues. The economy didn't come around, and an introspection set in."

Ronnie believed that if only the administration were given time, it would all work out. At news conferences and to staff members or interviewers, he continued to exude a profound faith in the programs. The anecdotes he told at his press conferences were often wonderful stories, but they sometimes didn't add up. When he spoke off the cuff, he often misspoke. "To hear him speak extemporaneously on domestic policy is to hold your breath in nervous anticipation of the unknown," wrote David Broder of the *Washington Post* in evaluating Ronnie's first year. "Too often, the thoughts he expresses have had to be corrected or reinterpreted by people who ought to be his subordinates, not his mentors."

The world was not as Ronnie would have liked it. The Polish government, with the support of the Russians, clamped down on the solidarity movement and declared martial law. If life were a Hollywood movie, Ronnie would have helped good Lech Walesa and the movement and they would have risen up and thrown the bad Communists out. But Poland was in the Soviet sphere, and any dramatic Western intrusion might well bring nuclear war. Moreover, Poland owed so much money to Western banks that if the nation defaulted, the world banking system would be in desperate trouble. So Ronnie settled for minor sanctions, an inspiring speech praising the will of the people, and asked Americans on Christmas Eve to put candles in their windows. Later the administration topped that when Ronnie's friend Charlie Wick put together a television propaganda program called "Let Poland Be Poland" to be shown around the world.

Ronnie and Nancy sought to celebrate the season among their friends. But there were various staff and press parties and ceremonies in the White House that Nancy couldn't possibly avoid. In early December, she showed the media the White House Christmas tree and decorations. There had been unverified reports of a Libyan hit team entering the United States to assassinate the president, and security in the White House was especially tight. Even here inside these precincts, Ronnie and Nancy could not be completely safe.

Nancy entered the Blue Room wearing a red suit and walked to the nineteen-and-a-half-foot Christmas tree. As she turned, the reporters pressed forward against the velvet rope. "I very much want it to be an old-fashioned Christmas," Nancy said in a tiny voice. She was nervous and tight as an overwound toy. She hated it when she didn't have a prepared statement, and there was no telling what the reporters might ask. It was the Christmas season, but to the seventy or so journalists, it was just another working day, another story. At the back of the group stood several male photographers talking and joking.

"We came down the other night," Nancy said, explaining when she and Ronnie had first seen the decorations. "And he came out and caught me under the mistletoe."

"What happened then?" boomed Sam Donaldson, an ABC correspondent, raising his Mephistophelian eyebrows as much as his voice.

Nancy laughed. "I'll never tell, Sam."

She showed the reporters the White House Christmas tree, the White House dollhouse and the White House gingerbread house. After it was definitely stated that this year's gingerbread house had a jelly-bean walk, the journalists were invited to have eggnog and cookies with Nancy.

As far back as any of the journalists could remember, no First Lady had invited the media for refreshments after the press tour. It was one thing to shout a question at Nancy, another to make small talk, and the group shuffled toward the decorated tables laden with crystal bowls of eggnog. As they passed under the mistletoe, Donaldson swept Sarah McClendon, a rotund reporter, into his arms and planted a loud, wet kiss on her elderly countenance.

"Bet you never knew he cared," Nancy giggled.

With that opening, Donaldson proceeded to tell the First Lady a dirty limerick, making himself far more the center of attention than Nancy had ever been.

As they stood drinking eggnog, the reporters didn't know quite what to say to Nancy. Practically no one thought of wishing her a Merry Christmas. Instead, four or five at a time, they clustered around her asking questions.

"What do you want for Christmas?"

"A safe Christmas," Nancy said, almost under her breath.

"Can you forget what happened?"

"I try to put it out of my mind."

"But *can* you?"

"From time to time," Nancy said, barely audibly, her eyes filled with tears.

Christmas Eve, Ronnie, Nancy, young Ron, Doria and Patti went to the Wicks' Watergate apartment for a buffet dinner. Every year someone played Santa Claus. This year it was young Ron's turn, and Nancy sat on her son's knee. "Now what do you want for Christmas, little girl?" he asked. Christmas Day, the Wicks came to the White House for an early dinner.

For New Year's, Ronnie and Nancy went where they did every year, to the Annenbergs' estate in Palm Springs. Sunnylands was ringed by six-foot-tall barbed-wire fencing and shielded from view by oleanders and eucalyptus trees. Guests in their limousines stopped at the entrance, where an armed guard checked out credentials. They stayed in two four-bedroom guest cottages where Lee left fresh flowers, a roster of other guests, and a schedule of that day's activities.

The day before the big party, the helicopter carrying Ronnie and Nancy swooped down on the 208-acre estate, the pink tiled roof of the great main house visible from high in the sky. Entering Sunnylands was like passing into an independent principality. The estate had its own flag, an orange Mayan sun god flying on the flagpole near the thirty-foot-tall Mayan column, a larger-than-life replica of the one outside the National Museum of Anthropology in Mexico City.

Ronnie and Nancy were greeted by their old friends and entered the house, which was colored pink to match the hues of the mountains off to the southeast. Just inside the entrance stood Rodin's *Eve* in the center of a pool, bathed in sunlight from the apex of the thirty-foot-high ceiling. Though Ronnie admired Walter, he didn't truly appreciate that Sunnylands housed one of the great private collections of Impressionistic art. As for Lee, Ronnie thought her unpretentious, gracious manner ideal. That was one of the reasons he had asked her to be his chief of protocol.

Jerry Zipkin roamed among the guests. He had learned to take pictures and he clicked gaily away. He caught Francis Albert looking almost bald, scarcely recognizable to an outsider. He shot Betsy against Ronnie's helicopter like a Fifties teen-ager posing his girlfriend beside his car. She stood there with her hands on her hips.

The Annenbergs had tried to make life at Sunnylands like a painting by Seurat, all grace and light. But darker, more realistic hues had begun to show through. A year ago they had all seemed so healthy and vital, as if they could go on forever. But now Walter was tiring of commuting between his Philadelphia estate and Washington. He didn't have that many years left, and he wanted to spend them with Lee, not have her run around as the chief of protocol. She had decided to leave office.

Betsy and Alfred still had their apartment near Lee and Walter's in the Watergate, planning to share the White House years with Nancy and Ronnie. But Alfred was dying of cancer. It was slow and painful, and as he approached death, everyone's mortality came into focus. Nancy had never faced such a death before, and as the New Year arrived, she was at times distraught.

—21—

"RAINBOW STEW"

O n a snow-flecked Friday afternoon in mid-January, an Air Florida jet crashed into the Potomac River on take-off, splitting open,
the broken pieces of the Lockheed 737 settling into the icy waters. It was just four o'clock and the highways leading out of Washington
were hopelessly jammed. The television crews arrived, and Washingtonians
in homes, bars and offices sat mesmerized, watching rescuers attempting to
save some of the passengers.

Over at the Washington Sheraton Hotel, preparations were well under
way for a party in honor of Lyn Nofziger, who was leaving the White
House to join the ranks of Washington consultants. Roy Pfautch, a St.
Louis businessman, was giving the party. He had plunked down over
$25,000. Mignon, the elephant, was already on her way. And it didn't seem
right to cancel. And so while the death toll mounted to seventy-eight people, Nofziger, the William French Smiths, White House staffers, lobbyists,
and journalists stood and talked while clowns passed out cotton candy and
peanuts and Mignon did tricks. Then it was time for dancing, and along
with the others, those journalists who had asked to bring their spouses
waltzed around the room.

Ronnie and Nancy were not scheduled to attend the party. Nancy saw
the television pictures, too, and she wanted to do something to help. "Visiting the hospital was really her idea," said Joseph Canzeri, then Deaver's
deputy. "Mike said, 'She wants to go. Put it together.' Her staff got pissed
off because they didn't know. We wanted no media. I saw Ike Pappas of
CBS in the hall and I made him promise not to use it. Nancy sat and cried
and squeezed this girl. We spent fifteen more minutes than we were sup-

posed to spend, and I planned it with plenty of time. She hugs the stumps. I have a hard time looking."

The first anniversary of Ronnie's presidency arrived a week later. In previous administrations, that date had passed largely unnoticed except by columnists and political buffs. But for the Reaganites, anything was an excuse for a party, and nothing was more worthy of a blowout than birthday number one for the new era. In fact, one party wouldn't do—there were three major events, plus scores of private parties. There was a major black-tie ball at the Washington Hilton attended by the Meeses and other officials; a $25-a-head blast at the Corcoran Gallery primarily for younger Republicans; and the biggest party of all, a gala at the Hilton for the Eagles, the big Republican contributors, that the Republican National Committee (RNC) put together as a fund raiser for the fall's congressional campaigns.

The RNC invited cabinet members and congressmen, promising those who bought tickets that they would be able to sit with one or more of the dignitaries. At $10,000 a table, the event sold out immediately. Even the president and the First Lady were assigned to a table. The night before, however, Nancy asked that Ronnie and she be sequestered at a head table, away from the crowds.

Nancy wore a black sequined gown with an enormous beaded star on the front, a dress that looked as if it had been designed by a repentant hippie. The dress was a Galanos in a ballroom that was a showroom for Nancy's favorite designers—Galanos, Bill Blass and Adolfo—and more diamonds were to be found than at Tiffany's.

As soon as Nancy and Ronnie stepped onto the floor to dance to Lester Lanin's music, the photographers and reporters pushed toward them, and fifty other couples jumped to their feet and began moving toward the president and First Lady in movements more akin to trotting than dancing. Nancy and Ronnie sat down.

"This is a very impressive gathering," Ronnie said as he spoke to the gathering, looking out on the gorgeous gowns set off against the black dinner jackets. "When I walked in I thought I was back on the set of *High Society*."

Despite the greeting the over 2,000 guests gave Ronnie, some of the Eagles were not terribly happy with the administration. When Richard DeVos, the Republican National Committee chairman, asked rhetorically, "Are you as confident tonight as you were a year ago?" the applause was hardly more inspiring than if DeVos had been introducing Ted Kennedy.

Ronnie and Nancy departed before the entertainment. Soon after, many of the other guests began leaving. Carrying away gifts of Jelly Bellies jelly beans and *A Great New Beginning* commemorative books, they were putting on their fur coats and overcoats as Marie Osmond sang "God Bless America."

Charlie Wick was in a great mood.

"Oh, Charles, Charles," called out Betty Adams, a Los Angeles socialite, as reported by Marie Bremer in *New York.* "Look," shouted the lady in diamonds and emeralds, clutching her Jelly Bellies. "I have my jelly beans!"

Charlie turned and hummed the last bars of "Make-Believe."

Charlie thought that "during the depression, when people were selling apples . . . they loved those glamour pictures showing people driving beautiful cars and women in beautiful gowns." And he was not about to cut down on his life-style. He traveled first-class all the way. He was all for Nancy and Ronnie and the administration continuing to do the same.

But there were those in the White House who had had quite enough of Charlie, Jerry, Betsy and the L.A. glitterati. The troika of Baker, Deaver and Meese knew that Nancy was the administration's main image problem, a lightning rod for criticism. In private, Baker could be very critical of Nancy, but Deaver remained her protector and keeper. Nancy was Deaver's best key to power. He didn't even complain when she kept him on hold on the phone for ten minutes or more.

In Nancy the administration had a more serious problem than mere image. In 1981 the Reagans had accepted free gifts that the White House itself valued highly conservatively at more than $30,000. That included a Waterford crystal wine cooler ($1,900), silver belt buckles ($500), two handcrafted belt buckles ($2,000), sports coat and slacks ($500), porcelain Boehm sculpture *American Eagle* ($2,500) and a music box ($125). But that didn't include the thousands of dollars in Nancy's dresses, and the "borrowed" jewelry from Bulgari and Harry Winston.

One high-ranking White House official felt that the administration should simply be honest about the dresses. A press release should be put out admitting that Nancy had accepted the gifts but that now it was felt it wasn't quite appropriate; and thus the gifts were being returned, and Nancy would accept no further clothes.

But a different approach was tried. First, on January 14, Nancy cabled the Parsons School of Design in New York City saying that she would be donating a group of dresses that the school would then distribute to museums across the country. In the meantime, the story of Nancy's "borrowed" dresses leaked to several reporters. Nancy went through her wardrobe, deciding which dresses she would return. Four days later, the White House announced that she had decided to take twelve designer outfits that had been "loaned" to her and donate them to museums.

Nancy would have been comfortable in the White House simply being

Ronnie's good and loyal wife, gossiping with Betsy and Jerry, buying clothes, overseeing parties and state dinners. Indeed, in retrospect, several aides wished now that a year ago Nancy had said that she was going to be the First Wife and not play any other outside role as First Lady. But that hadn't happened, and now Nancy had become a symbol of extravagance and unconcern.

This image hurt not only Nancy but Ronnie, and in the first few months of 1982, her staff sought to change that perception. Deaver brought in a new chief of staff, James Rosebush, a handsome thirty-two-year-old Republican who had been director of the Office of Business Liaison at the Commerce Department.

Nancy hated to leave Ronnie overnight, but she set out for a series of visits to drug rehabilitation centers. "Last year was a lost year," she told reporters flying with her to Florida and Texas in mid-February. "It was not the happiest year of my life." In Pinellas Park, Florida, Nancy sat among teen-agers and their parents involved in a drug-treatment program called STRAIGHT. PCP, THC, hash, pot, cocaine, D-Con powder, gasoline—these kids had tried it all. They had lied and stolen for these drugs, until they sank into a dazed morass. Theirs was a shocking litany and Nancy sat quietly, her eyes filled with tears. "My heart is filled with so many things I'd like to say to you, if I can get through them," she said. "I'm so proud of you and I love you, too."

Nancy visited other centers in Florida and Texas on her two-day trip, and in the next few months made similar sojourns. The administration was cutting down funding for drug rehabilitation programs as they were almost all social programs, but Nancy saw the problem as one to be solved primarily on a personal basis.

At first the reporters heralded Nancy's trips ("A 'NEW' NANCY STEPS OUT," "FIRST LADY FINDS A CAUSE"). But she herself didn't seem to learn anything from these trips, to broaden or deepen her perceptions. She always said the same things, the same way. The reporters tired of covering the same event again and again, hearing her familiar spiel.

What excited the Washington journalistic elite was Nancy's performance at the Gridiron Dinner. The Gridiron is a group of sixty journalists who are elected by current members. There are some distinguished journalists in the group, some who are not so distinguished and a few who consider being a member of the organization their stellar achievement. The Gridiron's primary function is to put on a private dinner each year attended by the president, top officials, and the *crème de la crème* of Washington. It is the one event of the year when official Washington lets loose. Nancy wasn't the first First Lady to perform. In 1975, Betty Ford participated; three years later, Rosalynn and Jimmy Carter jitterbugged.

At the white-tie dinner held at the Capital Hilton Hotel, Ronnie and Nancy sat among the 600 guests listening to the Gridiron members satirizing the administration in song and skit. One reporter imitated Nancy by singing new lyrics to the song "Second-Hand Rose":

> *Second-hand clothes.*
> *I give my second-hand clothes*
> *To museum collections and traveling shows.*
> *They were oh so happy that they got 'em,*
> *Won't notice they were ragged at the bottom.*
> *Goodbye, you old worn-out mess.*
> *I never wear a frock more than once.*
> *Calvin Klein, Adolfo, Ralph Lauren*
> *And Bill Blass.*
> *Ronald Reagan's mama's going strictly*
> *First class.*
> *Rodeo Drive. I sure miss Rodeo Drive*
> *In frumpy Washington.*
>
> *Second-hand rings.*
> *Donate those old used-up things.*
> *Designers deduct 'em.*
> *We're living like kings.*
> *So what if Ronnie's cutting back on welfare.*
> *I'll still wear a tiara in my coiffed hair.*

As the song ended, Nancy got up from her seat on the dais and dashed out. Some of the notables thought the joke had gone too far and she had left upset. Ronnie figured she had gone to the bathroom.

Within a few minutes, a bizarre-looking woman sauntered on stage wearing a white feather boa, an aqua skirt fastened with safety pins, white pantaloons graced with blue butterflies, a feathered hat and yellow rubber boots. When the audience realized it was Nancy up there, they broke into applause and gave her a standing ovation.

Holding a plate in her hand painted to look like the new White House china, Nancy sang her version of "Second-Hand Rose":

> *I'm wearing second-hand clothes,*
> *Second-hand clothes.*
> *They're quite the style*
> *In spring fashion shows.*
> *Even my new trench coat with fur collar*
> *Ronnie bought for ten cents on the dollar.*
> *Second-hand gowns*
> *And old hand-me-downs,*
> *The China is the only thing that's new.*

Nancy performs "Second Hand Clothes" to a standing ovation at the Gridiron Club, Washington, 1982. *(WH)*

Even though they tell me that I'm no longer
Queen,
Did Ronnie have to buy me that new
Sewing machine?
I sure hope Ed Meese sews.

In her stage career, Nancy had never received such an ovation. She sang an encore and to shouts of "bravo" broke the china plate.

On the evening of January 26, Ronnie walked through the Capitol with congressional leaders to give his first State of the Union message to a joint session of Congress. Michael Evans, the White House photographer, striding along beside Ronnie, noticed that while Senator Baker, the majority leader, and Congressman Thomas P. O'Neill, Jr., the Speaker of the House, appeared nervous, "the President was acting as if he were out for an evening stroll with a few of his buddies."

Although Ronnie was applauded warmly, there was nothing left of the emotional greeting he had received after the assassination attempt. His programs were in trouble in Congress now. The economy was not responding as quickly as he'd said it would. There was a projected $100-billion deficit for the coming fiscal year.

In the face of all this, Ronnie did not pull back one iota. Against the counsel of economic advisers who saw the specter of an enormous budget deficit, he refused to call for higher taxes. Instead, he pointed pridefully to the fact that "we not only cut the increase in government spending nearly in half, we brought about the largest tax reductions and the most sweeping changes in our tax structure since the beginning of this century." To make government more responsive, he called for "a single, bold stroke," giving forty federal programs to the states, in essence ending Washington's role in managing most major domestic programs.

Finally, he returned, as he almost always did, to his themes of patriotism and individual heroism. "Just two weeks ago, in the midst of a terrible tragedy on the Potomac, we saw again the spirit of American heroism at its finest," he said. "We saw the heroism of one of our young government employees, Lenny Skutnik."

Skutnik had dived into the frigid Potomac to save a woman. This evening he was sitting next to Nancy. The congressional audience interrupted to applaud Skutnik, who appeared every bit the shy young hero. On the administration's part, it was a neat bit of public relations. But as Ronnie spoke, his final remarks seemed once again to strike a chord within the American people.

"Don't let anyone tell you that America's best days are behind her— that the American spirit has been vanquished," he said.

In early March, Nancy and Ronnie went to Los Angeles, primarily for a vacation. On Sunday afternoon, March 7, they attended an outdoor concert starring Merle Haggard, the country-and-western singer. The performance was being filmed for public television at a ranch near Rancho del Cielo. By the time the Reagans were helicoptered over from their ranch, the other guests were already seated, on bales of hay in a big barn in front of the makeshift stage.

Ronnie wore a cream Levi's outfit, cowboy boots and a string tie with a fancy silver clasp. Nancy was in fitted jeans and a slick brown leather jacket. The other guests were duded out in western garb as well. The Reagans had invited their millionaire friends, other big Republican contributors and old movie stars, Fred MacMurray and Buddy Ebsen. There were no black faces, few ethnic types or people outside the financial elite, although Holmes Tuttle did bring his butler.

The reporters were held far back from the president, at one point being locked up in a cattle pen. Even some of the guests felt kept back from Ronnie and Nancy. "Afterwards, I said, 'Nancy, I want you to know I was there, but, honey, I couldn't even see you,' " Colleen Moore said. "Nancy said, 'After what happened, [with the shooting] it's great.' "

Nancy and Ronnie sat in the front row. Nancy clapped with the music while Ronnie tapped his boot. The country music that Haggard sang was as duded up as the new gentry in the audience, but beneath the chords of the electric guitars, there were the same old themes of hard life and hard love that have helped make country-and-western music so popular.

Haggard had served time in San Quentin prison for burglary. Though it had been twenty years since his release, he sounded like a man who knew firsthand the hardships of which he sang. A wiry man with a neat beard, Haggard looked out on the audience through small, piercing eyes. He sang the song that made him an icon among conservatives, "Okie from Muskogee," about a man fed up with all the crazy changes in America. He sang "Working Class Blues," about a man who has worked all his life with nothing to show for it. It didn't matter what the words were, it was all melody to his audience, and they applauded and applauded some more.

"I think the music we're hearing today reaches the heart of America," Ronnie said at the end of the concert. "As someone said, 'The political life of a nation is only its most superficial aspect. In order to know the inner life, to really understand it, you've got to feel the heart in the literature, the philosophy, and the arts. And there you will find the ideals, the passions and the dreams of a whole people.' Well, I would add in those dreams you'll find their future."

Then Haggard sang an encore. For his final number, Haggard sang "Rainbow Stew."

We don't have to get high to get happy
Just think about what's in store
When people start doing what they
ought to be doing
Then we won't be booing no more
When a President goes through the White House door
And does what he says he'll do
We'll all be drinking some free bubble up
And eating some rainbow stew

Eating rainbow stew
in a silver spoon
Underneath that sky of blue
We'll all be drinking free bubble up
and eating some rainbow stew

For the Reagans, these trips to Los Angeles were an opportunity for closer contact with Michael, Patti and Maureen. Patti loved music and she had been at the Merle Haggard concert. Despite her new high-powered agent, Norman Brokaw, and PR people, Patti's career had not taken off. Although she had vowed to be rich and famous, she didn't have the sheer *chutzpah* to take advantage of being the president's daughter.

Patti had the nerve, though, to publicly affirm her support for the nuclear-freeze movement. In June at the "Peace Sunday" benefit concert at the Rose Bowl, she stood on a stage with Joan Baez and Bob Dylan, names that were sheer anathema to her parents' generation, and spoke to 85,000 people, most of whom would boo at the mention of her father's name. She promoted the cause while at the same time trying to express her love for her father and her belief that he, too, cared just as profoundly about world peace.

Maureen loved Ronnie, too, but she had suffered further denials. Last spring her father had not been at her wedding. That had been understandable—it was Maureen's third marriage, and her mother, Jane Wyman, had been present. But then her father had tried to dissuade her from running for the Senate. When he had been asked if he thought she would run, he had said, "I hope not." And in March when she announced, he declared his neutrality.

Maureen had never run for public office before. On her own merits, she could have run for the House of Representatives and in several districts might well have won. But since her early years, she'd had an almost desperate craving for attention. One of her close friends found her a delight, one-on-one—generous, caring and funny. But to Maureen, two people were an audience; she went on stage, insisting on dominating any group. And so she set out in what from the beginning was a futile contest. Not only her father stood against her, but so did her uncle Neil, who had given her away at the wedding. Neil could be an irascible old man, and he did some radio ads for the eventual winner, Pete Wilson, the mayor of San Diego, including one saying that the Reagans were for Wilson.

Maureen was still very close to Michael and his family. Michael had been a further embarrassment to his father after he became vice-president of sales for Dana Ingalls Profile, Inc., a manufacturer of missile and aircraft parts. He had written a letter uncovered by the *Oklahoma City Times* in which he said: "I know that with my father's leadership at the White House, this [country's] Armed Services are going to be rebuilt and strengthened. We at Dana Ingalls Profile want to be involved in that process." Michael thought that he wasn't misusing his family relationship and he referred to the Oklahoma newspaper as "Pravda." He realized, however, that he was being used by people shrewder and more subtle in the ways of power than himself, and he resigned from the company.

For Nancy, these trips to California were also a chance to do some clothes shopping and visit old friends, always surrounded by her entourage of Secret Service and aides. When she went to I. Magnin's now, it was a major expedition. She usually arrived through a private entrance. "When she comes, she calls beforehand," said Miss Donahue. "She'll say, 'I need a special thing, Donnie.' "

Nancy still visited Rodeo Drive. Many of those merchants and salespeople who had known her over the years felt that the street was not the same. In a few years the leases had quadrupled and more, and the prices of the merchandise were so high that a person had to be extremely rich to shop regularly here; even then, one did far better at stores on less prestigious streets only a few blocks away.

Rodeo Drive had become an international attraction, though, and the street was full of what the merchants called "lookie-lous." On weekends the tourists walked up and down. They had read about the chauffeured limousines, the Rolls-Royces, the elegant shoppers, but for the most part what they saw were other tourists. "It's like Disneyland," said one clothing-store owner, who had designed what he considered the ultimate Rodeo Drive outfit, a unisex blue velvet straight jacket with gold trim. "People will only buy something that says Rodeo Drive. What you need is a tumbler with Rodeo Drive on it."

"There's too much luxury, too much wealth," said Dorothy Tupper of Amelia Gray's. "I hardly go out on the street anymore. It could have been beautiful, but I hate the strip. They call it the money street."

When Nancy wasn't shopping or attending to other duties, she saw her friends. They weren't coming to Washington so much any longer. Betsy had even given up her apartment in the Watergate. "These people thought that Washington would be Hollywood land," said one socialite close to Nancy's friends. "It was going to be wearing the dresses and every night there was going to be a party, the king and queen and all the lords and ladies of the court. The fact that there might be a war or a budget problem, well, they were going to solve that in the fourth reel."

Ronnie's early years in Dixon and Eureka were the wellsprings of his beliefs. As he faced a myriad of complex problems in the White House, he returned even more to those experiences. He had never been out of touch with his hometown and his alma mater, but now he reached back even more to those years. In the White House he had time to see people from Dixon, and keep appointments waiting while he did so. He knew the names of casual friends from fifty years ago and he could talk for hours about life in a small town in Illinois. He knew all about the young postman in Dixon who was leading the drive to turn Ronnie's old home there into a museum, and not with government money, either, but by private donations. When B. J. Frazer, his old drama coach, died, Ronnie couldn't go back to the funeral, but he sent flowers. And he wrote numerous handwritten letters to many old friends in Dixon, keeping up with life in his old town.

In May, Ronnie returned to Eureka College to give the commencement address. He chose his alma mater as the place to make an important foreign-policy speech, calling for dramatic reductions in Soviet and American nuclear weapons. To proponents of a nuclear freeze, the speech seemed merely an attempt to derail their growing movement. But if the plan for cutting missile forces by a third succeeded, then Eureka College would have a new, noble heritage.

"Some of the people in Eureka were surprised the way he was treated," said Neil Reagan, who is on the board of Eureka College. "It's a little bitty town. They set down the helicopter on the baseball field. He had to walk maybe thirty yards, but there's a limo to drive him.

"Afterwards he flew to Peoria to make a speech at the alumni dinner. I wasn't going to go. I don't hear very well. But the president of the college called me and said, 'You have to go.'

"So we go to the banquet room. I go to say hello to our old football coach, Mac McKinzie, who's ninety. Now Ron comes in. He says, 'I want to see my brother.' Pretty soon he's getting nasty: 'What about it! I haven't seen him yet.'

"He makes his speech and then they start to serve dinner to the rest of us. And here's one of the Secret Service coming up to me. He says, 'You're Neil Reagan. For ten minutes I've been looking the crowd over for you.'

"We go upstairs. Well, Nancy and my wife go over in one corner.

President Reagan's boyhood home in Dixon, Illinois, now a memorial. *(UPI)*

Ron, he's in an easy chair, and I'm pacing. We just talk. After we'd been there fifteen minutes, something like that, they give a signal. I say, 'Come on, Ron, on your feet or they're gonna throw me out.'"

More than anything, Nancy looked forward to her trip to Europe for a week in early June. This time Ronnie would be going with her to attend an economic summit meeting in France and, as one State Department official expressed it, "to give the Europeans a better sense of the man." For Nancy, though, it would be a glorious, triumphant journey from capital to capital.

Nancy wanted everything to be just right. According to one high White House official, the British would have preferred that the Reagans not stay at Windsor Castle; British soldiers were at war in the Falklands and it was no time for pomp and ceremony. "Deaver had to pressure for an invitation," said the official, "much to the dismay of the royal family."

As the departure date drew near, Nancy knew that she might not be able to go. For several years she had expected that her mother might die soon. Edith was in declining health. At their retirement home in Phoenix, Dr. Loyal had nurtured and protected his wife. Nancy had told friends that it was good and right that Edith go first; if Dr. Loyal died sooner, Edith would not live two weeks without him.

"Nancy had the Davises at the White House early in the year," said Colleen Moore, Edith's closest friend. "Nancy was with her mother alone. That was the first time she realized that her mother had moved into another world."

In the spring of 1982, however, it was Nancy's stepfather who was in the hospital with serious heart problems. "The doctor is very reserved, like Nancy," said Colleen. "He's not one to spill over emotionally. But Nancy called me and with a great choke in her throat said: 'I was talking to "Bopoo." I know that he's going. He said, "Nancy, I want you to know that I love you. I love you very much."'"

"I think that Nancy's problems have strengthened her. I can tell by the way she talks, especially in the way she handles her father. She is on stage. She talks to him about getting the night nurse for Edith, then to me she says, 'I have to go to Europe.'"

When Nancy talked to Dr. Loyal, she was strong and supportive. When she talked to staff members planning the European trip, she was as demanding and insistent as a Prussian officer. And when she talked to friends and acquaintances about the journey, she became a little girl, giggling and dreaming of castles and parties. The very week in mid-May that she was crying on the phone to Colleen Moore, she had talked to David Ladd, the film producer, for the first time, telling him about the trip. Nancy sounded so gay and carefree that Ladd never imagined Dr. Loyal lay dying.

In part, Nancy wanted to go to Europe so badly because so much had gone into the planning of her visit. Rosebush, the East Wing chief of staff, had made two trips to Europe preparing her way. Her wardrobe and itinerary were elaborately detailed. She was determined to go.

For weeks in the White House there had been an air of palpable excitement about the nine-day European trip. "Anyone or anyone's wife who wanted to go, and had the right pull, got to go along," said one staff member. "It was like the entire court going on a hunting party during Tudor times."

The White House party that arrived in Paris on June 3 contained 247 traveling members, not including the extensive advance staffs already in Rome, London, Bonn and Berlin. While Mrs. Baker, Mrs. Deaver, Mrs. Clark, Mrs. Meese and the other ladies could go shopping and attend fashion shows, Nancy had to maintain a serious image. To underscore that, a dinner in her honor planned by the Vicomtesse de Ribes was canceled.

Paris was a city of darkness as well as light. The explosive sounds of *plastique* were heard in the ancient streets more often now than at any time since the Algerian War two decades before. In honor of Ronnie's visit, a terrorist group, Action Directe, had set off a bomb in the early-morning hours at the American School. That afternoon, among the 300 Americans meeting Nancy at the embassy were the parents of students studying at the St. Cloud school. Among them, too, was Sharon Ray, whose husband, Lieutenant Colonel Charles Ray, had been killed by terrorists in Paris six months before. During the party, Nancy sat holding Mrs. Ray's hand as if they were sisters.

In the evening, Ronnie and Nancy hosted an elegant dinner in honor of President and Madame Mitterrand of France. To Nancy, Paris was still the capital of fashion, and she intended to show the French capital a bit of American style. For her debut she chose a black satin tunic and knickers by Galanos. "The group at the embassy was a rather elderly bunch," said one official. "It was a very fashion-conscious group, but more orthodox in their dress. When Mrs. Reagan came in, there was an audible inhalation of breath. She knocked them out."

It is an axiom of taste that a woman should wear a dress, not a dress a woman, and professional fashion observers were not charmed. "While Danielle Mitterrand looked *très chic* in a white Louis Feraud suit and ruffled blouse, Mrs. Reagan came across *très gauche*, " wrote Gwen Jones, fashion editor of the *Los Angeles Herald-Examiner*. "The tunic had all the style of a maternity top and the knickers made her calves look bloated."

The economic summit at Versailles was as elaborately planned as an Alfred Hitchcock film so that the three days would unreel without major surprises. In the midst of the meetings, Israel invaded Lebanon, underscor-

At the U.S. embassy in Paris, the First Lady greets French President François Mitterrand and his wife while wearing rhinestone-studded black satin knickers designed by Galanos, 1982. *(UPI)*

ing the brutal logic of politics in the Middle East, and the complex, morally ambiguous realities of Israel that Ronnie's own vision could scarcely encompass. At the end of the weekend summit, the seven leaders issued a broad statement of principle declaring their intention to work together to stimulate economic growth and fight inflation. At the top of Ronnie's agenda had been a tough economic policy toward the Soviets, but most of the other leaders did not view the Soviet Union quite as he viewed it. He had to settle for a statement calling for "a prudent and diversified economic approach" and "commercial prudence" in limiting export credits.

Then Ronnie headed off on a four-day trip to Rome, London, Bonn and Berlin. Mike Deaver had planned the trip like a frenetic travel agent shuttling a tour group from capital to capital with enough time only to buy picture postcards and move on again. "Logistically, it was a nightmare," said one of the participants. "There was only five hours scheduled for Italy. The trip was what the Secret Service calls a 'rat fuck.' No one was in the right place at the right time. It was unseasonably hot. The president was exhausted. There was this air of apprehension. It was all very unpleasant for the staff."

At the Vatican, Ronnie sat in the library with Pope John Paul II. Speaking in English to an audience that included millions watching on television, the pope had eloquent words about world peace and economic justice toward the developing world. But Ronnie was so tired that he appeared almost to be dozing off.

If it's late in the day, this must be Britain. By evening the Reagans and their entourage were in London. No American president had ever stayed at Windsor Castle. This was the part of the trip to which Nancy had most looked forward. Arriving at the Heathrow Airport a half-hour late, the Reagans found Queen Elizabeth and Prince Philip waiting. Nancy stood next to Ronnie as he and the queen reviewed the honor guard. When Nancy noticed that Prince Philip was standing behind, she would have stepped back, too, but the prince motioned that she was fine.

For her arrival, Nancy was wearing a two-piece beige outfit, her third costume of the day. At Windsor Castle, she changed into a gown for their dinner with the queen and Prince Philip and thirty-four other guests, including the White House aides and their wives, which British journalists referred to as "the Reagan court."

In the morning, Ronnie and the queen went for the most heralded ride since Hannibal rode elephants into Italy. Weeks before, the president's advance men had descended on Windsor Castle to discuss media coverage, sounding like Cecil B. De Mille planning the filming of the parting of the Red Sea.

And so the queen and Ronnie, dressed alike in tweed and jodhpurs, rode slowly out of the Royal Mews into the royal sunshine toward the common herd of journalists penned in an enclosure. Ronnie was riding eight-year-old Centennial, a mount as stolid and unexciting as a Checker taxicab. The American reporters shouted out questions. "Beautiful," Ronnie yelled back. "Yes, it does ride well." Then, "Better get out of the way," he shouted. "I'm going to ride on over."

The American reporters knew that *their* Ronnie was not about to run them down. But the British reporters, waiting half-expectantly for the American president to topple off the English saddle, were not so sure.

Before Ronnie had a chance to strut his stuff, the queen moseyed off alone toward the park. And Ronnie, gallant to the last, went to join her.

The entourage that followed Ronnie and the queen was as large a contingent as the cavalry troop that Ronnie had led into combat on "Death Valley Days." There was the queen's crown Equerry, the Windsor Castle stud groom, two mounted Secret Service men, and a Land Rover carrying six more security people. Behind that came a sedate duo, Nancy with Prince Philip driving a carriage pulled by four bays, with two postilions, a British security man in a bowler and an American in dark glasses. Behind them came another Land Rover.

Later in the day, Ronnie gave his address before Parliament, at an hour when the speech could be broadcast live to the morning news programs in America. He introduced a TelePrompTer to the august halls, and read a speech that was vintage Reagan: emotional, rhetorical, patriotic, simple and moving.

"I have often wondered about the shyness of some of us in the West about standing for those ideals that have done so much to ease the plight of man and the hardships of our imperfect world," he said, looking up from the TelePrompTer. "Let us be shy no longer. Let us go to our strength. Let us offer hope."

There is no legislative body in the world where in debate and discourse language is used so deftly, and a good speech is appreciated as an aesthetic as well as a political act. Ronnie was a great speaker, a great American speaker, and the parliamentarians interrupted him with shouts of "Hear, hear!"

Nancy heard the speech sitting next to Prime Minister Margaret Thatcher. Later in the afternoon, Nancy was supposed to go visit the children's cancer ward at St. Bartholomew's Hospital, but that was canceled; she wanted time to prepare for the state banquet. For the dinner, Nancy wore a white, long-sleeved Galanos, and a necklace and earrings that made her look regal. For all her social achievements in the White House, she could not have given a dinner like this one. There were footmen in scarlet livery, and Yeomen of the Guard in red uniforms. The 160 guests were seated on gold chairs at tables graced with golden candelabra. If there was one imperfection, it was that the queen, unlike the First Lady, did not have enough place settings for all the guests and had to use two different patterns.

And then it was on to Bonn for a meeting with NATO leaders. In five hours, the sixteen Western leaders considered a complicated communiqué that Prime Minister Pierre Trudeau of Canada considered "rubberstamp [ing] . . . a communiqué whose results have been precooked." At the end, while in the city 300,000 persons protested U.S. defense policies in the largest demonstration in postwar Germany, Ronnie gave a speech criticizing the detente of the 1970s and calling for "substantial and balanced East-West relations aimed at genuine detente."

Finally, Berlin. Twenty years ago to the very month, President John F. Kennedy had come to Berlin, nine months after the Soviet-backed East German regime had built a wall dividing the city. The young American president had stood and said *"Ich bin ein Berliner* [I am a Berliner]" and the West Berliners had cheered and stomped and tears had run down some of their faces.

As Ronnie stood before 20,000 on the grounds of Charlottenburg Palace, he surely would have liked to rouse the Berliners as Kennedy had two decades before. Since then, however, the Soviets had put down the Czech springtime of liberalization and supported ending the solidarity movement in Poland. And the political geography symbolized by the wall was as firm as ever.

A statesman's job was different now, and Ronnie gave a speech aimed as much at the technicians of arms control as at the people spread out before him. He talked of "proposals in such areas as notification for strategic exercise, of missile launches and expanded exchange of strategic forces data . . . [that] taken together . . . represent a qualitative improvement in the nuclear environment." That was not *his* language but State Department language, concepts about which he did not have the detailed comprehension of several of his predecessors.

Then, almost exhausted, Ronnie and Nancy flew home on *Air Force One*. In order to ensure a rousing welcome certifying the trip a success, the White House had sent out special tickets for the arrival ceremony at Andrews Air Force Base outside Washington. There is nothing Washingtonians like better than special tickets, and so on Friday afternoon, June 11, the lucky ticket holders headed out Suitland Parkway. The White House had printed a reported 50,000 tickets, and as the plane touched down there was an enormous traffic jam for miles around the airport. Enraged diplomats sent their chauffeured limousines inching up the shoulder. Loyal Reaganites abandoned cars and ran helter-skelter toward the gate.

At the arrival ceremony, Ronnie called the presence of the 15,000 or so well-wishers who had made it "a complete surprise." That brought the biggest laugh of the day.

When Nancy arrived back in Washington, Dr. Loyal was still hanging on, and she soon had a whole new set of unpleasantries to face. In July, Vicki Morgan filed suit against Alfred and Betsy. In her depositions and charges, the beautiful twenty-seven-year-old woman claimed that she had been Alfred's mistress since the age of seventeen. He had been paying her $18,000 a month, but in early July, as he lay dying of throat cancer, unable even to sign checks, she was cut off.

In depositions later made public, Morgan told of Alfred's "Marquis de Sade" complex. She said that he enjoyed tying up and beating nude women. During the first four years of their relationship, he allegedly applied English discipline to his young mistress, spanking her regularly. In southern California, there are as many therapists as real-estate agents, and Morgan claimed that she had provided "therapy" by no longer indulging in "sado-masochistic sex" and by getting Alfred to see a psychiatrist.

For readers of the tabloids, this was delicious stuff. But for the Reagans and their friends, it was a sordid business. To Nancy and Ronnie, the Bloomingdales weren't just friends, they were magnificent exemplars of the American system. All the friends knew that Alfred and Betsy did not have the closest marriage. As Alfred lay dying, Betsy still continued going to parties on both coasts. But this was public spectacle, bringing embarrassment to all of them. Worse yet was the prospect that Morgan might carry through her promise to write a book, detailing all that Alfred had said about Nancy, Ronnie and the group.

While the papers were full of the Bloomingdale scandal, Scott Meese, the nineteen-year-old son of Ed and Ursula Meese, was killed as he ran off George Washington Parkway in Virginia early one morning. Ronnie and Nancy had known Scott since he was a little boy. He was a freshman at Princeton, a fine young man, and the senseless, mindless death touched Ronnie and Nancy profoundly.

As they mourned over young Scott Meese, Dr. Loyal's condition was worsening. On August 19 he died. The next day, Alfred died. Less than a month later Grace Kelly was killed in an auto crash, and Nancy flew to her funeral in Monaco. The Reagans and their friends treated death as if it were a personal affront, but they were at an age when death is a constant. As often as not, they found the names of old friends not in the entertainment or news pages but in the obituaries. Another of the Reagans' millionaire friends had throat cancer, as did his wife. It was as if there were a plague of illness among them.

Nancy cherished the good times, the precious moments. She was proud that Ron, Jr., had been elevated to the main Joffrey Ballet, and said she was proud as well when he went temporarily on unemployment. Later, when he resigned from the company to follow a different career, she professed to understand that as well. One of the events she looked forward to was the big party late in October for her book, *To Love a Child,* profiles of twenty-eight foster grandparents. The Foster Grandparents program was one of Nancy's favorite causes. She hadn't written the book—that had been done by Jane Wilkie, a free-lancer who had been paid a lump sum for her work—and she had met almost none of the twenty-eight foster grandparents, but she considered *To Love a Child* very much her book. Indeed, according to one member of her staff, she at first wanted to keep the royalties, but was told that she'd better donate them to the Foster Grandparents program.

On October 19, Amin Gemayel, the new president of Lebanon, was supposed to come to the White House for a luncheon as part of his state visit. In the aftermath of the Israeli invasion of Lebanon, the administration considered Gemayel's visit crucially important. But Nancy had already scheduled *her* party that day, so the Lebanese president had to come to breakfast instead.

It was a lovely fall afternoon, and the 600 foster grandparents and children sat on the South Lawn looking up at the temporary stage. There stood Nancy, Frank Sinatra and a group of children. Nancy had gotten Francis Albert to record a song entitled "To Love a Child," and Nancy, Francis Albert and the children sang. Francis Albert had to read the words from a card and kept signaling to Nancy that she was flat, but the children did just fine.

> *As one human to another*
> *I'd like to question you.*
> *If it takes the sun and the rain*
> *to make a tree grow,*
> *If it takes the moon and the tide*
> *to make the sea flow,*
> *What does it take*
> *To love a child?*
> *To love a child.*
> *You start with a smile,*
> *And after a while,*
> *A hug and a kiss.*
> *It takes no more than this*
> *To love a child.*
> *To love a child.*

By all odds, Ronnie was the best salesman Washington had ever seen.

Nancy Davis Reagan and Francis Albert Sinatra sing "To Love a Child," 1982. *(Brad Markel)*

He could sell practically anything, and in the last months of 1982 he was proving it. With the whopping federal deficits facing him, in August he went on television to sell a $98.3-billion tax bill that amounted to the largest single tax increase in history. And Congress passed the bill. On September 28, he told a news conference that it would take a "palace coup" to get him to agree to any more tax increases. Yet two months later he was singing the praises of a five-cent-a-gallon gas tax that the administration called "revenue enhancement." He called Congress into a lame-duck session to push through social-security reform and his MX missile program, but Congress was not about to touch the explosive issue of social security when the administration itself didn't have a clear position. He said it was absolutely crucial to have a land-based MX missile program, but when that failed in Congress, he was ready to sell an alternative.

Meanwhile, month by month the unemployment figures rose, reaching 10.8 percent by the end of the year before declining. When prompted, Ronnie would call a man who was out of work and cheer him up. But he couldn't make twelve million phone calls. Even his closest advisers knew that there were millions of good, hardworking men and women out of work; the way things looked, they would probably be unemployed for months and months. But Ronnie was the same optimist in private as in public, pointing out all the want ads in the newspapers, as well as the rise in the stock market.

Ronnie was spending even more time thinking about the past. He wrote letters to his friends in Dixon. He considered the best moment of his week "climbing that helicopter to go to Camp David." At the weekend retreat he and Nancy had "taken to showing some of the 'golden oldies' " starring Lombard and Gable. He had been sent a complete print of *Knute Rockne—All American,* and he watched that again. "I'm not going to say it was the best picture we've seen," he told *People.* "I'm going to say I enjoyed it more than any other."

As the year drew to an end, there were seemingly endless parties at the White House. On the evening of December 5, the limousines and autos pulled up at the White House depositing some 300 guests for a reception before the fifth annual Kennedy Center Honors. Just across Pennsylvania Avenue in Lafayette Park stood a soup kitchen in an area that could be seen from the top floors of the White House. Here each night came scores of hungry, often homeless men and women, huddling against the cold.

Inside the White House, the men wore black tie, the women were magnificently gowned and bejeweled. As the ladies passed through the gauntlet of the media, the reporters shouted out asking for designer names.

In the State Dining Room beneath Healy's portrait of Lincoln an enormous buffet had been set out on a great table. There were immense loins of rare beef cut in thin elegant slices by white-coated chefs; trays of

Into the sunset . . . *(UPI)*

shrimp and pâté; fettucini in silver chafing dishes; cakes and other delicacies. Among the crowd passed pairs of waiters, one carrying a silver salver laden with liquor bottles, the other mixing drinks to order.

In the Green Room, Ronnie and Nancy chatted with the five honorees. Nancy talked to Lillian Gish whom she had known since her Chicago days. The silent film star appeared like a tiny porcelain doll. Ronnie had been friendly with Gene Kelly, another of the honorees, for years. Ronnie enjoyed talking about Hollywood far more than politics, and he was having a fine time.

Nancy and Ronnie greeted the other guests in the Blue Room, and everyone moved down the great hall to the East Room. There the guests sat on gold ballroom chairs.

Ronnie stood on a small raised platform. Beside him stood Nancy. In her tightly belted red gown, Nancy looked exquisite. But, as Ronnie said so often, the two years in the White House had aged her far more than him. Her speckled hands were as wrinkled as a crumpled bag, and when she was not smiling, she looked far older. Ronnie had aged, too, and when the photographers were not kind, he sometimes seemed to have lost much of his chin.

Then it was time for Ronnie to speak. "Someone once said that an artist is a dreamer consenting to dream of the actual world," he said. "The artists that we honor tonight have painted a panorama with their lives . . . allowing us from time to time to mingle our everyday world with their world of pageantry and dreams."

Although Ronnie was talking about the honorees, he might have been talking about Nancy and himself.

A NOTE ON SOURCES

Make-Believe is based on approximately 400 interviews, primarily with people who have not talked before about the Reagans. This includes most of Mrs. Reagan's housemates at Smith College, her childhood friends in Bethesda and Chicago, fellow workers at M-G-M, close friends and neighbors in Pacific Palisades, White House aides and others. For President Reagan this includes everyone from people in Dixon, Illinois, and Eureka to costars and colleagues, and political associates and cronies. It would be impossible to list all these people; and many of them have asked that they not be quoted by name.

The following people and institutions were particularly helpful: The Motion Picture division of the Library of Congress; the Museum of Broadcasting; UCLA film archives; Mary Trott, the Smith College archivist; Michael Reagan; Neil Reagan; Charlotte Ramage, Mrs. Reagan's cousin; Carrie Redebaugh, a longtime resident of Dixon, Illinois; Peter Sorum; Ursula Taylor Schacker; Nanette Fabray; Ann Sothern; Pat O'Brien; Patricia Neal; Kathleen Young, Mrs. Reagan's cousin; Rhonda Fleming; Letitia Baldrige; Helen Smith, Mrs. Nixon's former press secretary; Dean George Hearne at Eureka College; Diana Moore, the librarian at the *Los Angeles Times* Washington bureau; John Sears; Joe Canzeri; William Hifner, the *Washington Post* librarian; Wanda McDaniel of the *Los Angeles Herald Examiner;* Benny Thau; Diane Moore, head of the photo office at the White House; Dr. Paul Colombani, Kathy Ackerman, a librarian at the *Chicago Tribune;* Colleen Moore; and Clare Boothe Luce.

No sitting President and First Lady have ever had so much written about them, and it was a chore simply plowing through the bibliography. I have drawn on numerous newspapers, magazines and books and there is not the space here to list anything but their names. However, I would like to mention two articles that were helpful and that might not be easily found: "Hollywood Blacklist," by Tom Bourne in *Reader: Los Angeles Free Weekly* (February 13, 1981); and "The Other Man in Nancy's Life," by Jennifer Allen in *Manhattan* (November 25, 1980).

BIBLIOGRAPHY

BOOKS

Adler, Bill, with Norman King. *All in the First Family.* New York: G. P. Putnam's Sons, 1982.

Bacon, James. *Made in Hollywood.* New York: Warner Books, 1977.

Birmingham, Stephen. *California Rich.* New York: Simon and Schuster, 1980.

Boyarsky, Bill. *The Rise of Ronald Reagan.* New York: Random House, 1968.

Brown, Edmund. *Reagan and Reality.* New York: Praeger Publishers, 1970.

Brownlow, Kevin. *The Parade's Gone By.* New York: Alfred A. Knopf, 1968.

————, with Bill Brown. *Reagan, the Political Chameleon.* New York: Praeger Publishers, 1976.

Brownstein, Ronald, and Nina Easton. *Reagan's Ruling Class.* Washington: Presidential Accountability Group, 1982.

Cannon, Lou. *Reagan.* New York: G. P. Putnam's Sons, 1982.

————. *Ronnie and Jessie.* Garden City, New York: Doubleday, 1968.

Caughey, John and La Ree. *Los Angeles: Biography of a City.* Berkeley, California: University of California Press, 1977.

Cooney, John. *The Annenbergs: The Salvation of a Tainted Dynasty.* New York: Simon and Schuster, 1982.

Drew, Elizabeth. *Portrait of an Election.* New York: Simon and Schuster, 1981.

Edwards, Lee. *Reagan: a Political Biography.* San Diego, California: Viewpoint Books, 1967.

Evans, Rowland, and Robert Novak. *The Reagan Revolution.* New York: E. P. Dutton, 1980.

Ford, Betty, with Chris Chase. *The Times of My Life.* New York: Harper & Row and Readers Digest Association, 1978.

Germond, Jack. *Blue Smoke and Mirrors: How Reagan Won.* New York: Viking Press, 1981.

Graham, Sheilah, *Confessions of a Hollywood Columnist*. New York: William Morrow, 1969.

Heinsohn, A. G. (compiled by). *Anthology of Conservative Writing in the United States*. Chicago: Regnery, 1962.

Higham, Charles. *Warner Brothers*. New York: Charles Scribner's Sons, 1975.

Hobbs, Charles. *Reagan's Call to Action*. Nashville, Tennessee: Nelson, 1976.

Lewis, Joseph. *What Makes Reagan Run*. New York: McGraw-Hill, 1968.

Liepold, L. (ed.). *Governor and Statesman*. Minneapolis: T. S. Denison, 1968.

Lyons, Eugene. *Red Decade*. New Rochelle, New York: Arlington House, 1970.

McLellan, Diana. *Ear on Washington*. New York: Arbor House, 1982.

Moore, Colleen. *Silent Star*. Garden City, New York: Doubleday, 1968.

Murphy, George, with Victor Lasky. *Say, Didn't You Used to Be George Murphy?* New York: Bartholomew House, 1970.

Parrish, Robert. *Growing Up in Hollywood*. New York: Harcourt Brace Jovanovich, 1976.

Phillips, Kevin. *Post-Conservative America*. New York: Random House, 1982.

Reagan, Nancy, with Bill Libby. *Nancy*. New York: William Morrow, 1980.

Reagan, Ronald, with Richard G. Hubler. *Where's the Rest of Me?* New York: Duell, Sloan & Pearce, 1965.

Rotha, Paul, and Manvell, Roger. *Movie Parade*. London and New York: 1950.

Schwartz, Nancy Lynn. *Hollywood Writers' Wars*. New York: Knopf, 1982.

Thomas, Tony. *The Films of Ronald Reagan*. Secaucus, N.J.: Citadel Press, 1980.

Van der Linden, Frank. *The Real Ronald Reagan*. New York: William Morrow, 1981.

Washington Post, National staff of. *The Pursuit of the Presidency*. New York: Berkley Books, 1980.

White, Theodore H. *America in Search of Itself: The Making of the President 1956-1980*. New York: Harper & Row, 1982.

Witcover, Jules. *Marathon*. New York: Viking Press, 1977.

MAGAZINES AND NEWSPAPERS

Architectural Digest
The Atlantic
California
The Chicago Tribune
Fortnight
Harper's Magazine
The Hollywood Reporter
Los Angeles
The Los Angeles Herald Examiner
The Los Angeles Times
Manhattan (*New York Daily News*)

Modern Screen
Le Monde
Motion Picture
Movie Land
Movie Life
Movie Stars Parade
The National Journal
Newsweek
The New York Review of Books
The New York Times
People
Photoplay
Reader: Los Angeles Free Weekly
Sacramento Bee
Silver Screen
Time
The Times (London)
U.S. News and World Report
Variety
W
The Wall Street Journal
The Washingtonian
The Washington Post
The Washington Star
West
Women's Wear Daily

INDEX